"Lively discussions illuminate the personal histories and challenges of a vibrant era where women editors, graphic designers, and publishers working individually and with partners faced considerable hardships and challenges that entrepreneurial women often face. Before desktop publishing, grass roots publishers often worked at home on mimeograph machines to create magazines, journals, and books that celebrate a wealth of early literary, feminist, indigenous, and women of color writers and illustrators which laid the groundwork for contemporary BIPOC LGBTQ+ writers, audiences, and publishers to come." | Marilyn Stablein, author of *Houseboat on the Ganges and a Room in Kathmandu*

Praise for *Women in Independent Publishing*

"This long-overdue tribute to women publishers and editors in the small and independent press world is chock full of fascinating interviews and resource information. While creating 'presses of their own,' these women had a profound influence on the poetry, literature, and politics of the last half of the twentieth century. *Women in Independent Publishing* is a must-read for book lovers everywhere." | David Unowsky, founder of *The Hungry Mind Review*

"This book provides a hands-on, on-the-ground encounter with women editors of modern and contemporary small presses and literary journals. Their voices bring to life the vibrancy and commitment to their artistic and communitarian visions in real time with the implicit message that the torch is continually being passed to the next generation of cultural workers." | Maria Damon, author of *Postliterary America: From Bagel Shop Jazz to Micropoetries*

"Book artists will find in this work fascinating details about the publishing process, but every reader will be moved by the personal energy that drove these women to become publishers and the powerful network of friends and community that they helped to create." | Terence Diggory, author of *Encyclopedia of New York School Poets*

"Too much of our literary history has been lost or forgotten. This fantastic collection of interviews documents many of the important contributions by women writers, editors, and literary activists whose work changed our culture in so many ways. These singular stories, woven together, create a tapestry of memory and work, words that continue to sing to us, past, present, and future." | David Wilk, publisher

Women in Independent Publishing

Women *in* Independent Publishing

A History of Unsung Innovators, 1953–1989

EDITED BY **STEPHANIE ANDERSON**

UNIVERSITY OF NEW MEXICO PRESS | ALBUQUERQUE

© 2024 by the University of New Mexico Press
All rights reserved. Published 2024
Printed in the United States of America

ISBN 978-0-8263-6706-8 (cloth)
ISBN 978-0-8263-6707-5 (paper)
ISBN 978-0-8263-6708-2 (ePub)
ISBN 978-0-8263-6709-9 (webPDF)
Library of Congress Control Number: 2024941554

Founded in 1889, the University of New Mexico sits on the
traditional homelands of the Pueblo of Sandia. The original
peoples of New Mexico—Pueblo, Navajo, and Apache—since time
immemorial have deep connections to the land and have made
significant contributions to the broader community statewide.
We honor the land itself and those who remain stewards of this
land throughout the generations and also acknowledge our
committed relationship to Indigenous peoples. We gratefully
recognize our history.

Cover illustration: courtesy of Design Cuts
Designed by Felicia Cedillos
Composed in Alegreya

Contents

Acknowledgments   vii

A Note on Interview Format and Transcription   ix

Introduction. "It's Only Vanity If It's Not Good":
     Daisy Aldan and Women Midcentury Small Press Publishers   1

THE INTERVIEWS

Hettie Jones on *Yugen*   33

Rosmarie Waldrop on *Burning Deck* and Burning Deck Press   45

Margaret Randall on *El Corno Emplumado / The Plumed Horn*   55

Lindy Hough on *Io* and North Atlantic Books   71
     Interviewed by Zainab Farooqui and Tess Redman

Bernadette Mayer on *0 TO 9, United Artists,*
     and United Artists Books   85

Susan Sherman on *IKON*   111

Maureen Owen on *Telephone* and Telephone Books   129

Renee Tajima-Peña on *Bridge*   139

Maxine Chernoff on *Oink!* and *New American Writing*   151

Alice Notley on *CHICAGO*   169

Jaime Robles on Five Trees Press   185

Barbara Barg and Rose Lesniak on *Out There,*
     Power Mad Press, and Out There Productions   197

Rena Rosenwasser and Patricia Dienstfrey on
Kelsey Street Press — 225

Joanne Kyger on *Bolinas Hearsay News* — 245

Martha King on Two and Two Press and
Giants Play Well in the Drizzle — 253

Patricia Spears Jones on *W. B.*, *Ordinary Women*,
and the Heresies Collective — 263

C. D. Wright on Lost Roads Press — 271

Eileen Myles on *dodgems* — 279

Deborah Costello and Lisa Kellman on Black Oyster Press — 291

Barbara Smith on Kitchen Table: Women of Color Press — 297

Lisbet Tellefsen on *Aché* — 321

Lee Ann Brown on Tender Buttons Press — 333

Afterword — 343
    MC Hyland

RESOURCES

Additional Selected Women Editors and Publishers — 353

List of Selected Small Presses and Publications with Women and
Nonbinary Editors and Publishers, 1950s–1980s — 365

Notes — 369

Bibliography — 381

Contributors — 393

Index — 407

Acknowledgments

Many hands have crafted this project from the very beginning. This work began more than a decade ago, when I interviewed Alice Notley for a paper on her magazine *CHICAGO* and subsequently presented it at the Chicago Poetry Symposium on April 17, 2010, organized by David Pavelich (David also introduced me to *CHICAGO*). Notley's generous responses to my queries carried the paper and began this work. During the reception for that symposium, Nancy Kuhl had the idea for this book. MC Hyland was a constant cheerleader over the years, and her belief that this work should exist as a book made it so: she worked hard for it, and I am grateful. Always exuberantly community-building, Jennifer Karmin introduced me to Barbara Barg and Bernadette Mayer, and Sophie Seita and Cassandra Gillig offered ideas and assistance. Kyle Schlesinger and Jed Birmingham were early supporters, sharing research notes, and several people, including Ammiel Alcalay, Joshua Kotin, and Joshua Marie Wilkinson, made interviewee suggestions. The research about Daisy Aldan for the introduction was generously supported by the Fleur Cowles Endowment Fund at the Harry Ransom Center and a Travel Research Grant from the Modernist Studies Association, and Duke Kunshan University contributed to the project's research and publication. Elise McHugh steadfastly championed the book from first encounter, Denise Edwards did excellent copyediting, and I'm grateful to everyone at UNMP for their careful creation of the book as a book. I am also grateful for the incisive feedback from readers, including Chalcedony Wilding, Maria Damon, Terrence Diggory, and the reviewers for both *Post45* and UNMP.

Students at Duke Kunshan University saw this project through the last stages and motivated the publication of this book through their intelligence, persistence, and curiosity. Zainab Farooqui, Momoko Mandere, Tess Redman, and Xiaoxi Zhu created a fantastic website archive (https://sites.duke.edu/spiesintheaudience/) that also contains a glossary of small press

viii *Acknowledgements*

printing terminology and additional DIY resources. Karen Nielsen assisted with research at a key moment. Sydney Brown, Sadey Dong, Siyuan Wang, Flora Xu, Yilin Xu, and Xiaomeng Yan did formidable amounts of research, writing, and organization for the resources section of this book and also worked on polishing the website. Zainab's thinking about poetic sociality influenced the introduction, and with Tess, she interviewed Lindy Hough; Sadey and Xiaomeng also helped transcribe and edit that interview. Tess did additional work on the bibliography, and Sydney, Sadey, Flora, and Yilin worked on the transcriptions of the interviews with Barbara Smith and Lisbet Tellefsen.

Thank you as well to the editors (Andrew Peart, Steven Karl, Ching-In Chen, Andy Fitch, Christiana Baik, Nick Sturm, Jack Chelgren, Kai Ihns) who first published some of the project's pieces: the interviews with Hettie Jones, Margaret Randall, Maureen Owen, Patricia Spears Jones, and Renee Tajima-Peña first appeared in the *Chicago Review*; the interview with Bernadette Mayer first appeared in *Coldfront*; the interview with Susan Sherman first appeared in a Little Magazines cluster (edited by Nick Sturm) in *Post45*; and the interviews with C. D. Wright, Joanne Kyger, Alice Notley, and Jaime Robles first appeared in the *Conversant* (no longer accessible online). Additionally, the interview with Joanne Kyger was reprinted in *There You Are: Interviews, Journals, and Ephemera* (Wave Books, ed. Cedar Sigo), and the interview with Margaret Randall was reprinted in *Talking Stick* (Editorial Igneo). The introduction first appeared as an article in the "Editing American Literature" special issue of *Post45* (edited by Evan Brier and Tim Groenland).

The interviewees are, of course, the authors of this work, and were patient as they taught me about the role of interviewer, the genre of the interview, and the histories glimpsed here. This book is for them, and for current and future students.

A Note on Interview Format and Transcription

These interviews took place in person and over e-mail, phone, and video-call platforms. The medium for each interview, the timeframe, and the name of the press or publication on which the interview ostensibly focuses are provided in the interview header. The book centers on women and non-binary editors and publishers who ran independent small presses and little magazines that began between the 1950s and 1980s, and here it is worth emphasizing that the interviews are arranged in chronological order by the publication/press's start date. A header's date range indicates the years the press or publication has been active, regardless of the timeframe for an interviewee's involvement; several of the interviewees were involved in press or publication projects that are *not* listed in the header, as the interviews did not encompass all an editor/publisher's projects and the header reflects ones discussed in the interview. Editorial terms of tenure are usually addressed in particular interviews, or occasionally in clarifying endnotes.

There are several reasons for foregrounding the timeline of the press or publication in this way. First, editorial handovers are not always linear and prompt. Second, because the interview format here most frequently involves a single interviewer and interviewee, the book emphasizes individual editors-publishers; the headers' shift in focus to the timespan of a publication or press allows the reader to glimpse an overlapping network of publications, especially in instances of collective models, where an individual's participation might be more or less compressed. And third, many (though not all) of these interviewees established the presses and publications they edited and later handed the projects to successive editors-publishers; highlighting the publications' dates of operation can emphasize a sense of ongoingness.

In considering how heavily to edit the interviews for publication, I generally have tended to think about these pieces as written documents that, in cases when they are transcribed from a conversation, retain traces of orality. I have thus edited for clarity and concision, while attempting to preserve some of the spoken (and, in one case, note-taking) elements. However, I have also attempted to follow the desires of the interviewee regarding transcription fidelity and the degree of editing. Finally, in this era of fast information, the reader can decide when to disrupt an interview's conversational flow by pausing to investigate a reference. As a result, endnotes are used sparingly in the interviews themselves and tend to identify a supporting source or a reference the reader might not be able to look up quickly.

INTRODUCTION

"It's Only Vanity If It's Not Good"

Daisy Aldan and Women Midcentury Small Press Publishers

"Well, if you're a woman you put yourself somewhere near the beginning & then there's this other place where you put yourself in terms of everybody."

—ALICE NOTLEY, *DOCTOR WILLIAMS' HEIRESSES*

I. Predecessors, Siblings, Successors, Friends

Anthologies have a way of changing over time. Despite aspiring to be summative resources, few remain so; the rest become curious sorts of artifact, neither book nor periodical, a record of departed interest. Historical comparison can help restore their original context. For example, if I tell you that an editor named Daisy Aldan published an anthology called *A New Folder* in 1959, the year before Donald Allen published *The New American Poetry, 1945–60* with Grove Press—and that the latter has sold "more than 100,000 copies," according to the most recent edition's cover[1]—you might get a quick sense of Aldan's role as a crucial literary precursor to Allen. And regardless of whether you know Aldan's anthology, you may be frustrated to find her framed in terms of Allen at all—especially given that her work has faded into obscurity and his, at least partially inspired by hers, is still regarded as canonical and field defining.[2]

Here, we can see parallels with Virginia Woolf's now-famous Judith Shakespeare thought experiment. In *A Room of One's Own*, Woolf demonstrates how the social expectations of and strictures on women make it impossible for Judith Shakespeare, sister to William, to succeed in her chosen work autonomously; in Woolf's fictional account, Judith is recognizable, if recognized at all, because of her name and genealogy. Must William always eclipse Judith—and must his work always be present as the standard by which to measure her success or failure?

This question of relation and lineage is one that the heirs of modernism like Aldan (1918–2001) and other midcentury, US-based small press women editors and publishers take up with ambivalence, often conceptualizing ways to value work other than by comparison with their male peers.[3] For Aldan's younger contemporary Alice Notley (b. 1945), seeking a lineage of writers in the lecture *Doctor Williams' Heiresses* in 1980, imagining Judith means imagining her as part of deliberately imprecise relations: "From out of the West came Gertrude Stein, the daughter of the guy who wrote the 800-page novel & the girl who thought maybe rightly that she was Shakespeare."[4] We can read Stein here as the daughter of the novelist and the woman "who thought maybe rightly that she was Shakespeare"—or as "the girl" Judith, sister to Shakespeare—or as Shakespeare herself. The qualifier "maybe" in the phrase "maybe rightly" reveals how occlusion can make it hard to see these relations and lineages.

Following Notley's ahistorical and aesthetic concept of inheritance, this introduction uses the words relation and lineage, especially the latter, to loosely indicate a sense of affiliation or continuity that is not always coterie based. As the epigraph suggests, midcentury women editors-publishers often have a sense of singularity or lack—that they are on the vanguard, and/or that women writers are not adequately represented in the publishing scenes. When I interviewed Notley in 2010 about her editing of the little magazine *CHICAGO* (1972–1974),[5] her complaint then was not that her editing work had been framed by her relationships with male poets but that she had not received recognition for her small press editing and publishing at all. During our correspondence, she pulled the magazines out of storage "under the bed," writing, "They are extraordinarily beautiful and wonderful, and I can't believe what amazing poets I published. And why have I gotten no credit for this whatsoever?" she asked. "Why doesn't anyone ever mention them?"[6] Of course, being overlooked and being on the vanguard are not the same thing; however, they both imply actively being "near the beginning," one in terms of production and one in terms of reception. For midcentury women editors and publishers, this sense of being "near the beginning," is often concurrent with the creative claiming of relationality with other women editors-publishers as peers, predecessors, successors, and friends, suggesting lineages and alternative ways that women frame their relationality.

In addition to the interviews, archival material and small press publications—especially anthologies like Aldan's and Allen's—provide a snapshot, albeit an imperfect one, into literary scene gender dynamics. It is difficult to know whether or not Aldan might have had the same complaint as Notley about the lack of attention to her publishing activities, given the recognition of her accomplishments in her lifetime.[7] However, her proximity to *The New American Poetry* and her absence from later discussions about it are indicative of the ways in which women editors working between the 1950s and 1980s have been overlooked. Aldan's *Folder* magazine (1953–1956) and *A New Folder* anthology (1959) occurred at an important historical juncture—in the postwar period right before the interviews start, at the beginning of the "anthology wars" of the late fifties and early sixties.[8] Contemporaneous publications helmed by women were scarce in these years, though Aldan is not exactly solitary—Lita Hornick ran *Kulchur* from 1961 to 1964, Hettie Jones was involved in *Yugen* from 1958 to 1962, Diane di Prima coedited *The Floating Bear* beginning in 1961, and so forth. However, given the continuity between *Folder* magazine and *A New Folder*,[9] combined with the relative lack of women-involved publications in the fifties and Aldan's direct connection to other women modernists—she went on to edit *Two Cities* with Anaïs Nin (1961–1962)—Aldan's editorial work stands out.

Nonetheless, much of Aldan's work—especially on *A New Folder*—is absent from the scholarship about the era, and when Aldan and *A New Folder* are discussed, it is often in the context of comparison with Allen's anthology. This context is an important first step, and scholars who have written about *A New Folder* have brought it back into the conversation by suggesting its influence on *The New American Poetry* and calling for additional attention to it. In what follows, I am also not able to avoid comparing Aldan and Allen. However, this introduction aims to bring Aldan out of the footnotes, proposing her as key figure in a nongenealogical lineage of women small press editors and publishers and exploring some of the ensuing characteristics of

4   *Women in Independent Publishing*

such a lineage. Furthermore, in tracing such a lineage or lineages, we can also begin to see how these women constellated community and groups in various ways, allowing the participants to view themselves both as heiresses (to use Notley's word) and makers of lineages, a vantage Aldan embraced in her early editing and publishing.

When I began to interview women midcentury small press publishers and editors from the nexus of "Second Generation New York School" poetry, it was admittedly driven less by conceptualizations of lineage and more by Notley's sense of occlusion. I wanted to get the accounts of women editors into the historical record, and had the sense that the "often tacitly gender-blind allegiances of the postwar poetry community," in Anne Dewey and Libbie Rifkin's words, was enabling the exclusion of women from the historical record, even if unintentionally, because treating gender as inconsequential perpetuates the ongoing recognition of male editors and lack of attention to women.[10] Furthermore, the continuing legacy of these allegiances was contributing to a lack of documentation about women in independent publishing between the 1950s and 1980s. Although recent and less recent scholarship has explored the publishing work of not only Woolf (Hogarth Press, 1917–1946)[11] but also other women at the vanguard of modernist small press publishing,[12] in 2010, when the interviews began, the dynamics of "tacitly gender-blind allegiances" were being replicated in scholarship pertaining to the so-called Mimeograph Revolution, the period of DIY and small press publishing that resulted in a flurry of little magazines and books[13]—though it is important to mention that there were several earlier discussions about gender and publishing in small press and poetry contexts, notably 1994's Editorial Forum on women poets, editors, and critics published by Jena Osman and Juliana Spahr in *Chain* and 1999's Page Mothers Conference at UCSD.[14] Additionally, despite the fact that the small press scholarship contains a small but growing collection of texts devoted to interviews with and accounts by little magazine and small press publishers, women are largely underrepresented in these volumes.[15]

I intended the interviews—occurring between 2010 and 2023 with twenty-five women and nonbinary editors-publishers—as well as the accompanying resources, to partially address these elisions. In the period between the fifties and the eighties—the decades implied by the long "midcentury" in this introduction's title—women conceive of a nongenealogical lineage constellated around inclusion/exclusion in spaces and technologies, professionalization/self-publishing, geographical proximity or mobility, friendship, and gender and identity politics. The period occurs after much of the activity of influential modernist women editors-writers and ends in the widespread technological shift to computers (and Xerox machines) and the brilliant profusion of third-wave feminist zines and other publications. This period also sees the start of the growth of MFA programs and the ways in which the professionalization of creative writing both codifies and challenges modes of publication. In this context, small press publishing might attempt to disrupt or actively participate in such professionalization—or anywhere in-between, dependent also on the particular historical vantage point.

In the long midcentury cultural context, the legacy of gendered institutional disenfranchisement was both recent and ongoing. Aldan printed *Folder* magazine surreptitiously in the fifties because women were not allowed in the printer's union[16]; Notley was the only woman in the fiction workshop at Iowa in 1967, saying, "There were just so few women around, in fact"; Rena Rosenwasser describes how "supporting organizations such as the Book Club of California and the Roxburghe Club did not allow women to be members, or even come to functions except for once or twice a year. They were just snooty men's clubs, like old British gentlemen's clubs." Through these four decades—importantly, the ones in which second-wave feminism was also shaping the larger cultural context—women used publishing in various ways to push against the sexism and misogyny of literary scenes writ large.

How that resistance intersects with the women's movement more generally differs across the interviews. Some editors-publishers overlapped at spaces associated with the movement or thought of their publishing activity as a component of it; Lisa Kellman and Deborah Costello (Black Oyster Press, 1981–1984) had both spent time at the Women's Building in LA, and Susan Sherman (*IKON*, 1967–1969 and 1982–1994) became increasingly involved in the movement through the Fifth Street Women's Building in New York. Kitchen Table: Women of Color Press's (1980–1995) editor Barbara Smith describes the urgent role of the press in building the LGBTQIA+ and

6   Women in Independent Publishing

women's movements, which in turn provided the audience for the press's publications, though she often found herself "more comfortable" in a Black publisher's consortium, where other publishers were "engaged in the same challenges of being Black publishers, publishers of color, in an inhospitable publishing environment." Some editors, like Patricia Spears Jones, edited important movement-adjacent anthologies, while others were more skeptical of anything they saw at the time as related to identity politics, or changed their minds about this issue later. In locating the interviews initially in the "literary" scene of the Second Generation New York School, I was also following certain "allegiances" somewhat "tacitly," especially those regarding literariness and value, and much more work remains to be done on the overlaps and distinctions between movement-oriented and small press publishing circles.

Aldan is one of several editors-publishers who were often wary of projects that foregrounded gender or race, especially in the early decades, seeing such projects as further marginalizing their participants instead of shifting the center or the terms of participation. Though perhaps well-meant politically, these "race-blind" stances often had the consequence of replicating white-supremacist structures of exclusion—white women involved, especially those affiliated with New American and innovative poetry, often published white authors, many of them friends. That said, poetry publication in the era wasn't entirely segregated by race. Several of the previously mentioned publications and publishers featured women writers of color, especially into the 1980s, but as in the contemporary publishing scene, diversity in editorial positions was slower than diversity of writers featured, a fact relevant to the founding of Kitchen Table and later projects like *Aché: A Journal for Lesbians of African Descent* (1989–1995), which featured a calendar of events and articles as well as poetry and art. The editorial work of women of color extended to scenes like the Poetry Project, as with Patricia Spears Jones and her coeditors Sara Miles, Fay Chiang, and Sandra Maria Esteves's work on *Ordinary Women*, and the circles surrounding the Nuyorican Poetry Café, though Lynn Keller and Christanne Miller point to the ways in which scholarly framing of feminism further marginalized innovative writing by women of color.[17]

In sum, the vital work showcasing women of color is often adjacent to

Introduction   7

codified literary history, echoing the tacit refusal to acknowledge gender, and women of color often pursued editorial roles in scenes organized around race more than gender. Janice Mirikitani, editor of the foundational Asian American literary magazine *Aion* (1970–1971) and the bilingual *Ayumi: A Japanese American Anthology* (1980), pursued social justice through her work with Glide Memorial Church and urgent anthologies like *I Have Something to Say About This Big Trouble*, an anthology of writing by children affected by the crack cocaine crisis, published in 1989.[18] In her interview, Renee Tajima-Peña articulates how, like her subsequent filmmaking practice, she viewed *Bridge* as "a cultural organ of the [Asian American] movement," and how "Asian American publications have served that function since the earliest immigrant publications." Small presses also helped drive the Black Arts Movement. In Detroit, Naomi Long Madgett founded Lotus Press in 1972, now Lotus Broadside Press, and the aforementioned Kitchen Table: Women of Color Press was founded in Boston in 1980 by a group of women that included Audre Lorde and Barbara Smith. Some women like Tajima-Peña pursued editorial or publishing work as part of a trajectory that led away from purely literary scenes to other media and communities, their professional lives informed but not exclusively guided by their work on little magazines. It is urgently important to showcase these projects while not overreaching for commonalities across lineages and scenes or denying how race-based exclusions functioned in artistic scenes.

Because of the importance of these and other historical particulars, I do not want to pose the commonalities sketched out in this essay as imperative across all the interviews. In considering the interviews themselves as both literary texts and historical accounts, we must resist generalizing across moments and experiences. In these four decades, US-based literary communities were often fairly geographically mobile; editors pursued publishing agendas specifically designed to query the notions that schools and movements had fixed perimeters and magazines reinscribed these boundaries. Some editors found it useful to flag these groupings in order to publish across them; others sought to question the groupings themselves. However, in the sections that follow, I draw out several commonalities. First, this lineage suggests a long view of literary value and its independent quality over time, offering forms of literary valuation outside of comparison to

8   *Women in Independent Publishing*

established literary male predecessors and peers. Second, women in these scenes often saw friendship as a component of publication and distribution, suggesting adaptable relations in which friends shift among creating, critiquing, and publishing their own and each other's work. As Dewey and Rifkin note, "Friendships function not only as buffers against and wedges into poetic institutions whose exclusive gender politics would otherwise stifle women's poetic identity and practice, but as microsites from which these institutions can be challenged and transformed."[19] Finally, the shifting writer-critic-publisher roles support a symbiotic understanding of writing and publishing as components of a holistic process. Women small press editors and publishers therefore often had dual goals, which were to publish work that would accrue value while simultaneously developing as writers themselves.

II. "You Put Yourself Somewhere Near the Beginning": From *Folder* to *A New Folder*

Though Aldan stayed involved in literature her entire life, she is an example of someone whose editorial and writerly scenes and practices changed over time. She was born in New York City in 1918 and had a long career as a poet, teacher, translator, and editor-publisher.[20] She authored more than a dozen books of poetry, fiction, and nonfiction, and was also a prolific translator; she published the first English translation of Mallarmé's *Un coup de dés*. She was nominated—twice—for a Pulitzer Prize, was a member of the National Book Critics Circle, and was an influential teacher to thousands of students. In our correspondence, Gerard Malanga, a collaborator of Andy Warhol's, credits her with introducing him to poetry and guiding his poetic career.[21] Furthermore, even her teaching was in line with her several hyphenated roles; another former student, Renee M. Roberts, remembers her requiring her students to create little books of their own work,[22] and Aldan's first book of poems (1946) resulted because one of her students was talented at calligraphy and Aldan "thought it would be nice to put my poems in calligraphy."[23]

Throughout her interviews and correspondence, Aldan talks about her teaching as a way to support her publishing endeavors. Her initial impulse to self-publication quickly changed form, from single-author pamphlet to a magazine that included her as one author among many—a shift partially influenced by her PhD work at New York University on French surrealist poetry and its American inheritors, research that would have included little magazines in which editors published their own work. Some recent scholarship discusses her work on *Folder*, a magazine of art and literature published between 1953 and 1956 and coedited with Richard Miller, and a current literary magazine has even named itself *Folder* in homage.[24] *Folder* ran for four issues, each of which contains work either by or translated by Aldan. Perusing it, you can see why it merits attention: Its portfolio format (a result of not having the money for binding[25]) works beautifully with the enclosed silkscreen prints and letterpress text, and the table of contents now reads like a who's who of the midcentury New York art and poetry

Figure 1. "A Party for *Folder* Magazine" (1955). From left to right: Daisy Aldan, Richard Miller, William Fense Weaver, Grace Hartigan, John Ashbery, Frank O'Hara, James Schuyler, Kenneth Koch. Daisy Aldan Papers, Box 1, Folder 2, Harry Ransom Center, The University of Texas at Austin.

10   *Women in Independent Publishing*

scenes, especially those intersecting with French symbolism and surrealism.[26]

In moving from a magazine to a bound book, Aldan practiced the editorial criticality described by Sophie Seita in *Provisional Avant-Gardes: Little Magazine Communities from Dada to Digital*, which underscores the ways in which both editors and writers historicize and reflect upon their publishing work. "Editors and contributors," Seita writes, "became and still are theoreticians and pedagogues of the little magazine." These magazines, she argues, in being serial to some degree, or "aim[ing] toward periodicity," share the qualities of "provisionality, periodicity, multiple authorship, [and] heterogeneity of contents."[27] As an anthology that is both an extension of the earlier magazine—in his work on *Folder*, Ian Patterson calls the anthology a "coda" to the magazine, and a 1960 article in *Mademoiselle* calls the book "actually *Folder 5*"[28]—and something new, as the title suggests, *A New Folder* embraces some of these characteristics and suggests how the genre categories of magazines and anthologies shade into each other. In a 1991 interview, Aldan emphasizes the less ephemeral qualities of the anthology. She says: "I felt that *Folder* had finished its mission, and I wanted to put out instead a book, a bound book . . . [It had] about 50 poets, three-quarters of them women and about 50 pages, their works. And it got a lot of attention; you can imagine how much this is worth now."[29] It's hard to imagine how much *A New Folder* was worth in 1991, but in 2015 I acquired a copy for twenty dollars; at the time of writing you could find one on Alibris for fifty dollars. Aldan exaggerates not only the book's appreciation in monetary value but also the number of women included, which is one-third of the total poets and artists, or twenty-two of seventy-seven.

Though one-third is significantly different from three-quarters, as previously discussed, we might compare it to other anthologies of the moment to understand the more general trend. *New Poets of England and America* (1957), which provoked both Allen and Aldan's anthologies, published six women out of fifty-two, or about one-eighth; *The New American Poetry* published four out of forty-four, or one-eleventh. *A New Folder*'s relatively better numbers are one reason behind the impulse to compare it with *The New American Poetry*. In a short 2011 talk on *A New Folder* later published in the online forum *Jacket2*, Michael S. Hennessey resurrects Aldan's anthology for critical

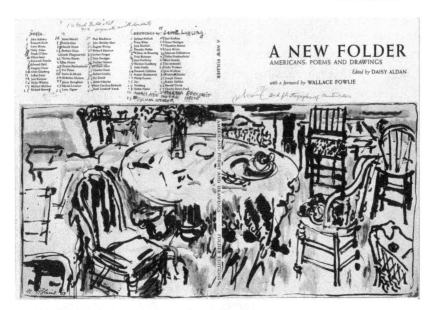

Figure 2. A *New Folder* Cover Proofs (hardcover edition, front and back, 1959). Daisy Aldan Papers, Box 2, Folder 2, Harry Ransom Center, The University of Texas at Austin.

attention, largely by comparing and suggesting it a precursor to Allen's.[30] More recently, Stephan Delbos's *The New American Poetry and Cold War Nationalism* uses Allen's archive to show how Aldan's anthology was "something of a touchstone" for Allen[31]; he finds that in Allen's correspondence about *The New American Poetry*, several other writers bring up Aldan's book, motivating Allen to make somewhat contradictory statements about his own editing in contrast with hers.[32]

Despite the fact that Allen's correspondence contains these exchanges with others *about* Aldan, the two do not seem to have directly corresponded at length. Their papers contain a small exchange about permissions: Allen tried to avoid using poems Aldan had published, though he had "slipped up in three cases."[33] But if Allen was not as generous as he might have been about acknowledging Aldan's influence, Aldan did not consider the anthologies to be in competition. Delbos's book mentions another letter, in which Aldan alludes to, as Delbos puts it, "the shared affinities between the anthologies" and commiserates with Allen after a negative review of *The New*

12 Women in Independent Publishing

American Poetry.[34] And Aldan went further than commiserating. In 1960 the magazine *Trace* published a negative review by Curtis Zahn of *The New American Poetry.*[35] In response, Aldan wrote a strongly worded letter to the magazine's editor, James Boyer May, which opens, "I rarely write letters of protest, but I was shocked by the vindictive review of Donald Allen's anthology, written by Curtis Zahn. [. . .] I don't believe that I have ever seen a review of any book that was less objective, reeked of [sic] personal vindictiveness, and which gave a false picture of the contents of the volume."[36]

Here Aldan takes up the "shared affinities" between the two anthologies and savvily positions her own anthology alongside Allen's. She continues, "I do not know Curtis Zahn, and there are portions of Mr. Allen's anthology which were not to my personal liking. However, I must say, that it IS one of the most exciting collections, containing excellent work, which has appeared since A NEW FOLDER: AMERICANS: POEMS AND DRAWINGS, my own anthology." In aligning her own anthology with Allen's maligned one, Aldan makes the interval between their publications sound much longer than one year, writing a version of literary history. If the anthologies are different, she suggests, it is less that they are in competition and more that Aldan's provides a fuller picture of the same scene: Near the end of the letter, she concludes, "My only argument with Mr. Allen is that more work by American women poets of which there is quite a number of excellent ones, was not included. His anthology included only three, I believe. Mine included eighteen, all worthy and fine writers."[37] Aldan sees herself as a predecessor to Allen and also as a protector, perhaps like a sibling—yet tensions of that relationship are downplayed, because she and Allen are working together against critics like Zahn. Aldan is fully aware that the disproportionate number of men to women being published does not reflect who is actually writing—and she insists on positioning herself, her editorial work, and women's writing in the discussion about what would become known as the New American Poetry.

And yet she doesn't stay in the discussion. Her work on *A New Folder* in particular becomes present as a spectral version of Allen's; Delbos follows Hennessey in writing, "As a document that suggests a path not taken, a path that was in fact completely obscured by Allen's anthology, *A New Folder* is fascinating."[38] From this starting point, we can consider strategies for bringing Aldan out of the margins. How can we put her in the historical record without reinforcing an opposition between Aldan and Allen (and Judith and William) or a story of one anthology winning out over another? One provisional answer places Judith in relation to other women writers and publishers—and thus focuses on documenting a community of Judith Shakespeares. Aldan becomes an editor in part to publish her own work and create her own community. This founding, or putting herself "near the beginning," is a repeated action across the history of midcentury woman publishers-editors; Aldan need not directly inspire other women in order for us to see this action as a commonality that both puts the women in relationality and allows them each the founder spotlight in turn. In order to pursue this idea, we will now turn to Aldan's production and selection practices in relation to those of women small press publishers who came after her.

A New Folder was printed in an edition of 1,000, the first 125 of which were hardcover—a small but respectable print run for poetry. Always attentive to production, Aldan decided when she saw the proofs that she wanted better paper and a hardcover edition, but the books then cost six times the original estimate. She hoped to recoup some of the funds through the June 1959 release reading at the Living Theatre, but the theater was also in a hole, and finally sent her twenty dollars—in March 1960.[39] Her correspondence reveals that she was adamant about tracking down money owed Folder Editions in the years after *A New Folder*—a necessity perhaps born out the experiences of publishing the anthology. Much of her correspondence involves badgering booksellers and others for payments. In the years following *A New Folder*, Folder Editions increasingly turned away from the New York scene and more toward translation and poetry from other cultural contexts, as well as Aldan's interest in the work of Rudolf Steiner and the anthroposophy spiritual movement.

What is somewhat surprising, given the years and contexts covered by interviews with Aldan and the *Women in Independent Publishing* interviewees, is that activity that might now be seen as separate from "professional" publishing was nonetheless taken quite seriously. Despite financial pressures— she says the "greatest [difficulty publishing *A New Folder*] is trying to do everything with very little money—all earned in teaching"[40]—Aldan remained a staunch advocate for self-publishing throughout her life, and

14   *Women in Independent Publishing*

even saw losing money on publishing as part of the vocation of being a poet. In 1970 a poet she had published, Virginia Brady Young, wrote to complain about sunk costs. Aldan responds, "Some people spend money for fur coats, antiques, stamp collections. We poets spend ours on our work if we want it out in the world. . . . Its [the book's] presence in the world defines you as published POET. That was the purpose of the publication."[41] In the 1991 interview quoted earlier, she refers to the tendency to call self-publishing "vanity" publishing, saying, "Yes, I believe it's only vanity when it's not good. As a matter of fact today, especially in poetry—today, they won't publish your work if it's called literature. . . . Poets must publish their own work! And they mustn't be ashamed. It will find its way in the world if it's good."[42]

The *Oxford English Dictionary*'s first example of "vanity publisher" comes from 1922, though the first examples for "vanity publishing" and "vanity press" appear in the sixties,[43] and all three terms seem to have risen substantially after the fifties up until the nineties.[44] Given the legacies of Whitman, Dickinson, Woolf, and many others, it's obvious to say that some of the stigma around self-publishing is a relatively recent phenomenon. Less obviously, the interviews suggest that regardless of historical moment, much of this stigma has to do with the social and cultural spheres surrounding publication contexts. When I asked Bernadette Mayer (0 *TO* 9, 1967–1969, and United Artists Books, 1977–present) about the dislike for self-publishing, she said, "Nowadays there is. But you know what, there was then too. But you'd just ignore it. I mean, it's the stupidest thing. I mean, what is that all about? Capitalism, perhaps?" Aldan's notion that the quality of the work will lead to its long-term circulation and valuation—that it "will find its way in the world if it's good"—echoes in other accounts. Sometimes, like in Aldan's idea of value, this sense is optimistic and future oriented, as when Hettie Jones, who coedited *Yugen* (1958–1962) says, "I do think the best kinds of work will finally come to the fore," and when Patricia Spears Jones says, "Go for excellent, that is what lasts." Other times it is a historical truth; about poetry readings, so often tied to the business of publishing through release parties, Eileen Myles, who edited *dodgems* (1977–1979), says, "And later on you learned that more people heard you than you knew. There was a nice thing of not trying hard but still feeling connected." In both of these instances, through readings and some small press publications, something that is almost ephemeral accrues value, primarily at the local community level but potentially expanding across time and place, in a series of moves so minor that they are often invisible. In some scenes, this value comes primarily from a participant's continued engagement with writing scenes; in others, it comes from surprising circuits of circulation and readership. The publishers are suggesting that the fact of whether or not the publisher and writer are the same person has very little to do with the accrual of value.

III. "You Print by Hand": Typesetting, Typing, and Production Technologies

Noting this accrual reflects an attunement to the gendering of production technologies and women's labor across periods of history longer than the midcentury. The affective and sensorial histories suggested by the use of various publishing technologies and their embodied use by women are often not linear. Midcentury publishers and editors alternately describe them as limiting and liberating in regard to gender. Because of this connection to haptic collective histories, the interview questions are sometimes repetitively interested in the nitty-gritty details of production—stencil typing, collating parties, distribution details—suggestive (though not always illustrative) of gendered labor histories and their alternatives. One place where gender historically intersects with book production is in typesetting and typing. In an interview with Dennis Barone, Aldan describes how she "set the type by hand" for *Folder* magazine, first using a "Kinsey press"[45] purchased by mail and later via Linotype, printing surreptitiously at a shop on 82nd Street. "When someone entered the shop," Aldan says, "I had to stop work because women were not allowed in the union then and the printer would have been suspended or fined."[46] These labor restrictions contributed to the blurring of domestic and production spaces; many women editors and publishers describe setting up presses in their homes, a choice that, in later decades, was often attributed to financial considerations, but one that should also be seen in historical proximity to labor restrictions and gender bias in publishing.[47] This context also informs the sense of accomplishment with which some women discuss typesetting and printing, actions through which you determine the look of the page. Aldan says, "I think I was the only female linotype setter in New York at the time."[48] In secretly doing

16   *Women in Independent Publishing*

something women were not permitted to do, Aldan was connected to both predecessors and successors. Rena Rosenwasser and Patricia Dienstfrey describe working "under the influence of the famous photo of Virginia Woolf setting type for the first printing of *Ulysses* at Hogarth Press" when Kelsey Street began in 1974, and accounts of women being both implicitly and explicitly marginalized in print shops persist into the 1980s.[49] As part of a professional world from which women had been excluded, typesetting and printing could be considered an empowering or exciting form of labor.

Running parallel to the labor of setting type is that of typing stencils—often involving pressing forcefully on typewriter keys to cut letters into a wax-coated sheet—for mimeograph machines. Both typesetting and typing stencils were activities widely discussed as pedagogical, one of the ways in which writing and editing strengthened each other, especially in contexts where women were less frequently involved in the formal study or informal conversation surrounding writing and often taken less seriously as writers. Rosmarie Waldrop (Burning Deck Press, 1961–present) describes setting type as "the greatest lesson in close reading I ever had" and "helped make my own poems very lean." Likewise, Jones credits typing stencils with teaching concision.[50] She says that "the act of typing and retyping" allowed her to hear "the rhythms of everyone's poems" and taught her to "simplify [her own] lines and really absorb what it meant to write a good poem." The rhythm and sound of typing is often linked to the musicality of the poem, but the sound itself as pedagogical builds on Friedrich Kittler's description of the sound of the typewriter as reflex loop motivating more writing.[51] Maureen Owen, who edited *Telephone* magazine (1969–1984), says that after the heightened attention required by typing "each word and space and line break" would make the poem "embossed on [her] brain": "I became one with the poem in a way that doesn't happen when one is just reading the work." Notley sums up this sentiment, calling typing "very educational" for learning to write poems. This education was about discovering your own poetic process alongside the poetry of the moment.

However, as the typing of stencils loses any associations with typesetting—an off-limits part of the production process—and becomes, in the midcentury, a rote task performed by typists and secretarial workers who were often women, some interviewees talk about the action as gendered and devalued.[52] Spears Jones describes having "to type out each of those darn pages" for *W. B.* (1975), and Mayer refers to typing stencils as "a very womanly reaction, or role to play" that she performed when coediting *0 TO 9* (1967–1969). When asked about typing stencils for *United Artists* magazine and United Artists Books, she exclaims, "[Coeditor] Lewis [Warsh] could type stencils! Isn't that great?" Finally, both Barbara Barg and Myles talk about typesetting changing with the use of computers, specifically the Compugraphic 7500 (first produced in 1977), and how "typesetting helped people make a living," again shifting the possible gender dynamics of typing and typesetting.

In the decades between the fifties and the eighties, available technologies for book production mixed to an unprecedented degree. Letterpress, mimeo, offset, computers—production decisions had different aesthetic implications across contexts. Mimeo, lending its name to the era's wide variety of publications as the "mimeograph revolution,"[53] was the most polarizing among women editors. Waldrop states, "Mimeo was never an option: it faded too quickly," and Maxine Chernoff (*Oink!*, 1971–1985, and *New American Writing*, 1986–present) explains, "At that time there was the whole movement and history of printing on mimeo machines, and all kinds of sub-par printing that was fairly widely used back then, and widely disseminated and maintained." Considered to be ephemeral, the appeal was one of rapidity and collectivity; Owen says, "Mimeo was immediate. It inspired and supported spontaneity. It captured that fabulous feeling of folks coming together and just doing it." Or the immediacy got folded back into the material text *as* aesthetics; she also says, "I'll never forget the feeling of that first issue coming off the gestetner and the beauty of the rich black ink lifting the poems off the white page." For Mayer, one of mimeo's staunchest advocates, the appeal was both tactility—"touch[ing] each piece of paper"—and instantaneousness, so much so that other modes of production, like letterpress, began to appear precious.

For letterpress advocates, like Aldan, the technology offered "sensuous pleasures," as Rosenwasser and Dienstfrey call them, more associated with fine art. Kelsey Street began to explore these pleasures through their writer-artist collaborative projects, while Martha King and Susan Sherman's chapbook press Two and Two (1975) attempted to keep things "low cost, very

18 *Women in Independent Publishing*

cheap, easy to produce"—though, as King stipulates, "that does not mean cluttered or ugly." Myles disliked the romanticization of mimeo's ease and economy to the point of calling it "cheap and poor," saying, "I never had any sentimental attachment to [the poetry magazine's] scarcity aesthetic," and had a memorable exchange about the topic with Mayer in two subsequent issues of *The Poetry Project Newsletter* in 1982.[54] Additionally, embedded in the debates about aesthetics, the value of immediacy, and cost, is a series of associations between particular production modes and countercultural values, and these associations are not necessarily stable across moments and contexts. For Smith, paper choice of a press release could help subtly indicate the press's identity and catch the eye of the audience. And of *IKON* (Series 1, 1967–1968), Susan Sherman says:

> On the other hand, we got all kinds of criticism from some of the movement people about *IKON* magazine supposedly looking too slick. It was work that made it look that good, not money. It didn't cost more except for using decent paper. We had a really good printer who printed on a huge press sixteen pages at a time . . . Just because you're doing a movement thing doesn't mean you should have to do it on newsprint—unless it's a newspaper, of course!—and make it look messy. I mean, even when we used the mimeograph—and we used it a lot—we tried to do it as nicely as possible.

In other words, the technology did not necessarily predetermine the amount of care and attention devoted to particular publications, despite aesthetic assumptions associated with different modes of production.

Of course, there were reasons apart from aesthetics and political alignment to produce something that looked more like a conventional codex, and these had largely to do with the practicalities of distribution. In many of these publication contexts, handmade production qualities excluded a book from certain types of circulation, further contributing to the stigma against self-publishing. Aldan says she wanted a book "because when the *Folders* were in bookstores, people would take them up, and they would look at them and all the pages would fall out on the floor."[55] However, distributors—and some bookstores—also wanted spines. As Mayer says, "A lot of people that I met have this idea that mimeograph books are not as good as—what we used to call them at the time—'books with a spine.'" Jones confirms that, in the *Yugen* years, distributors required a spine (though the rule might have been flexible—one distributor "agreed to take on our magazine" because "he liked us"), and Barg turned to books with her press Power Mad in 1979 "because the thing was, back then, you couldn't really get your book . . . into the bookstores unless it had a spine . . . So I decided I would start publishing books with a spine." If not having a perfect-bound spine was often the mark of community and a more inclusive DIY aesthetic process—"No spine, hand-sewn by press members at a dining room table," as Dienstfrey says—this mode of production also kept the books from circulating in more well-worn commercial tracks, excluding them from certain spheres of readership. Other editors-publishers, like Myles, became skeptical of the limits—in terms of both production values and audience—of the "scarcity aesthetic" of spinelessness, in terms of both production values and audience. Owen says, "As gratifying and as satisfying as it was to 'make' the books myself through mimeo, it was famously exciting to be able to afford to do a perfect-bound publication."

Even when she was making books by hand, Aldan never was interested in the "scarcity aesthetic." She wanted to make beautiful books, and she wanted them to be distributed. As evidenced by the success of her own self-published poetry, Aldan could get books into the hands of reviewers and readers; her correspondence is full of compliments from readers who were artists and not, in fact, poets. However, like many, she also struggled with distribution and publicity beyond her circles and was frustrated by the lack of reviews—or by getting good reviews in places where there was no market for the books. In a November 1, 1959, letter to Fowlie, she mentions "very enthusiastic letters from [all] over" in response to *A New Folder*, but then states, "However, I must still go myself to bookstores and I find this a most unpleasant job,"[56] unpleasant due to the time involved in peddling the books. Additionally, she actively collected addresses and possible review venues for *A New Folder* in her correspondence with contributors.

Aldan's reliance on address mailing lists was fairly standard for midcentury distribution. Mayer, Owen, and others describe how distribution took place through "various bookstores and people, individual people," Owen explaining that "mailing book rate was very inexpensive in the seventies and eighties." Even for a slightly later magazine like *New American Writing*, which did have "a couple distributors," much of the work of sending it out "to libraries and subscribers" was done literally in house. Chernoff says, "But for a few weeks every late spring or early summer, the dining room looked like a warehouse—we'd have many copies to send in envelopes to people." Additionally, Aldan's dislike of the actualities of distribution was also fairly widely shared, with Smith a notable exception. C. D. Wright (Lost Roads, 1976–present) says, "Actually selling the books was not my forte. Nor is it of most small press editors. Distribution is limited to the outfits designed to serve the small literary press and we did not publish enough titles for the ones who actually had reps." King admits, "I was supposed to do promotion. Ahem. Which is why I still have a stash of *Women & Children First* in my basement." And when I lament to Barg that such issues persist, despite the ubiquity of publicizing and distributing through Internet platforms, she responds, "Give them to the poets, tell them to distribute them! Why should you do all the work? You're putting the book out!"

Of course, distributors could decline to carry a publication for reasons other than the fact that the books lacked a spine. Series 1 of *IKON* ceased because it "depended on three major distributors nationwide" to get it to newsstands, and after Sherman published an issue about the Cuban Cultural Congress in 1968, the distributor did not send out the magazines. She says, "I can't prove the government was responsible, but it was pretty obvious when we got the returns of the magazine I put together about the Cuban Cultural Congress I had attended back from the distributor. [The distributor] hadn't even unpacked it." Even an irreverent or seemingly countercultural title could put off distributors. Chernoff says that because distributors refused to take *Oink!*, when they began to publish again after a brief hiatus they renamed the magazine: "So our trick was that we'd give it a big name, *New American Writing*, but it's really still just *Oink!* inside. And we didn't really change anything else. . . . And so our distribution went way up—at one point we went from distributing about 1,000 copies to almost 6,000 copies."

Regardless of whether you were using a distributor, the mail was an effective mode of getting the publications out, and some publications, like

Introduction 21

Lisbet Tellefsen's *Aché* (1989–1995) and Martha King's *Giants Play Well in the Drizzle* (1983–1992) embraced a newsletter format at first. Margaret Randall, editing *El Corno Emplumado / The Plumed Horn* in Mexico City (1962–1969), says, of circulation, "Our ambitions weren't only global; they were universal!" and Owen exclaims about how "folks you didn't know would now be reading your work." Notley similarly used the magazine to expand her aesthetic circles, saying, "I had a lovely list of readers—I just sent *CHICAGO* . . . to them without requiring payment, as I remember it—abstract expressionists and second-generation NY School artists for example, all the major NY poets, etc., everyone in San Francisco and Bolinas." The mail helped constellate scenes when the participants were moving about and changing locations. Aldan especially relied on her correspondents to suggest other poets and give her the addresses of poets who were strangers to her, soliciting work based on word-of-mail recommendations. She was, in fact, quite a bit more interested in expanding the circle of her authors beyond her immediate friends than other postwar small press publishers—perhaps confident in the knowledge that, given the local orientation of distribution, even if you were committed to publishing strangers, they often became friends.

IV. You Print Your Friends: Group and Community

Friends helped you make magazines and books and wrote the contents of said publications; friendship, with all of its tensions and flexibilities, oriented conceptions of community. The party, in various forms—the collating party, the release party, the post-reading party—was one of the most exuberant versions of community. And parties there were. Jones says, "I mean, our parties were generally the collating parties. But we had a party every weekend!" Collating parties, in which magazines were assembled by individuals picking up single pages from piles of copies, often made the authors included in table of contents part of the publishing process; Aldan describes how she and "the poets" collated *Folder*.[57] Later, these collating parties were part of the larger poetry scene surrounding the Poetry Project at St. Mark's Place. Owen says, "Everyone who was local and in the issue would come to help collate and bring friends . . . It was truly a community effort. We would buy pizza and cokes and wine, and it was a hands-on working party that would continue until the last copy of the issue was stapled and put on the stack." Parties provide a glimpse into the shifting, constellating, and participatory characteristics of community. Barg describes a similar scene "for anything that had to be collated."

On the West Coast, both Jaime Robles (Five Trees Press, 1973–1978) and Dienstfrey emphasize release parties: "And there were lots of release parties. Great parties to which everyone would bring ephemera, broadsides, and booklets to be shared"; "We were into release parties. We viewed the publication of a book as a cause for celebration with food and wine. We were also into food. And wine." Aldan, too, understood the ways in which a good release reading party could shore up a sense of community, and her release reading for *A New Folder* at the Living Theatre began at midnight. The recording of the event reveals it to have been an efficient affair, with each reading synched with the projection of an artist's work and Aldan succinctly announcing everyone. She closes the reading by saying, "*A New Folder* invites you into the lobby for a reception where you may meet the poets,"[58] both positing the poets as separate from the audience (despite making up a good portion of it, given the number of readers) and simultaneously suggesting that the poets are accessible for intermingling. When she talks about this reading in 1991, she remembers it as the initiating event for subsequent readings at the Living Theater, as a broader art world event, and as a blast: "It was packed! It was a who's who of dancers, painters, poets, opera singers . . . They were all part of the circle. 18 books were stolen, so that showed that it was a success. And champagne, and . . . we began at midnight and we left at about 4 o'clock in the morning."[59] When Frank O'Hara attempted to drop out of the reading because he wanted to leave the city for the weekend, Aldan used both friendship and an appeal to his "public responsibility" to convince him to stay and participate.[60]

If O'Hara already drew an audience in 1959, one would not necessarily glean that fact from *A New Folder*'s table of contents, where he comes fifth in the list of poets—after John Ashbery, Kenneth Koch, Larry Rivers, and Aldan herself, a fact to which we will return in the next section. As evidenced by this list, the poetry is certainly New York centered, though it productively crosses generational lines and schools.[61] At the same time, we must note that LeRoi Jones is, as he so often was, the token writer of color. Delbos considers the anthology unique for mixing "academic" and avant-garde poetry,[62] though Aldan herself did not conceive of it thus: She considered the anthology as part of avant-garde publishing. In a May 3, 1958, letter to Madame Caetani, she suggests that, like other contemporaneous editors, a desire to create a more exciting anthology than Donald Hall's—which helped instigate the "anthology wars"—partially motivated her: "Donald Hall has edited one that has been published recently, but although it contains some finely cut jewels, it is a dull affair."[63]

Before considering a scholar's introduction for the anthology, Aldan tried to involve a matriarch of the avant-garde: Alice Toklas, whose imprimatur would reflect the contents, which Aldan thought of as more innovative than traditional. In an undated letter responding to this idea, Eugene Walter writes, "[Toklas's] preface—if she agreed—could give a cachet of civilized pleasure which would indicate to a large segment of the public that this is not another Donald Hall let's-be-professorpoetpals-together anthology!"[64] Yet Aldan ends up asking a professor, Wallace Fowlie, to write the introduction, presumably after Toklas declines the invitation, and Aldan's avant-garde has more to do with selectivity and modernist innovations than social groupings. In a January 27, 1959, letter to Toklas, Aldan explains, "[The anthology] is to be very selected—not a million American poets, just SOME. It seemed to me that the anthologies I have seen include mostly poems in the traditional idiom, as if nothing had happened to poetry—and especially American poetry—since 1900, so I felt compelled to remedy that."[65] And in a January 25, 1958, letter to Carol Hall, she writes, "I am interested in the most exciting things you have—ones which, perhaps, you have had difficulty publishing elsewhere—not because of inferior quality but on the contrary, because they were more than traditional."[66] A constellated lineage, one that becomes visible through self-publishing practices, both stands and accrues value apart from the "traditional." Was Aldan, like Alice Notley, "[not] very interested in the idea of groups"? Aldan might have had a somewhat capacious sense of community, but she definitely relied on networks and connections; for instance, she and Elliott Stein agree to exchange blurbs—and though he had not seen *A New Folder*, Aldan asks him to write a blurb anyway, asserting, "It's the only [anthology] so far that's any good."[67]

Other women editors and publishers are both more and less circumspect about the interpersonal connections that motivate and result from small press publishing. Chernoff takes a long view when she says, "People publish each other—it's the same activity that happened when I was young, only it's a new group and several generations down the line of young people coming aboard and publishing each other." Robles says, "I think that remains the model for most presses: you print your friends . . . I'm not a big fan of the presses who won't publish the people they know, who are their friends, believing that that makes the press somehow more democratic or more objective and therefore somehow more politically correct or aesthetically true or fairer in some sense . . . I recommend publishing the work you love by the people you love . . . Make it a gift, or an act of love."

What is the difference between a group and a community? Perhaps counterintuitively, the way the interviewees use the latter suggests that it moves beyond the local, is always plural, and functions more like a constellation—communities vary in size, are nestled in each other, overlap, and so forth—than the fixed perimeters of a group, and that small press publications make communities dialogic. For many of the women interviewed, editing small press publications did not so much create as enable participation in and expansion of communities. In "Space Occupied: Women Poet-Editors and the Mimeograph Revolution in Mid-century New York City," Rona Cran demonstrates how women editors associated with the Second Generation New York School assert themselves in "material, textual, and cultural spaces in which their presence was registered or negated."[68] Notley and others tend to phrase this assertion in terms of communication and community—and enlargement, balancing out the exclusivity of the group: "The magazine was a way of really joining the poetry community, of getting to read a lot of poems." Chernoff also speaks of the magazine as "[keeping] us in touch with a larger community," and Tajima-Peña says, "Publishing *Bridge* was a communal experience . . . It was a community. Wright says, "We were still publishing writers we knew, but the sense of the local expanded, because of being at a university where any number of writers filtered through; because we were both more in touch with writers by mail and travel, the press took on a somewhat broader character." Tellefsen, importantly, points to the ways *Aché* facilitated opportunities for "you [to] see the entirety of your community, from the fresh out baby dyke to the 90-something with her partner."

Finally, Spears Jones suggests the necessary interplay of community and audience: "While there will always be poets who veer towards monasticism, solitude, the carefully tended garden, there will be others who will speak to, speak of and speak out about specific communities. The trick is to create work that can do that and reach farther than one's own tribe."

However, small press women publishers and editors did not come to univocal conclusions regarding *how* the community is expanded through publishing or how best to set up inclusive publishing practices. After *A New Folder* and the continued lack of women in other anthologies of the period, Aldan thought about putting together an anthology of just women, even sketching out a table of contents. But the project was never realized, and later she would declare herself to be against any identity-based forms of publishing, wary of tokenism and the ways in which such projects could be marginalized.[69] To return to the idea of value, her belief in quality as some sort of abstract, depoliticized criterion is both typical and problematic. Spears Jones points out how the "poetics" mindset "allowed white poets to question the 'quality' of the work of poets of color," and Sherman describes how the NEA uses the term "uneven" about a piece titled "The Vietnamese Lesbian Speaks" to justify the withdrawal of funding. This is one of several ways in which liberal gatekeeping reinforced exclusions, particularly around race.

Temporal distance can help provide clarity about factors contributing to exclusion. Waldrop was one woman who, in 1994, was wary of projects that focused on publishing women. By 2015, however, she had modulated her opinion: "I think I was wrong about the 'ghetto'-problem. The women-only mags and presses were a leavening and helped raise awareness." Owen and others have sometimes cast the gender imbalance of the seventies as uneven access to ambition: "I remember talking to Anne [Waldman] about women poets who weren't getting published. They just weren't knocking on the door." Her focus, like that of so many of these publishers, was getting the work out to an audience instead of focusing on the causes of the dynamic. For Chernoff, supporting women students meant creating publishing opportunities; for Notley, publishing was both a way to give women writers power and to get power, "since men wanted to be in All the magazines." Rosenwasser and Dienstfrey, "driven to erase the absence of women in the poetry world" and also to connect

26   *Women in Independent Publishing*

to a historical lineage, reiterate, "Again, there were many women who did not want to be part of gender-based projects."

Myles had the contents for an issue of *dodgems* 3, which was going to feature more work by women, but never published it. Despite their focus on gender when soliciting submissions, they say, "All these men gave me poems either dedicated to me or about me and then they wanted me to publish it. I thought I'm either going to look like a huge narcissist or offend them by not publishing it. It was definitely not something they would put on a man. Like my magazine would be filled by all these little China dolls of me." Notley experienced this sort of dedicatory (and predatory) practice as well, and though it gestured toward inclusivity by suggesting friendship or camaraderie, as Myles so succinctly articulates, it often actually functioned to exclude woman and non-binary writers' work with a gesture that recast the subject as a precious object or as valued in the community precisely for their gender difference, potentially too "fragile" if they attempt to call out an act that others might assert was a compliment or "joke." Here the dedicatory practice, writing *for* another, also marginalizes their labor.

V. You Print Yourself in Terms of Everybody: Editing and Writing

In addition to being potential dedicatees, Notley, Aldan, and others saw themselves in oscillating and flexible roles as editors, publishers, and writers. In an early moment of the history of Burning Deck Press, Waldrop describes her role in a 1959 University of Michigan prank performance called the Beatnik Hoax as that of being a "spy in the audience."[70] Editors and publishers are, to varying degrees, already in a special espionage category, scoping out work and poets for their journals at readings and in discussions with friends. This phrase is especially apt for illustrating the role of women editors and publishers in this period. But by the early 1980s, women were calling out men in some poetry spaces, particularly those around the Poetry Project, vividly described by Rose Lesniak when she talks about heckling men who "were just out there dreaming in their sexist wonderhood." Women midcentury editors and publishers were not only spies in the audience but also hecklers in the crowd, organizers in the wings, and—importantly—writers reading onstage. If, as the subtitle of this book suggests, they were "unsung innovators," they were also never not singing.[71]

In addition to the simultaneously inclusive and exclusive gesture of publishing friends, they also published their own writing, connected to espionage in that self-publishing is sometimes disparaged as a way of "sneaking" into a publication or book catalog. Throughout this introduction I have been referring to much of the publishing activity I describe as "self-publishing," with good reason; many of the interviewees published their own work to be in conversation with that of other writers they admired. Aldan published herself not only as a contributor to *Folder* and *A New Folder* but also as the author and translator of individual volumes with Folder Editions. Waldrop describes how Burning Deck's first letterpress chapbooks, published in 1967, were by herself and Keith Waldrop. Many of the editors of magazines especially included their own work. Myles says, "I put in my own best work and also work by people I wanted to be in conversation with. Including my own best poem made me more excited about distributing *dodgems* widely, me to be in such great company." Aldan's understanding of her own group is visualized in the author and artist photographs at the end of *A New Folder*, where her picture—smiling, gazing up out of the book—tops a hexagon of young poets.[72] Regardless of her role as an editor, she always also saw herself as a writer and translator, and she published her poems or translations in every issue of *Folder* and in *A New Folder*. In revisions to a 1993 pamphlet for Folder Editions, which lists titles written or translated by Aldan available from other presses, she crosses out "editor" under her name to shift the emphasis to her role as writer and translator.[73]

Aldan's blurry oscillation between editor and writer is shared in practice by other women small press publishers, though they have different articulations of the degree to which writing and editing overlap. Sherman sees the selective skills of the editor as similar to the ones the writer uses in writing: "I mean, we edit our work, don't we? We make choices all the time. I mean, a writer knows how to make choices!" For many publishers, in a small press context, editing is a catch-all word for everything required to shepherd a book to publication; others hear in editing the process of locating and selecting manuscripts. Mayer describes mostly "happen[ing] on [manuscripts] by chance." Notley says, "Now that I think about it, I realize that my editing was quite aggressive. It was hard for me to know what it was like at the time, I was so young and there was so much sexism in the atmosphere . . . I didn't necessarily accept what I was supposed to accept, I picked and chose—for example I might accept one part of a poem in several parts." Aldan saw providing feedback as one aspect of editing, asking some writers to significantly cut their pieces (she told Ginsberg that "Howl" was "uneven").[74]

In a broader conceptual sense, the role of the editor comes out of the "sneaky" ways in which we think about order and disorder,[75] of organizing a jumble while simultaneously creating one. In small press publishing, editorial work is often seen as ferreting out and gathering work, rather than sorting it. This vision influences how pieces are placed together in a volume and even in a series. King says of *Giants Play Well in the Drizzle* (1983–1992), "The pages were intended to flow and to set off some resonances from one work to another. Counterpoint? Contrast? Dissonance??" On a personal level, though, editing allows the writer to showcase herself as a writer—and an editor, however an individual differentiates and elides those positions. King calls editing *Giants Play Well in the Drizzle* a "an important survival tactic besides being a wonderful opportunity for me to work with words and be in touch with interesting writers on my own terms" during the grind of an everyday job.

When women and nonbinary midcentury editors-publishers are connected to "interesting writers" on their "own terms," they can create the kinds of relations and lineages that then constitute so much of literary history. As this essay has been suggesting, for midcentury women editors, publishing *felt* like beginning, a fact Aldan implicitly acknowledges when, in telling an audience the practical steps to becoming a publisher, she ends by "kick[ing] her foot into the air and saying, 'GO AHEAD AND DO IT.'"[76] Aldan's anthology might not have survived the test of time, but recentering it despite—or even precisely because of—its current minor status allows us to, in scholarship, articulate the new beginnings she and other midcentury publishers-editors examined in this essay have been modeling for us all along. In other words, if women and nonbinary editors are asserting a porosity in their lineages by putting themselves at the beginning but also always in relation, it behooves us to imagine a literary history that does similarly, suggesting new beginnings and nongenealogical relations, attempting to see Judith without William.

So what does a literary history that sees Aldan and *A New Folder* as a major forebearer for postwar poetry look like? It highlights the work and stories of women who were involved with small press publishing, even when they were copublishing with men.[77] It is present and future oriented, and not (only) focused on encapsulating the recent past. In this way, it is desirous of change, though not all the editors in the interviews that follow would phrase it thus. The change might be political or social—the interviewees had very different aspirations for their publications and broader societal change. Or the future-orientation of the editor might be general: Aldan called editing "fore-intuition"[78]; Myles says, "I'm always convinced of the poetry & prophecy connection so same goes for editing. Same flow." Editing is a place where you have to have optimism about the future, though it does not remedy the exclusions of the present and recent past. A literary history that sees Aldan and *A New Folder* as a major forebearer for postwar poetry sees these conversations as texts occurring in the literary present; we can continue to have them again and again. It is by no means equitable, and, especially in a friendship model, is fed by many of the exclusions that characterize US-based literary history more generally. Its intersectionality means that it includes white queer participants much more quickly than women of color, whose publishing communities were often separate, and it requires attention to how the dynamics of race and class excluded writers and editors from small press communities, as well as an additional critical lens focused on undercurrents of marginalization. It requires a more critical assessment of our affective responses to self-publishing as an important component of small press publishing, and a more transparent look at gatekeeping and the insider/outsider dynamics created by so-called schools and artistic groups. And while contemporary interest in Folder Editions might seem nascent, the press was featured in two exhibitions in New York libraries in the 1990s, reminding us of that the process of shifting literary history is always recursive. In bringing up neglected examples there is eventually power in the accrual, a sort of sine wave formation of research and minor stories becoming major ones.

THE INTERVIEWS

Figure 3. *Yugen* Issue 6 (1960). Cover by Basil King.

Hettie Jones

Coeditor and Copublisher, Yugen *(1958–1962, New York)*

SEPTEMBER 10, 2014, VIA THE TELEPHONE

Stephanie Anderson: I had a little bit of a hard time coming up with questions because your memoir, *How I Became Hettie Jones*, does such a wonderful job of describing your role in the publishing of *Yugen* and Totem Press. So I thought I would start with a really simple question, which is: What was your favorite part of the magazine production process?[1]

Hettie Jones: Let's see, what was my favorite part. Being alone with the poems, and typing and retyping the poems so that they were perfect on the page. Because everything—as you can tell, everything was done by hand, and it was done by *me* by hand. So the poems were very personal to me. I can recall Frank O'Hara's "Personal Poem"—I don't know whether you know that poem—do you?

SA: Yeah.

HJ: Oh, okay. So I eventually in my later life wrote a sort of rejoinder to that poem, about my own process in it. It sort of goes:

> Over and over the mind returns
> to the bent shoulders of the young woman
> who types, over and over, the poem
> until it is perfectly placed
> on the page, the name
> of her husband, the name
> of her lover
> the guilty thrill
> of juxtaposition
> as each gives

> to the poet
> what he keeps
> in his pocket
> in her arms she holds them
> over and over.

The only reason I remember that by heart—I'm not reading it from a book—is that I just read it at a tribute to Frank O'Hara at the St. Mark's Church. We read all of the poems that were published in *Lunch Poems*, and I read "Personal Poem" from that, and then I read my rejoinder . . . I talked about what it meant to me. Anyhow, it wasn't only *that*—that was the most personal—but it was just the act of typing and retyping. I got the rhythms of everyone's poems in my head, and I believe that's how I learned to simplify my own lines and really absorb what it meant to write a good poem. Because I was really just out of college, only a year or two, before we started *Yugen*, and I was really what they call "wet behind the ears." [*laughs*] I was young, I was very young and very green and hadn't had much exposure—I was a drama major; I hadn't studied the history of poetry or anything. But I learned so much. And that was my favorite part.

SA: I love that typing influenced you both as a reader and a writer, and I'm wondering about the other physical work that was involved with producing the magazine. In another interview you say, "I did all the work. I did the real physical work."

HJ: Not only did I type and retype but in the early issues of the magazine I cut stencils, which were very laborious. And then I remember doing work over a light box so that everything was precise. So it was a matter of not only just typing but designing. Then of course when we got the early issues they were just in pages, so we had parties—stapling parties. [*laughs*] You know, both LeRoi and I really organized those parties—set people up so that they would pass pages to one another and then somebody did the stapling on the spine—we got a long stapler. It was all of that.

SA: You talk about one of those collating parties in your autobiography, which is another scene I absolutely love.

HJ: Yep, that was exactly the way it was. And we got drunker as the night went along. But it's amazing, those little magazines—they survived! Which is quite amazing to me.

SA: Did it help engender a sense of community, having so many people's hands on the physical objects?

HJ: Oh, of course. That was the very idea. You know, we were all young, we were all used to living communally in some fashion because a lot of our friends had been at Black Mountain College, where everything was done communally, and we were no strangers to cooking communally and having people sleep over when they got too drunk to go home—things like that. When you're young and haven't got very many responsibilities that's just fun and a great pleasure. I'm sure it still goes on in many places.

SA: Yeah, we sometimes have sewing parties when we're putting together a chapbook.

HJ: [*laughs*] Of course, of course! Of course like that.

SA: There's a passage in your memoir about going to get a diaphragm and being asked about LeRoi's race—and then right after that is the moment where the magazine is discussed. And the secondary title of *Yugen* is "a new consciousness in arts and letters." So I was wondering if you would talk a little bit about what that secondary title meant for you, and if it was purely aesthetic or also sociopolitical.

HJ: Well, you know, not political in the sense that now I think of myself as a political person. I hadn't lived long enough to have an input into politics. I had sociopolitical views from having gone to college in the South, right from New York, and being appalled at segregation. I went to college in 1951, which was before *Brown v. Board of Education*, and everything was segregated—everything. And I had no experience with things like that. Also, as a Jew, I was not really welcome in a lot of places in the South either. So I experienced what New York never shows you, that I was an other in a way that I did not understand. So the "new consciousness"—I don't think I provided that, that was probably LeRoi—it was more of a redefining. I had read certainly a certain amount of poetry, American poetry, and found it academic and unappealing and very stiff—and very middle class.

And one thing that we, the group of us all, one thing we weren't was we weren't middle class. A, we had no money, and B, we were living in a way that would never have approached being middle class. We lived with cast-off furniture; we hadn't the middle-class attachment to money and material objects that was the common ground of the fifties, which was really in response to World War II. Everyone after the war—the economy was booming—and everyone was told to go live in the suburbs and have 2.5 children. And we were not part of that; we were living in Greenwich Village, which made us bohemian. We didn't really have a name for ourselves at all. We weren't always the Beats—you know, there were other people who weren't Jack Kerouac and that particular circle . . .

SA: There are lots of other people in the magazine too.

HJ: Yes, that's true. So I think that's probably what "a new consciousness" meant to me, was that the emphasis almost on a more spiritual aspect of things, not in terms of churchgoing but in terms of finding out what is truly important: independence and free-thinking and certainly a kind of art that was free from the old structures. Don't forget that we were also friends with abstract expressionist painters—so it all fit together. Theirs was a new consciousness in painting. You know, action painting, and we were action poetry.

SA: It also sounds though like you personally were very good at the practical aspects of running a magazine—you were juggling, as far as I can tell, being a typist, a typesetter, an editor, a designer, a distributer, a publicist . . .

HJ: I was also working at the *Partisan Review* at that time, and I was responsible—I mean, they hired me as what they called a subscription manager, but once the editors saw what I could do, they just entrusted me with everything and went to the country. [*laughs*] But I liked to work. I still like to work. It gives me some kind of satisfaction. So I didn't mind at all; I would go to work during the day, earn some money, and then come home and work at night on what I loved. But what artist hasn't done that? I just was lucky to have a day job that I really liked! So that made a big difference.

SA: Will you talk a little about your experiences at Grove Press and the *Partisan Review*, and how they influenced your editing and writing?

HJ: At *Partisan* the two editors were very kind to me. When we got the proofs for the magazine, William Phillips showed me physically how, if we were one or two lines over what would fit, to take out unnecessary words from a piece of writing so that you didn't destroy the meaning and coherence of the sentence, but you could search for something that would help the type fit into its allotted space. So that was one thing that I learned; it was a very useful thing. The other editor, Philip Rahv—he said, "Here," and he handed me something and said, "Copyedit this." I said, "What does that mean? I've never done that." And he said, "Oh, just make it *right*. And change it from English to American." [*chuckles*] The fact that these men, who were a good generation older than me, saw that I was smart and that I could be trusted and that I could do the right thing—that gave me great confidence. I was, I think, very ambitious and proud of myself for getting along in New York. I was madly in love. And all of that helped. The work gave me respect from not only those guys but also the New York School of poetry, like Frank O'Hara and Kenneth Koch and people like that. They didn't just see me as somebody's old lady. I had this job, and they knew what I did. And they respected it. So I wasn't just anybody's little secretary either; they knew I was taking care of everything there and that I had some say in things. *Partisan Review* let me read the slush pile! So I could choose and bring to their attention things that I thought were good. Now that really was a great privilege. And Grove Press—I did that later, or maybe interim, or maybe at the same time—you know, I was always working. But Grove also trusted me, not only to proofread some of their famous authors but to copyedit them as well. You know, copyediting is not just fixing commas and things like that. There's a little bit more to it than that. But I felt that my innate good sense had been recognized, and I felt happy about it. Because I was learning things, and of course who wouldn't be delighted to read the best literature coming out of the most avant-garde press, which Grove Press was then. Jean Genet and Marguerite Duras and people like

38   *Women in Independent Publishing*

that. I wrote to my friend Helene [Dorn] that it was like getting paid to be interested. It was just a wonderful, wonderful thing. [*laughs*]

SA: Did you have the same kind of say over either content or editorial choices when it came to *Yugen* and Totem Press Books? Was the content all the responsibility of LeRoi?

HJ: He was the one who asked for contributions. And he had the time to do that! Also, given the fact that most of the people we published were men, as usual, he was the one who met them at the Cedar Bar. Truth to tell, I was not interested in hanging too much at the Cedar Bar, or any other place. I'm really a very small person and I can't drink a lot. And I was never interested in drinking a lot. I didn't grow up that way, so I had almost no tolerance for alcohol. And besides that, Cedar was a place where . . . you know, sometimes I enjoyed myself there, just hanging out and listening to people and occasionally having a conversation. But when people are drinking, they're not really talking shop all the time. Maybe some of the artists did, but usually they're talking trash! [*chuckles*] And I didn't want to hang out and flirt with people.

SA: In the first three issues of the magazine, you're listed as an editor. And then in issue four you become the assistant editor.

HJ: I think I did that. Because I really kind of wanted to withdraw a little bit from it—that, I believe, was after the people who owned the Eighth Street Bookshop gave us money to have it printed, which was a great, great boon.

SA: That's why the look of the magazine changed with issue 4?

HJ: Yes, because I didn't have to do the typing anymore. And besides that, I had my day job and I had one child and one in the belly at that time. So there was a whole lot going on in my life.

SA: Do you remember an issue of the magazine that you were particularly proud of?

HJ: I was very proud of them all. But it was the very first one. I just loved it because it was so real to me. It was a real thing; it was a real magazine. The distributor for *Partisan Review* became a good friend of ours; he just sort of liked us. His name was Bernhard DeBoer, and he had a business distributing all these little literary magazines to colleges and universities all across America. And you had to have a spine, and ours was stapled. But even so, he liked us, and he agreed to take on our magazine, and that's how we got known in places like Madison, Wisconsin, and Chicago and San Francisco—just places where there were universities. San Francisco it probably would have gotten there through Lawrence Ferlinghetti, but there were colleges on Bernhard DeBoer's list, and when he offered things—you know, the more established magazines, like *Partisan* and the other literary magazines that had been around for a while—he would show people or mention to people that he knew *young* people who were publishing. I never think about that, usually, but people remind me of it, and I know that's how we got outside New York. Because it was easy enough for LeRoi, who did the walking, because I was working—he would take copies around to all the local bookstores and leave them there for sales. But we couldn't just mail them to bookstores in Chicago and say, "Hey, take this." So people at the universities found out about us that way. That was very important for us getting somewhere.

SA: You've written about the release party for issue 1, and how ConEd cut the electric in the building.

HJ: Oh! [*laughs*] Yeah, you know we borrowed somebody's studio; we didn't have it in our house because we were just living in one little room—sort of what they called a one-and-a-half-room apartment in the village then. I guess LeRoi got somebody to give us a loft. And ConEd cut the lights—I don't know how, maybe somebody sort of jerry-rigged the lights on, but when the lights came back on—everybody had lost each other in the darkness. And when the lights came on, I remember spotting him and he spotted me and we just sort of fell together; that was so nice. I still remember that; that was a very nice moment.

SA: Do you remember if there were other release parties?

HJ: I don't believe there were. I mean, our parties were generally the collating parties. But we had a party every weekend! A lot of people stayed over. We were always giving parties. When we moved to 14th Street we had a huge space, and we had parties there often too, because it was such a big space. Why not fill it with people, after all!

40   *Women in Independent Publishing*

SA: Exactly. And have them make the magazines! I'm wondering about the frequency of the magazine. It seems like it was more frequent in '58 and '59, and then it kind of slows down in the last three issues, between '60 and '62.

HJ: Well, the chief—how did we use to phrase it—the chief cook and bottle washer was busy having a baby! [*laughs*] I was working . . . I worked the day that my second child was born. I worked that day, and then I went home, and then I went into labor, and then I went into the hospital, and I think I came home two days later, and I went back to work a week later. Yeah, I know, I left my little baby. But nobody else was earning any money, and I had to have my salary. Then shortly after that the *Partisan Review* people were so nice to me; they let me collect unemployment insurance again, and then I got to stay home and from then on I didn't have a regular job. I had worked at *Partisan* for five years. That was enough. And that's when I got all the proofreading work from Grove, and the copyediting eventually. Then LeRoi started to earn a little bit of money, so we just sort of managed, without my having a regular job. It was a great relief in a certain sense. But I liked working at home, too, on these wonderful books that I didn't mind reading.

SA: Did you know that *Yugen* issue 8, from 1962, was going to be the last issue of the magazine?

HJ: No, not really. It's just that so many things happened that we were not prepared for. LeRoi began to write plays and then his plays were being produced. And I had to—don't forget that was in the days when there were no such things as answering machines, and so I was an answering machine. I just also read Peter Orlovsky's letters. When Peter came back from India, at a certain point—I don't know where Allen [Ginsberg] was—Peter came and stayed with us for a couple weeks, and he wrote somebody, "Hettie is not only the mother and the wife but she's the secretary." [*laughs*] You know, in 1962 we had already moved to the house where I am talking to you from right this moment. So it just was physically impossible—I didn't really have enough room to do the magazine anymore, and with two little kids, you just can't do what you used to do. Besides, I don't regret not doing the same thing all the time. I like new challenges, and new experiences, and I didn't mind not being the designer and all of that. And, also, I was getting older, and thinking of my own career, which I was sort of putting off by having children and doing everything for everybody else—I think something was nagging at me then. You know the letters to my friend Helene Dorn that are quoted a little bit in my memoir? I wrote to her all the time late at night when everything was quiet, and that was the writing that I did. We wrote for forty-four years. I made a selection, and that's to be published by Duke University Press.

SA: I feel like I have a pretty good grasp on *Yugen* and the timeline, but I don't feel like I have as good of a grasp on Totem.

HJ: Oh, okay. We did the very first couple of Totem books, one was *For Fidel* by Fielding Dawson, I think? And then maybe one other? But by that time, the people who owned the Eighth Street Bookshop had become friends and were interested in us. And they gave us money to have those books printed.

SA: Is that the partnership with Corinth Books?

HJ: Yeah, the partnership didn't happen until afterward. The first books were simply Totem. And I've forgotten which ones those were—maybe something by Gil Sorrentino, and maybe Ed Dorn. But anyway, then it just got to be too much, you know, there was just too much for two people to do. And we also couldn't keep asking for money from those people, so that's when Totem/Corinth came into being. They wanted to add their imprint to it and all we wanted was for our friends to get published so it didn't make any difference, really.

SA: Recently—I'm thinking of the last ten to fifteen years—there's been a lot of small press activity, especially around chapbooks. I was wondering if you've been taking note of that, and if it feels really different from the small press stuff you were involved with. What do you think the similarities and differences are between small press publishing now and in the fifties and sixties?

HJ: With technology there's so much more possibility. I mean, everybody and his brother can be an editor and put out a magazine, or people can do online stuff. There's so much to choose from. I do think the best kinds of work will finally come to the fore. Also, the rise of spoken-word poetry and poetry readings—I just gave a lecture at a local state university; it's not my title, but I was offered this opportunity, "How the Beats Gave Birth to the Spoken Word." Before, we participated in poetry readings in the fifties in a few little places in the Village and maybe out in San Francisco. Poetry wasn't read aloud; it wasn't an entertainment for anyone. Maybe at the university level there were a few people, but it wasn't a popular—it wasn't like going to a concert. But then, gradually, that kind of spoken word escalated until now you have poetry readings—in New York, anyway—you could go to two or three or ten poetry readings within a week, you know, and still not cover every one!

Everything is influenced by pop culture, ultimately, and I think poetry is definitely one of those things. In the fifties poetry wasn't anything that was put out to people who might not be readers. But spoken-word poetry has become very influenced by hip hop and that kind of music. Take poetry slams. Some of that stuff is good. Some of it wouldn't work if you put it on paper, but it allows people who wouldn't ordinarily get to speak their minds to speak their minds. You know, I teach everywhere. I mean, I've taught in prisons, in community centers, in senior centers—everywhere. Anyway, I like to teach people who don't have a literary background and who aren't interested in being literary themselves but are interested in expressing themselves. And I find that very gratifying to me, and it is to them too.

Are you familiar with the Nigerian writer Chimamanda Adichie? She gave a TED Talk titled "The Danger of a Single Story." She explains that when she first came from Nigeria, what she knew of the United States was maybe Disney and Coca-Cola. The danger of our knowing only one story, in the reverse of other countries, limits us. And it limits what other people think about the United States and what we think of other cultures. So I like to encourage people to contribute their story. The people that I worked for at *Partisan Review* had been young people during the Depression, and they were partially supported by giving writing workshops and teaching people for the WPA. It's very important that those kinds of stories of ordinary life see the light of day, and that they be collected somewhere. I worked this past academic year at a place called the Lower East Side Girls Club, and I taught mothers from the housing project, which happens to be across the street from there. And other women from the neighborhood. I put out a little pamphlet of their work—you know, that's very important—they were so pleased! As was I.

SA: I think about when I used to teach in an after-school program in Brooklyn, and we would put together, every semester, a little Xeroxed booklet of what the kids had written that semester. And they were so proud of that book.

HJ: Everyone should have an opportunity to express themselves like that.

SA: It seems to me like it actually isn't that far away from your role as an editor and publisher—you called yourself a facilitator at some point when talking about the magazine. It's like that interest has stayed with you, that role of bringing new work into the world that's important.

HJ: Yeah. Somebody—a guy I was talking to this afternoon—he said, "You seem to have mentored people." But facilitating—I think that's more what I do now, because I teach, but then I have to come home and do my own work. [*chuckles*] So.

SA: Maybe we can close on the question of what advice you'd give to a young woman who wants to start a magazine?

HJ: Sure. The advice is: Just go for it! But make sure that you have time to do it. And make sure you get advice from people who are in touch with people who are writing, or painting, or whatever. So that you have a good bit of material to choose from, and you don't have to print every single thing that you are handed, even if you don't really like it. And be super critical, and take your time. Because you don't want to say, "Well, I need to fill up a page . . ." and then put in it something that isn't really worthy, you know?

SA: Right, or "This person is my friend, so. . . ." Is there anything else you want to say about *Yugen* or Totem?

HJ: No. . . . I haven't talked about it in a long while, so it's been a pleasure to really remember all of that. As I've been talking, I've had my eyes closed, and all of those memories are just floating around in my brain—which is fine. At least they're there. [*chuckles*] You know?

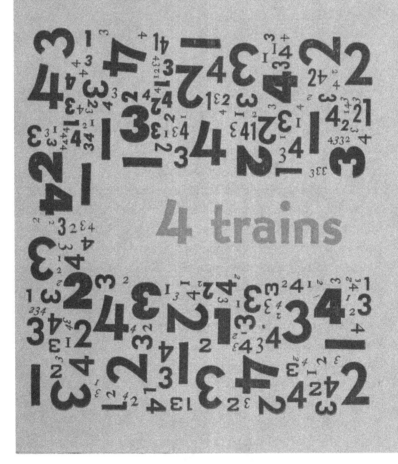

Figure 4. Four Trains, 4–5 December 1964 (1974) by Jackson Mac Low. Designed and printed by Rosmarie Waldrop.

Rosmarie Waldrop

Coeditor and Publisher, Burning Deck *(1962–1964) and*
Burning Deck Press *(1961–2017, Michigan and Rhode Island)*

MARCH 2014 TO JULY 2015, VIA E-MAIL

Stephanie Anderson: Where does the name Burning Deck come from?
Rosmarie Waldrop: It comes from the poem "Casabianca" by nineteenth-
century British poet Felicia Hemans, which starts:

> The boy stood on the burning deck
> Whence all but he had fled;

Casabianca was captain of one of the French ships in the Battle of
the Nile. When the ship was hit by the British, he went to check on
the damage, telling his ten-year-old son to hold on to the steering
wheel until he'd come back. The captain is killed immediately, and
the boy keeps holding the wheel, crying, "Papa, must I stay?" and
eventually goes down with the ship.

It was an immensely popular poem that kids were made to
memorize from the time of its publication (1826) till about the middle
of the twentieth century. There are many parodies, like

> The boy stood on the burning deck
> Eating peanuts peck by peck

including one by Elizabeth Bishop ("Love's the boy stood on the
burning deck . . .").

A burning deck seemed to us an appropriate image for poetry.
And standing at the press cranking out pages I often felt like crying
out, "Papa, must I stay!"

45

SA: Matthew Timmons's article about Burning Deck says that the press started when you bought "a secondhand 8 x 12 Chandler and Price platen printing press for $175." As an owner of a dining room platen press, I know that neither they nor the materials you need to print are exactly . . . small and portable. Where did you print in those days? How did you learn? Why letterpress over mimeo?

RW: We were graduate students at the University of Michigan. The press was (with the help of friends) put in the basement of the tiny house we rented. (It knocked out several steps in the process.) We learned from a high-school manual, by trial and error, by occasional input from a printer ("use less ink"). Mimeo was never an option; it faded too quickly.

SA: In an interview with Jared Demick, you explain that Keith wanted a magazine, and that you started Burning Deck because you "couldn't get [your] own poems published." Will you expand more on that statement? What were some of the factors at play in the poetry world of the early sixties?

RW: It's true that Keith couldn't get his poems published. But Burning Deck didn't change that because the editors (Keith, James Camp, Don Hope) decided they would not publish their own work. A more accurate reason for starting the mag was what became known as "the war of the anthologies," between "the Donald Allen" and "the Hall-Pack-Simpson." Both anthologies claimed to represent current poetry, and not a single poet appeared in both of them. *Burning Deck* magazine ignored this too-clean dividing line and in this represented the more inclusive (and also divergent) tastes of the editors. Which resulted in several letters that said more or less: I appreciate your printing me, but how can you also print that awful X . . .

SA: How did you solicit submissions for the magazine?

RW: Keith wrote to the poets he admired, promising "payment on acceptance." He didn't say how much—I think it turned out to be five dollars per poem or perhaps per person!

SA: How did distribution work?

RW: Badly. As far as sales went. But word spread anyway because there were soon tons of submissions.

SA: You did a lot of reviewing for the journal. How else were you involved?

RW: Keith and I did the printing. It was our first printing project—hence the first issues are messy. I and a friend, Jeanne Longyear, did a bad job of proofreading—here is a note in one of the issues: "proofreaders' names withheld by request"!!

SA: The first time I see the note ["proofreader's name withheld by request"] is in issue 3, below a large list of names who "printed and collated" the issue. Actually, since the first issue, that list of names is substantial. Were the typesetters all friends? Did any undergrad students work on the journal?

RW: I don't recall anybody actually helping with the actual printing, but we used to have collating parties where a bunch of us walked around a table assembling copies while a couple of people at another table folded and stapled.

I looked at the list of names again. They were all friends and grad students except for Amy Miller and Betsy Wagman, the only undergrads. Amy was in one of Keith's freshmen English classes. (She later became a stunning photographer. We only lost touch a few years ago.) I don't remember how Betsy connected with us.

SA: Did you like the physical process of printing?

RW: Yes. It was a LOT of work, but also very exciting to make a physical object. Also, hand-setting the poems letter by letter was the greatest lesson in close reading I had. And it helped make my own poems very lean.

SA: In issue 2 there are three poems by Rosmarie Keith. I suspect this isn't some crazy coincidence?

RW: No. At the time both Keith and I were trying out various names. Keith was "Bernard Keith"; I was "Rosmarie Keith" for a while.

SA: I love the experimentation with names. How long did that go on?

RW: Not very long. Keith had always gone by Keith Waldrop, but wanted to have a separate name for anything he did, say Bernard Keith for poetry, Bernard Waldrop for critical essays. It was a nice idea, but we soon realized neither of us was likely to write enough to support more than one name.

48   *Women in Independent Publishing*

SA: How did the shift to books happen? There's an ad for the anthology *The Wolgamot Interstice* in issue 1; were books being printed alongside the magazine?

RW: *The Wolgamot Interstice* was actually the first Burning Deck publication. It was an anthology of poets who were at that time in Michigan. Mostly at the U of Michigan in Ann Arbor (Heath-Stubbs taught there for one year) and Detroit (D. C. Hope, Snodgrass): Donald Hall, X. K. Kennedy, Dallas Wiebe, James Camp, John Heath-Stubbs, Bernard Keith (i.e., Keith Waldrop), D. C. Hope, W. D. Snodgrass. It also had, as introduction, a report of the Beatnik Hoax we performed, "How to Swallow an Aardvark and Other Movements." It was composed and printed by a friend of Don Hope's in Detroit, who wanted to learn to use a linotype machine.

SA: Keith's account of the Beatnik Hoax—the readings by fake poets of the San Francisco Renaissance, the world premiere of the play *The Quivering Aardvark and the Jelly of Love*—is a pure delight. What was your role in that event?

RW: Very minor. I wrote some of the poems the fake poets read, using German Dada texts as a base. In the performance itself I was a spy in the audience.

SA: "How to Swallow an Aardvark . . ." lists, at the end, some sincerely positive reactions from audience members, one of which ("It changed my whole life. They were so free.") "made some of us shudder a little." Were these genuine comments? Did much of the audience fail to understand the event as parody?

RW: Absolutely. This took us all by surprise.

SA: The report states that the Wolgamot Society, "dying [. . .] because we cannot tie our spurious beginning to our constantly moving ends," has performed a few plays, and that the poems presented in the book "provide something more." Will you talk a little about the group's interest in both drama and poetry?

RW: Poetry and theater were Keith's twin interests. He founded the Wolgamot Society as a student organization so that we could use University of Michigan venues. The first play he gave was Alfred Jarry's *Ubu Roi* (which he and X. J. Kennedy translated as *Gopotty*

Rex). Word got around that this play had caused a riot when first performed in Paris (Yeats was there and reported cheering for the livelier side). So the grad students who were not part of the cast decided to duplicate that. They threw rotten tomatoes and Polish sausages. Needless to say, the Wolgamot Society was never allowed to use the University theater again. But at other places Keith directed Paul Goodman's *Jonah* and Christian Dietrich Grabbe's *Comedy, Satire, Irony, and Deeper Meaning*—a great German Romantic comedy, really Dada *avant la lettre*.

SA: *The Wolgamot Interstice* is fairly impressive for a first book—nice graphics, handsomely printed, with many of the poems appearing in previous publications, including the *New Yorker*, the *Paris Review*, and Robert Bly's the *Fifties* and the *Sixties*. Did Burning Deck—both the magazine and the press—particularly admire any other publications and/or publishers when it was founded?

RW: Of publishers, New Directions was always our model. Of magazines, we followed *The Fifties* and *Sixties* (still, I think, Bly's major achievement), the *Floating World*, Clark Coolidge's *Joglars*, a bunch of mimeographed ones like the *World* from the Poetry Project in New York, *0–9*. Of larger ones especially *Evergreen Review*, the *Drama Review* (actually *Tulane Drama Review* at that point).

SA: When did you move into a more editorial role with the press?

RW: When we gave up on the magazine and started to print chapbooks instead. From then on it was just Keith and me.

By this time we had moved to jobs at Wesleyan University in Connecticut (and taken the press with us), James Camp to New York, and Don Hope to Pennsylvania. Beside the geographical scattering of the editors, we found we couldn't keep a regular schedule for the magazine. Also, the linotype for the reviews was three times as expensive in Connecticut. Chapbooks we could do whenever there was time.

SA: What year was this? I see that the last issue of the magazine was in 1965.

RW: *The Wolgamot Interstice* in 1961 had been an anomaly as far as production goes. It had come about because a friend of Don Hope's wanted

50   *Women in Independent Publishing*

a project for learning to use the linotype machine. The first letter-press chapbooks came out in 1967 and were by Keith and myself.

SA: A WorldCat search suggests to me that the first few chapbooks were by various editors or former editors—you, Keith, James Camp. Is that right? Was publishing the editors a way to "test drive" book publication?

RW: Exactly.

SA: And were you still printing on the Chandler and Price platen press?

RW: Yes, and we moved it a second time, to Providence, and used it as long as we were doing chapbooks or broadsides.

SA: I'm looking at some of the chapbooks you printed in the seventies and eighties and they're so astonishing—done in several colors, letterpress throughout, and in runs of 250 or 300 (by today's standards, not an insignificant run for a home studio). How long did it typically take to do a chapbook?

RW: All I can say at this point in time: it was very slow. Also, sometimes it went smoothly, other times there were constant problems.

SA: The colophons of the chapbooks I have here usually refer to either you or Keith as the designer and printer. Sometimes (as with Elizabeth Robinson's *My Name Happens Also*) one of you has designed the cover and one has done the interiors, but overall it seems like one of you spearheaded each chapbook. Is that right? How did you divide editorial and publishing labor and decisions?

RW: We both read all manuscripts and often agreed. If one of us liked a manuscript very much that was sufficient reason to print, but the person who wanted it had to do the labor.

However, very often I did the inside, which was more time-consuming, because after 1970 I taught only occasionally, hence had more time than Keith who from 1968 on had the steady job.

Keith also has the stronger visual sense and so tended to do covers.

SA: Do you remember any chapbooks from the seventies and eighties of which you were especially proud? (I guess I'm also thinking that printers invariably have "disaster stories," in which something went wrong and an entire book component had to be redone—and how finally seeing those books completed can be really satisfying.)

RW: There were some instances where we did things you weren't supposed to be able to do in letterpress.

Keith's cover for William Bronk's *Utterances* was a real triumph. In letterpress printing everything has to be straight, rectangular, but he managed to bend two rules into sort of asymptotes without them breaking or falling out during the print run.

I am still proud of my cover for Jackson Mac Low's 4 *Trains*, for which I made an assemblage of the numerals 1–4 in all different sizes and headed in all four directions. It was very difficult to keep the smaller numerals from falling out, but it was worth it.

SA: What was the basis for the decision to move to full-length books?

RW: Anthony Barnett showed us the ca. sixty-four-page manuscript of *Poem about Music*. We liked it a lot and proposed a chapbook of about a third of it. He said: No, it's all or nothing. After some hesitation we took the plunge and printed it in 1974.

SA: I image that doing full-length books was both more and less time-consuming than doing letterpress chapbooks. Is that true? How did your role(s) in the press change—or not?

RW: Except for the short fiction books we started adding, the first twenty or so full books were still printed letterpress. Definitely more time consuming than the chapbooks!

In fall 1985 we drove the printed sheets of four full books to our bindery in Vermont and found that they had automated over the summer and could no longer bind our small 2-up sheets—they would simply slide through the machine. We could not find any other pre-automation bindery. Those four books had to be handbound, which cost a fortune.

From then on full books had to be offset printed. I did practically all the design and layout for the full books on the computer. Keith wanted as little as possible to do with the computer.

SA: Wow, I can't imagine how time-consuming letterpressing the full books must have been. Did you like working with the computer, when you switched to that?

RW: It was easier and a lot faster.

52 *Women in Independent Publishing*

SA: Quite a few of the chapbooks are from post-1974, so I assume there was an allure to continuing with the letterpress as well?

RW: Right.

SA: Did your manuscript acquisition process change at all?

RW: No. Except once when we had miraculously managed to clear the slate (I think it was in 1984). We announced in Poetry Project Newsletter and I forget where else that we would be reading manuscripts—and got five hundred submissions.

SA: Will you talk a little about the press's commitment to publishing works in translation?

RW: Both Keith and I have been translating poems as long as I can remember. In fact, when I met Keith (who was then a GI stationed in my hometown in Germany), it was the project of translating German poems into English that really brought us together.

September 1970 to September 1971 we spent on grants in Paris and met Edmond Jabès (whose BOOK OF QUESTIONS I had already begun translating) and a number of younger poets, most importantly Anne-Marie Albiach and Claude Royet-Journoud, whom Keith started translating immediately.

Then Paul Green of Spectacular Diseases Press in England asked me to edit Série d'Ecriture, a series of French contemporary poetry books in translation for him. The first five titles (by Alain Veinstein, Emmanuel Hocquard, Joseph Guglielmo, plus two magazine issues) were published by Spectacular Diseases. However, the production quality was so poor that I decided I'd have to take on that part of the job also. Paul let me keep the series title and continued to distribute the books in England. A few years later we added the German series "Dichten=."

SA: In the *Chain "Editorial Forum"* (1994), you write:

> No, gender is not a basis for Burning Deck decisions. Some years we publish more women (1993: 4 women, 1 man), other years, more men. I must admit that I read mss. by women with extra attention, but my first commitment is to poems. I am sometimes bothered by the large role that happenstance plays (who sends a ms.

at which moment, etc.), but prefer going with it to, say, a quota system.

Women's mags and presses have been necessary and useful, but the "ghetto"-problems are obvious. I was delighted with the first issue of *Big Allis* which, without comment, printed all women poets plus 1 male poet—a nice reversal of the usual tokenism.

Twenty years later, do you still agree with this assessment? Has the "usual tokenism" changed, in your opinion?

RW: It has changed. I also think I was wrong about the "ghetto"-problem. The women-only mags and presses were a leavening and helped raise awareness. Also, we've had such a flowering of women poets for such a long time now it would be extremely hard to ignore us at this point.

SA: Would you say that you still "read mss. by women with extra attention"?

RW: Yes.

SA: Who are some contemporary women writers and editors you admire?

RW: Writers: Susan Howe, Mei-mei Berssenbrugge, Lyn Hejinian, Rae Armantrout, Cole Swensen, Norma Cole, Juliana Spahr, Ann Lauterbach, Tina Darragh, Lisa Jarnot, Marjorie Welish, Pam Rehm, Joan Retallack, Jena Osman, Elizabeth Robinson, Elizabeth Willis, Rusty Morrison . . .

Editors: Lisa Pearson (Siglio), Kathleen Fraser (*How2*), Tracy Grinnell (Litmus and *Aufgabe*), Rachel Levitsky (Belladonna*), Sandra Doller (1913), Rebecca Wolff (Fence) . . .

SA: What do you think are some challenges and opportunities for contemporary publishers?

RW: I suppose navigating the space between print and electronic media.

SA: What does the future hold for Burning Deck?

RW: Alas, nothing. High-end birthdays and illnesses make it too difficult to continue. So at this point we're just trying to publish the backlog. But SPD [Small Press Distribution] will continue working with our titles.

Figure 5. Margaret Randall. Photo by Magdalena Lily McCarson.

Margaret Randall

Editor, El Corno Emplumado /
The Plumed Horn (*1962–1969, Mexico City*)

OCTOBER 2014 TO JANUARY 2015, VIA E-MAIL, UPDATED 2022

Stephanie Anderson: Your website bio mentions that you lived "among New York's abstract expressionists in the 1950s and early sixties." What took you to Mexico in the sixties? How was the artistic scene there different from the one in New York?

Margaret Randall: What prompted my move from New York City to Mexico City in the summer of 1961 was largely personal. New York had been exciting and very productive for me. When I arrived, I had that feeling many young creative people must have had at the time, that it was the only place to be. But after several years, it became harder (economically) and I also began to understand that I could live and write anywhere. In fall 1960 I gave birth to my son. His father and I weren't married, not even really in a relationship (although he was attentive to Gregory's life, and they became close many years later). Being a single mother, in New York in the 1960s, wasn't easy. There were few daycare centers, few services of any sort. I worked all day, long hours in order to support the two of us, and rarely was able to spend time with my son. I had the notion that this might be different in Mexico, that I would be able to earn a living and spend more time with him. So, impulsively perhaps, when he was ten months old, we boarded a Greyhound bus and headed south.

This is what took me to Mexico. How the artistic scenes differed is more complicated. There was a wonderful scene in New York, and I found a wonderful one in Mexico as well. In both scenes, writers, visual artists, theater people, singers, dancers, and others interacted.

Perhaps the biggest difference was that in the United States the chill of McCarthyism was still very present; writers especially were made to feel that we could only write about certain things, that only some subjects were safe. Certainly, political, or socially conscious writing, was discouraged. While in Mexico any topic was legitimate; writers wrote about what moved them most, and that was very often the situations of injustice that plagued the world. Perhaps one reason there was such a mix of intellectuals and artists in Mexico is because that country has had a long tradition of giving political refuge to people fleeing political persecution. When I arrived in the early sixties, many of the great poets and artists who had fled the Spanish Civil War or Nazi-occupied Europe were still alive and active. While I lived there, they were joined by many who fled the brutal Latin American dictatorships of the 1970s and eighties.

SA: In your article for *The Little Magazine in America* you talk about the title *El Corno Emplumado / The Plumed Horn* as coming from "the simple urge to speak, to be heard, to be felt." Whose idea was the title?

MR: Although I am no longer absolutely certain, I believe the idea for the journal's title was Harvey Wolin's. He was only with us for the first couple of issues. I know we talked about creating a title that would reflect the best of the creative contributions made north and south of the border. In the US, we felt that jazz was a major contribution, thus the jazz horn or *corno*. In the south, cultural history was still very much influenced by the pre-Columbian gods and myths, thus the plumes of Quetzalcoatl. At the time, many artistic groups took names that paired unlikely terms in interesting ways; I remember the Cross-Eyed Cat, the Crazy Coyote, the Roof of the Whale, and so forth. So, *El Corno Emplumado / The Plumed Horn* seemed like a good name, representing as it did major elements from both hemispheres.

SA: In the same article, you write, "We understood the alienation between two continents, but neither its colonialist nor its imperialist nature. We removed cultural expression from politics, falling easily into the enemy's trap of compartmentalization." The article was published in 1975; do you still feel the same way? Will you expand on how the first issues of the magazine "removed cultural expression from politics?" (I suspect this changed over the course of the magazine's existence.)

MR: When I spoke about understanding the alienation between the two continents, I was referring to popular culture: the long-held feelings of superiority in the North and inferiority in the South, the jealousies, the fact that Latin Americans hated their northern neighbors but still frequently wanted to look like them, be like them, or immigrate to live among them. When I said that we didn't understand its colonialist or imperialist nature, I meant that we didn't really understand the complexities. The truth was, we ourselves didn't yet understand how complicated the relationships were, the ways in which inequality was woven into all areas of life, or the lengths to which the US government and its representative bodies would go to infiltrate and dominate cultural expression in the south. The McCarthyite dictate that literature be free of politics was certainly part of that. In 1975 we understood all this very partially. Sometimes it was more intuitive than scientific. Today we know the extent to which institutions made this influence a priority, and the lengths they went to exert their control. So not only do I still believe this today but I can see much more clearly how it manifests itself, how it works.

The whole point of the journal was NOT to separate politics from cultural expression. To this end, we published work by Communists, guerrilla leaders, Catholic priests, mystics, "hippies," and those of other persuasions. What we wouldn't publish was work by fascists, racists, etc.

SA: Later in that paragraph, you write, "We were more concerned with form, perhaps, than we should have been, and we really thought we could all be brothers. (We didn't think, then, about being sisters. We were a few women, a minority among mostly men. Our intellectual pretensions took care of that ratio—women's consciousness was not part of us then.)" What was it like to be a young woman—and a young mother—in these artistic scenes? Did it end up being true that you were able to "earn a living and spend more time with [your son]" in Mexico, as you hoped when you left New York?

58 *Women in Independent Publishing*

MR: It did turn out that I was able to spend more time with my son. In Mexico, as throughout Latin America, even working-class people had access to domestic workers, who often lived in one's home. In that sense I never lacked for a babysitter, but I also was freer to spend more time with Gregory. Sexism definitely ruled our lives, though. Perhaps as a foreigner I was less subject to the subservience expected of women. In general, because we were all young artists, we proclaimed men and women equal. In practice, of course, it was much more complicated. I definitely felt that I was my own person in the realm of poetry, editing the journal, and so forth. But this was the 1960s, before the second wave of feminism, and Sergio [Mondragón] still expected me to be his "wife" in every domestic sense.[1] I always rebelled, and eventually this was one of the things that ended our marriage.

SA: You've also written about the importance of Philip Lamantia's apartment as "a meeting place for artists and writers from several countries." Will you describe what an evening there was like?

MR: After all these years, my memories of those evenings at Philip Lamantia's apartment are not so clear. I know we gathered there almost nightly. People would drop by, arriving whenever they could, and stay into the early morning hours. I'm sure there was food and drink . . . and probably good weed, since we all smoked back then. One or another of us might be excited by something he or she had written or read, and we'd read out loud to one another. Indeed, these informal readings were what pointed to the need for a bilingual journal. Most of those who frequented Philip's apartment only spoke and read Spanish, or only spoke and read English. We needed a way to understand each other's work more deeply. My most vivid memories of those evenings at Philip's include Ernesto Cardenal, Raquel Jodorowsky, Juan Bañuelos, Sergio Mondragón, Carlos Coffeen Serpas, Juan Martínez, Harvey Wolin, Howard Frankl, and a few others.

SA: Did you know Spanish when you arrived there?

MR: I did know Spanish when I got to Mexico. I had spent almost two years in Spain, in the 1950s, which is where I learned the rudiments of the language. Then, in New York, I worked part time as an interpreter for the New York City courts: mostly eviction cases and the like. My Spanish was elemental but pretty fluent, and it improved immensely in the world of poetry and culture I inhabited in Mexico City.

SA: How did the three editors divide responsibilities for the first issue?

MR: I don't think there was a formal division of labor leading up to *El Corno*'s first issue. I'm sure Sergio took the lead, as he was a native and knew better than Harvey and I did where to go for financial support, advertising, what poets and artists to approach for work, and so forth. But we all did everything. We put the word out, begged help of all kinds, solicited work, read manuscripts, made decisions, translated when we could, found a small independent print shop . . . and when we had the issue in hand, we delivered copies to bookshops and bundled them up to send outside the country. Harvey quit, as I say, after the first issue, and then it was just Sergio and myself. We more or less assumed responsibility for our native tongues; in other words, Sergio made decisions regarding what to print in Spanish, and I did the same in English. Initially he had more contacts in Latin America and I had more in the US. Soon we were in touch with young poets in Europe, Asia, and Australia as well. I remember those eight years as frenetically active. We both did everything . . . and with only the slightest of sporadic help from others—for instance, someone who might volunteer a few hours a week now and then. After Sergio left the magazine, Robert Cohen came on board to edit the last three issues with me. As a US American poet, he took responsibility for some of the journal's English side, but I had taken responsibility for the Spanish side by that time and was also making decisions about the English submissions we received.

SA: Will you expand on the nitty-gritty of doing "everything"? What part of magazine production was your favorite?

MR: By everything I mean soliciting manuscripts, reading them, choosing which ones to publish, carrying on an overload of correspondence with people throughout the world, raising money for each

60 *Women in Independent Publishing*

issue, designing the issue, translating what we could, overseeing the printing, sitting down on our living room floor and packing up copies to be sent to individuals, poets, subscribers, exchanges with other magazines, bookstores, and our representatives in each country, doing the billing; and then starting the whole process over again for the next issue. By far my favorite part of the production was reading new work, discovering great poets, and letting them know their work would be included in a forthcoming issue.

SA: I love the fold-out pages (with poems by Rochelle Owens and Raquel Jodorowsky) in the first issue. Was it hard to find a printer who could do what you wanted with the book—and print without errors in both languages?

MR: Mexico City was full of small print shops in the 1960s. Each one had at least one linotype operator, and he (it was always a man) simply copied what he saw in the texts we gave him. There WERE errors in *El Corno Emplumado*; far too many of them. But I think these were due to our failures as proofreaders rather than to any fault with the printers we used. As we were almost always only two people doing everything at the journal, we probably worked too fast, and too carelessly. What became more problematic insofar as the print shops were concerned, and what caused us to move from one to another, was the sexual explicitness of some of the texts—not every print shop owner accepted that—and toward the end also the political fear that reigned in Mexico. Just before and after the Movement of 1968, and because we openly supported the students, I remember a print shop throwing us out into the street mid–printing job. We had to search for a print shop then that was willing to risk being visited by the police.

SA: The copyright page lists "representatives," artists and writers who represent the magazine in various places. How did you develop this network? Did people write and volunteer? Was it a mostly epistolary correspondence, or did it also rely upon visitors to Mexico City?

MR: We selected representatives in each country, and they also self-selected. Poets would write telling us they wanted to distribute the magazine in their country. They would talk to us about their poets, and often offer to gather an anthology of poetry for us to publish. Sometimes poets visited us in Mexico City, and we got to know them in person. It was all voluntary, of course; no one ever got paid for anything.

SA: Who did you get to know especially well through this kind of trans-national (transcontinental!) exchange?

MR: Too many poets, writers, and others to name, really. I could start by listing the following: Ernesto Cardenal, Rosario Castellanos, Laurette Séjourné, Leonora Carrington, Paul Blackburn, Allen Ginsberg, Lawrence Ferlinghetti, Felipe Ehrenberg, Miguel Grinberg, Roberto Fernández Retamar, Anselm Hollo, Octavio Paz, Raquel Jodorowsky, Julio Cortázar, Susan Sherman, George Bowering, Nancy Morejón, Russell Banks, Ted Enslin, Cid Corman, Diane Wakoski, Edward Field, Carol Bergé, Agustí Bartra, Walter Lowenfels. . . . The list is a very long one. Bear in mind that *El Corno Emplumado*, over the eight years of its life, published more than seven hundred poets and artists from thirty-seven countries.

SA: Your 1965 book *October* contains a small portfolio of photographs of sculpture and some short pieces of prose. Was it Ediciones El Corno Emplumado / Plumed Horn Editions' first book? How did it come about, and did publishing it through the press allow for the cross-genre inclusions?

MR: The photographs were by the Japanese sculptor Shinkichi Tajiri, and I suspect that those photos—which include his sculptures as well as a woman's body, which may have been that of his wife, Ferdi Jansen, also a sculptor—were fairly scandalous in the Mexico of the 1960s. I remember that the printer where we put the book to press refused to finish the job, literally throwing the photographic signatures into the street. The poems were mine. Shinkichi and Ferdi, along with their young daughters Giotto and Ryu, had come to Mexico that year, along with two assistants whose names I no longer remember. One was also Japanese, the other German. It was an international family, and very creative. We always loved having guests from other places, and this collaboration came about quite naturally. I suppose I just thought the photographs worked with my poems, and

62 *Women in Independent Publishing*

Shinkichi agreed. *October* was not our first book; there were others before it, and many afterward as well. But cross-genre works were always interesting to us.

SA: Unlike the magazine, which often published English and Spanish works side-by-side without translation, several of the Ediciones El Corno books—Walter Lowenfels's *Land of Roseberries*, Jerome Rothenberg's *The Gorky Poems*, José Moreno's *Prontuario* (this last one translated by Elinor Randall; your mother?)—are bilingual. Why was that important for the press?

MR: Translation was always important to us. Good translation was one of our main motivations for doing the journal. We would like to have been able to make every piece in every issue bilingual, but that didn't turn out to be possible. Along with reading hundreds of submissions, choosing what we wanted to publish, raising money for the endeavor, promoting and distributing *El Corno*, there wasn't much time left over for translation. And we didn't know many others whose translations satisfied us. We did what we could. In the case of the books, sometimes we made an extra effort, or someone else did. And yes, Elinor Randall was my mother. She occasionally translated something for the magazine, or one of our books. She did *Marsias & Adila*, our issue number 4, which was by the Catalan poet Agustí Bartra. And she did *Majakuagy-Moukeia*, the book-length creation story according to the Indians on Mexico's western coast, collected by Ana Mairena (a pseudonym, as she was married at the time to the governor of the state of Nyarit). Later my mother devoted herself to translating the Cuban revolutionary writer José Martí, work she was doing up to a few days before her death at the age of ninety-seven.

SA: Is there an issue that you find especially memorable or remarkable, either because of its content or its production?

MR: There are several. One would be number 18, dedicated to Mexico. Another would be number 23, dedicated to Cuba. Our very first issue is also noteworthy, because although we had yet to make our name as a known journal, we had unpublished work by such as Laurette Séjourné, Leonora Carrington, Elaine de Kooning, Ernesto Cardenal, León Felipe, and Robert Kelly.

SA: The Cuba issue seems vibrant and vital, and I know you moved there in 1969 (and published a memoir about these years, *To Change the World*). Had you visited previously? Will you talk a little bit about your relationship, both personally and through the magazine, with Cuban poets and artists prior to 1969?

MR: Cuba was a revelation to me personally, and a revelation to *El Corno*. And through our pages, the revolution was revealed to a US readership that had been prevented from accessing the poetry and just about anything else coming out of that country then. The cultural blockade, after all, was as important as its economic and military counterparts. Early on in the life of the journal we made contact with Cuban poets, writers, and artists. We devoted a section of our issue number 7 (in July 1963) to work from Cuba, and then dedicated our entire issue number 23 (in July 1967) to it as well. That latter issue was also illustrated by some wonderful Cuban artists. So yes, Cuba and *El Corno* are intimately entwined.

In response to the first part of your question, I *had* traveled previously to Cuba, and those trips strengthened my relationships with Cuban poets. In January of 1967 Sergio and I were invited to El encuentro con Rubén Darío (The Meeting with Rubén Darío), a gathering of poets from a number of different countries who got together to celebrate the 100th anniversary of the great Nicaraguan modernist. I stayed on for an extra couple of weeks and took the Cubans up on their offer of going to Santiago de Cuba in the eastern part of the country. That trip really sparked my interest in the revolution, and a year later I was invited back again, this time to El congreso cultural de la Habana (The Havana Cultural Congress), an immense event that brought together more than six hundred intellectuals, artists, writers, philosophers, scientists, religious leaders, and others, as well as more than a thousand journalists.

SA: At the Cultural Congress you discovered that Fidel Castro had read *El Corno Emplumado*. You also coincided at the Congress with Susan Sherman, a lifelong friend. What has been the importance of the relationship with Sherman for your creative and political development?

MR: I met Castro on a couple of occasions, and I was always surprised

64 *Women in Independent Publishing*

that he knew about the magazine, and was so up on cultural matters in general. Susan Sherman and I became good friends at that 1968 conference in Havana, and her friendship continues to nourish me. We are women of a particular generation, who shared our feelings about the importance of artistic creativity, the need for social change rooted in justice, the role of art in social change, and the identity politics that two lesbians who subscribed to socialist ideals came by naturally. Susan is a marvelous poet and writer, whose work has not received the attention I believe it deserves. But this is true of so many women writers; despite important advances we are still underrecognized by publishers, literature professors, grantors, and those who decide who gets invited to perform in the major reading series.

SA: Your interest in Cuba actually began much earlier; in 1961, from New York, you and several other artists and writers—LeRoi Jones (later Amiri Baraka), Elaine de Kooning, Diane di Prima, Lawrence Ferlinghetti, Marc Schleifer (later Suleiman Abdallah), and Norman Mailer—wrote a "Declaration of Conscience in support of Cuba's sovereignty." How did that group of people come together, and what was the experience of writing the Declaration like?

MR: Elaine de Kooning and I were close friends. I also knew Diane di Prima, Marc Schleifer, and Norman Mailer because we frequented similar circles. And of course I knew Ferlinghetti's work. The Cuban revolution had a big impact on all of us. We were encouraged by a small island country standing up to US domination. At first it seemed as if the US, at least in the press and on campuses, was going to be supportive of the Cuban initiative. But we soon heard the inevitable cries of "Communism!" and understood that the Eisenhower administration was making plans to blockade or even invade the island. I worked at Spanish Refugee Aid at the time, in a small office at 80 East 11th Street in Manhattan. We attended to the needs of those refugees displaced by the fascist takeover in Spain. The Fair Play for Cuba committee had its offices in the same building. I was not a member of Fair Play for Cuba but was in touch with people who were. I think this was how the seven of us came together to write that declaration. I can't really remember what the experience of writing it was like, except that we got several hundred signatures without half trying. Most writers and artists supported the Cuban revolution back then.

SA: More generally, did you travel a lot in the 1960s, while editing *El Corno*?

MR: Yes, although mostly throughout Mexico and to the United States. Sergio and I were often invited to read our poetry at a university or in some other setting. The network of poets that was created around *El Corno*, and through other small literary magazines of the era, meant we always had a place to stay and vital creative colleagues to talk to. And our home in Mexico City also became a magnet for poets coming from the US, Europe, many Latin American countries, and occasionally farther afield. I can hardly remember a time, during the journal's eight years, when someone wasn't staying with us for a few days or weeks. This was important because communication was much more difficult back then than it is now. We didn't have the Internet or e-mail. A letter or envelope of poems typically took three months to get from Buenos Aires or New York to Mexico City. We didn't have the money for long-distance phone calls. So we had to depend on the regular postal service and these personal visits. Today it would be hard to imagine running anything like a magazine without e-mail. But the way we did things back then had its advantages: We looked each other in the eyes, shared meals, got high together, read our poems out loud to each other, and generally got to know one another in ways almost forgotten now.

SA: The editors' notes are a really intriguing aspect of the magazine, especially when the Spanish and English don't seem to map onto each other or be direct translations. Did you often write the English notes? A quotation from number 18 reads, "and this editor's note remains the place where we, the makers of this magazine, may speak." And then in number 25: "25 issues of a little magazine: they are pieces but not broken, fragments of a whole every day more tangible, every day closer to the hand, clearer to the eye." The magazine always seems aspirational to me, but in an everyday way—the world as it could be. What do you think?

MR: The editors' notes are interesting. I always wrote the English note, Sergio the Spanish. At the beginning, when our visions were practically one, I might end up writing the note and he would translate it into Spanish, or he might write it and I would translate it into English. For a while, as you've probably noticed, it was the same note in both languages. As our visions began to diverge, though, we began writing different notes. At first this might have been due to the fact that each of us thought a different topic needed editorializing. Gradually, though, the fact that Sergio was moving toward a more mystical, Eastern current in poetry and I was moving toward a more revolutionary stance meant that our notes were completely different. By that time, it almost seemed as if we were publishing different magazines between the two covers. For this reason, some critics have suggested that the journal's history can be read in the editors' notes. I've always thought this was a bit too simplistic an interpretation, though.

SA: Did your work as a midwife intersect at all with the editing of *El Corno*?

MR: Not really. It was always something I did on the side, sometimes more, sometimes less.

SA: Will you talk a little bit about your involvement in the 1968 student movement and your harrowing move from Mexico City to Cuba in 1969?

MR: I took part in the Mexican student movement of 1968 like so many young people and others. I worked with a group at the University of Mexico's School of Medicine. I passed out leaflets, translated materials for distribution outside the country, and eventually—when the repression came down—hid and fed people for a while. *El Corno Emplumado* also declared itself to be on the side of the students: in our editorials, and in what we published. The Mexican government put a brutal end to the movement on October 2, 1968, when its forces shot into the crowd at a large, peaceful rally, and hundreds of participants were killed. Around the same time, the magazine lost much of its funding; at least that which we got from Mexican government sources.

The repression I personally faced came almost a year later, when in July of 1969 we were preparing to commemorate the movement's first anniversary, to honor our dead and missing in some sort of commemorative event. That's when a couple of paramilitary operatives came to our home, stole my passport at gunpoint, and I myself had to go into hiding. I was living with American poet Robert Cohen by then, and we had just had a daughter—my fourth child. Ana was three months old when the repression hit. Robert left his job, we had to shut down the magazine, and it was clear that we weren't going to be able to stay in Mexico. But finding a way out, without my passport, wasn't going to be easy. I have told this story in much more detail in several of my books, most explicitly in *To Change the World: My Years in Cuba* and in my memoir, *I Never Left Home: Poet, Feminist, Revolutionary*. Here I'll just say that it took some time, several months, and enormous effort to make our escape. We felt that our children were vulnerable (the bodies of a number of sons and daughters of movement people had been found on the outskirts of the city), so we sent the four of them to Cuba ahead of us. The Cuban government took them in and protected them as it did many children in those years. A few months later, we were able to join them. And that signaled the end of *El Corno Emplumado* and the beginning of my eleven years in Cuba. In 1980 I went on to Nicaragua, but my two oldest children remained on the island much longer than I did.

SA: *El Corno*'s copyright page says, "A magazine from Mexico City." "From," instead of "in" or "out of," highlights the idea of circulation. The magazine as emissary. Would you say that your ambitions were global?

MR: Our ambitions weren't only global; they were universal! If we could have been in touch with life on another planet, we surely would have sent the journal there. We were young, idealistic, and recognized no boundaries or barriers. We believed that poetry—art in general—was powerful and could change human inclination: away from violence and war and toward brotherhood, justice, and hope. The fact that we would have used the term "brotherhood" simply reflected the fact that feminist ideas had not yet touched our consciousness. When it did, at the end of 1969, everything shifted yet again.

SA: In *To Change the World* you write, "Feminism redirected me. And as was the case each time I discovered a powerful new truth, its influence on my work and the changes it provoked in my personal life were profoundly intertwined." While living in Cuba, you translated some essays on feminism, published as *Las mujeres* (The Women), and began an oral history project that became *Cuban Women Now*. How did your work on *El Corno* prepare you for working and writing in Cuba?

MR: Actually, I put *Las mujeres* together while I was still in Mexico, toward the very end of my time there. The book was published in 1970, after I had moved to Cuba. But *Cuban Women Now* was a book I undertook after my arrival in Cuba, and it was published there in 1972, as *La mujer cubana ahora*, as well as two years later in English in Toronto (by Women's Press). I don't know that either project was directly influenced by *El Corno*, although of course the magazine gave me some very useful editing experience.

SA: While we've been conducting our interview, the US has changed its policy toward Cuba. What is your reaction to that news?

MR: Like most people who have followed the Cuban revolution all these years, especially those of us who have respected Cuba's right to sovereignty, the news that the United States and Cuba had renewed diplomatic relations moved me to tears. To be honest, it wasn't something I thought I'd see in my lifetime. Such a succession of US administrations have held firm in the absurd Cold War policy that erected the blockade and waged attacks on the island ranging from outright military invasion to a series of covert sabotage actions. It is hard to imagine that policy is beginning to crumble. We are two people separated by a slender arm of water, and who share a common history, good and bad. So I reacted to the news with joy. At the same time, I know this is not the end of the problem. Congress must still dismantle the blockade. This change will have challenges. I am hoping that from the US point of view it is not merely a change in method but rather a change grounded in the respect of which President Obama spoke. From the Cuban point of view, it will be up to them to limit resultant chaos and retain as many of the revolution's socialist advances as possible. In general, isolation isn't good for anyone, and islands can be terribly isolated. Increased communication with the rest of the world can only be good for Cuba. Increased trade will mean necessary farm machinery and parts. It will be interesting to see how it all unfolds.

SA: We're reviewing our interview now in 2022, almost six years after this conversation first took place. What would you now add to the 2016 discussion of the US's changing policy toward Cuba? How has it "all unfolded" so far?

MR: I was hoping we could do a retake on that. The rest of the interview is up to date, but after the Trump administration we need to take a new look at many issues. Obama made a courageous move by opening the US to Cuba after decades of bad policy by one administration after another. There was a lot of hope on both sides. And things were moving in the right direction. Even large sectors of the US corporate society were happy with the changes because it meant new outlets for their goods. But when Trump came in, bowing to the most retrograde interests in Florida, he reversed Obama's changes. He tightened the screws again, dashing US hopes and making life harder for people on the island. That was to be expected, of course. It was in line with all of Trump's other policies. But the sad thing is that when Biden was elected, Trump's policies stayed in place. Biden has not made a single move to secure a rapprochement with the Cuban revolution. Add this to the economic downturn internationally, and Cuba is suffering now more than ever from the US blockade and from years of pushback from the North.

SA: I know that you just returned from a big celebration of *El Corno Emplumado* that was held in Mexico City. What was that like? Who staged it?

MR: Yes, and it was life changing. Several students at the cultural center of the Tlatelolco campus of the University of Mexico participated in curating an exhibition called *Siete.de.Catorce* (Seven of Fourteen). Their part of the exhibition was about the 1960s, which of course was a turbulent and creative time in Mexico. In the context of this exhibition, which is really wonderful, they began to think about other activities. They invited me down to be on a panel, along with Sergio Mondragón and Felipe Ehrenberg (an artist who did several of our covers).[2] I also took part in a daylong curator's seminar and gave a poetry reading. These students are extraordinary. Mexico today is plagued with violence and the frustration of protest that doesn't seem to bring change. The students look to those of my generation for answers. But of course we are mostly just asking questions: we as well as they. Our exchange stimulated me to move forward, and also gave me hope, great hope, for a better future for us all. And it strengthened my conviction that art has an important role to play in the struggle.

Figure 6. Lindy Hough. Photo by Lindy Hough.

Lindy Hough

Coeditor and Copublisher, Io (1965–1977; Amherst, MA; Ann Arbor, MI; Cape Elizabeth, ME; Plainfield, VT; Berkeley, CA; Bar Harbor, ME) and North Atlantic Books (1974–present, Plainfield, VT, and Berkeley, CA)

AUGUST 11, 2021, VIA ZOOM AND SUBSEQUENT EDITS OVER E-MAIL

Lindy Hough: Hi, it's nice to see your face, what you look like.

Stephanie Anderson: It's nice to see you. So, I'm Stephanie, and I'll let the students introduce themselves.

Tess Redman: I can go first. Hi, my name's Tess, and I'm a rising sophomore at Duke Kunshan University.

Zainab Farooqui: Hi, I'm Zainab Farooqui, I'm a junior at DKU, and currently I am in Lahore, Pakistan. Press publishing has always been very interesting to me so I'm also very, very excited to have this opportunity to speak with you about your experiences; thank you for coming. To start, do you have any particular memories of the first issue of *Io*, when it was published through Richard [Grossinger]'s fraternity?

LH: Sure. I was a sophomore at Smith College in Northampton, in western Massachusetts, when I met Richard Grossinger, also a sophomore, but at Amherst, a college just seven miles away. We became friends and kindred writers—he wrote nonfiction; I was a poet and fiction writer. The existing literary magazines of our colleges seemed staid, given the explosion in writing, visual arts, avant-garde filmmaking, dance, and theater in 1962 to 1966, the years we were in college. We met through mutual friends and bonded over writing and the desire to travel and see theater, films, poetry readings in New York. He was from New York; I was from Denver.

We decided to start an interdisciplinary magazine to publish

Women in Independent Publishing

writers we admired and were influenced by, and new writers from the four colleges in the Pioneer Valley right around us—University of Massachusetts, Smith, Amherst, and Mount Holyoke. This was before Hampshire College was started in the seventies. Our interest in founding a journal was to create a literary community for ourselves, our colleges, and the national literary-artistic world. Smith had a literary magazine called the *Grecourt Review*, which published academic, more formalistic poetry. We became identified with "New American Poetry," the term created by Donald M. Allen's anthology *The New American Poetry: 1945–60*. My middle sister, Polly Hough, five years earlier had edited the *Grecourt Review*.

Our vision was to gather modern poetry and short fiction from the writers we admired, embedding these in an interdisciplinary context with pieces on science, math, geology, and geography. Richard was able to take funding from the arts budget of Phi Psi, his arty fraternity. This was in the last dying days of fraternities at Amherst. Phi Psi had money to pay for an 8 mm camera, student short films, a film series, and a literary magazine. He ordered films from the Filmmakers Cinematheque in New York and had film nights, which I came to that fall of 1963. Richard was very enterprising; he sold ads to Amherst shops and businesses to make enough money to print the fledgling journal.

We called it *Io*, after the moon of Jupiter—a metaphor of size and scale; we were making something small (a literary magazine) in the orbit of large planetary bodies, a national vision and account of contemporary poetry in an interdisciplinary context, Jupiter.

That first issue began a long personal and publishing collaboration. After college, Richard and I married and moved to Ann Arbor, Maine, Vermont, and finally, in the midseventies, to California, for forty years, where we raised our children. In 2014 we moved full-time to Maine. *The Io Anthology: Literature, Interviews, and Art from the Seminal Interdisciplinary Journal 1965–93* was published in 2015 by North Atlantic Books. This doorstopper tome is a useful and important compendium of *Io* contributors, both the magazine and, later, Io Books. We had no idea that *Io* would continue for twenty-eight years. *Io* lasted from 1965 to 1993, counting the Io Books that it published in the late seventies and early nineties. In 1975 we moved to Berkeley, and in 1981 incorporated North Atlantic Books (NAB) as a nonprofit publishing organization. *Io* had been publishing book-length, perfect-bound books. Terry Nemeth, a friend at Book People, the small press distributor in Berkeley, said in 1975, when we were living in Vermont and thinking of moving to California, that if we came to Berkeley and the Bay Area, we could effectively publish there and likely be distributed by Book People. We had been teaching at Goddard College and spent three nonresident winters in Berkeley.

I had a dance background. I studied ballet for eight years, from eight to sixteen, then modern dance, in Denver. When I got to college, I realized I just wanted to write and gave up dancing—though I often took class in the places we lived, especially when we lived and taught at Goddard College in Plainfield, Vermont, in the early seventies. A close friend was head of the Vermont Council on the Arts; she told me NEA had opened up a new program called Audience Development. Would I like to be one of about fifteen dance critics in rural states where dance companies weren't coming because there was no audience? I would be able to find work as a dance critic. I was already writing arts pieces for the local Montpelier, Vermont, newspaper. I said yes, and flew to Oakland, California, and attended a three-week seminar on this at Mills College, taught by Marcia, where noted choreographers and performers were invited. This was my first exposure to post-modern Judson choreographers: Douglas Dunn, Valda Setterfield and David Gordon, Lucinda Childs, and Meredith Monk. I fell in love with writing dance criticism. Worn out from the intense snow of Vermont, we stopped teaching at Goddard and moved full-time to Berkeley.

ZF: In both your and Richard's introductions to the *Io Anthology*,[1] you mention that a very important part of *Io* was that it published different materials, always changing, always evolving. How did you solicit submissions for the magazine?

LH: Great question. Editors start magazines to publish their own work, writers they admire, and new voices. The poets we most admired and were friends with were Charles Olson, Robert Creeley, Robert Duncan, Ed Dorn, Gary Snyder, Denise Levertov, Joanne Kyger, Diane Wakoski, Jerome Rothenberg, the prose writer Fielding Dawson, Anne Waldman, and Bernadette Mayer, the latter who was associated both with the Language poets and the New York School groups of poets. I was hungry to find women poets and fiction writers in the generation above me: Leonora Carrington and Gertrude Stein. We solicited material from writers we admired, and asked others to introduce us to writers from whom we wanted submissions.

We tried to meet Charles Olson, a major influence, when he was a visiting professor at the University of Connecticut at Storrs. He became sick there and returned to Gloucester, where he died. We came very close. Have you and your students heard of him and discussed his influence on poetics, perhaps?

SA: I don't think we've discussed Olson in this group, but we have talked a little bit about projective verse.

LH: Okay, absolutely. That was his gigantic contribution to poetry. *The Maximus Poems*, *The Distances*, everything he wrote was important and beautiful. Projective verse was a different theory of how to organize and structure the poem: by the breath—determining line breaks not by an arbitrary structure of stanzas, but by where the breath naturally broke the line. It was an open verse, using the page freely. Olson was the link between the modernists and another generation of poets, as well as the experimental filmmaker Stan Brakhage, whom Richard and I visited when we went to see my family in Denver.

It became obvious to me at Smith that neither Olson nor any of these later poets were being taught; academic poetry dominated. I was very interested in the Black Mountain writers and artists: MC Richards's *Centering* on how throwing a pot was a metaphor for life. I longed to bring these new poets to the campus so that Robert Lowell, Anne Sexton, and confessional poetry would not be regarded as the sum total of poetry in America in the sixties. I brought Stan Brakhage my junior year. I was identifying as a poet, which was not a possible thing to be then; the entire emphasis was on New Criticism and becoming a critic. In the seventies Smith realized that being a poet or a fiction writer was as important as being a painter or musician, and hired visiting writers, but not in the midsixties. This was before MFA programs began and the possibility of making writing your vocation was feasible. We were being educated to be critics in the fifties and sixties, not writers. I was a writer discovering my own voice, believing writing was what I was meant to do with the same dedication and determination I had brought to dancing.

ZF: Speaking of the sixties to seventies and how it was a very turbulent time, a lot of the other interviewees have also talked about the sheer amount of change that was happening, and how there was an impetus for them to begin their own presses—because there was so much to talk and write about that they couldn't just see what was happening and then not write about it. Will you talk a little bit about whether writing served as a way of dealing with the changes that were happening around you?

LH: Writing has always been a way of dealing with hopes, dreams, sadness, and anger for me, but it is not therapy—it's a creative act with the satisfaction of making something lyrical, beautiful, surprising, or ironic which can embrace complex and often contradictory layers of meaning.

In Europe, the UK, and America, the sixties and then the transition to the seventies were a tremendous period of social change. I was once on a Smith College panel of students representing four classes for a reunion presentation. The goal was to elucidate how the college responded to these years of turbulence. A student from every four years: '61, '66, '71, and '75. I represented the class of '66. It was fascinating how the eras abruptly changed after my year—the sixties became the looser seventies, and so too the earlier fifties cascaded into the much more radical sixties, so young people either were sensitive to this change and embraced sixties values or identified more with the earlier decade. David Bowie's 1971 song

76 *Women in Independent Publishing*

"Changes" captures the change of eras, as well as the constant change of musical styles—it and all of Bowie's music embodied this chameleon-like quality.

In 1962 to 1966 Richard and I became fellow writers and artists, piling into his yellow Thunderbird to go to New York and check in with his family, but also Allen Ginsberg reading in the Village, off-Broadway theater, new dance, new art. Richard's inspiring high school friend Charles Stein said, "Go see Robert Kelly at Bard." Kelly was a magus who led to all the other poets we met and revered in these years; it was Kelly who suggested we create a collegium by founding a literary magazine of our own, and he led to scores of poets, including Olson and Gerrit Lansing, Paul Blackburn, and Jerome Rothenberg, among many.

After college, during the early years, *Io* won grants and funding from the Coordinating Council for Literary Magazines, the National Endowment for the Arts, the Vermont Council on the Arts, and the California Arts Council. We incorporated North Atlantic Books as a nonprofit in 1981; we both wrote grants for some years for the magazine and the publishing company.

ZF: Was there any particular issue of *Io* that you now find very memorable?

LH: The issue I edited by myself, *Mind, Memory, and Psyche*, was special in terms of editing and content; it gave me a greater degree of control. I could reach out to more women writers and explore the intellectual and artistic connections between the psyche and the conscious mind, as well as the role memory plays in creative work. We were traveling quite a bit doing readings, so much of the work came from host poets on the road: at Kent State, in West Virginia, in Lawrenceville, Kansas.

How did we get this magazine out to anyone? Submissions, subscriber lists. Mailing a lot of Jiffy bags, whole cartons of Jiffy bags. We had a long subscriber list to *Io* in a tall ledger book; among it were the Coordinating Council of Literary Magazines in the US; fifteen to twenty public, college, and university libraries that had literary magazines collections; and many bookstores.

ZF: I'm sure that North Atlantic Books is doing its best to reach farther abroad, so you achieved the goal at some point.

LH: Yes. A key difference between a literary magazine and a publishing company is the latter has distributors. There are some distributors who take literary magazines, but often only very established ones—the *Paris Review*, *Granta*, *Ploughshares*, et cetera. We took part in a distribution collective in Berkeley and had national sales reps for some years. With North Atlantic, we had Book People and UK and European distributors connected to Publishers Group West, in the years we were with them. Now Penguin Random House does all the distribution, national and international.

ZF: One of the issues that I found very interesting was your book *Changing Woman*; it's issue number 11 of *Io*.

LH: It was my first book (1971), written during the winter of 1969 to 1970 when Richard and I were married and had come east to Mount Desert Island in Maine. After Smith and Amherst we went to Ann Arbor where Richard did the course work at the University of Michigan toward a PhD in anthropology. He had won an NSF Fellowship for the domestic fieldwork which would support us for a year. I wrote the poems in that book when we were living in a small house on a pretty deserted road.

ZF: Indian Point Road?

LH: Yep. In Ann Arbor, our son Robin was born in June of 1969. In September we moved with him to a house on Indian Point Road called The Gatehouse, owned by a wealthy woman from New Jersey who had a magnificent house on Green Island, her family's island. I nursed him for nine months in a rocking chair and wrote the poems in *Changing Woman*.

Each of the poems has different inspirations. I was teaching English at the University of Southern Maine and had a student who had just come back from Vietnam; I was amazed to hear some of his stories ("Three Poems Greeting April & Maine"). We did a lot of flying between Maine and California in these years, and I wrote in the second part of that poem about the oddity of seeing one's fairly rural home geography again from the plane.

78   *Women in Independent Publishing*

"Emu Ritual Dance" was about a dance from an anthropological film.

Why does one pick certain poems and not others? The goal is to work with a poem until it works to one's satisfaction. The poems that didn't make the cut of this book? I still have them; they're in my big, black, typed-up binder. You have a rough page count, and you work within that.

ZF: In the *Io Anthology*, only two poems from *Changing Woman* were included: "Beach Baby" and "A Botany of Love Poems."

LH: "Beach Baby" carries a whiff of Olson and maybe Alfred North Whitehead's process reality in the first stanza: "okeanos, and fertile / friendly inland crescent thalassa." Thalassa is the primordial pre-Greek goddess of the sea. The poet has an intermundane sensibility, watching the two-year-old see the ocean again a year later; the poet sees that the child is no longer the "unconscious baby of one who does everything / to please." He gets that the waves are large, and at two is a warier child—no longer a baby. And yet he is "1000 hydra eyes all open alive / to resounding echoes of pleasure/ pain . . ." The toddler is traipsing about exploring his world. "A Botany of Love Poems" is a ten-part poem about the dynamic of a couple.

What governed the choice of contents for the *Io Anthology* was the necessity of having to draw from so many different issues and books that *Io* had published as a literary journal. My work is best found in my four books (*Changing Woman*; *Psyche*, a long narrative poem; *The Sun in Cancer*; *Outlands & Inlands*) and *Wild Horses, Wild Dreams: New and Selected Poems 1971–2010*, published by North Atlantic Books in 2011.

ZF: "Beach Baby" links to other themes in *Changing Woman*, which has many poems that talk about building a house and building a home. I was curious as to how life in the domestic sphere affected your writing language. Is *Io* another home you built?

LH: Sure. A journal is a home for the work, much as books are. Domestic life does not influence me overly, any more than for men—we don't expect to read about domestic life in *Moby Dick*.

It's the backdrop, much as it is in Dickens or Turgenev. My work has close personal poems and poems more influenced by content. When I lived in Berkeley and taught at UC Berkeley, I attended lectures by philosophy faculty on Wittgenstein and Alfred North Whitehead's *Process and Reality*. Ideas and content from philosophy are useful in poems. I intuited from the sad ends of women poets I admired (Anne Sexton, Sylvia Plath) that a poet needed subject matter outside one's self. The poems usually mix the natural world, history, geography with conceptual or intellectual thoughts.

Io was something of a home for my work in these early years, but so were other literary magazines: *Sulfur, IS, Sixpack, Truck, Tooth of Time Review, Llama's Almanac, Toothpick, Lisbon &the Orcas Islands*, et cetera. It had our own work but much more was a vehicle for others; a work of editing, of getting ourselves and others' work out there. I quickly looked to the sustenance of publishing my own five books.

There's an interesting difference between writing the poems and then publishing the book of poems or editing an anthology like the *Io Anthology* or later *Nuclear Strategy and the Code of the Warrior*, Richard's and my anthology of antinuclear writing, interviews, and a symposium featuring many different writers. When you edit an anthology, there's a tremendous amount of material to get into it. The prose tends to dominate in that anthology—long pieces by authors Richard was involved with.

As I said, I was at home during that winter, nursing and taking care of Robin. There were not many places to go. We weren't even aware of Acadia National Park that winter. It was usually very cold and snowing. Richard drove to Southwest Harbor interviewing fishermen when they came in at 4:30 in the afternoon with their catch, gathering data and research for his PhD thesis. He was also writing his own nonfiction: the Cranberry Island series, many early books. This was fieldwork. I'd been to dinners of anthropology students bound for the field and heard how rugged it was, how the wife or spouse had to be supportive and help get through it. We had it easy, staying stateside to do domestic fieldwork. My world was creative and artistic, involved in reading Pound and H. D., Charles Olson, Denise Levertov; Marguerite Duras novels. Keeping my interior world alive.

One of the things that has always amazed me about that winter was that I had no women friends at all! Later, I looked back and thought: Weren't you lonely? Didn't you die for not having anyone to talk to? I was involved in caring for the baby, prizing times when he was asleep for writing. I had no problems writing and typing up (pre-computers) the poems; they came easily. Do I write for myself? For myself and other people. Eventually they get published and I read these poems at readings around the country.

TR: How did gender affect either your writing or your work on the magazine?

LH: Gender didn't affect my work on *Io*. We both did what needed to be done: editorial, acquiring pieces and authors, business-financial, and marketing. I wrote grants and raised money. Once we had two children, born in 1969 and 1974, I was occupied more with childcare, transportation, et cetera. We worked together at North Atlantic Books for fourteen years. I taught technical writing in the College of Engineering for nine years also at UC Berkeley, then went to graduate school in Social and Cultural Studies at UC Berkeley in the late eighties and early nineties, completing the coursework for a PhD, but not the dissertation.

I'm a bi woman who is attracted to men and women both. I was raised in the more conservative fifties, came of age in the sixties. Those were not decades which gave as much choice for gender roles as later. As a result, I've always been interested in lesbians, lesbian writing, films, et cetera. At seventy-eight, it's hard to know if I'll be able to live out this unlived life or not. I write with a certain sensibility that is mine alone, about what I want to say in ways that I've found to express myself. I have always been interested in women emotionally and identified more with women than men, though I've also had a long, satisfying marriage. I have a grandchild who is gender fluid and have several trans friends.

I've finished a novel called *Radon Daughters*, about a love affair between two women in the early fifties against the backdrop of uranium mining in New Mexico and Utah—a lesbian burlesque artist who performs in Europe and across America, and a Denver collage artist who teaches at a school for "retarded and handicapped" (the term then) children. Their union and desire for agency grows out of a tired despair and exhaustion with men.

I was culturally pressured as a child of the fifties and sixties into getting married right after college, by my family and my generation. Also, the war in Vietnam was ramping up to recruit all US college-aged men in 1966; graduate school, being married, and having children were initially deferments.

TR: Do you have any advice for young women trying to get into self-publishing now?

LH: Self-publishing (now known in this country as hybrid) can work well. I'm most familiar with payment to a publisher to cover the editorial and design. On Jane Friedman's blog, Brooke Warner, founder of She Writes Press, a Berkeley hybrid publisher, describes it well. As she says, it's a nuanced and complicated issue. There are excellent hybrid publishers who are far above your average paid publishing service. *Poets & Writers* magazine has articles on this.

One of the things we haven't touched on is the importance of reading your work and performing it out loud to people, giving readings of your work, having a blog, and reading/performing your work on YouTube and Instagram. When you publish a book, you have to do marketing and publicity for it. One thing that helped us as writers was to develop a network of writer friends around the country whom we could link up with to perform our work and sell books. I would definitely invite writers to come to wherever you're teaching or going to school and read their work; there is absolutely nothing like hearing a writer's work read by the author in person.

Writers should also grapple with who you're writing for. How much are you writing for yourself, how much for other people? How much are you reaching out in a really positive way to connect to other

82 *Women in Independent Publishing*

people through your work? Work that is too solipsistic or narcissistic doesn't happen too often, but sometimes, at a reading, you do feel like the writer is pretty much just preening.

I think that for young writers, self-publishing and publishing in literary magazines are both important. Putting out a magazine yourself is a way to reach out to the world and circulate your own work. Self-publishing isn't necessary if you somehow make enough contacts with editors and publishers of literary magazines or independent publishing companies to do your work. Virginia Woolf was a good example—you learn a lot from the process of publishing—setting type, having a typesetter, taking the work to be printed, et cetera.

TR: What type of printing technology did you and Richard use for the magazine and/or the books you published?

LH: Offset printing initially, taking sheets of typesetting, which had to be incorporated with a designed copy and sent to offset printers in the Ann Arbor area. We used Lithocrafters a lot. The copy came back to the office and was proofread, then taken back to the typesetter for the corrections to be put in. Now corrections can be made online; discs with hard copies are sent to the printer. Print-on-demand publishers have proliferated and gotten better in recent years. You pay for this, but not being stuck with many copies you can't sell is the greatest advantage.

TR: I just had sort of a philosophical question before we wrap up. Do you think there's an inherent difference between written poetry and oral poetry?

LH: You write the poem, then read it aloud; it becomes oral. I think when you're writing poems—and writing anything—it's great to read it out loud yourself. Written and oral seem to me almost like the right and left hand, and orality is just as important as the writing. The urge to perform one's work, to articulate it and throw it out there, is strong. You come into your own when you are performing your poem. You don't even have to think of it as performing, but there is a difference between reading a poem aloud to an audience without any eye contact or dramatic ability and performing it. I have sat through too many boring poetry readings in stores, colleges, and universities, where the poet is unable to risk really communicating, or trying to communicate.

I don't believe in that at all. I believe that the audience is there to be reached, and your work and your voice is the transit that can reach them; the vehicle that can make that transition happen.

Figure 7. Bernadette Mayer. Photo by Philip Good.

Bernadette Mayer

Coeditor and Copublisher, 0 TO 9 *(1967–1969, New York),* United *Artists (1977–1983), and United Artists Books (1977–present, Lenox, MA, and New York)*

NOVEMBER 1, 2013, IN EAST NASSAU, NY

Bernadette Mayer: I always like the way that trees like that look on gray days. So my view is of a skeleton.[1] I can see three skeletons. Actually, the tree looks more yellow today than it does on other days. And all the green parts are gone.

Stephanie Anderson: So. You say that you and Vito [Acconci][2] started 0 TO 9 because you wanted to envision a space where you could publish? It was more eclectic than some of the other mimeo mags of the time.

BM: Yeah, and it was a perfect environment. [It was] just interesting to mix poetry with conceptual art in a particular way. We couldn't really get *all* the conceptual artists we wanted to be in the magazine.

SA: How did you try to get them?

BM: By letters. Yeah. [*chuckles*]

SA: Do you feel like doing the magazine changed how people reacted to you?

BM: [*laughs*] No! I think they continued to be totally crazy, refusing to accept [me], you know, because they figured, "Well, she's really young, you know, doesn't know what she's doing." I couldn't have been more than twenty. I think I was younger than that. It was the poets I had the most problem with. Our problem with the conceptual artists was that they just wouldn't accept us because we were weird and we were these . . . poets. And we weren't even typical poets; we were like these weird, idiosyncratic, Catholic . . . you know. I mean, who . . . The person who did accept us lovingly was Jerome

86 *Women in Independent Publishing*

Rothenberg. Which, I thought *o TO 9* was very much like his magazine, *Alcheringa*, except that there was more poetry in it.

SA: Yeah, I mean there's the kind of anthropological work in the first few issues.

BM: Well, that's where we found the great poetry that we could, you know, ensconce everything in. Poetry of the American Indians. Our audience, whoever they were, didn't really know it that well, so . . . I always thought that was great poetry.

SA: Do you remember how you and Vito divided the editing responsibilities? Was it pretty equal?

BM: I wouldn't say it was equal, but how it was divided—I don't know the answer. Vito did a lot of work ferreting out manuscripts. And I just used the ones I happened on by chance, and I didn't really seek them out. Which was probably a mistake, but I didn't know how to do it.

SA: Was the poetry scene really centered around the Poetry Project at that time too?

BM: Probably; I really don't know. I really didn't have much to do with it. My world was the different world of, at that point in time, the weird conceptual art and performance work—kind of "happenings" type art, and not really poetry.

SA: What was your favorite happening?

BM: Oh god. Oh god! I'm sorry I mentioned that. [*laughs*] My favorite happening was when the Living Theater got possession of this storefront in downtown Manhattan and lived in it. I thought that was so great. I used to go and look at them every day, living their lives. What could be finer? [*chuckles*]

SA: You've always been fascinated with humans, it seems.

BM: Oh, yes. Well, how could I not be? It's all we have, when we have no money. We have other humans. Or ourselves.

SA: Do you think of the Street Works as the culmination of *o TO 9*?

BM: Oh, no, by no means. They were great, though. I loved [them]. We had whole different performance things going on as part of that world. It was the street works, the theater works. And they were all very interesting ways to get writing things away from the page, pretty much. But—"culmination". . . funny word. Sounds like a car crash, right? [*laughs*] "It all culminated in a car crash . . ."

SA: Speaking of words you don't like, why don't you like the word "performative"?

BM: Oh, performative! I hate that word! Performance, I don't mind. Performative . . . it's like a made-up, unnecessary word. It's like you suddenly want to seem a certain way. That's all I'll say. [*laughs*]

SA: Do you feel like being an editor-publisher changed your status as a woman, or a woman working in the scene?

BM: [*pause*] You mean . . . in what way?

SA: I don't know. I guess I'm asking what it was like to be a woman. [*laughs*]

BM: Oh! Well. When we were editing 0 TO 9, I typed all the stencils. This was a very womanly reaction, or role to play. [*laughs*]

SA: Right. I feel like so much of the talk of typing stencils is, like, it's in the domestic sphere, it's at home. But I guess then you have to go find a mimeograph machine somewhere. You guys were going to some place in New Jersey, right?

BM: Well, we did for the magazine, because we were using Ed Bowes's father's mimeograph machine in his law office.

SA: Did people help?

BM: Oh, yeah, we had to have helpers. As soon as we ran off the pages, we had to collate them, because we only had one night to do it all.

SA: Was there an army of young poets to help?

BM: Well, there wasn't an army, though; my sister helped, I can't remember who else helped . . . Ed helped . . . Hmm. We must have had other people. We had at least four people. We didn't want to have so many people that it would . . . it was a very small space. So it would seem too crowded.

SA: You didn't want it to turn into a party?

BM: Well, there was that aspect of it, too, but since we just had that one night, we were very covetous of our time. It could have turned into a party, I guess. [*chuckles*]

SA: Because Maureen Owen talks about the mimeo collation parties for *Telephone* being kind of . . .

88 *Women in Independent Publishing*

BM: Yeah, they were fun!

SA: Did you guys have release parties for o TO 9?

BM: No, no.

SA: It just got distributed?

BM: Yeah. We would pack it up and send it out pretty much as soon as it was printed. To various bookstores and people, individual people.

SA: Alice [Notley] talks about sending *CHICAGO* to all the people she admired and wanted to be friends with. [*laughs*]

BM: Yeah, exactly! [*laughs*] It was fun. It was fun to have the magazine *finished*.

SA: I can imagine. Would you turn around right away and start a new one?

BM: Well, we'd start gathering work for a new one. I mean, some work we had left over from previous issues. So. Definitely. I don't know how people do a *lot* of issues—like, of *The World* there were a lot of issues. I don't think I would even want to have that stamina.

SA: o TO 9 petered out after what, six issues?

BM: Six. Yeah.

SA: In the introduction[3] both of you say, like, you don't remember deciding to stop; it just kind of stopped . . .

BM: It just kind of ended; I think Vito's reluctant to explain that he just completely lost interest. And I couldn't see any point in continuing on, because I was doing all these other things, too, so . . . We still had no place to publish, though. [*laughs*] So it didn't work, as you might say.

SA: Did Hannah [Weiner]'s work get more attention through o TO 9?

BM: Gee, you know, I have no idea. I don't think o TO 9 had that kind of effect on anybody. You think?

SA: I don't know, but . . . because it's now reprinted by Ugly Duckling in that big, beautiful book, I think people think of its impact as being really important.

BM: Yeah. Well, it's much more important now than it ever was then. [*chuckles*] When we were doing o TO 9, this magazine started coming out . . . well actually, it might have started after we finished. It was like a glossy art magazine, called *Avalanche*, and the publishers

Bernadette Mayer 89

had lots of money, and they had ads . . . and it was like this conceptual art magazine. And I was jealous. But you know, not really. [*laughs*]

SA: How did you keep in touch with the New York scene when you were living up here and in other, more rural places?

BM: Well, different times, different ways. When I first moved to the country, I rented somebody's summer house in Great Barrington, and I rented it for the winter. It was the only thing I could afford. And I started inadvertently writing, so on the desk where I had my typewriter, I put the pages that I was writing in reverse order. So it wasn't really an intention to do anything, but a lot of the poets, including Anne Waldman and Gerard [Malanga] and I don't remember who else . . . Actually, John Weiners visited once . . . [they] came to my house because they really wanted to get away from the city, and they knew that they could stay at my house, for free. And I welcomed the company because I was living there alone by myself, so it was kind of fun to have people around then. But anyway, Anne came to visit me once, and she saw all these pages, and she started reading through them. And she decided that she would like to publish this work. So that became *Moving*. So that's a way that I kept in touch with them—or with some representative of them. But I didn't really see too many other people. I saw a lot of Hannah at the time, and . . . I didn't really see too many people at all in the house in Great Barrington. People thought I was crazy. Like, "Why is this young woman living by herself in the middle of nowhere?" I mean, this is insane.

SA: This is before Lewis [Warsh][4] and kids and *United Artists*, but after *0 TO 9*?

BM: Oh, yeah. Grace [Murphy][5] came to visit me, and one day we were inhabiting the house, and a raccoon started hanging upside-down from the screen door of the kitchen. So we went to the door, because it was banging, and we thought it was a bear! [*laughs*] Because it looked so tall! Its head was . . . [gestures up high] We had never seen a bear before! So, we had fun. Ed Bowes, who I was living with at the time, used to come up whenever there was a hideous snowstorm, of which there were many. And he would try to induce me to come back to New York City. And I would say, "This is the moment when I would most like to stay here!" But eventually I did come down, and you know what? I regretted it. Because you drive on the Taconic Parkway—there's not even any car tracks to follow. It was terribly maintained at the time, and probably still is. I don't know why I did it. It took us maybe . . . nine hours to get from there to New York City? And I said to myself, "This is not worth it." I was a nervous wreck the whole time. [*chuckles*]

SA: Did you ever miss editing a magazine, or books, while you were in Great Barrington?

BM: No. Not at all. I mean, I knew I could do it any time I wanted. Or any time I could afford to. Yeah. "Miss"—funny word. What I *missed* was human companionship. But, at the same time, it was a great pleasure not to have any. [*chuckles*] The people next door to me— whenever there was a big snowstorm, they would get together with their neighbors and play cards. So they invited me over one day to play, and I very—probably, in retrospect—impolitely, refused. Declined.

SA: That seems like a situation, though, that might be hard to escape from once you're in it.

BM: Well, I didn't really like the playing of cards. But it was really quite beautiful there. I was there from September through May. So I got to see, right before I left, the apple blossoms. I took a lot of photographs there. I was very happy there. I would have stayed longer, forever maybe, if I could've gotten a job. But I really didn't know how to look for one; nobody that I knew wanted me to stay, so they didn't help me . . . I don't know, I just blew it somehow, and I had to come back to New York City.

SA: What did you do when you got back?

BM: I was living in a loft on Grand Street, like SoHo area before it was SoHo, and . . . nothing. I just thought to myself, "How horrible the city is." I was ready to leave it. [*laughs*]

SA: How long was it before you left again?

BM: Well, I stayed in the city until Marie was born. Yeah. A long time.

Bernadette Mayer   91

But I was busy; I had to figure out how to have Marie, how to get pregnant, you know, this was not something that would take a small amount of time. I had to find the right man that I wanted to be pregnant with. So it turned out to be Lewis because he was so hot to have a baby. I mean, he was the only man I knew who really wanted to have children. So it wasn't that difficult to figure that one out.

SA: United Artists started when you were living outside of the city? Or it was just what Angel Hair morphed into?

BM: No . . . it became an extension of Angel Hair because of Lewis. Because he had been involved in Angel Hair Books. And I always thought that Angel Hair was really stupid, because they did all these really precious things, like with the letterpressed covers, you know, and I thought that was dumb. I was not a very . . . you know, a kind of person who's tolerant of others. [*laughs*] Especially things like that. I mean, part of Vito and I, our . . . impetus to start 0 TO 9 was this idea that the poem doesn't belong on a page surrounded by white space, like a precious object. And that was what was going on in that other part of the world. They were going in that direction. Not the mimeograph books so much. But just the tendency of poetry toward that kind of thing. I felt that very strongly. And I couldn't understand why nobody understood how strongly I felt about it. [*laughs*]

SA: So what did you envision for United Artists? How did you want it to be produced and be different?

BM: I thought it was kinda great the way it was. I mean, I didn't really have any desires for it. Except that everybody would contribute to it that we thought of. You know, I've always had this problem. I always think that any of my thoughts . . . that everybody knows what they are, so I don't even have to say them. [*laughs*]

SA: [*laughs*] You're not an extremely transparent person, Bernadette.

BM: [*laughs*] I know, I know! Well, that's why I started writing things down. Vito was very mad—well, I wouldn't say mad, that's probably the wrong word—when I showed an interest in continuing to write only. Because his tendency was to get away from writing and my tendency was to get more into writing. But I mean, there was no way to tell when I first met Vito what was going on with him. And

92   *Women in Independent Publishing*

I don't think he knew either. Because he went to the Iowa Writer's Workshop and all that. I mean, I didn't really object to that—although I did in retrospect.

SA: Is there a United Artists book you did that sticks out in your mind?

BM: Hmm. I really liked . . . I don't know what year this was, but Jim Brodey's book *Judaism*. I thought that was a great book. And everybody kind of doubted . . . Well, I was a big fan of Jim's work, even though it was the first time in my life I realized that there could be a poet that you really didn't like personally who wrote great work. [*laughs*] I don't know. I hated all that. Well, hated is maybe too strong a word. I didn't like the poets who were accepted in that realm as poets, because it always seemed like their work was . . . kind of thoughtless, and maybe sometimes at its very worst, cynical and . . . weightless. You know? I mean, I'm reluctant to say anything that will be horrible. [*laughs*] The whole New York School scene just seemed flimsy to me. I didn't like it.

SA: Did you have a hand in typesetting the books?

BM: Oh, the books. Probably. We just did it by mail. McNaughton & Gunn. There were these same [street] corners adjoining three different publishers who were all printers for all these poetry magazines. So McNaughton & Gunn was one of them. I never went there. I've just heard about this. No, the nice thing about any form of publishing, including mimeograph, is that you feel like you can do anything you want. Mimeograph extremely so. Because you can do it instantly. But other forms of publishing . . . I mean that's kind of what people want, is to have a book published. It's a weird idea, but yeah, we've learned to live with it.

SA: But by the time you reprinted Berrigan's *The Sonnets* . . . that was all offset, right?

BM: Yeah, it was all offset. All those books were offset.

SA: Did you allow the people you published to have a lot of say in how they wanted the book to look?

BM: Yeah, as much as they wanted!

SA: Do you feel like editing—having a hand in all that process—changed your own work at all?

BM: Well, actually it was great to get to know, so intimately or so thoroughly, all those kinds of poems. So it was useful in many ways. But yeah, I don't think it really affected what I was writing. But I liked it; I enjoyed it very much. I never could understand why anybody thought then, or thinks now, that a manuscript for a book is valuable in any way.

SA: You mean the actual manuscript?

BM: Yeah. I loved it; I loved what I was doing. But if I were doing it by myself, I would have done it completely differently. I would have published different things. I mean, because it seemed like, with United Artists—presses are always seeming this way—that it seems like you have to publish this or that. And it's like you never even *think* about it. You know what I'm saying?

SA: Yeah. It's not even like pressure from a single person, it's just, like . . .

BM: Yeah, weird. It's weird.

SA: How did United Artists get funded?

BM: For *United Artists* magazine, we would get these little grants. It was an organization at the time called CCLM—Coordinating Council of Literary Magazines. We would just apply for a grant every year.

SA: It seems like a lot of little magazines in the seventies and eighties were funded that way.

BM: Yeah. It was pretty inexpensive to keep it going.

SA: Who thought of the name United Artists?

BM: [*chuckles*] Well, you know, we did a little catalog, and we used on the cover the drawing that Paramount Pictures does? We thought of it together. I mean, that was the idea. But I don't think anybody ever noticed the joke we were making. [*laughs*] Nobody ever mentioned it.

SA: Did you do other books like Ted's *Sonnets*, reprinting things that had gone out of print?

BM: Gee. Probably not. I don't remember doing anything like that. Oh! We did print—not as a United Artists book but in *United Artists* magazine—a serialized version of a work called "The Relation of My Imprisonment." Russell Banks was responsible—it was an imitation

94 *Women in Independent Publishing*

of an old seventeenth-century manuscript. So we thought we'd try, in *United Artists*, serializing something. But like all those things, you don't get much response. I mean, you would think . . .

SA: Oh? It's not like Dickens?

BM: Yeah, people would write to you and say, "Oh, I always thought you should do serializing . . ." Right? [*laughs*]

SA: Did you like doing the books better, or the magazine? It sounds like you liked doing the magazine better.

BM: I liked doing the magazine better because you could really touch it more. I mean, you touch each piece of paper. Pretty interesting. I mean, pretty great for paper on which is printed writing. [*chuckles*]

SA: You like concrete objects.

BM: Yeah, I do.

SA: Did you ever work with writers to edit the work?

BM: Probably. But I can't think of any instances. It was fun. We had fun. It never seemed really overwhelming, to be doing all these things. I don't know.

SA: And raising kids?

BM: Yeah, right! [*laughs*] Yeah.

[*after a break*]

SA: [*adjusts the telephone, which is recording the conversation*] I get nervous with the device.

BM: Yeah, having a device. And we decided that yours was the kind of device where you can get apps, right? [*laughs*] Apt to get an app.

SA: There should be more poetry apps.

BM: Are there any?

SA: There must be, but . . . I bet there are some really cheesy ones.

BM: Yeah. Well, I'd be happy to . . . If I knew anything about designing an app, I'd be happy to design a bearable poetry app.

SA: What would your ideal poetry app be?

BM: You'd just get introduced to a new poem. Every day, or how often you felt it was usable. Right? Wouldn't that be fun? To have on your device a poem. Your device has room enough to read a poem on it?

SA: Yeah. So, do you remember any particularly memorable stories about working with writers that you published?

BM: When we published this book by Clark Coolidge, the cover was a picture of Floyd Collins, who is a famous old spelunker—which means cave explorer. You know, I have to get straight his story. I think he was buried alive in some cave somewhere, and it was a big publicity thing. Maybe in the thirties? forties? But anyway, the book is called *Own Face*, so everybody wonders if that's Clark's face. [*chuckles*] Simpleminded, right? But I really enjoyed doing that book. Nobody was really publishing Clark's work at the time yet. So.

SA: And you and he had a cave project.[6]

BM: Oh, we've worked together on many things! But yes, that one was published. We went to explore this cave in West Stockbridge, because he was living up here at the time, and in order to get to it—it was on somebody's private land—so in order to get to it we had to first get permission. And then we had to do all this bushwhacking to get to the cave, because nobody knew how to tell us where it was. But we knew approximately where it was. And when we got there, I couldn't go in. I was terrified. And we went with Ed Bowes, who was going to make a film in the cave, and Clark's daughter, Celia, and his wife, Susan, and I had my period. And I started bleeding so profusely . . . You know? Have you ever had a period like that? [*chuckles*]

SA: Yeah.

BM: And then later on Clark read, in some nineteenth-century book about exploring caves, that women who have their periods should never go into caves. For that same reason. Interesting. I don't think anybody knows that. So when everybody came out of the cave, I was sitting on a rock, bleeding. I mean, it seemed to me like that was all I ever did, was bleed. I got into Clark and Susan's car, which was a Volkswagen camper-type car, and they put down a towel for me on the back seat, so the blood wouldn't get all over the car. [*laughs*] And we went back to Clark's house, and Clark and Susan gave me a brandy. Because everybody thought if you lose that much blood . . . it's kind of threatening, maybe. I felt fine. But yeah, it was kind of scary for others. You know, did you ever notice that? When something happens to you, and it's scarier for other people than it is for you?

SA: Oh, yeah, totally.

96   *Women in Independent Publishing*

BM: I've never gotten used to that. Jennifer [Karmin][7] did that to me once. We were walking around here, and I fell in the creek over here, the Kinderhook creek. And it wasn't very deep at all. And the worst thing that happened was that I got my cigarettes wet! So I get out of the creek, and that's all I'm thinking of. I mean, it was the kind of creek, you know, where the water was like up to here or something. [*gestures low*] It wasn't a big deal. But Jennifer made such a big fuss about it, and I've thought ever afterward that it's really scary, other people's reactions to what happens to you. So nobody wants to be responsible for your injury. [*chuckles*] I think that's weird. I still think that's weird, and I'm old.

SA: Did you and Clark do other collaborations that aren't published?

BM: Um. Not actually written down. Yeah, I can't remember what they all were. Mostly we talked. We just talked incessantly.

SA: And wrote letters incessantly.

BM: Yeah.

SA: Was he your main correspondent about poetry then?

BM: He was for a while. Because I didn't really agree with anybody else. So Clark and I had great conversations.

SA: You were both kind of . . . on the fringe of things.

BM: Well. If that's . . . if that's something that has a fringe, yes, we were. [*laughs*]

SA: Did you publish any of your own books with United Artists?

BM: Oh, quite a few! Yeah.

SA: Your audience, like, was fine with you publishing them yourself, right?

BM: Oh, yeah.

SA: Because there's such a stigma around self-publishing now.

BM: Nowadays there is. But you know what, there was then too. But you'd just ignore it. I mean, it's the stupidest thing. I mean, what is that all about? Capitalism, perhaps? [*laughs*]

SA: This idea that if someone else likes your work enough to publish it, that it's, like, valid or something?

BM: Yeah. I've talked to a lot of people in the history of my time being a poet, and they would all say they would prefer to have a book, and they would say, uh, and I would say to them, "Publish it yourself!" And they would say to me, "No, no, no. I want somebody else to publish it." I mean, even Phil [Good][8] says that to me. I can't believe that. I mean, why? That is so insane. Plus the fact that who cares if somebody else likes your work enough to publish your book. But I'm saying this as a total spoiled brat, because when I was a kid, not a kid but like, in my twenties, I got a letter from Barbara at New Directions asking me to be a New Directions author. So I said, "Wow! This is great! I'll never have to think about this again!" [laughs] And it turns out that it's true. Yeah. I was happy. To be a New Directions author. My first thought was, "Wow, I get to be in that great catalog, with William Carlos Williams, and isn't it amazing." I get to occasionally look in New Directions's office, where they have all the books by New Directions authors, and . . . it's amazing to see them. And one of the great things about being published by New Directions is that you can get any of their books for free! So it's hard for me to walk out of that office and be able to carry what I really want. [chuckles]

SA: Yeah, I always thought that when you are a publisher you should keep sending free books to the authors you've published. But it gets hard when you're doing little books, because the print run is so small these days . . .

BM: Well, you figure that into your print run, how many you need to send to all those people.

SA: How did you guys distribute your books?

BM: Well, it's always different every time. I used to save envelopes with return addresses on them. I had this *huge* pile of envelopes. And I would just use that and hand-address . . . well, typewriter-address all the books. But, you know, then Phil threw them away, because I had these overflowing—maybe falling over—piles of envelopes. So now I just use my address book. But, I mean, that's doesn't include everybody. Someday I'll figure it out. [chuckles]

SA: Were there release parties for those books?

BM: No, we never had any parties. I mean, I was always someplace else . . . And if there was a party, it probably should be in New York City,

98   *Women in Independent Publishing*

and I was never there, and I didn't have any money. So, that's why we probably never had . . . but I mean, we *would* have had a party. Just for the sake of *party*. Right? [*pause*] I always felt sorry for my kids, because they grew up in these houses filled with books, with all this publishing activity. I mean, they must have thought that their parents were kind of . . . remote from them.

SA: How so?

BM: Because we were doing all these other things. [*chuckles*] I'm sure they had fun, though.

SA: So you typeset *0 TO 9*, but were you also the one who typeset the United Artists magazine and books?

BM: No, because Lewis was able to do that. He could type stencils! Isn't that great? So I shared that work with him.

SA: He wanted to have babies *and* type stencils! He's like the dream guy!

BM: [*laughing*] Yeah! Well, when I first met Lewis, he had edited a magazine with Bill Corbett called *Boston Eagle*, and that's how we bumped into each other the time before we had kids together. Because he had put something of mine in the *Boston Eagle*. And I was really impressed by his ability to type stencils. [*laughs*] I don't know, easily impressed, right? Or *weirdly* impressed. [*pause*] But Bill Corbett and a lot of people that I met have this idea that mimeograph books are not as good as—what we used to call them at the time—"books with a spine." [*laughs*] Right? That would be a good title for a poem. "Spineless Books." There *is* a publishing company called Spineless Books.

SA: Was anyone interested in sewing books?

BM: Well, we sewed . . . when Phil was editing this magazine called *Triangle Shirtwaist Fire*—it was like a small size. And we sewed the bindings.

SA: Nice. And he called that "the last mimeo magazine"?

BM: No, no, that wasn't mimeograph; that was offset. It was on a kind of folder paper, really small. "The last mimeograph magazine" that he was talking about is a magazine called *Blue Smoke*. Which was done on my mimeograph machine. Phil and his friend Bill DeNoyelles asked me if they could have it. And I said sure. Because then we knew we weren't going to use it anymore. And Lewis said, "Well, how much are you going to pay me for it?" So I think in the end they did pay Lewis something for it. But what it was, I couldn't tell you. Anyway. I knew . . . it's like your children, right? I [always] knew where the mimeograph machine was. [*laughs*]

SA: It was an extension of you. But you've never had a desire to edit a magazine with Phil?

BM: You know, it's never come up. Yeah, it's a good idea. I'll mention it to him. We have a little money now, so we could do that. I don't know if he'd be interested. And now editing a magazine is really kind of negligible. You just collect the manuscripts, put them in Xeroxable order, and bring them to Staples. And you design a cover. There are a lot of people these days doing sort of imitation mimeo magazines. Meaning, offset magazines that are stapled. It's a cheaper way of doing it. Because Staples does charge you money for binding something. I mean, all of that, too, is a negligible cost; everything's kind of cheap at Staples. Did I ever tell you that Staples is a business of that guy [Mitt] Romney?

SA: Yeah. That's too bad.

BM: It's kind of disconcerting. I have this magazine called *The Tasawassans*, and I've done two issues. The whole magazine—to make, like, I don't know how many copies I make; maybe two hundred?—[costs] a hundred dollars. But if I put a color cover on it, it's three hundred more dollars. But it would be great to have every page be in color.

SA: You've always been always a fan of writing in color, right? I feel like your letters were always in colored pens . . .

BM: Well, it's because I have that funny form of synesthesia, where you see every letter in color. You know, but I realized the other day that—you may have heard me telling somebody this. I bought some delphiniums—I was going to raise them in the garden—because I have great memories of delphiniums . . . somebody down the road. Oh, look, the sun. Wow, it's going to get even hotter! [*chuckles*] They were raising them down here, and they were beautiful—blue, bright blue delphiniums. So I bought some thinking that they were *all* blue. Well, the ones that I got were kind of this funny shade of pinkish gray. So I realized after that that all I care about in the world is color. I mean, I get so profoundly disappointed when something's the wrong color. This is insane. It's not the way humans are supposed to be.

SA: When you see letters in color, does it mean that each letter . . . like, *e* is always green, or does it change?

BM: No. It's always the same. But it's not the same for anybody else who sees letters in color.

SA: What's your favorite color of letter?

BM: Lately I've been liking the *s* best. Which is a bright yellow. I don't know; I just like the shape of it and the way it looks when it's yellow. Sort of like a tree. Not really. This time of year drives me crazy; nothing is in color. I mean—terrible! [*chuckles*]

SA: Now I'm going to think about the *s*'s of my name in bright yellow forever on and that's lovely.

BM: Yeah. You have a great name. Because the *e*'s are green, the *a*'s are red . . . so, it's a really pretty name. And the *r* is orange. I have a great name for that too: "Bernadette Mayer." It's a very colorful name. Some people have just, like, yellow and brown names. [*laughs*]

SA: Did you ever tell Joe Brainard about your colors, your synesthesia?

BM: I don't think we ever talked about it, no. Joe and I didn't really talk that much. Neither of us liked to talk. So we'd just hang out together. I would see him in front of St. Mark's Church; he would come to the readings. He had terrible social anxiety disorders, and so did I, so we would just stand there together and smoke cigarettes. I never felt any need to talk to Joe. I mean, unless something vital had to be said.

SA: How long had you had the idea for *Midwinter Day*; do you remember?

BM: Oh, god, forever! I had the idea forever, and I couldn't figure out how I would ever do it. So what I had to do beforehand was figure out . . . I figured out I could probably do it there [in Lenox, Massachusetts,] because I was more settled down in one place. And so I could plan everything ahead of time. And it seemed possible to do. But I had that idea hundreds of years ago. My life was always just so crazy that I never felt like I could really do it. I mean, actually it probably would have been more interesting to do it in a crazy life, for a crazy life. Don't you think?

SA: I don't know. That would have maybe taken away some of the meditative quality of it . . . I think you need it in that book.

BM: Yeah, it would be gone completely. A very interesting fact about that book—when I wrote it, it was . . . you have this experience when you write, or I do, sometimes, where you're writing, but you're feeling like the writing is already there, and you're just kind of tracing it.

SA: Do you think it was that you had, like, meditated on the idea for long enough that you had accumulated all these things?

BM: Yeah, I guess. [*pause*] No, I think it's more . . . probably more weird and spiritual than even that. But I'm not even going to get there. Go there. Whatever people say nowadays. [*laughs*] Because if you quoted me, people would say, "Mmm, I never thought she was that crazy." [*pause*] No, when I visited once, a hundred years ago, Bill Corbett, in Boston—where he used to live—he said to me . . . he made the mistake of saying to me, "So. What are your plans? For writing, I mean." So I said, "Mmm. Very interesting. Now I'm going to put all these things into words." I didn't say any of this; I thought this. And so I delineated all these different projects, among which was *Memory*, and I've done each of those projects.

SA: Wow.

BM: This is scary. Right? [*laughs*] Well I was in a real hurry when I was growing up, to write as quickly as possible. Everybody in my father's family died as the result of a cerebral hemorrhage at age forty-nine. So, stupidly, it never occurred to me that I could get brain surgery, right? And survive. I just figured I'd die when I was forty-nine, so I'd better hurry up. It was a very unemotional decision. And so, I hurried up. But then I didn't die! [*laughs*] So I did all these things, and wrote all these works, and had all these kids, and . . . what am I doing now? What am I doing? [*laughs*] Talking to you about the *past*. It's funny.

SA: Well, and the future a little bit too. [*pause*] What would you tell a young woman who was wanting to do a magazine now?

BM: Oh! Hmm. Well, I think it's a great thing, and it's much easier now, so it's possible. I would talk to her about money, mostly. Because

102 *Women in Independent Publishing*

you need some money to pay for it. And—this is true of anybody who's writing poetry too. So that would be your main concern, I would think. But I think [it's] possible to do it nowadays if you can afford it.

SA: Were there other magazines from "way back then" that you liked and were reading especially?

BM: I used to read *Alcheringa* all the time. I don't know what other magazines I read. Well, I read *Avalanche*, when it came out, because I was interested in that whole world. Magazines of poetry . . . Good question. I don't think I knew of any that I read all the time. I just read them all. At least once, to find out . . . It was like this hungry desire to make sure you knew what was going on. Right? [*laughs*] But I mean, I never really, excitedly, thought, "Oh, what's going to be in the next issue?"

SA: I almost find that, like, working on a magazine makes me have less energy for reading other magazines.

BM: Mmm. Really? Why? You have less time . . .

SA: Yeah. And because, living in that world of discussing contemporary poetry so much within the confines of the magazine . . . I don't know. I get tired. I come home and I want to read noir or something.

BM: Yeah, right? *People.* I like schlock magazines. Those magazines that they have in the supermarket check-out lines. I mean, they're pretty engrossing. [*laughs*] We should publish a gossip magazine for poets. Wouldn't that be great? I would love it. Imagine collecting work for it? You could write it all yourself! In the magazine we would treat poets like celebrities, right? That would be so great.

SA: I think it would be fun to have a magazine where you could put, like, ephemera in. Like leaves and whatever else you want to do.

BM: Different ones in every issue. Yeah. [*chuckles*] It would get kind of messy. People would say, "Oh, give me a copy of that messy magazine . . ."

SA: Was it you or Alan [Casline][9] who was talking about the two-issue problem? He was saying that people sometimes get stuck after the second issue, but if you keep going, you're good.

BM: Well, you could say kind of anything. But I guess that's true. [*pause*] Well, I have the third issue of *The Tasawassans* somewhere in this house . . . I tried to publish it about four different times, and Phil kept saying to me, "Don't do it now, we don't have any money." And it was true, we didn't, but I was going to do it anyway. Because, you know, you can put a lot of stuff on credit cards, and you know, what the hell. So after about the fourth time, I just thought to myself, "I'm never going to try and do this magazine." And I lost all the manuscripts. And the cover. So, I mean, if I ever find them, maybe I'll do it again. So maybe Alan is right. I have the . . . it's the third-issue hurdle, or the second-issue hurdle, really bad. [*chuckles*]

SA: We'll have to go on a treasure hunt through the house for *The Tasawassans*.

BM: Yeah. Well, I've looked every place that it could possibly be, and I haven't been able to find it.

SA: Who was in it?

BM: It was a "Bill" issue, so it was all poets named Bill. And on the cover was a picture of Bill DeNoyelles as a child on the shoulders of his father, whose name is also Bill DeNoyelles. And then, I was . . . I had some poems by William Carlos Williams, and a poem by Shakespeare . . . and then I was going to let anybody who wanted to be Bill whatever their last name was be a Bill too. [*chuckles*] So it was a well-planned issue, and the only reason I'm sorry that I never did it now is because the issue after that is so interesting. So maybe I should just skip ahead and do it anyway! [The next issue] is like *The Tasawassan's* version of the *New Yorker*. You know in the *New Yorker* they have that About Town column? I was going to have it be all about trees. And have pictures of all the different kinds of trees.

SA: [*pause*] It seems like it's always been important to you to publish older stuff alongside contemporary stuff. You guys were doing it in *0 TO 9* . . .

BM: Well, there's no reason to discount some writing because it's old. I mean, some of it is actually more interesting than anything anybody's doing right now. [*pause*] But also there's the idea that your own writing doesn't have to be *written* by you. It can have al-

104   *Women in Independent Publishing*

ready been written by somebody now or a long time ago. So you want to appropriate for your own this older writing. I mean, why not? When you do a collaboration, it doesn't have to be by you and Jennifer Karmin. It can be . . . just everybody's writing. There's this form, I'm sure you've heard of it, called—it's a poetic form called a cento. Which is one line, out of a hundred lines, by other people.

SA: Right. And you like to make up blurbs by other people.

BM: Oh, yes! Making up blurbs is one of my favorite things to do. [*chuckles*]

SA: Are they always John Ashbery's blurbs?

BM: No. I mean, they can be . . . I like to use John's name to get a rise out of people.

SA: Does he know that you do that?

BM: Oh, yeah. It makes him laugh. He especially likes when I say that I'm him. [*laughs*] I'll give you a copy of *Utopia*. I wrote all the blurbs on the back. And they're from people like Plato. I had so much fun writing that. It just seemed so easy.

SA: [*pause*] Are you still involved in United Artists?

BM: No. Lewis is still keeping it going, though. He keeps saying, every time I see him, that he's not going to do it anymore. Then he keeps doing it! I don't think he can contain himself. [*chuckles*] Yeah, I have nothing to do with it anymore, but . . . But it's still happening, as far as I know. It could end at any moment. [*laughs*]

SA: Was almost everyone you knew in the seventies publishing or editing somehow?

BM: It seems that way, right? Probably. Yeah. [*chuckles*]

SA: Was there ever extra conflict, because you were editing with your partner, at all?

BM: I don't think so. I'm nice. I don't say, you know, to my partner, "That's a really stupid opinion! Go take a walk!" [*laughs*] My god. [*pause*]

SA: [Holds up *Utopia*] What color is *u*?

BM: *U* is a grayish-black kind of color. Yeah. Not a beautiful color.

SA: Did you pick the [red] cover paper?

BM: Yeah, because I wanted it to look like the colors of anarchy. [*chuck-*

les] I don't know if you're going to read this book, but I hope you do. It's kind of funny. Clark said to me . . . I gave him a copy. He said, "That is your worst book," when he read it. Any idea why?

SA: Why?

BM: Because he doesn't like . . . he didn't like books that were *about* something.

SA: Speaking of your books, I must admit that I haven't finished the *Studying Hunger Journals*. Is the original *Studying Hunger* in there as it is?

BM: Yeah, that's it. And it was originally written by me in these journals that were like 11 by 17. And with colored pens. My original plan . . . well, I guess it was to attempt—through writing it, but maybe after writing it—to color-code emotions. Of course, I didn't do it. I couldn't do it. But that was what was in my mind. [*pause*]

SA: Hannah [Weiner] was doing something kind of like that in her notebooks; she would circle something and say "yellow" or "yellow means . . ."

BM: Yeah. She did. But, you know, recently I've learned more about synesthesia, and I think that what Hannah was expressing with the words written on your forehead was a form of synesthesia. And that her relationship to color was based on some—I can't explain what, how—synesthetic reaction. Because what else could it have been? I mean, people would say that she was schizophrenic, but she really wasn't schizophrenic . . . well, I don't know. She was just treated by everybody, including her doctor, as if she was. But I don't think Hannah was schizophrenic. I did for a while think that. When she did *The Fast*, she had a bottle of liquid LSD in the refrigerator, and I thought, "Hmm, well, if Hannah's not schizophrenic she might be later, *now*." Right? I don't know. I don't think she was. Anyway, I learned this from . . . well, a lot of reading but also from this TV show, *Criminal Minds*. They have an episode about a guy whose words come out of his head. And each letter is a different color. It's worth seeing. And the character on that show, he says, you know, very wisely, "This is a form of synesthesia." And apparently it is. But you know what is interesting to read? Oliver Sacks's new book, *Hallucinations*. You should check that out if you have a moment. Or

106 *Women in Independent Publishing*

many moments.

SA: Maybe I will only read the right-hand pages.[10] [*laughs*] It would be especially hallucinatory.

BM: Well, the only hallucinatory thing about reading the right-hand pages is just the beginning of the top line. Because that's pretty funny! Like, it says "-ing," right? Hmmm.

SA: It's like the most intense line break ever. [*pause*] Have you noticed that doing that has influenced your poetry lately?

BM: No. It's a weird thing about being old. I don't think something like that . . . It might have influenced my poetry in the past, but at this point in time . . . I mean, I see "-ing" on the top of the page, I just think to myself, "Oh! This is good! This is nice!" But I don't think, you know, it's something new. It's something that I've already known about. Boring to be old, in that sense. [*pause*] Well, I'm going to have a glass of wine.

[*after a break*]

SA: I think Jen said that your favorite book of your own work is *Scarlet Tanager*?

BM: It is now, yes. Took me a while to figure that out.

SA: Why is it your favorite?

BM: I was giving all these readings and I realized that that's the book I always read from. So I started looking at them, realizing that it's a very interesting book, for me to do that.

SA: Do you like giving readings?

BM: I do now. I used to hate it. I used to be so nervous. I remember when I gave my first reading—that I had a twitch in my, uh, ass. And I kept thinking, "I wonder if anybody's noticing this." I mean, it was out of my control, obviously. [*laughs*] I never understood why other people weren't nervous too. The most nervous person I ever saw was Jim Carroll when he would sing. When he first started singing . . . He used to just read poetry before then, and then all of a sudden, he was singing, and he would be shaking, visibly. And it was painful to watch. I always enjoyed Jim's singing, but I hated watching him sing.

SA: What's your favorite time of year to write?

BM: You know, I was thinking about that the other day. I used to write mostly in the winter, but in this house, I like whatever season I can sit and have my typewriter out on the back porch. Which is usually the warmer months. So that would be spring, summer—sometimes it gets even too hot to sit out there. So, fall. But when I have to move in here [to the winter study], lately I'm not liking it. But that might change. I don't feel inspired to write here yet. But I just moved here, so who knows? There's too much stuff in this room. Too many pieces of furniture, and . . . I mean, it's like a storage room now. Phil and I, whenever we say we don't know what to do with something, "Well, put it in my winter office." Right? [*chuckles*] It's kind of ridiculous. But yeah. I always liked writing, you know, in living rooms, when there were a lot of other people around. I always thought that was fun.

SA: Was that something that happened a lot?

BM: Well, whenever I arranged it. I think [it's] fun to arrange to—I like writing in the middle of the action, you know. Because there's a lot of words to overhear. But ideally nobody would care that you were there, writing. Right? [*chuckles*] Maybe it's time to tell you—hope I didn't already tell you this—my ideal house.

SA: Okay.

BM: It would be this house, but it would have to be relocated in the middle of the woods. And rebuilt a little bit so that there would be porches on all sides of it. Wouldn't that be great? And, if you really had the leisure, all the porches—well, not all of them, but some of the porches—would have to be glass-enclosed. Like the ones facing south and I don't [know] which others . . . You'd have to figure out from where you moved it. And in the house would be an indoor swimming pool. And outside the house, an outdoor swimming pool. And nearby, a glass-enclosed walkway for walking in the winter. You would have your neighbors walk there too. And at one end of the walkway, where people would finish their walks, I would be sitting there fixing them grilled-cheese sandwiches. To allow them to get on with their day. And we would have really excellent bottles of wine available. Or, you know, Coke, I guess, if people needed it. Wouldn't that be great?

108 *Women in Independent Publishing*

SA: It would be amazing.

BM: Yeah, that's my ideal house. [*pause*] But, you know, I have other ideal houses. I mean, my ideal house would also have a tree growing in it. So, you'd have to arrange it so that the top of the tree was outside.

SA: When you were a kid, did you have much access to nature in New York?

BM: No, not at all. There was a park in Ridgewood, in Brooklyn, where I grew up. And it's called Forest Park—and it's still there, my kids tell me—but to me, it always seemed like a kind of a wasteland-ish park. I mean, it didn't seem beautiful to me. I don't know. Maybe it's just me. Maybe I just had a horrible childhood. I mean, I know I did. But maybe that's why. I hated everything about my childhood. Including the park, which I might, under normal circumstances, have loved.

SA: It seems like you read a fair number of books about nature, or natural things . . . It seems like a big part of your work.

BM: Yeah. [*pause*] Well, my project now, I think, might be to accumulate the rest of the field guides that I don't have, and read them all. But not like just read them but really immerse yourself in them. And then write a field guide to field guides, which would not really be about these other field guides at all. And what it would be, I don't know yet. And my other project, with Jennifer, is to write a history of science in poetic form. She and I have already written poems about neutrinos and poems about the Higgs boson particle. But that's more like news kind of poetry. But anyway, this would be the whole history of science. I think we could do it easily. We just have to come up with the right table of contents. Like, to know what aspects of science we want to write about. And then you do some research on them. And I write the poem. I mean, do you realize the bad science poems that exist in the world? This would be *so* fun to read. And to write.

SA: I really like doing that kind of work. Using field guides and science books.

BM: I know. What could be finer? [*pause*] So that's what I'm planning. But I think the field guides . . . I mean, I'm thinking to myself, "Am

I just planning projects that don't involve walking around anymore? Because I broke my arm?" It's possible. [*chuckles*]

SA: Well, you're adapting maybe, then. [*pause*] What are the earliest projects you can remember that involve walking around?

BM: Well, I think they all did, really.

SA: Do you write while you're walking?

BM: No, I can't. I never do. I've tried to tape record, and . . . I hate it. So really what I do is—when I'm walking around—is just memorize things that I want to write down. And what percentage of them I remember wind up in my poems.

SA: [*pause*] It would be fun to do a science magazine. A poetry science magazine.

BM: Wow, yeah. That would be interesting.

SA: Last year I met a doctoral student who was writing her dissertation on . . . I think about you and Clark and science.[11]

BM: Mmm. Once, I was hearing about all these papers being written about me, and I said to somebody in conversation, "Boy, I wish they would all send me a dollar." So the next request I got from a person for more information for her thesis, I said, "Okay, I'll send it to you, but send me a dollar." So she sent me . . . I think it was twenty dollars, because her advisor was Lyn Hejinian, and they put their money together. And she said, "This is for your oysters and raspberries fund." [*laughs*] And I thought, "Wow." So maybe on the Internet, the thing to do—for me to do—would be to make a plea for money to buy oysters and raspberries. Right? Don't people always go for, like, more luxurious things? As opposed to not paying my heating bills—so boring.

SA: So, do you have any parting wisdom on small press publishing?

BM: Nope. [*laughs*] Nope.

SA: I wish that there could be a CD insert with the text of this conversation and it would just be you laughing. [*laughs*]

BM: [*laughs*] Exactly.

Figure 8. IKON Series 2 Issue 5–6, Art Against Apartheid: Works for Freedom (1986). Artwork by Carol Byard.

Susan Sherman

Editor, IKON *(Series 1, 1967–1969; Series 2, 1982–1994; New York City)*

OCTOBER TO NOVEMBER 2014 AND JANUARY 2020, VIA E-MAIL, AND
SEPTEMBER 17, 2015, VIA SKYPE

Stephanie Anderson: The first series of *IKON* ran from 1967 to 1969. Will you talk a little about the New York art scene during those years? What was the context for the journal, broadly speaking?

Susan Sherman: The New York art scene then was so vibrant, at the peak of artistic activity. For me personally, there were poetry readings at Les Deux Megots Coffeehouse and then Le Metro, theater at the Hardware Poets Playhouse and La Mama Experimental Theatre Club. [I was] going to the Living Theatre, avant-garde movies, and on and on. However, the context for *IKON* was not only what was going on in New York but my two trips to Cuba in 1968 and 1969 and my friendship with Margaret Randall, who was publishing *El Corno Emplumado* in Mexico City at the time. Both Cuban trips introduced me to people, material, I would never have had access to, drastically changing my relationship to activism as well as directly influencing the content and focus of the magazine.

SA: Let's talk a little bit about how the magazine started. In your essay about *IKON* for the Society for Educating Women's (SEW) conference that appears in the *IKON* Series 2 (1982–1994) archive,[1] you talk about how you were originally supposed to be the book and theater critic for *IKON* Series 1, headed by Arthur Sainer and Thomas Muth.

You write, "After a year of meetings with no actual magazine, I finally said that I would make sure the magazine came out, but I had to be the editor. They agreed, and *IKON* was born." Had you had previous experience in publishing? Did it feel natural to take over as editor?

SS: Except for doing some chapbooks through Hardware Poets The-

112 *Women in Independent Publishing*

ater and being on the school newspaper in high school—where I learned the technical as well as the journalistic parts of putting out a paper—I had no "formal" publishing experience. But then neither did probably 90 percent of the people involved in alternative media in the 1960s. I don't know what made me have the guts to announce I would take over the magazine. I somehow had the confidence I could—and, in fact, I did!! As far as I know, *IKON* is the only American alternative journal that had women in charge in 1967. By the time the second series of *IKON* came out in the early 1980s, I had a lot of experience producing a magazine, and a magazine run by women by then wasn't that unusual. I must say that the first series of *IKON*, pre-feminist movement, didn't have nearly enough representation in content by women; that took a lot of growing and learning on my part.

SA: You had already been in New York for, what, maybe five or six years, when you started *IKON*?

SS: Yes, but even so it was a big step. To elaborate on what I said before, in the original meetings about publishing a magazine, nothing was getting done. I was tired of the endless meetings, and I didn't want to do the work and have others take credit for it, because I knew I would wind up doing all the technical work. And then finally after the first issue Arthur dropped out. There was no fight or anything; he just wasn't that interested. Tom did get us $1,500 to fund the first issue and was very supportive. We started *IKON* primarily because we were fed up with critics saying they were the ones who knew about art, not the artists who created it, and you had to depend on them to explain your work, and you couldn't talk about anyone you knew because you couldn't be objective. The magazine was always anti–Vietnam War but, of course, became more political as I became more politically involved. That's all detailed in my memoir, *America's Child: A Woman's Journey Through the Radical Sixties*.[2] *IKON* became much more political after I returned from Cuba. And then Series 1 ended when we lost most of our distribution. I can't prove the government was responsible, but it was pretty obvious when we got the returns of the magazine I put together about the Cuban Cultural Congress I had attended back from the distributor. They hadn't even unpacked it. We depended on the money from the previous issue to fund the next one. And the next one was already at the printer. So that was the end of *IKON* Series 1. Also five hundred copies of the issue that I sent to Margaret Randall in Mexico never reached her at all.

SA: Yeah. That's crazy.

SS: Well, the best way to stop you was economically. You know, if they tried to do something more openly it might cause too much trouble for them. We also had problems years later with lesbian material in the second series, with the NEA (National Endowment for the Arts). I mean, the way they can get you without causing a big fuss and having pickets and letters of protest is just to cut off your funding. We received no government funding at all for the first series.

We got NYSCA (New York State Council on the Arts) funding which paid for printing essentially and finally had gotten some funding from the National Endowment for the Arts for the second series. With the second series, *IKON* 9, the Asian/Asian American women's issue, *Without Ceremony*, I thought we were a shoo-in to renew the funding we had gotten from the NEA for the previous issue. It's a wonderful issue done in collaboration with the Asian Women United Collective, who were the ones who gathered the material and did the design. They had already been working for some years collecting and putting together an anthology when they got in touch with us to see if we could help them complete the project. We helped put all the elements together and published it for them. It was only the second time another group had almost total control over the issue and its design—the first was the *Art Against Apartheid* issue—but the final reward was an incredible issue including everything from a sexuality roundtable, to a working mother's roundtable, to a veteran political activists' panel.

SA: It's great!

SS: I was really shocked when we were denied the funding, so I called

114   *Women in Independent Publishing*

the NEA, which you could do, and asked, "What happened?"
The reply was, "Well, the writing was uneven," which was crazy;
it was a beautiful issue—you have it. The woman on the phone
didn't know why specifically. She looked it up, and she only had
an author's name, Huong Giang Nguyen. She happened to be the
author of an essay titled "The Vietnamese Lesbian Speaks." That's
when I realized what had happened. During that period, the NEA
was under heavy pressure not to fund any lesbian and gay material. Something they obviously didn't want to directly state, only
using the author's name in their notes. Anyway, so that's what
happened with the ninth issue, second series. It didn't stop us,
but we were hoping to be able to fully fund the magazine and pay
a little to ourselves, for all the work we put in. We always tried to
pay the contributors and designers a little if possible. So I wound
up funding a lot of the issues with my salary and my credit cards.
I carried the interest on the debt for a long time and finally had to
declare personal bankruptcy around 1997. It took me a long time
to get my credit back. I don't know how I did it all, to tell you the
truth, because I was working the whole time, at the equivalent of a
full-time job.

SA: I think in the article you say that the circulation was around 8,000.
Which was, you know, pretty impressive for a little magazine!

SS: That was only for the first series that was sold on the newsstands.
The original *IKON*. The second series we distributed in bookstores.
A much smaller run. Around 1,500. Except for the *Art Against Apartheid* issue, which went into a second printing when the first printing sold out. Do you have copies of the original Series 1 *IKON*?

SA: Yes. [*Stephanie shows her the magazines.*]

SS: Well, then you can see that it was geared toward newsstands.

SA: The covers are very attractive in that way; very eye-catching.

SS: Nancy Colin, who was one of the cofounders of the magazine, was
an artist, and the integration of graphics was one of the important
points of the magazine, and although she left the magazine after
Series 1, the second series also integrated graphics and text. I mean,
this was pre-Mac. I can't remember any other literary journals in

1967 that were doing that. The alternative news media, however, was very creative design-wise.

SA: Speaking of graphics and text, in the first series, the title *IKON* has a dot between *I* and *KON*. Was there a significance to this gesture? It makes me think of how the "I," the artist, can (kon?) "understand and write about" his or her own work.

SS: Actually, it had no significance. The dot between the I and the KON was just a choice by the people designing the first issue—probably Nancy. That is also why *IKON* was spelled with a K instead of a C. Purely because Nancy felt it looked better.

SA: That's a good enough reason! Continuing with the title, in the SEW Conference essay, you talk about its genesis: "For us the word *IKON* symbolized synthesis—words and pictures, art and politics, creativity and change, the separate parts fused as one into an organic unity in which all the parts could be perceived simultaneously, the way you perceive a picture. We believed there was no conflict between theory and art, art and action, that 'there was no place for the middleman,' that artists were perfectly capable of understanding and writing about their own work." I love how this synthesis can really be felt in Nancy's design work.

SS: Actually, the design of the magazine was the work of a number of people and varied from issue to issue. When everyone except Nancy left the magazine when I returned from Cuba, Nancy and I both did the layout as well as the design. Nancy left after the first series, and I did most of the design on the second series, along with a number of very talented women who helped. Remember it was almost all "volunteer." I and many of the others were not paid, and in the first series after the first issue, we supported the magazine with our own money and the money we got from sales and subscriptions. Because of the content of the magazine in the sixties, government funding was out of the question.

After I got back from Cuba, the issues got even better graphically, because I learned a lot being in Cuba, where they were doing amazing work design-wise with posters, films, and even their newspapers and magazines. My mother had actually gotten a scholarship—she never used it—in graphic arts, so maybe it's in my genes somewhere because I picked it up fast, and then later when I lost my job teaching, another result of my Cuba trip, I got a job typesetting and doing the graphics at a typesetting place at minimum wage, I might add.

And after that I got a job at Cooper Square Tenants Council doing bookkeeping; I learned doing the books for *IKON*. So I learned all different kinds of skills because of experience on the magazine. But it was very hard. People don't understand how hard it was in the sixties; they have this romanticized picture.

SA: So everything was really related organically. You write in the memoir, "These were not just pieces in a magazine. Each represented an activity in which we were either directly or indirectly engaged. The magazine was beginning to fulfill its initial intent in a way I had certainly never conceived of." Is that because you planned the content of the magazine to also symbolize synthesis?

SS: That really relates to the way the content of the magazine generated activity as well as being the result of activity. For example, my trip to Cuba, which then became a causal factor of political activities I became involved in and changed the way I looked at things and, therefore, my own art as well as the work that we published. We also tried to go outside set boundaries. For example, we also had, if you notice, tried to create a new tarot deck—this is pre–New Age, you know. I went to UC Berkeley where I first got involved with poetry and a lot of artists and poets in San Francisco were really into reading the tarot, and then there was Samuel Wiser's bookstore here in New York where you could buy a lot of great books. I still have a great library, lots on alchemy, the tarot, Jewish mysticism, and other things. So one idea was to combine that with radical political activism. You know, to really put them together within the same context, like we did with the artwork, and not have one in one corner and one in the other. That was one of the things I think that also made *IKON* different.

SA: It's similar to your initial kind of impulse behind the magazine, which was that serious theory and artists and critics don't necessarily need to be divorced—that artists are capable of commenting on their own work.

SS: Shouldn't be divorced. I originally met Arthur Seiner because I had been doing plays at the Hardware Poets Playhouse and La Mama and he gave me a really nice review of my first play. And he also wrote plays as well as being a critic. I started reviewing plays for the *Village Voice* when Michael Smith, who was one of the theater critics, went on vacation, and I took over for him, and saw, like, two plays a week for a long time. But once again the whole point was that we were sick and tired of critics, professional critics, saying that we weren't qualified to make "objective" judgments. Like, you know, unfortunately, although I like some things about Jung, this Jungian thing that there's the sensitive artist types and then there's the intellectual logical types—of course the women were the "sensitive types" who can't think objectively for themselves, and when the artist works that somehow your unconscious takes over and you don't know what you're doing! Because if you read Van Gogh's letters, for example—and many, many other artists, you know all of these artists were *very* involved in thinking about and critiquing their and other's work. I mean, we edit our work, don't we? We make choices all the time. I mean, a writer knows how to make choices! It's really very dangerous to think you have to depend on someone else to make the serious choices, both about your work and your life for that matter!!

SA: And so many writers I think do it as they're writing instead of afterward, or that the editing brain and the writing brain aren't as separate as people like to make them sound.

SS: Of course, you can do it as you're writing, or separately, whatever. Even stream-of-consciousness—I bet *Ulysses* didn't just flow out of James Joyce. I'm sure he worked and worked and worked at it. And, please, that's not the same as controlling or manipulating your work to make it say what you want it to. Sometimes the words seem to take on a life of their own. The work is an expression of whatever you are. In a sense you are an instrument that the work flows through. But

118 *Women in Independent Publishing*

you're not an unconscious instrument. It's hard to explain. Everyone works differently.

So that was one thing. And at the time in the late fifties and early sixties the idea of the separation between critic and artist was really bad. I write that vignette in the memoir about how I was at Berkeley and they were talking about there was no more creative artistic work being done, that the critics were the creative people. At the very same time the San Francisco Renaissance was going on across the bay. Which is very, you know, reminiscent of postmodernism, that somehow all the original work is over and you collage. Suddenly the critic becomes the philosopher-king. You know, that critics can not only tell us what art is about—it also means they'll tell you what you're allowed to produce, what's valid to produce. So that was really the main reason that we started the original *IKON*. And then because Nancy was involved, I think that's why the graphics became so involved. Working together. And there were also three different friends from Cooper Union working on the original magazine. I became very involved in the graphic aspects when everyone but Nancy left—I also painted a little bit on the side. I can show you a couple things I did.

SA: Nice!

SS: But, you know, we got the idea of putting these things together. Again, that's where the meaning of the name *IKON* came from. Remember this was way before the computer representation of the word *icon*. And not the religious version of it, but *icon* as a symbol in which, like a painting, you take in all of this information at once, not linearly. It's not separated out. So we started the magazine to try to bring these things together, and have artists . . . I remember the other thing was that artists weren't supposed to—and this is still true—critique friends. If you knew somebody you weren't allowed to write about them. And that was crazy because that would mean that I couldn't write about *anybody* I admired, because I knew so many people. But usually you pick out people that you feel simpatico with and why not write about them?

So it was for those two things. One, we wanted people to write about people that they knew and admired if they felt like it, like Yvonne Rainer's article about the dancer Deborah Hay, who was her friend. People that were involved in the same groups. So that was the idea, because who would know *better* what somebody's work was like than somebody who was close to them. It was this whole phony sense of objectivity. So that's why we started *IKON*. A lot of that was Arthur Sainer's ideas too.

SA: I mean, it's also really just how a scene gets built, right, is the participants kind of reflecting on each other?

SS: Exactly. So that started it off. I knew Margaret Randall because she had published some of my poems in *El Corno*, much earlier, though. I think maybe '63, '64. And she wrote a column from Mexico for the first issue. But that's how we got started, and then of course when the eighties came I started the second series. I had been writing Margaret about doing a magazine with her, but she was in Cuba—we had been together there at the Cultural Congress, and then Nicaragua—which made it very difficult [*laughs*] to correspond and work together. And I got this five thousand dollars when my stepfather died and used that for seed money. So anyway, that was the genesis of the second series. Starting with Series 1 *IKON* had obviously gotten progressively more political. For the first series we refused to take any kind of funding from the government, as a matter of principal—not that we would have gotten it, since they were more intent on getting rid of the magazine than giving us money! Which actually represented to me that the counterculture—if you want to call it that, I mean, it's such a misnomer—was important, because at a certain point that's one of the first things they tried to defund.

SA: Speaking of genesis and funding, I was kind of curious about the things you were doing before and in-between the two series.

SS: Right. In grammar school I did a little cut-out magazine. I started reading in the first grade, like we all did then. Alphabet in kindergarten, reading in grade one. But I was very sick that first year in

120   *Women in Independent Publishing*

school. You know, in those days they didn't have vaccinations for measles so the way you got vaccinated was that my sister had the measles and my mother put me in the room with my sister. It's very contagious. Because if you get it when you're five, or six years old, it's supposed to be not as deadly. The vaccinations now are certainly a much better idea!

SA: Yeah, the kind of chicken pox parties they used to have when I was a kid in the eighties.

SS: So I had chicken pox and I had measles. And I had scarlet fever.

SA: Wow.

SS: That was much more dangerous. They didn't do that on purpose! Or chickenpox either for that matter! So I was stuck in bed a lot. Of course, with measles you can't read, because they're afraid it's going to get in your eyes, so you have to wear sunglasses and be in a darkened room. So I listened to records of stories. And I listened to the radio. That's probably where I got my love of science fiction. [listening to the radio dramas] *X Minus One* and *2000 Plus*. But I did a lot of reading when I could, and I leapt way ahead with my reading. I just loved to read, so that's why when I was in the fifth grade, as an art project, I did my own magazine. I think that what gave me the most practical experience, though, was the high school newspaper I was on for two years. They actually had their own printing facility so what we would do is we would do the editorial work and then a preliminary paste-up and then on Thursdays we would go to the print shop where they had a linotype machine, a big machine where one metal line of type is produced at a time.

People don't realize that the reason the type is justified (lined up) on both sides is because the old metal type actually fit in a form with wooden panels on the side which you put type into and locked it up, so it had to be straight on both sides and justified. First, I was the third page editor and then the associate editor. So I edited the material, did the paste-up, and then went to the press for the final proofing, and actually laid it into the form myself. Then we took the proof and made a final paste-up and put the page together. That gave me a huge amount of experience, including being able to read type backwards and upside-down, which is what the metal looks like when you're standing over it until it's pressed onto the page—this was before offset printing.

SA: I do some letterpress printing . . .

SS: Well, then you know what it is. So I already had that experience when I started doing the magazine.

SA: And then you were the poetry editor of the *Village Voice* very briefly.

SS: I also took over for Denise Levertov for a while choosing the poems for the *Nation*. And for the *Voice* it was the same thing. I chose poems and reviewed plays and some books. The *Voice* was quite small when I first started working there. They got much bigger when the newspapers went on strike, and there was no place for people to get classified ads except the *Village Voice*. Their circulation and number of pages shot up enormously during that time.

SA: I didn't know that; that's really interesting. I assumed it was a kind of protest literature increase.

SS: No, it was the newspaper strikes. I mean, the *Voice* was always well-regarded in terms of content. They had an office on Sheridan Square at the time. The poet Bob Nichols got me that job. He was married to Mary Nichols at the time, who was one of the editors. Later he married Grace Paley. That's how I met her. He and Grace were involved with the Greenwich Village Peace Center, and I worked there at nights in the early sixties selling peace buttons and generally just keeping it open. It was very quiet at night, and I wrote a lot of poems during that time.

SA: What was working on the little chapbooks with the Hardware Poets Playhouse and Hesperidian Press like?

SS: I worked on those with Allen Katzman, who edited a magazine out of the Judson Church called the *Judson Review* through his and his brother's press, Hesperidian Press. Besides my chapbook I have a copy of Jerry Bloedow's *How to Write Poetry*. Did you get that?

SA: I think I've seen that one actually. . . .

SS: I have only one copy of my chapbook *Areas of Silence*. James Nagel did the drawings. I think we did one of his books. But just, you know, typed them. This is just cheap offset printing. It's pretty

122   *Women in Independent Publishing*

faded now.

SA: The issue that I sent you of the *Hardware Poets Occasional* is . . . I think it must be mimeo, but it's pretty hard to read at points.

SS: This is definitely offset. There was a little place on Eighth Street that used to do printing really cheap. You know they did just 8 ½ by 11 on a small offset printer. You could get, I don't know, five hundred copies of one side of a page for like eight dollars or less. And we bound them ourselves—mine is an attempt to have a perfect binding (flat back cover)—it didn't work out so well.

SA: Oh, I see.

SS: We only did four chapbooks. You know, we were having a lot of problems then, because around 1963, '64 the city tried to close down the poetry and experimental theater venues—we were doing the readings at Café Le Metro then—saying that we needed to have a liquor license to do poetry readings using an outdated cabaret law. Who knows the real reason. Whether they were trying to clean up the city, which was ridiculous, I mean these were hardly dens of iniquity. I mean, we smoked cigarettes and that was about it—there weren't any drugs or even alcohol around. We thought that it was commercial, because it was right before the World's Fair. We felt that it might be a conspiracy on the part of the people in the West Village, because at one point readings in the East Village and what was known as off-off-Broadway theater were becoming very popular and taking customers away from commercial venues—I think the first reading I came to at Le Metro there was a line out the door that was over a hundred people.

And the plays—we had full houses at the plays. The theater venue I was associated with was the Hardware Poets Playhouse. You have one of the newsletters. It was uptown over a hardware store—hence the name! It was composed mostly of poets who read at Les Deux Mégots and then later Le Metro, which were in the East Village. It was at the protests that I met Ellen Stewart from La Mama where I also did plays. They were very experimental. In fact, the full name is La Mama E.T.C., standing for experimental theater club.

There's an interesting story most people don't know. Even

though they might've used the term East Village once in a while,
it became very popular because of the *Voice* ads and real estate interests. They couldn't rent property under the original name of the
Lower East Side, because it reeked too much of immigrants, poor
people, working people, you know. So they coined this term the East
Village to rent apartments. I knew that because I worked at the classified section of the *Voice* when Rose Ryan, who was the head of the
ads, promoted the term.

SA: Was your bookstore, IKONbooks, in the East Village?

SS: Yes, it was a nice, large, open space next to La Mama. On 4th Street
between 1st and 2nd Avenue. That was the late sixties, early seventies where we did everything but sell a lot of books! We carried
mostly alternative publications. We had poetry readings, music
events, and political talks, and one night a benefit for the Panthers.
We supported it with our salaries and designing and printing the
programs for La Mama. The rents weren't anything like now. If I
remember correctly the rent was about $125 a month.

SA: And you put out an anthology of Vietnam War poetry . . .

SS: Actually, general protest poetry. It's called *Only Humans with Songs to
Sing*. It was all done using an electronic stencil maker. We could put
photos in and thin metal mimeo stencils would come out, and then
we also had a Gestetner electronic mimeo. We actually mimeoed the
whole book. But I made the terrible mistake, because it looked nice,
of using construction paper for the cover, and it's disintegrating.
Like *literally* disintegrating. The ones I have, the construction paper
is literally turning into dust. Newsprint is the same. I had a bunch
of copies of the *East Village Other* in plastic protective sheets and you
can't even take them out of the plastic.

SA: Yeah, that old acidic paper.

SS: On the other hand, we got all kinds of criticism from some movement people about *IKON* magazine supposedly looking too slick.
It was work that made it look that good, not money. It didn't cost
more except for using decent paper. We had a really good printer
who printed on a huge press sixteen pages at a time. I remember
walking into the deli on 2nd Avenue and the counter person say-

124 *Women in Independent Publishing*

ing, "Oh, this is such a nice-looking magazine. Can I take a look at it?" I thought that it was such a disparaging kind of thing to think that somebody who was a worker wouldn't like something beautiful and well designed to look at. It attracted people's attention because it looked so nice! Just because you're doing a movement thing doesn't mean you should have to do it on newsprint—unless it's a newspaper, of course!—and make it look messy. I mean, even when we used the mimeograph—and we used it a lot—we tried to do it as nicely as possible. When I did *Only Humans with Songs to Sing*, I just sat there all night with poems that were typed up and scissors, cutting out different little pieces of photos from magazines and newspapers to make designs for it.

SA: Do you think that doing projects like that—like that kind of anthology idea—is part of why the second series of *IKON* actually refers to itself as an anthology?

SS: No, the reason for that with the second series was that some of the issues were double issues and were anthologies. Also the issues only came out once or twice a year and were quite big, averaging around 130 pages. The double issues were larger. The ones we specifically called anthologies also had an ISBN number which you use for books and were sold both as magazines and books.

SA: Oh, okay, that makes sense.

SS: The *Art Against Apartheid* issue, for example—I hope you have that issue. That was the incredible issue that we did with the Art Against Apartheid committee with sponsorship from the UN. We also sponsored a reading around the issue.

SA: I have a copy from the library; I don't have a copy of my own.

SS: I only have about five copies myself. We went into a second printing on that issue. We didn't do much newsstand with the second series. The first series was almost purely newsstand, which in a way was our downfall since we depended on three major distributors nationwide, so when the time came after the Cuban issue it was easy to cut us off. There was some bookstore distribution, but there weren't as many alternative bookstores. Now there're almost none. Even St. Mark's Bookstore, which is the last of them, is gone.

So it was definitely mostly bookstore distribution for that second series—and then, of course, much fewer magazines. I think we ran maybe 1,500 copies. The *Art Against Apartheid* issue we did about five thousand because we went into a second printing; we sold out that first printing. And we had money from the UN, and a bunch of people contributed money to it. We were also getting funding then. Nobody got salaries, unfortunately, but we got funding that covered printing from the New York State Council on the Arts Literature Committee, which then was being run by this wonderful gay man, Gregory Kolovakos, and for one issue from NEA, which is why it was such a shock when the NEA didn't renew.

SA: Right!

SS: You know, you asked me a while back what I was doing both before and after the first and second series of the magazine. I spoke a little about my trips to Cuba and their influence on me and on the first series of the magazine. After we stopped publishing the first series of *IKON* and the IKONbooks, which closed mainly because it just got too hard to sustain both in terms of energy and money, I became much more involved in the women's movement and gay liberation struggle particularly through the Fifth Street Women's Building in 1970, which was a combined women's liberation movement and squatter action, and then Sagaris, an experiment in women's education. I traveled to Chile during Allende, and Nicaragua during the early days of the Sandinistas in the seventies and eighties, and continued to write and get jobs wherever I could find work—mostly low-wage jobs doing things like typesetting—until I finally got an adjunct position teaching at Parsons School of Design, where I still teach. All of which contributed material, connections, and inspiration that led to revisiting *IKON* again in the eighties.

Then in the early eighties came *IKON* Series 2, which followed pretty much the same philosophy as the first series except now it was consciously feminist and exclusively published women, with the exception of the *Art Against Apartheid* issue and the last issue that came out in 1994 and one essay by Henry Flynt in the first issue.

126   *Women in Independent Publishing*

Some of the issues were done in collaboration with groups such as the *Art Against Apartheid* issue, the Asian/Asian American women's issue *Without Ceremony*, and the *Coast to Coast: National Women Artists of Color* issue. Even when the magazine stopped publishing, we still continued with a series of chapbooks by authors that included Hettie Jones, Harry Lewis, Ellen Aug Lytle, Chuck Wachtel, and later poetry books by Bruce Weber, Rochelle Ratner, Paul Pines, Gale Jackson. I had also done a series of chapbooks with Martha King between the two series of *IKON*.

SA: What do you think the value of reading *IKON* now is?

SS: First of all, as Audre Lorde so eloquently put it in "Poetry is Not a Luxury"—an essay that was really my inspiration to begin publishing *IKON* again—when she characterizes poetry "as illumination . . . The farthest external horizons of our hopes and fears . . . carved from the rock experiences of our daily lives." That is something without price and without age. *IKON* in both series is history, an archive, but it is more than that. As are magazines like *Sinister Wisdom*, which is still publishing, and *Conditions*, to name only two, and all those many books and magazines that are exemplars of the epigraph we put on the covers of *IKON* Second Series—Creativity and Change. They should be preserved, and even more they should be read. They contain our history and aspirations more than any textbook ever could.

Figure 9. Telephone Issue 16 (1980). Artwork by David Morice.

Maureen Owen

Publisher and Editor of Telephone *and Telephone Books (1969–2003, New York, Connecticut, and Denver)*

OCTOBER 2013 TO OCTOBER 2014, VIA E-MAIL

Stephanie Anderson: In a 1999 interview with Marcella Durand, you say:

> I was meeting a lot of terrific writers, a lot of them women who were around, who were writing, who were writing seriously, and weren't really getting published anywhere, despite the Project's magazine *The World*—there was never enough room in it for everyone anyway. People who didn't feel part of the group weren't getting in, were intimidated by the scene even though the Project was quite open. I was meeting a lot of poets, especially a lot of women poets, whose work I liked a lot. I remember talking to Anne [Waldman] about women poets who weren't getting published. It seemed they just weren't knocking on the door. I thought, well shoot, I could do a little magazine. I knew zip about it. [I asked Anne] if I could put it together, could I use the Gestetner. She was totally generous.

Will you expand on what the "scene" was like then, especially for women? I've heard it said, about contemporary publication, that women don't submit nearly as much as men, or don't "knock on the door," as you say. Why do you think that is/was? Who were some of the women you wanted to promote, and how did you meet them?

Maureen Owen: Well, the "scene" at that time on the Lower East Side was tremendous. It was a moment in time, but a moment that went on for quite some time. When I arrived it had been going on, been building, and now it was in full swing. It was a phenomenal gathering of creativity. It was as though some magical force had

130 *Women in Independent Publishing*

brought us all together. Poets, writers, artists, performance artists, from everywhere had gravitated to this low-rent geography in New York City where a thriving community had settled in and around the Poetry Project on 10th Street and 2nd Avenue. The Poetry Project always seemed a radiating center, a hub where this community could gather for workshops, readings, collating of books and zines, discussions, or just visit the office and hang out. Everyone's generosity to assist one another with publications and events filled us all with a tremendous power; we all had help and support.

I was so excited to be a part of what was generating there. I would just meet women writers at the park with my children, or at a party, or sitting on the stoop, or at a reading, or at another poet's apartment. And I'd ask to see their work. I was so inspired by what I was seeing and hearing. But often the work was not getting published. I became not so concerned with the "why" of that as I was with that I found myself thinking excitedly about how I, myself, might print these terrific pages. I began to think about designing my own zine and who I might ask for cover art and who to contribute work. I wanted to bring together the eclectic-ness of the community. It was the work that was being done that interested me. *Telephone* invited contributions of innovative process. It wasn't limited to publishing women by any means. It was open to everyone. That was one of the inspirations for the name. Ma Bell was big in NYC at that time and the thought of being so inclusive was invigorating to me. My thinking was that I would aspire to getting all the powerful writers I was meeting into its pages. I loved the idea of getting these works into the hands of readers.

SA: One contemporary complaint is that we're so glued to our cell phones that we fail to interact with people around us. Can you talk more about how Ma Bell was a tool of "inclusivity"? How did you then make sure that production and distribution also reflected that goal—of getting the works "into the hands of readers"?

MO: I was thinking of Ma Bell in terms of that enormous publication of names and numbers, the telephone directory or telephone book. I wanted a magazine that would include everyone like the telephone directory did. An alternate telephone book, a zine big enough to publish all the prodigiously powerful work I was hearing and seeing.

SA: Who was involved, and what were the collation parties like?

MO: The collation process reflected the generosity of participation that was so abundant on the Lower East Side then. Everyone who was local and in the issue would come to help collate and bring friends. And then others would just come and join in. It was truly a community effort. We would buy pizza and Cokes and wine, and it was a hands-on working party that would continue until the last copy of the issue was stapled and put on the stack. Then everyone would take copies to distribute around and even mail to folks out of town. I would send contributor copies to everyone in the issue, usually two copies. Mailing book rate was very inexpensive in the sixties and seventies. And I would take copies around town to various bookstores to leave on consignment. Because *Telephone* was the odd telephone booth–shaped size of 8 ½ by 14, some stores would sigh as they tried to find a spot to display them. But most stores were very lovely, and the 8th Street Bookshop was especially kind. The folks there would always say: "Oh, a new issue of *Telephone*, how exciting!" I loved them. So in these collective ways entire issue runs quickly became available and were being read.

SA: Can you clarify what you mean by "process" when you say, "*Telephone* invited contributions of innovative process"? How did the aesthetic goals of the magazine relate to mimeo technology?

MO: When I posit that *Telephone* invited contributions of innovative process, I mean that through mimeo, the work could move so quickly into print. If your poem or work seemed to still be in process, you could publish it via mimeo, maybe receive feedback or just have that opportunity to see it in print and then make changes from the printed perspective. Mimeo was immediate. It inspired and supported spontaneity. It captured that fabulous feeling of folks coming together and just doing it. Not waiting for

132 *Women in Independent Publishing*

approval from the publishing mechanism, but just coming together and printing it. The mimeo zines and books that proliferated during that time (of which *Telephone* was but one) were a tremendously liberating force. They fostered creativity and inspiration and created an atmosphere of breathless excitement. Poems were bouncing off the sidewalk.

SA: I love the idea of revising the work based on responses to its publication in the magazine. How did editing the magazine and seeing your poems alongside others change your work?

MO: Seeing their work in a print zine, formatted on its page, afforded the writers a new perspective on how the type displayed in that context. Line length, spacing, enjambment, and punctuation showed fierce and stark in that position of availability. Folks you didn't know would now be reading your work. It allowed a time to pause and consider before finalizing.

For me the excitement of putting the issue together, creating a table of contents, placing the works, typing everyone's poems onto the stencils, was not only a heady involvement but a physical infusion of energy as well. Often after typing a poem carefully onto the stencils, my attention so intently drawn in to each word and space and line break, I would have to get up and walk madly about the house reciting the poem now so embossed on my brain. I became one with the poem in a way that doesn't happen when one is just reading the work. I also experienced such freedom putting *Telephone* together. Being a single editor I had complete artistic control. I chose the cover artist. I had great fun embellishing pages with illustrations I found in old nursery rhyme books and dictionary illustrations and children's primers. I'd place the illustration against a window, laying the stencil over it and tracing it with the stylus. Often, I would alter the drawing or collage with it.

SA: Will you talk about your decision to publish your own poems under a pseudonym after the first few issues?

MO: I loved the idea of having some mystery poets that no one would ever know. Again, it was the freedom and the fun of being able to write some works and invent authors. Actually, that was during the earlier issues. Later I had so many submissions I wanted to include that I had no more room for the mystery works. I did continue to include poems from mine and others' children. And under their actual real names.

SA: Issue 7 of the magazine, especially, has a wonderful mix of lyric poems and syntactically difficult, experimental works. Were you actively thinking about crossing various aesthetic "camps"?

MO: Yes, definitely. My plan from the beginning was to be as inclusive as the telephone (Ma Bell) directory. Eclectic was the theme. Quality fabulousness of the work was my only criterion.

SA: How long do you think it took the magazine to settle into its own style? Or does it change with each issue?

MO: *Telephone's* constant change and flux was its style. Change was what it was all about. Poets were boldly experimenting, traveling in marvelous directions. I wanted to present and document that process and its progress.

SA: The magazine didn't publish as rapidly as other little mimeo magazines of the era—but it did publish longer. Were there advantages and disadvantages to publishing at a slower and steadier pace?

MO: I would have published more often if I could have afforded to. I published as soon as I had enough money to bring out a new issue. I was a working mother and that slowed the production with respect to time and money, but I think it also kept it steadier and stronger too.

SA: Do you have a favorite or especially memorable issue?

MO: Each issue has aspects and works that make my heart sing. Production-wise I'll never forget the feeling of that first issue coming off the Gestetner and the beauty of the rich black ink lifting the poems off the white page.

SA: Why did you stop publishing the magazine?

MO: I could no longer afford the cost of publishing it. Had I the money and time I would never have stopped. I loved publishing the work that excited me and making it available for others to see and read. I felt a singular mission in introducing work that had no other publishing venue.

SA: When and why did the magazine decide to branch out into publishing books as well?

MO: It seemed a natural progression. I felt such passion about the work. I wanted to publish more than just a few poems in the zine. With the books I wanted the writer to have complete control over the cover, illustrations, size, et cetera. Telephone Books are in a variety of sizes. I was able to add some of my own creative touches to the books too, though. I found cutting slices from glossy commercial magazine ads provided gorgeous, multicolored end pages, each one uniquely different.

SA: Some of the books I have are side-stapled and some are perfect-bound. How did the publication process work? I love the idea of unique endpapers; could you add your own end-pages only to the stapled books, or were you able to add them at the binder's?

MO: I delighted in producing the staple-bound books, as I had complete control through the entire process to add a rubber stamp or use cut-up, colorful pages from a commercial magazine or newspaper. The *New York Times Magazine* ads were a fabulous source for end pages, and each one was completely unique: They were individual cut-outs, no reproducing to match. This was a hands-on process. One was truly "making" a book.

As gratifying and as satisfying as it was to "make" the books myself through mimeo, it was famously exciting to be able to afford to do a perfect-bound publication. I still did all the preparation work and discussed with the authors how they wanted the book to appear, but the complete freedom that mimeo offered was something I had to relinquish. My glorious end-pages were no longer possible. I am a hands-on person and love the actual process of "making" the book one by one. But of course with the perfect-bound titles we were able to print more copies with much more commercial flair and gloss, and we looked much more respectable in the bookstores. That was an important step in giving the books accredited status among their peers.

SA: You pretty consistently published about three books a year between 1972 and 1984. Did you have three in mind as the ideal number for the year? How long did each book take? Did you work on more than one at once?

MO: I had a job and two then three children, so I just worked mostly on one book at a time whenever I could. It was an organic process. Very spontaneous, on the street, in the moment. I'd read someone's work in a zine or hear them at a reading, and on the spot, I'd talk to them about doing a book with Telephone. It was an incredibly exciting time. I was endowed with an amazing amount of energy, and I used every bit of it. My book *Zombie Notes* is themed around sleep deprivation. I worked after the boys were tucked into bed until about 2 a.m., and then I got up at 6 a.m. to get them off to school and me to work. I was also so fortunate to have a devoted partner, Ted Mankovich, during a number of those years, and he was invaluable in sharing care of the children and cooking and other family responsibilities and chores. Telephone will always be indebted to him.

SA: How did you acquire manuscripts, both for the magazine and for book publication? When did the rate of submissions begin to accelerate so much that it was necessary for the magazine to contain a note about submission backlog?

MO: I kept the book manuscripts under control by being the sole solicitor. But as the magazine grew in readership, I began to receive submissions from far and wide, which was wonderful. Still, because of time and finances I could only do a certain number of issues a year. So it was with a heavy heart that, at some point—I don't recall exactly with which issue—I decided I had to put in a note for "no unsolicited submissions." This was a huge decision for me, as the whole idea of Telephone was its openness and inclusion. I had a post office box at Chelsea Station for the magazine, and when I went to pick up my mail the postal workers would all joke with me as they brought out a huge, stuffed USPS mail sack. It was too heavy for me to lift, so I would literally drag it down the street, onto the subway, and lug it up the five flights of stairs to our apartment on 13th Street. I put off placing the note as long as I could and then finally had so many back submissions, about three issues worth,

SA: There's a long lapse in book publication between 1984 and 1999. In that time, did you intend to restart the press later, or did the desire to see a particular work in print motivate the press's reemergence?

MO: In the truly organic tradition of Telephone Books and *Telephone* magazine, it was life events that shaped progress. In 1984 my partner, Ted Mankovich, and I went separate ways. I had one son still in high school and two in college. I had to take on three jobs to support and facilitate their education. It seemed the end of an era. Publishing was becoming more expensive, and though over the years I had received some grant monies to keep the press and zine going from the New York State Council on the Arts, CCLM [Coordinating Council of Literary Magazines], and the National Endowment for the Arts, I now did not even have the time to apply for them.

Telephone brought out a last mimeo publication. A terrific little book of poems, *Strange Rain*, by my son Patrick Owen.

In 1999, still hungry to publish, I decided to do a pocket-sized series of Telephone Books. (Rose Lesniak suggested too late that I should have called them Cell Phone Books.) I was able to bring out Janet Hamill's stunning *Lost Ceilings* and the absolutely astounding, posthumous *A Found Life* by Elio Schneeman.

Then a most wonderful poet and prose writer passed away from us, Susan Cataldo. Steve Spicehandler, her husband, and I produced two gorgeous titles of works she left for us all, *The Mother Journal* and *Drenched*, published in 2002 and 2003 respectively.

I do miss publishing and highly recommend it.

Figure 10. Renee Tajima-Peña. Photo by William Short.

Renee Tajima-Peña

Editor, Bridge *(1971–1986, New York)*

NOVEMBER 2021 TO JULY 2022, VIA E-MAIL

Stephanie Anderson: Perhaps we could begin by situating your work with *Bridge* in the context of the journal's history and the larger historical moment. How and when did you become involved with *Bridge*?[1]

Renee Tajima-Peña: I'll start with the larger context of what was going on then with Asian Americans and culture through my personal experience. I graduated from Harvard in 1980 and wanted to become a filmmaker. That was akin to an Asian American woman deciding to play point guard in the NBA. I tried to get nonpaid internships at every studio and network I could think of and never even got calls back. I had white male classmates who landed paid work in the business, sometimes even in the writer's room, but that was the industry at the time. Even at PBS with its public media mission— Grace Lee has a great podcast on PBS's legacy of whiteness, *Viewers Like Us*—there were only a handful of Asian Americans who weren't doing maintenance or clerical jobs. Karen Tei Yamashita, who was just honored with a lifetime achievement award from the National Book Foundation, was working at KCET–Los Angeles as a secretary.

I also got a job as a secretary—for the "Mr. Bill Show," the Claymation character on *Saturday Night Live*. I lasted six months. Since I'd been a student activist, I got involved with Asian American movement work in New York, and found out about the Chinatown media arts center, Asian Cine-Vision. It had been all-volunteer, and they were hiring their first paid director position and I got the job, $2.50 an hour, if that. ACV mounted the Asian American International Film Festival, did community video training, and had a Chinese-language public access program; we did film screenings in the Chinatown pub-

140 *Women in Independent Publishing*

lic library across the street.

Bridge had already been published since 1971. At some point, we began administering Basement Workshop and also took over the publication of *Bridge*. I became the managing editor—as the director of a bare-bones community nonprofit, I wore a lot of hats! I didn't have any professional experience; I was only about twenty-one or twenty-two when I became the editor in 1981. I had edited an alternative newspaper when I was in high school, but that was about it.

Bridge had an all-volunteer editorial board and contributors that thankfully included people with real skills—my sister Marsha, who had a PhD in art history from the University of Chicago, the poets Kimiko Hahn, Luis Francia, and Walter Lew, the activist Rockwell Chin, the photographer Corky Lee, various artists and writers. Shanlon Wu was also on the editorial board—he's now a high-powered attorney and CNN legal analyst who briefly represented Rick Gates, the Trump campaign aide.

Anyway, in the early 1980s the Asian American political and cultural movement was not new—it goes back to the 1960s—but it was still in a fairly nascent, grassroots stage. And it was evolving. During the 1980s and '90s, it continued to grow. Demographically the Asian American population was really booming, and to an extent there was a "professionalization" of people and structures within the movement—Asian American studies was fighting for legitimacy, academics were trying to get tenure, filmmakers were going into MFA programs and slowly making broadcast or theatrical films, organizations were getting boards of directors—that kind of thing.[2]

And an activist brand of cultural organizing continued to resist, such as the Godzilla Asian American Artists Network, which included a number of Basement Workshop veterans. In 1991 Godzilla called out the homogeneity of the Whitney Museum of American Art Biennial and its "conspicuous absence of Asian American visual artists." Artist of color criticism of the Whitney led to a very different Biennial in 1993, the one that got the white establishment critics up in arms. I was a part of a collective installation in that show, *Those Fluttering Objects of Desire*, that Shu Lea Cheang put together as "tales of postcolonial interracial desire through reconstructed red phones, appropriating the 900-phonesex and 25-cent-per-peep pornography apparatus."[3] My contribution was a phone sex audio remix of James Brown to quotations from Mao Tse-tung's *Little Red Book* as performed by the *Dogeaters* playwright Jessica Hagedorn and the writer–performance artist Robbie McCauley.

Anyway, back to the Asian American arts community in New York. We started to get small grants from the NEA, the New York State Council on the Arts, donors, businesses, and the like to publish *Bridge*. Kitty Carlisle Hart, the actress and wife of the playwright Moss Hart, was the chair of NYSCA at the time, and she famously thought it was a magazine about the card game bridge. She was actually really great. She would charm all of the upstate New York legislators and get them to approve budgets that funded artists and organizations of color and controversial work. She was a real champion for the arts.

As in the previous decade of *Bridge*, we covered arts and politics. I think we were more multiethnic and included a larger proportion of US-born Asians than *Bridge* had in the 1970s. For example, Kimiko is mixed-race Japanese, Luis is Filipino, Walter is Korean. It was a time of growing pan-ethnicity in the Asian American political and culture movement. I want to emphasize that it wasn't the beginning of that pan-ethnicity—for example, the 1940s labor movement in Hawai'i and the ethnic studies strikes of the late 1960s involved Filipinos, Chinese, Japanese, and Koreans, and others. Keep in mind that up to the 1970s, the Asian American population was small and overwhelmingly Chinese, Japanese, and Filipino. That all changed with the impact of the 1965 immigration reform and migration from Southeast Asia after the American War in Vietnam. In the late seventies, the Chol Soo Lee case, and beginning in 1983, the Vincent Chin case, mobilized pan-ethnic Asian American organizing and drew from the pan-ethnicity of the continuing labor movement, ethnic studies, and other struggles. *Bridge* captured a lot of what was going on at that time and came out of that ferment. Everyone was living it.

SA: What was your sense of *Bridge*'s legacy at that point?

RTP: I didn't think about legacy. I thought about the moment, and the role of *Bridge*—like filmmaking—as a cultural organ of the movement. Asian American publications have served that function since the earliest immigrant publications. In New York in particular, it was actually a great time for Asian American journalism. There were Chinese-language newspapers from left, right, and center perspectives, there was a Japanese American paper, there were in-language Asian publications. On the East and West Coast, there were publications of left formations, and alternative papers like *Gidra* and *New Dawn*. I think the UCLA Asian American Studies Center "Mountain Movers" project talks about those publications.[4]

SA: How was the editorial staff of *Bridge* organized?

RTP: All volunteer. People primarily took on roles related to their skill set. I'm fuzzy about the details, but you can ask other people on the editorial board who have better memories than me. I just remember it was a lot of work.

SA: How varied were your responsibilities?

RTP: Everyone did everything. I would regularly work until 2 a.m., 24/7, but not only on *Bridge*, so it's a bit of a blur. I had to do fundraising, writing, editing, finding images, keeping on top of logistics. But we were all doing everything. We were a barely funded Asian American nonprofit operating out of a walk-up in Chinatown, pre-Internet, when things were typeset manually and the layout had to be done by hand.

SA: Of the many things you were doing—"fundraising, writing, finding images, logistics," and so forth—what was your favorite?

RTP: Fundraising and logistics are dirty jobs that somebody has to do, and not my favorite. But we all had to do everything in our careers apart from making art or films or writing or performing. The late great Corky Lee was a photographer, but he also worked at Expedi Printing, and that's where we printed *Bridge* and our film festival posters, protest flyers, everything. We'd call Corky. I learned a lot of skills about publication layout and prepping for printing that you can just do on your Mac now. I did love seeing the magazine come off the press, because it was always so exciting to see the covers.

Publishing *Bridge* was a communal experience. We met in person, put it together, and schlepped it around to sell it in person. It was a community.

SA: Volume 7, number 4, the Winter 1981–1982 issue, contains your special report on the First Asian American Media and Humanities Conference (East Coast). Was this a significant event for you?

RTP: Yes. At the time we were building the National Asian American Telecommunications Association (NAATA), which is now known as the Center for Asian American Media (CAAM). I'll refer to it as CAAM. It was a big deal—for the first time, Asian American media makers organized on a national scale. We had chapters in different cities, and we were advancing an Asian American independent film movement that had been building since the late sixties–early seventies with seminal formations like the UCLA EthnoCommunications Program and Visual Communications. I was just out of college at the time, but I jumped in feet first. I cowrote the CAAM founding proposal and was the first paid staff person and director of Asian Cine Vision. It was 24/7, low-paid, mostly volunteer work, so perfect for a clueless recent grad. Like many people involved in the conference and creating CAAM, I had been involved in student and community activism for a long time, so the ideological basis and organizing principles that we discussed at the conference were an extension of that media activism. Just as Godzilla was an extension of Basement in the arts and literature sphere.

SA: One of the things I love about *Bridge* is "its iconic blend of Asian American political issues, critique, art, poetry, and fiction."[5] The pieces are in conversation to an astonishing degree. And the pages are often packed! What were some of the editorial strategies that ensured this effect?

RTP: *Bridge* reflected what was happening in those worlds because everyone contributing to it was immersed in Asian American politics, arts, literature, intelligentsia, community, imagining. That's a lot different from the conventional writer who lands in a space and interprets what they see from an outsider's lens. We were insiders. And that in itself was an act of resistance, to stake

144   *Women in Independent Publishing*

a claim to our own stories. At the time, insider knowledge wasn't respected, of course, because outsiders wanted to reproduce the status quo. In academia, scholars of color were accused of doing "activist" research. In filmmaking, there were suits in the PBS system who were suspicious of us as Asian American filmmakers taking on an investigation of a racially motivated killing for *Who Killed Vincent Chin?* But the power of *Bridge* was precisely because we were insiders.

SA: In the essay "Moving the Image," you discuss the importance of eclecticism and the "plurality of cultural influences" in seriously considering Asian American filmmaking aesthetics, and one can see how these resonate in the pages of *Bridge* as well. How did literature and your early involvement in writing and filmmaking all influence each other?

RTP: I never went to film school and never got any formal training. I learned filmmaking on the job, so I didn't have many influences other than the culture at home, in the neighborhood, at school; the TV shows and movies I saw, the music I listened to, the books I read. I had grown up in a multiracial community near Los Angeles: Asian, Black, Latinx, white. It was a totally hybrid cultural existence. I once wrote about how it was, "feeling as much at home with the Delfonics as the Shigin; even closer to the Black Power movement than the Cultural Revolution. So it seems to me the natural order of things, as a filmmaker, is to use jazz and rhythm & blues in films about Asian Americans, as it is to draw from the style and sensibilities of the German-born [Charles] Bukowski, who wrote about the neighborhood milieu where my mother grew up."[6]

When I started out in the 1980s, a lot of documentary practice drew from genres of journalism, direct cinema, and ethnographic filmmaking. But not knowing any better, I just went by what I liked. And I was really drawn to literature, fiction, and scripted film and television. I brought that mix into my filmmaking, partly as a strategy of necessity in locating relatable cultural reference points for non–Asian American audiences: the murder story, the humor of a road trip, the melodrama of a family reunion.

In the documentary *Who Killed Vincent Chin?* (1988), I drew on literary and dramatic influences to negotiate an Asian American experience that most viewers probably knew little about. The dramatic structure and fractured storytelling approach is based on two fiction-based works that really influenced me—the multiple perspectives of the play and movie *Rashomon* and the parallel story lines of the 1980s-era television drama *Hill Street Blues*. Was the killing a barroom brawl or a hate crime? Using a narrative strategy like the one in *Rashomon* makes it possible to explore the subjectivities and social locations of witnesses to the crime and its aftermath, and to maneuver through ambiguities of perception and fact. In *My America . . . or Honk if You Love Buddha*, I was influenced by Jack Kerouac's *On the Road*, and by the outsider's quest for humanity along the peripheries in Carlos Bulosan's novel *America Is in the Heart*.

SA: Your work is sometimes called lyrical. What do you think about the relationship between poetry and film?

RTP: That's a compliment! Not sure I've heard that before. I'm interested in people's interior lives, which is often memory or dreams, and so I think about the poetics of a scene. I do wish I could be as concise as a poet, though. Poetry is very cinematic, very descriptive. There's an internal visual and rhythmic logic to a film's construction. Really great editors know how to construct a film that way, and I've worked with some amazing editors like Holly Fisher, Johanna Demetrakas, and Jean Tsien. I think of it as the choreography of the edit. Documentary editors don't get half the credit they deserve for making a film sing.

SA: Will you talk a bit about your work with the *Village Voice*, as the only Asian American woman film critic in the late eighties?

RTP: I wasn't on staff, but I was a frequent contributor. Those were the old days when we actually went to screenings. I had a little pocket flashlight for taking notes in the theater. I don't remember ever getting wined and dined like the screenings during awards season these days. Which is for the better because it was really uncomfortable that people were so nice to me because I had some kind of power as a critic. It's one of the reasons I stopped. The funny thing is you'd see the filmmakers all fixated on Vincent Canby's reaction to their movie. They would just stare at his every move during the screening. He was the lead film critic for the *New York Times* and he was known to make or break a film, especially an indie or international film. Anyway, there I was quite often the only Asian American at a screening. I really appreciate my *Voice* editor Howard Feinstein because he kept on giving me assignments even though I was always bringing race and ethnicity into my reviews, which wasn't fashionable at the time. Like the anti-Black racism of one of the *Chucky* movies. I was reviewing all kinds of stuff—anything from *Chucky* to Meryl Streep vehicles to the Asian American film festival.

It was weird, my being a film critic for a publication like the *Village Voice*. I was a raised-in-the-West Coast populist and the *Voice* was definitely an urbane, New York intellectual vibe. But I liked movies about immigrants and families and I didn't mind sentimentality. I had grown up watching Japanese soap operas with my grandma. I didn't fit in with those rhetoric department–trained critics wielding trenchant quips and French new wave references. I mean, I gave a positive review to the Steve Martin movie *Parenthood*. I thought it was touching. That's how un-*Voice* I was, but Howard kept on giving me movies to review.

SA: I believe you did your last issue as managing editor of *Bridge* in late 1983, and you and Christine Choy made *Who Killed Vincent Chin?* in 1988. What led up to that important film? What are some of the joys and difficulties of collaboration, for you?

RTP: I was sitting in our office at Third World Newsreel when I opened an envelope that had been sent by a local activist. Inside, there was a newspaper clipping and a note describing the murder of Vincent Chin. This was in the spring of 1983. In March, his killers Ronald Ebens and Michael Nitz had pleaded guilty to manslaughter, so there was really no trial; there was a plea agreement. Judge Charles Kaufman sentenced them to approximately three years of probation and a $3,000+ fine. They would not spend a day in jail.

I was shocked at the light sentence for such a brutal murder. I had been hearing about incidents of anti-Asian violence, and of racial violence in general. But like many cases of racial violence, Vincent Chin's killing wasn't getting the attention it should. Chris and I were filmmaking partners at the time, and we decided to make a film about the case. We teamed up with WTVS/Detroit Public TV and really lucked out that the station general manager, Robert Larson, and the head of cultural programming and special projects, Juanita Anderson, came on as executive producers. Juanita was one of the handful of Black women production executives at PBS during that time, and she really got the story and the politics of an Asian American film team taking on the investigation of the case. She was also a Detroit native and knew the city beyond the "murder capital" stereotypes that were so prevalent at the time.

Juanita and Bob insulated us from the PBS suits who didn't trust that Asian American filmmakers could be "objective," as if professionalism is biologically determined. Our main funder, the Corporation for Public Broadcasting, wanted us to be overseen by a white male journalist. Juanita and Bob told us, just make your film and we'll deal with him. It was a great team. The filmmaker Nancy Tong was associate producer, and she conducted all of the Chinese-language interviews, including with Lily Chin. Nancy and I spent three months in Detroit researching the case, meeting all of the players, and developing the story. When I talk about an editor choreographing a film, I think of our editor Holly Fisher. She's brilliant. And her provenance as an experimental filmmaker really made a difference. She understood how to choreograph the layers.

SA: At the end of "Moving the Image," you suggest that "it may be time to look back" to get new perspectives and move forward. What forms of this "looking back" might you suggest to an aspiring young filmmaker or writer-scholar?

RTP: I was just in Detroit for the Vincent Chin 40th Remembrance and Rededication, a four-day convening that was launched by the original activists of American Citizens for Justice (ACJ), including Roland Hwang, Jim Shimoura, and Helen Zia. There was nothing nostalgic about the event; no one was fixed in the past. It was all about figuring out what that collective experience of the Vincent Chin case tells us about the fight today.

The justice for Vincent Chin campaign was seminal: It was the first time Asian Americans were recognized as a protected class in a federal civil rights criminal prosecution. It was a recognition that Asian Americans experience systemic racism, that we are not the "model minority," and going forward, the question of race could be factored into incidents of violence toward Asian Americans. It had to be considered when a white supremacist murdered Joseph Ileto, it had to be considered when Balbir Singh Sodhi was murdered after 9/11, it had to be considered when six Asian immigrant women were gunned down in the Atlanta area this past March. But today those civil rights protections are being rolled back, one by one.

It took an engagement with history to change the narrative of the Asian American model minority in the first place. The ACJ activists framed Chin's murder as a part of a long history of racial violence and scapegoating. Asian Americans have always fought to define ourselves and tell our own story. That hasn't changed. Right now we're in a golden age of the Asian American story and presence, from K–12 curriculum requirements to blockbusters like *Shang-Chi and the Legend of the Ten Rings*.

At the same time, however, there is a right-wing backlash to our story wrapped up in anti–critical race theory attacks and banned books. Even children's and YA books like Lawrence Yep's *Dragonwings* have been banned by school districts. We can't assume that we'll be able to teach the Vincent Chin story, or the truth of our history, unless we wage that fight.

SA: What are you working on now?

RTP: I'm working on narrative-shift initiatives with different AAPIs in media, activism, philanthropy, education, cultural strategy. Also developing more documentaries!

Figure 11. *New American Writing* Issue 1 (1978). Artwork by Darragh Park.

Maxine Chernoff

Coeditor, Oink! *(1971–1985, Chicago) and* New American Writing
(1986–present, San Francisco)

SEPTEMBER 18, 2015, VIA TELEPHONE

Stephanie Anderson: It was really fun to look through some of these old issues of *Oink!* and *New American Writing*.[1]

Maxine Chernoff: I've been doing this for a long time.

SA: I'm in Chicago, so it's especially fun for that reason. I was interested in the overlap of the beginning of *Oink!* with Ted Berrigan and Alice Notley's time in Chicago—though I think *Oink!* started before that?

MC: It did, but it actually started without me; I wasn't one of the founders of *Oink!*. It was started by three grad students at the University of Illinois at Chicago: Dean Faulwell, who has recently passed away, Jim Leonard, who became a missionary, and Paul Hoover, who stayed a poet. And all three of them were in the program for writers, and the first four issues of the magazine were published there through university student funds for activities such as that. They met in a graduate workshop that Paul Carroll was teaching.

SA: Okay.

MC: But a lot of the activities that subsequently happened were during Ted's sojourn in Chicago. And starting with *Oink!* number 5, I was involved, and by the time number 5 happened, I believe that the other two—Faulwell had moved to Berkeley, where his wife was getting a PhD in German, and Jim Leonard had become religious. I believe that Ted Berrigan was in Chicago by then and he was an important person in our lives, and also that Paul and I were the only two people working on the magazine.

SA: And then you became an editor with issue 11—or you were an associate editor of 9 and 10.

MC: I don't even remember. I mean, I was around—we were together and I was around. [*chuckles*] I think he put me officially on the masthead maybe at that point. I'd been involved since issue 5. We used to do everything by ourselves in Paul's apartment, which became A. B. Dick Central. We would feed the paper into the printer and do the cover and everything ourselves. Then we would have evenings when people would come and help us collate everything, and we would make it—at that time it was five staples. We had a big cup and huge stapler; the cup would make the line to indent the magazine, and the stapler, an industrial-size stapler, is what we would use to put it together. The first issue that we had professionally printed was the one with the part man and part elephant on the cover. And we switched to a printer because a lot of small press machines can't do humidity, and we were having a terrible problem printing that issue. We gave up in the middle on it. And then we called the printers and found a local guy who would do it for not too steep a price, but then when he saw our cover, which was half elephant half naked man, he hesitated, but then I think he just decided on a cover charge. So from then on, we had it professionally printed, but not with that local guy. [*chuckles*]

SA: Yeah, that was number 11. The issue actually—I got interlibrary loan books from Iowa, but number 8 is funny because I think in the binding, maybe at Iowa, they must have split the issue in half and accidentally reversed the order, so I spent a long time looking for the table of contents.

MC: Weird. Yeah, we had all kinds of printing escapades before we turned it over to a professional printer. I think as far as 9 goes—it has a rainbow looking cover in silver—

SA: Yeah.

MC: We were very proud of it because it was the first time we used color in our very own professional way—at that time there was the whole movement and history of printing on mimeo machines, and all kinds of subpar printing that was fairly widely used back then, and widely disseminated and maintained. So we thought we were pretty fancy but we really weren't. [*laughs*]

SA: Well, I was actually thinking of Alice Notley's little magazine *CHI-CAGO* that she was doing around the same time, because there's so much overlap between some of the people who you were both publishing . . .

MC: We had similar interests and also a similar group. Poets would want to come to Chicago to give a reading, and they would typically be people who Ted knew, so they would see Ted, and then they would read at the Monday series at the Body Politic, which was run by Yellow Press and Richard Friedman, Darlene Pearlstein, and Peter Kostakis. They did the *Milk Quarterly*, the magazine, for a while. So visiting poets would come, and then Ted would get them a reading at Northeastern Illinois University, where he was teaching, and then they would read in the series at the Body Politic. We'd all get to hear them, and then all the same people would be asking them for poems—thus the overlap with Alice's magazine. Mostly universities would have people in. I remember a University of Chicago reading, actually, being Kenneth Rexroth and Robert Duncan, and many other fine events in the seventies. But a lot was happening at the Body Politic on Monday nights, which was where the young poets would habitually go to talk to the older poets. I got my first reading at the Body Politic. It was 1975; Ted was there and would interject, but in a kindly manner for the most part.

SA: Okay.

MC: He was a big fixture on the scene, and Alice to some degree—but because she was home a lot actually with kids, and he would be out, she wasn't as much on the scene. And then the other person of note at all these events was Bill Knott, who was teaching at Columbia College in Chicago.

So the two big guys in the room were Bill Knott and Ted Berrigan. And often particularly Ted would be commenting all the way through. [*chuckles*] Every Monday night was really interesting. I saw so many poets there for the first time, not only Alice and Ted but [Robert] Creeley—tons of people came through—[Gregory] Corso, everyone eventually came through that series sometime in the late seventies, early eighties.

154   *Women in Independent Publishing*

SA: Was *Oink!* doing any of its soliciting through the readings?

MC: We would often go, and we would ask people for poems. Actually, to get Ted's poems is the funniest story . . . So what Ted would like to do was have you come to his apartment, where he would be lying in bed without a shirt on—I don't know if he had anything else on, actually; all you could see was his naked chest—and he would show you these big black folders of poems, and basically let you pull out what he said was available. There was an immediate selection, like the Ted poetry bazaar.

SA: Oh, okay. That makes sense. Because I did notice a sonnet in one of the issues, and I went back to my copies of *The Sonnets* and realized that it was one of the ones that he had not included in the original *Sonnets*.

MC: That was fun, and then, of course, if you got to go over to Ted's, you'd see more of Alice—I'm not sure when Anselm and Edmund were born, but at some point there was a very little person and a baby and they'd all be just around the kitchen, often at a table, and Ted would be lying in bed smoking, with his manuscripts. [*both chuckle*] There were three or four groups of poets at that time in the seventies. There were people who were studying at Northeastern with Ted, and they did a magazine for a while called *Stone Wind*; that included Terry Jacobus and a few other guys. And then there were the *Milk Quarterly* people, and then the *Oink!* people. That was kind of what was happening. Also at University of Illinois at Chicago there was Michael Anania, also a poet influenced by [Charles] Olson and his young followers. He and Paul Carroll pretty much liked the same poetry, but at that point two groups didn't mingle all that much. Notable people under him were Jim Ramholz, John Rezek, Brooke Bergen, and Jennifer Moyer, who became head of the Illinois Arts Council for a while and has since passed away. She founded a press, Moyer Bell, that was in operation for a while and did beautiful books. Years later I am good friends with Michael, my first professor.

The other thing that brought us in contact with poets was that around 1975, '76, Paul Carroll and one of the other poets founded the

Poetry Center that was then at the Museum of Contemporary Art. And people got on the board of that—Paul Hoover was on the board, and Art Lange would have represented the interests of the group you're interested in—eventually I was on the board too. We would get to arrange one reading a year: two poets that we would care to see. So we might've brought in Russell Edson that way. We brought in . . . oh, we brought in a ton of people; that's how I met Kenward Elmslie to begin with, and Joe Brainard . . . so many people who we would not have had a chance to meet had they not been coming in to read for the series, and who we became good friends with after. So that was an important way, too, for us to meet people and get them published. Then Paul was teaching at Columbia College Chicago and he arranged many readings, some of people we'd seen at the Body Politic before. I remember seeing Leslie Scalapino early on in her career, both at the Body Politic and then at Columbia College Chicago—he brought her the second time. A lot of the Language-based poets got brought in through Paul's department at Columbia. And so that was another source of meeting writers we would ask to be in the magazine.

SA: Oh, okay. I was wondering about that, actually—the fact that there's this kind of amazing mix in the early issues of *New American Writing*, especially between what later became known as the Language poets . . .

MC: In the late seventies—now we've been here in California since '94—but in the late seventies we were going to San Francisco probably once a year or more. My sister was nearby, and we would come out and meet the poets—we were friends in much earlier days with Carla Harryman and her husband, Barrett Watten, and Bob Perelman when he was still out here, and his wife, Francie Shaw. But then we were also friends with people who weren't their friends, like the Objectivist poet Carl Rakosi, and George Evans and August Kleinzahler, people who were not SF Language poets. Because we weren't from here, we weren't as encamped as the people who lived here. So we were picking up interesting voices from various schools of experimentation all at the same time. We weren't territorial, living outside the territory.

156 *Women in Independent Publishing*

And then I taught part-time at Columbia College and Paul taught full-time there, and we had some really good early students—like, Elaine Equi was one of Paul's first students. They would come to our house to have independent study, so we would all hang out a lot. And Sharon Mesmer, who's still active in New York, and Lydia Tomkiw, who had moved to New York and later passed away. It also included Kimberly Lyons and Connie Deanovich. There was a scene that developed. A woman named Lorri Jackson, who died of a heroin overdose and was a pretty wonderful poet. So a lot of young women poets were coming out of those classes Paul or I taught at Columbia. Those were people who we published quite a bit in *Oink!* and then in *New American Writing*. And we would go to New York probably twice a year or so. We developed good friendships with some people—we were very good friends with Kenward Elmslie and Joe Brainard, and I had become really good friends with Ann Lauterbach—and they introduced us to people, so, for instance, some of the visual artists who we have in a few issues, or on the cover, Donna Dennis, for instance; a lot of collaborations with Kenward and other artists; Alex Katz agreed to do two covers; and we didn't know Larry Rivers, but we knew people who knew Larry Rivers, and we got a cover from him . . . So we had connections in all the major cities where poets were doing important work and had people whom we'd regularly see.

SA: The word Chicago still appears very prominently on the title page of *Oink!*, at least, so it does seem like you were kind of trying to position Chicago as a place where all these different kinds of innovation could come together.

MC: Right, well, it wasn't dispersed, but the base wasn't as solid and as school based as it ended up being when the Language poets became more prominent. I think of the seventies as being more of an undefined space in terms of what was influencing one's writing or how you were moving in your writing. We had more openness in Chicago because of this central location in terms of people coming in, but not central location in terms of defining what poetry was. We felt open to all the different schools that were possibly writing anything of interest at the same time. So we never were the Language

Maxine Chernoff 157

poetry–only magazine or the New York School–only magazine—it was all kinds of experimentations under one cover. We also always liked to be able to take people unsolicited. Even now, about a quarter to a third of the magazine is people who just send in and we take over the transom. Because there are so many people who are just interesting loners—doing what they do. So over the years we've published a lot of people who would fit that description as well. Who aren't really affiliated but are interesting, unaffiliated, experimental people. And often we've published people of note for the first time.

SA: How did you kind of divvy up the technical duties for the production of the magazine?

MC: The front side of doing things was Paul. I did almost all the screening. And what happened would be that if you passed my first read—and I would do that fairly fast, because quite soon you can often tell that someone isn't going to be chosen. I would hold anything that I knew we would both find interesting, and then eventually we would sit down, often on a Sunday evening, and have a big reading session. Sometimes I would even put the manuscripts in order of what I thought were the most interesting. Not always. And we didn't always, of course, agree on everything. But that's how we would get down into the reading—we had this big basket that we would hold people in, for a while, like months, before we could sit down together to review our order for the issue. Then we would go back through them, we'd sit down and do all that together, and we would see how the issue was shaping up. If the issue was shaping up in a way that we thought we needed or wanted more of this or that, or it was thinner than we wanted, or we had a lot of young people and we didn't have a lot of major figures yet, then we would solicit and get more and fill the pages that way. At some point still when it was *Oink!* our interests also turned to translation—eventually Paul got into the Hölderlin translation with me[2]—but way before that, we started to be interested in also publishing translators in the issue. So that would happen.

At the point when we had put the magazine together, did the table of contents together, and figured out the order, Paul would take over getting it typeset. We would find a cover together usually.

One of us would see something we liked and the other one would say fine, or think of a better thing, and we'd choose together what the cover was. But in terms of sending it to a designer, a printer—all of that Paul would do, with the estimates and getting it actually physically sent and typeset. Then when it came back in boxes to be distributed, we would work again together to send it out to libraries and subscribers. We had a couple distributors who were sending larger orders to magazine distributors, like Ingram, and Ingram would send hundreds of copies out that we didn't have to come to our house. But for a few weeks every late spring or early summer, the dining room looked like a warehouse—we'd have many copies to send in envelopes to people. We did that all ourselves—we always did mostly everything ourselves, except for a few times when we used first readers. We found it not useful because we then had to check everything they did. One of our first readers, without our knowing, was sending "how to write" notes to people who weren't expecting it, which we would never do. You know, it was easier for the two of us to do it fast and efficiently. We always were doing many, many things, because we were both teaching, and we ended up having three children. Everything was happening so we were trying to get the magazine done the easiest way possible, and it seemed like the fewer people doing it the better.

SA: Yeah, I understand that. I mean, it sounds sort of remarkably—I mean, not exactly harmonious, but practically harmonious.

MC: We very much—we pretty much agreed on who we chose. Sometimes one of us or the other was more interested in a person than the other, and then we just said fine, take what you want from them. I don't think we ever had a fight or an argument about "This person can't be in the magazine. . . ." That would never have happened. We always had a tacit agreement that, okay, if one of us feels strongly enough about something, then it's in. And our tastes are similar enough that that was never very shocking to the other person. [*chuckles*]

SA: It's a really nice change to hear that Paul was taking over some of the more nitty-gritty production stuff, because often, with women I've interviewed, it's been the women typing stencils and stuff like that.

MC: He was always more of a detail person. I have this speed about everything I do—so I am not a good detail person. I wouldn't be a good copyeditor. I like making quick decisions. So choosing the materials, finding an order, approaching people, finding cover art, all of that good stuff I enjoyed more than the copyediting/typesetting part—that he was better with.

SA: So why was there the transition . . .

MC: Between *Oink!* and *New American Writing*?

SA: Yes, exactly.

MC: So in 1985 we had twin boys, and that kind of pushed us over the brink for about a year, in terms of how much we could do a night. When we had the boys, we couldn't stop being parents, and we both were teaching, so there was a year hiatus where we didn't do the magazine. And we thought maybe we wouldn't do it again; *Oink!* 19 was the last issue of the first group of things. When it was called *Oink!* we had had some distributers not want to take it because it was called *Oink!*.

SA: I'm sorry, because of what?

MC: Because they thought *Oink!* was a silly title, we were having trouble with some distributors. We started thinking, well, if we do the magazine again—because we'd been missing doing the magazine during that year in which one-year-olds were toddling around here and driving us insane—he said to me, let's do the magazine again, but let's revive it in a way that makes the claim that no one can refute in terms of distributing. So our trick was that we'd give it a big name, *New American Writing*, but it's really still just *Oink!* inside. And we didn't really change anything else.

SA: Yeah.

MC: A few people were upset at us. Dean Faulwell, who was one of the original founders, didn't like that we called it *NAW* and Andrei Codrescu was upset for some reason. At one point Dean Faulwell actually did an issue of something called *Boink!*. But other than that the transition was smooth. That was the time, like 1985, '86, when there were still a lot of bookstores in America. Way more than now. And so our distribution went way up—at one point we went from distributing about one thousand copies to almost six thousand copies.

SA: Oh, wow.

MC: Before the bookstores started all closing. Like the first three hundred Little Professor stores closed in college towns, and then Borders. In Chicago, Kroch's and Brentano's went out; all these bookstores closed. It went down from a peak of about 6,000 being distributed in the late eighties to about 1,500 being distributed just a few years later.

SA: Okay.

MC: That really pretty much followed the story of publishing. And publishing as a bookstore-related enterprise was being swallowed up by the online sources for books, Amazon, and all the big places. Our "take" got smaller and smaller, and we sent out fewer and fewer, and continued our lives. So that's what happened when we called it *New American Writing*, either because of this boom in bookstores at that time or because the name actually did change the reception of the magazine—I'm not sure which. I don't know really what happened. Now we're printing about one thousand copies.

SA: I see. Speaking of the importance of the times—I don't know if you have recently read the opening note in the first issue of *Oink!*, about the title?

MC: Oh, yeah; that predates me.

SA: Yeah. You know, it's really quite funny but as one gets older it's a little bit harder to see as funny because it's—they're "founding the Male Chauvinist Pig School of American Poetry," you know?

MC: That was 1971. That was a really long time ago, and that was guys in their twenties . . . It was a whole different time and place. And I think it was also a sign of the times that there was no real reason to call it that. They never really had a chauvinist poetics about them; one of their first issues had Anne Waldman in it, and Brooke Bergen, who was a student in the program. I think that in terms of continuing in publishing, it had very little to do with that first silly statement they made when they were founding the magazine as boys in 1971.

SA: Yeah, it was one of the things that reminded me of that kind of Second-Generation New York School humor . . .

MC: It's deadpan and "hee-haw funny." Reminiscent of some of Ron Padgett's work tonally. And they hugely admired Ron. But we've always been very open, and happy to publish women, obviously. There's never any agenda in the magazine past issue number 1 where that gets spoken or felt in any way.

SA: Have you, over the years, paid attention to the gender balance in the magazine?

MC: We have when I've made attempts, sometimes like thirty-one women and twenty-eight men. We're often pretty close. Sometimes it's been more women, sometimes a few more men. I have never edited by any kind of quota system. And we've published big sections by a lot of women, and we've always been big supporters of our students and their further work in the world. I care very much about women being published, but no, it was never a case where I had to push for it, or there was anything to push for. We naturally had many good women poets to include all the time.

SA: That's great.

MC: Yeah. Maybe one editor being a woman helped that; I'm not sure. But I think it was always very pretty even and fair that way. There was never a consideration of, you know, we need to put her in because she's a woman. They're just good writers so we published them. I know there's much more attention to that now, and I know that with VIDA,[3] people are really looking at that. But it was just natural through who submitted to us that we always had really excellent women to publish.

SA: Were you ever doing release parties for the journal?

MC: Yeah, we did sporadically. Sometimes we were more active in terms of trying to give it a public face in a community. So we had some big release parties for it, and we actually, at one point, formed a board. I remember a release party that we had—I can't remember the name of the place, but it was a club in Chicago—and Kenward Elmslie read and sang, and a bunch of people, and it was a big fun event with good attendance. And it was a benefit, of course, for the magazine. Sometime in the early eighties; I don't exactly remember when.

SA: Fun.

162   *Women in Independent Publishing*

MC: But we never did some of things that you would think people should do as professionals who publish a magazine. We never did subscription drives, we didn't take out big ads or anything . . . we just kind of did the magazine. It was one of the many activities that we had in our lives, which have always been pretty busy. But yeah, of course we had big parties. The two years before we left for California, '93 and '94, we started a board. It was a board of fancy fundraising people, associated with the arts in Chicago. One of them was the president of the Harvard Club. It's strange; I don't remember quite how we got them. One was a lawyer named Hugh Schwartzberg, who's still in Chicago and goes to a lot of events and videotapes them—or used to, at least. The board would meet at Columbia College. We had one big benefit at the Union League Club where Robert Creeley and Charles Simic read for the magazine, and we raised a couple thousand dollars and fancy people came. Then the board started wanting us to do things that we didn't want to do. You know, they started being too active. [*chuckles*] Having ideas that weren't very interesting to us. And we thought, well, I don't know, we made a few thousand dollars, but this is kind of a pain. We didn't want to become *Chicago* magazine, or some glossy, slick thing.[4] We wanted to be how we were, and somehow get money for the magazine. At that point, Columbia College was contributing about $5,000 an issue while Paul was still there. Eventually, when I came out here and started at San Francisco State, the College of the Humanities was contributing $2,500 a year. And then, through Z Press, Kenward Elmslie was contributing. So at some point we stopped having to write grants; through Z Press and through one college or the other, we pretty much had the publication covered. As an annual, we didn't have to do a lot of writing Illinois Arts Council grants and things like that. Which is what had led us to form a board—we kind of expected when we applied to the Illinois Arts Council that we would get money, and one year we didn't—and then we said we better start a board and we better find ways to finance the magazine. We've always done a serious job that's "serious-casual."

SA: Yeah.

MC: I think the early wisdom around "do-it-yourself," coming of age in the late sixties/early seventies, that model, you know, sustained more than the professionalism of young people who came around later and did magazines, you know, in a bigger, fancier way from the start.

SA: Yeah, yeah.

MC: To try to look fancy from the beginning. I'm reminded of *Fence*. But many, many magazines. We've held different views about how to do the magazine, but I think our simplest philosophy is in the way that's the least annoying. [*both chuckle*] And that's also kind of why we went to an annual publication. We started with more frequent publication but doing it once a year, anthology style, started to make sense with our time and the other requirements of our life.

SA: It definitely feels more like an anthology or a book, later.

MC: Yeah. Putting it together once a year, people know to submit from September to January; January, February, March we put it together, publishing by May or June every year—that ends up being the cycle for us.

SA: I know that there were a couple special issues; there were some single issues of *Oink!* that were dedicated to—one to Paul's work, and single-author issues, and there were some special issues of *New American Writing* as well. How did those tend to come about?

MC: At some point toward the end of *Oink!* we were kind of tired—sometimes you'd grow weary, and you'd think of ways of reinventing yourself. I know that we did a Russell Edson issue, we did a Peter Kostakis, and then we did special issues that were related to places, and they were places where we ended up traveling to as writers. In 1988 I went to Australia, sent by the state of Illinois. It was the centennial year of New South Wales, and so eight Chicago poets got sent to Australia, and that's how the Australian issue got made.

SA: Wow.

MC: We did a Chinese issue after a trip to China in 2004 or '05, we did a big British issue—we were in England around 1990, '91. We went to read in Scotland, and were visiting Ric Caddel, a British poet who's now passed away, in Durham, England. We asked him to edit a section of *New American Writing*, which I believe is number 8–9—it has a bunch of British poets, so that came out of that trip. Paul Hoover

164   *Women in Independent Publishing*

went by himself to Vietnam two times, and he put a lot of Vietnamese poets in the issue. Issue number 5 was a themed issue around censorship and the arts. And that came out of the big deal with the Mapplethorpe censorship, and the Serrano *Piss Christ*, and all that was happening then. People were losing grants for publishing what Jesse Helms thought was edgy art, so we decided to do an issue based on that topic. I think that's our only topic issue: number 5, with the Mapplethorpe cover. Basically, because it's been the two of us, and because sometimes our adventures and interests guide us, we've done special issues. And sometimes people have approached us; in *New American Writing* we've had a Canadian and a Quebecois—two different sections of Canadian writing. I remember very early, in one of the *Oink!s*, there's South American writing. That was done after someone from the University of Chicago approached us who had a few people in mind who he had already translated. So people came to us sometimes for special sections and sometimes it was based on our travels—in a recent *New American Writing* there's a Mexican section. We tried to reach out to other poetries and include translation a lot, particularly when Paul and I, from 2004 to 2008, worked together collaborating on the *Selected Poems of Friedrich Hölderlin* and were getting involved ourselves in a lot of translation. Our attention turned more to translation, and we *consciously* included it more in our magazine.

SA: Do you have the feeling that the work you did over the years on the magazine influenced your own writing in kind of vague ways or specific ways?

MC: Definitely; I've always felt that the way to stay active in writing is by declaring yourself a member of a community. You know, I felt that in a couple ways. We were really the first ones to publish some people who became more well-known, like Elaine Equi, Noelle Kocot, Susan Wheeler, Mary Jo Bang—who became prominent writers. Mary Jo Bang, before she went to New York and kind of got discovered, took some classes from Paul at Columbia College in Chicago, when she was barely yet a poet. Then they became famous and that was nice to see. As Chicago writers, the magazine kept us in touch

Maxine Chernoff   165

with a larger community. We had openness to a lot of things, but it was a way of being connected to poetry communities while living in Chicago, where the community was a little sparser at that time. Although there are probably more poets there now than there were when we were younger people.

SA: There are—you know, just in the last ten years there has been, I think, an explosion of poets here.

MC: And I think that with the rise of the Internet, and people communicating in other ways, most anywhere can have a poetry scene. Like the Facebook poetry community, and all kinds of poetry communities. Now I notice among my students at San Francisco State that younger people these days, I think they only attend readings by their peers and younger people. [*chuckles*]

SA: Yeah.

MC: And I really have to bring them out for these fabulous older poets; mainly it's older poets who come to see the older poets and younger people. Audiences seem to be more age-based these days than they were when I was younger. Like when I was young, if Kenneth Rexroth was going to be somewhere in town, I would run to see him. But I think—I don't know if people go out as much, or if people think of poetry more as something they do online. And they communicate that way and enlarge their communities that way as well. When I was younger you had to go there to do it. [*chuckles*]

SA: I get the impression that it's also that younger people coming through MFA programs feel like they come out of MFA programs with their community already established, or something like that.

MC: They find their peers; they find their group. They're comfortable that way, and that's fine. They support each other and they start presses—any number of presses have been started in the last ten years by various former students of mine, and that's great! People publish each other—it's the same activity that happened when I was young, only it's a new group and several generations down the line of young people coming aboard and publishing each other. And then someone young will step forward and do things for other people. I think that there are really kind of two models—in life, not

166 *Women in Independent Publishing*

just in poetry: the people who do things for other people and the people who get things done for them. [*both laugh*] I've always been in the first group—I've always felt that there was a reason to be active in that way, as a supporter of other writers as well as a writer myself. The same people tend to do that all the time, and the people who don't do that—I won't name people—but they seem to do *that* all the time. The people who are taken up by others, but then take others up with them.

SA: I loved that phrase you used, declaring yourself a member of a community. There are people who would declare themselves members of a community to get resources, right? And there are others who would declare themselves members of a community to provide resources.

MC: Right, right. I think that it's a richer life if you are the former rather than the latter. Because then you feel that you're reaching up and you're reaching down, and you're holding people together in interesting ways. The magazine really has always done that. We've reached up so that we could have Carl Rakosi when he was ninety-eight years old lifted up, being published in the same magazine as well as a twenty-four-year-old who just got a program.

SA: Yeah. Obviously, the Internet provides a lot of opportunities for people to connect in ways that were previously impossible, but I do worry about what you're talking about in terms of age and the stratification of poetry scenes.

MC: Right, because it's bad if you think you invented yourself and nothing changes your poetics, ever—that's kind of imprecise and sad.

SA: Yeah. Or even—I run a little chapbook press, and it's actually hard for us to get submissions outside of my generation *because* we only do online promotion.

MC: Yeah, that's the other thing. A couple years ago I had an online chapbook for the first time. There's a series that's called Beard of Bees that's published, and Paul Hoover and a few others—

SA: Oh, yeah; I love Eric Elshtain's press.

MC: Yeah, they do nice stuff. So there's all kinds of ways that people might get their work out, which is great. You know, students come

Maxine Chernoff   167

in and say, "Well, how do I get published?" And there's a million ways to get published. How do you get published in a way that's important to you and healthiest is the question. [*laughs*]

SA: Yeah, yeah.

MC: So there aren't really—New York isn't like *the* publishing place or anything, and if it weren't for small presses that do wonderful work . . . Coffee House, or MadHat, a small press that acts like a large press, basically—presses like that, that started small and become more ambitious, outside of the university presses that are diminishing their publishing. I was a judge for the Akron Prize last year. And when the press was going to fold, it looked like the person who I'd chosen's book would never be published. But now, again, it's on to be published. So, you know, you have to worry about this, the security of poetry in the world. Small presses are where everything starts, but it's unstable—so there's an ongoing nomadic population of poets going from small press to small press. We know students who've started a new press for women, and then we know presses like Kelsey Street Press, who have only published women for decades. People redo this experiment again and again and keep the poetry scene alive, in various different iterations and generations.

SA: Yeah.

MC: So that's good! Being someone who looks to the world, and not just your own page. People need publishers, and people need people committed to the very task of publishing poetry, which is a financial burden. Except Christian Bök apparently had *Eunoia* published in a million copies or something.

SA: Oh, wow.

MC: It's very popular. But that's an anomaly, someone actually making money off of poetry. My eighteen-year-old freshmen students: "I'm going to be a poet! Can you make a living—" No! [*both laugh*] You need to do something else too.

SA: Yep.

MC: You know it can't be work. And that isn't why anyone writes poetry, which is what is kind of wonderful about poetry. No one really cares if you do it, so you have to care.

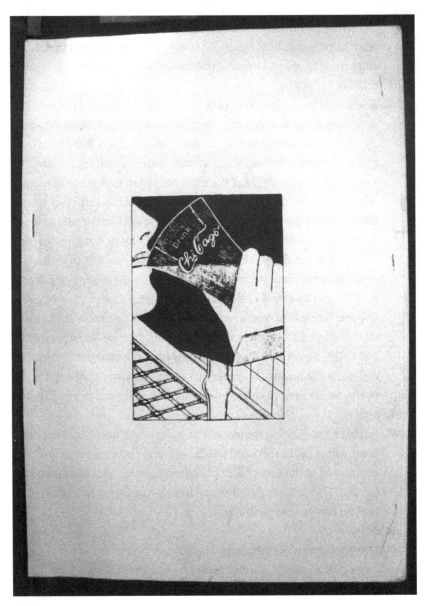

Figure 12. *CHICAGO* European Edition No. 3 (1974). Artwork by George Schneeman.

Alice Notley

Editor and Publisher, CHICAGO *(1972–1974, Chicago and the UK)*

FEBRUARY TO MARCH 2010, VIA E-MAIL

Stephanie Anderson: How long had you been living in Chicago before you started the journal *CHICAGO*? Did you decide to publish it immediately?

Alice Notley: I started the magazine immediately, as soon as Ted [Berrigan] and I moved to Chicago. I was twenty-six years old and pregnant. I hadn't written very much poetry and was in danger—I saw it that way—of not becoming a poet. The magazine was a way of really joining the poetry community, of getting to read a lot of poems. You actually typed the poems in those days, so you studied the work you published quite closely.

SA: I've noticed that the first few issues contain quite a few New York poets. How much (if at all) were you thinking consciously of publishing as an activity spanning geographies?

AN: I wanted most to be in touch with the poets in New York. However, I also had an idea about picking and publishing consistently a core group of poets, most (but not all) of whom lived in New York. I was particularly interested in Anne Waldman and Bernadette Mayer, Lorenzo Thomas, Ron Padgett, Tom Clark, Anselm Hollo, Ted, and myself. In fact, that's four in New York, one in California, one in Iowa, and the two of us in Chicago, so I guess quite a bit of geography was covered.

SA: Did you actively solicit poems? I suspect that a kind of community of poets was exchanging work and collaborating—did you find material this way?

AN: I solicited work as well and asked for work from people who came through Chicago to give readings. There were several reading venues

170 *Women in Independent Publishing*

in Chicago at that point, and after a reading I particularly liked, I
would ask to see work.

SA: Do you have stronger memories of a particular issue or issues of the
journal than others?

AN: I liked all the issues, and I was always excited about George
Schneeman's covers—he did all of them, and the first six, the
ones from Chicago, are organically interconnected. The magazine
changed—changed size and content and cover content—when we
moved to England. A lot of English poets were then included . . . a
different geography and a sense that the core group might be larger. I was pregnant again in England; I associate the whole process
of the magazine with being pregnant. But let's see, particular issues. There was one issue that Ted edited in order to prove that he
wasn't the editor of the magazine in general! This was a very sexist
time, and everyone thought he was doing it, not me. So he edited
issue 5 to show what the magazine would be like if he edited it. It
is different, though I'm not sure our friends were smart enough
to see that. Also, it is the issue that came out just as I gave birth—I
really needed a different editor for that one. I very much remember the issue you don't have—the first European one—because it
contained the interview between Ted and George Oppen (I think
that's the one; it's hard for me to find my set of the magazines this
morning) and a special selection of Oppen's work that I made. He
had come to England for a festival and I met him and Mary, which
was lovely.

SA: Did you do all the mimeographing and stencil-cutting?

AN: I did all the stencil-cutting, Ted did the mimeographing in Chicago
(it's very poor, I'm afraid—we destroyed two church mimeos that
shouldn't have been printing that many copies). I just couldn't do
everything; I was pregnant. I did all the collating, stapling, and mailing. I kept the mailing list, etc. I did all the correspondence. Bob
Rosenthal helped Ted with some of the mimeographing in Chicago.
In England the people at the University of Essex did the mimeographing—there was a machine in the literature department—and

the mimeographing got a lot better. I still did all the stencil-cutting, collating, stapling, mailing, and letter-writing.

SA: Did you work with writers to edit pieces?

AN: I did all the editing myself. Occasionally I took input from Ted, but not really very often. I very decidedly had my own taste, after I did the first issue and learned what the process was like (he initiated me, basically—I didn't know anything). I never worked with the poets themselves that I remember. Now that I think about it, I realize that my editing was quite aggressive. It was hard for me to know what it was like at the time; I was so young and there was so much sexism in the atmosphere. I've participated in—edited and coedited—three magazines now (four if one counts the scurrilous and anarchic mag *Caveman*), but you are the first person to ask me questions, as if I had actually accomplished something in the field. There are other kinds of prejudices involved, of course—aesthetic, for example.

SA: Can you expand on now realizing that your editing was aggressive?

AN: I didn't necessarily accept what I was supposed to accept; I picked and chose—for example, I might accept one part of a poem in several parts. I'm not sure I would dare do that now. I didn't necessarily take pieces of froth sent to me by famous people—Donald Hall once sent a set of variations a class of his had done on Williams's "Red Wheelbarrow," and I rejected it. I published things that had already been published in books because I liked them or because I wanted to make a point. That sort of thing. I wrote to people and asked them for particular works or particular kinds of work—I looked around a lot. I exercised the editing muscle. Once Ted put a lot of pressure on me to print something by someone, who will go unnamed, and I finally did it—it was the "nice" thing to do—but it made me want to vomit. I think he was nicer than I was. I was young and opinionated. I thought a magazine shouldn't relax that much or be that inclusive. (This was, in fact, a way that we had different editing styles.)

SA: It seems ridiculous, but it's a little hard for me to have a good sense of the sexism of the time. I feel a fair amount of it still in the air in academia these days, though I try to tell myself it must be so much less blatant than it used to be—that intentionality "makes up" for most of it. How blatant and/or insidious was it then?

AN: There were just so few women around, in fact. When I went to Iowa in '67—to the fiction workshop—I was the only woman admitted that year. A woman was also admitted into the poetry workshop, and the two of us were a really exceptional event. The previous year a woman had been admitted into fiction, and no women into poetry. The problem was, in New York, that the few women might be as bad as the men; I mean as sexist. Everyone was defending some abstract territory. I remember the whole thing as perpetual gauntlet, except when I was writing. The men never let the women talk, and Ted was bad himself about this, being a speed freak and never letting Anyone talk—he would make up for it later by admiring my poetry, which he did truly and whole-heartedly. His ability to appreciate poetry, without prejudice, was one of his great talents. But if you want to imagine it, imagine everyone being the way the Language poet men still are (or some of these newer, mostly male "movements")—totally territorial, but imagine them without their concomitantly acknowledging that some women poets are important. You must get a sense of it, that we have political correctness now. At that time women poets were considered to be girls pretending to be poets. However, the magazine was a place where you could get a little power, since men wanted to be in All the magazines. Anne Waldman, Maureen Owen, and I were all editing (legal-sized) magazines at around the same time, and there was a reason for that! But so much of it was and is about territoriality—I had the good fortune of hooking up with Ted at a time when he was expanding his sense of what the poetry world was like, how large and various it was, how big the territory actually was "So Going Around Cities"—and we managed to escape for some years the primary, fabulous territory of New York. I did my apprenticeship in Chicago and England, and I am different for that. But everyone was

Alice Notley 173

sexist—maybe not in Chicago, per se, because everyone was just so naïve there. It was a nice trait.

SA: I love that the magazine was a way of staying connected to/joining the poetry community. This very much has been my experience in small press publishing as well. Do you remember any reactions of people not immediately involved in the community? I guess I'm wondering how seriously audiences took these publications, if you have a sense of that—and even how seriously the participants themselves took the publications.

AN: These magazines were taken very seriously. They were enormously entertaining to everyone, for one thing. They were aesthetic statements as well—magazines now seem boring in comparison. That's probably to do with computers; no one types up anything themselves, everything sprawls and seems unoverseen, one's never sure that editors actually read your work, since they don't have to type it. I had a lovely list of readers—I just sent *CHICAGO* (the magazine name must be in caps) to them without requiring payment, as I remember it—abstract expressionists and second-generation NY School artists, for example, all the major NY poets, etc., everyone in San Francisco and Bolinas.

SA: Do you remember how carefully you ordered the pieces in the journals? Were you thinking about the arc of the whole?

AN: I paid a lot of attention to the ordering of poets and poems in the magazine. One tried to put enough space around everything, like in an art gallery.

SA: Were there release-reading events for any of the issues?

AN: There were no release events. I wasn't trying to make any money or, really, to get the magazine around all that much except to the people on my list. I think the release event for a magazine is relatively new.

SA: Did your sense of yourself as an editor-writer change as you continued?

AN: I think my sense of myself as editor and poet probably did change a lot. And when I did the subsequent magazines—*SCARLET* and *Gare*

174　*Women in Independent Publishing*

du Nord, coedited with Doug Oliver—I was so much an other. We had "features" in our mags—something missing from everything I read now. It feels to me, at this moment though, as if *CHICAGO* had something metaphorically like features—a sense of continuity that was comment and commentary. As well as a dramatic sense of change—Chicago to England? But *CHICAGO* came out really often in its rather short lifespan—a few years—and that was important.

SA: Sometimes I think that one of the best ways to really examine a poem is to write or type it out. Did cutting the stencils further internalize the poems for you at all?

AN: Typing the stencils was very educational. I typed up other people's poems a lot anyway—it was something Ted had suggested, but I took it further than he had (he had sort of invented the typing of poems as a way of studying them). I typed up a lot of longer poems, particularly in England: I typed up all of Jimmy Schuyler's "Hymn to Life," a good portion of Williams's "Of Asphodel That Greeny Flower," and O'Hara's "Ode on Michael Goldberg's Birthday (And Other Births)." Also Milton's "Lycidas." This is probably how I learned to write long poems. But I really enjoyed cutting the stencils.

I finally got all the magazines out from under the bed. They are extraordinarily beautiful and wonderful, and I can't believe what amazing poets I published. And why have I gotten no credit for this whatsoever? Why doesn't anyone ever mention them? There were copies of the first six in that show at the New York Public Library—they didn't even bother to find out there were nine! Is Europe that far away? Why wasn't I invited to be in the Page Mothers conference, as if I had never edited anything? (I was in the middle of my third mag at the time)—etc., etc. Pardon me. Obviously, you have to publicize yourself, and I didn't.

SA: I really appreciate the link between editing and power. It resonates with my own experience—that *some* want to be in *all* the magazines. Was the decision to go legal-sized a practical or an aesthetic one, or both?

AN: Ted had invented the legal-sized concept for *C*. It is practical—you get much more per page—but it is also a great size for longer po-

Alice Notley 175

ems and open-field poems, the kinds of forms we were all working in. It gives a feeling of lavishness and generosity, of openness.

SA: I have to admit that I'm envious of the seriousness with which these magazines were received. The magazines, too, are serious and also enormously entertaining (I think it's Reva Wolf who talks a little bit about this in her book on gossip). It reminds me of Ted's statements that poetry is twenty-four hours a day. Do you think the broader community had that attitude as well? Did the entertainment factor come from the humor in the poems? From a kind of collaborative milieu?

AN: I think more people were operating then on the principle that being a poet or artist was continuous and all-encompassing. Not as many people were teaching, for one thing, or if they were, the job wasn't as time-consuming and brain-destroying as it is now. Rents were relatively cheaper, and there was perhaps more extra money around, though I think it was really about the rent. The entertainment factor comes from the humor and wit, but also a certain gossipiness about and in the poems themselves—you could always figure out who was sleeping with who from what you were reading, for example. This is not necessarily a bad thing—it's probably a little bit better (in terms of readability) than the Look Ma How Innovative I Am mood of much of the now contemporary work. I myself didn't like collaborations all that much and didn't do it often; they didn't entertain me except for when they were really funny or striking.

SA: I've thought a bit about the ephemerality of such publications, and their immediacy, but I'm not sure I had really yet conceived of the importance of frequency until you mentioned it. I must admit that I love that about *CHICAGO*—a kind of vibrancy resulting (perhaps?) from speed and immediacy. Do you think other contemporaneous publications shared that feeling? Would you be willing to expand on the idea that *CHICAGO* contained a kind of comment and commentary? Across the issues (via content), or within a larger publishing community, or both/neither?

AN: Coming out often was the whole thing. I think *CHICAGO*, though,

176   *Women in Independent Publishing*

came out more frequently than any other magazine. This was how the sense of comment and commentary was created: The same poets from issue to issue providing a sense of continuity—it's like an aesthetic diary. But also, there's so much variety of form in these issues: not just poetry and kinds of poetry, but prose and a travel journal, an excerpt from a pornographic novel, art, an interview, translations, etc. The first issue contains Jimmy Schuyler's latest poems written as a consequence of his most recent stay in a mental institute: He had wigged out again and written the works. That has very deep gossip value, aside from the fact that the poems are amazing.

SA: I would love to hear more about the dramatic sense of change from Chicago to England. Certainly, the European editions feel much different, even based simply on size and production alone.

AN: The European *CHICAGO*s are in A4 size, which is the longest European size. So the magazine became more compact. But it also included British writers (including my second husband to be, Doug Oliver). I am able to get poems from different kinds of people coming through—I see that I published Allen Ginsberg here, and [George] Oppen, for example. These are people coming over for international festivals; a different tone. Carl Rakosi. And I catch up some more with the younger Chicago people; it's kind of all coming together. And George finally decides to put the word *CHICAGO* on the cover (now that I'm in England).

Do you have *The End of the Far West* by Frank O'Hara? That was Ted's contribution to the European editions, an edition of eleven poems of O'Hara's that were intended to go together but were never published together in his lifetime. I published them—but Ted typed them, he really wanted to, and they were influencing his writing, then in process, of the sequence *Easter Monday*. You can see that it's his typewriter, not mine. I did the covers.

SA: I love that the legal-sized paper is associated with the open-field technique. I had a sense, when reading around, that poets were moving in this direction (kind of post Ted's *Sonnets*), but I wasn't certain. Do you think this influence came directly from Olson or

Alice Notley 177

more circuitously? I also love that it links the typewriter/mimeo-graph with poetic technique.

AN: The open-field technique. Olson was partly in mind but nobody got it directly from him. For someone like Ron Padgett Mallarmé was involved, for Ted there were Paul Blackburn and Philip Whalen—but we were all heavily affected by William Carlos Williams. Some-one like Anne would be getting it from Ted a lot—and from Phil, and there were some people off to the side who liked Duncan. Also, of course, there were the open-field works of O'Hara, certain of the Odes and "Biotherm"; he was getting it from Williams, I think. Wil-liams died in '63, and just prior to that *Pictures from Breughel* (with *The Desert Music* and the variable foot poems inside) came out, which totally influenced O'Hara. I myself wrote a paper on "Asphodel, That Greeny Flower" when I was an undergraduate circa '66 and had never heard of any of my future friends, and I've never gotten over the influence of that particular poem, though I don't write open-field poetry much. Oh, and some people were influenced directly by Pound. I think it was all mixed up.

SA: How much was a kind of "professionalization" part of the more uto-pian (that's not the right word, but it gets near what I want) idea of poetry 24/7?

AN: I don't know how to answer that one. Anyone had a sense that they were professional poets and were owed consideration as such. One insisted on oneself as a professional. Some people sent out a lot and some people waited to be asked . . . No one sent out to places like *Poetry*, at least after the very beginning, before they found friends and friendly journals. I think I may have done so once.

SA: I am still thinking about frequency, and the idea that the poets created continuity across the issues. I get the definite impression that by issue 4.6 the geography spreads out farther. The European editions seem kaleidoscopic in their inclusiveness—more authors, etc. Did the stay in England feel differently global than that in Chicago? By which I mean: Was it easier to meet a variety of po-ets?

AN: I felt much more isolated in England, much less taken seriously as

178 *Women in Independent Publishing*

a poet. England was very very painful. It's hard for me to be specific about this; I did meet a lot of poets, but I didn't get to see them as much as part of the daily flow of things. I lived in a village in Essex, I had a bad post-partum depression, I had one small child and was expecting another. However, I managed to do a lot: I wrote my first long poem there, *Songs for the Unborn Second Baby*. I did three issues of the magazine. I read all the contemporary poetry books in the library of the University of Essex. I have very little memory of the festivals, though I do remember seeing W. H. Auden read his poems in his bedroom slippers (he always wore them), I remember when Ted genially insulted Robert Bly onstage, and I remember Oppen's reading voice. These are two different festivals. In different circumstances I met Basil Bunting, who liked me, Anselm as baby, and my reading with Ted. One time Ted and I gave a reading together, when I was about seven months pregnant, and he told me afterward, very solemnly, that I had won the reading. I, of course, hadn't known, but I think it was true; I had an unfair advantage being pregnant, and there were a lot of young women in the audience (this was in Wales).

SA: The overlay of genres does seem to me to be incredibly important; I feel like it didn't happen as much in other small journals of the time (though that's a generalization of which I'm uncertain; I'm thinking of *C, o TO 9, Angel Hair*). Were you editing with the intention of including many genres? Or was it more about exciting work in general?

AN: I read every kind of book there was, I liked all kinds of genres and still do, and people wrote in a lot of different ways then. People tried out all sorts of things in case they could do it—usually they couldn't; they were just poets.

SA: I've been thinking lately about how many of the poems in *CHICAGO* seem to fall into spaces of transition (not as much temporally, since they're often quite specific in dating the poems, but spatially). How they sometimes present location as kaleidoscopic. Were the authors generally moving around quite a lot? Was there a lot of talk of travel?

AN: The authors were traveling around a lot, and it is perspicacious of you to see that. We were, mostly, young and in motion, trying out different cities. People's relationships broke up often, no one was that sure of who they were or wanted to be. That wasn't the same as traveling as in tourists—I don't remember people voyaging to see different places so much as changing addresses. It was easier to be mobile then, too; rents were a lot cheaper, people stayed with each other more easily, residences were roomier, etc. And a certain amount of discovery of Europe was going on; there was an English scene that Americans could connect with; a perhaps smaller French one.

SA: I'd like to bring up some particular pieces. With the Brownstein poems in 2.2/3, I adore how the small poems are arranged across pages, so that the page acquires its own rhythm-space. (I assume this is your layout and genius.) I was also thinking about how some of these longer sections (like Brownstein's here) are chapbook-length. One gets such a feel for the poets' projects.

AN: Michael Brownstein did not appreciate my layout; he had wanted a straight-down-the-page presentation and was angry after the issue came out. I was, however, working with a different page size than he was. He may still be mad at me.

SA: The Harris Schiff piece in 4.6—!!! Do you remember choosing to place it first?

AN: I don't remember choosing to place Harris's piece first, but it is an obvious read-me-right-now choice. Though I know one might also place it last. Readers have more energy at the beginning of a volume, don't they? But I was very taken by the piece; it seemed like "the news."

SA: Volume 6 seems to me to be a culmination of sorts. It's called a "double issue" (though I haven't counted pages and am uncertain how much larger it is than other issues), and I see that the cover utilizes images from the previous covers. Did you (and George Schneeman) know you were leaving Chicago when you put it together? Were you thinking about it as a final issue (of sorts)?

AN: Yes, it's a double issue because I (and George) knew we were leaving for England and didn't know if I'd be able to continue publishing the magazine. It probably contains everything I had on hand and needed absolutely to publish.

SA: I ran across more mysterious "for Alice" poems today in the European edition number 3. The Tom Clark sequence is for you, of course, but is the Berkson ("Camera Ready, Like A Dream") as well?

AN: The Tom Clark sequence is dedicated to me for obvious reasons, but Tom is from Chicago and he's writing about himself. The Bill Berkson poem has to do with the fact that he published my book *Phoebe Light* (Big Sky Books)—he's talking about that. I think this book is very rare now, but they might have it in the collection you're working with. This will tell you even more about the small press publishing world of the time!

SA: "Great Balls of Fire," in the European edition number 2, seems like an interesting shift for you, though I may be (totally) mistaken on this. And I am very much taken with "Your Dailiness" in number 3—partly because of its form and partly because I've been thinking about ordinariness and everyday life (and various forms of domesticity) alongside editorial work and mobility/dis/relocations oh my, etc.

AN: I have absolutely no memory of writing "Great Balls of Fire," which is obviously an allusion to Ron's book by that title, which itself alludes to Jerry Lee Lewis's song. "Your Dailiness," though is one of my best poems; it was next published in my book *For Frank O'Hara's Birthday* and has appeared in both of my volumes of selected poems. I've never written better than that. It came to me rather miraculously: I saw the whole poem one morning, word for word, and then gradually wrote it down. I mean that literally—I saw all the words of it.

SA: I'm starting to see some difference between the European editions and the others. For example, there seems be a kind of multigenerationality in European edition number 3, and perhaps a more determined overlay of different forms. Do you remember what made you decide to end with the reprint of the Kerouac piece? As with volume 6, did you know that it was going to be the last issue in this edition?

AN: It's so hard to remember anything. The Kerouac piece would have suddenly come into my possession; maybe Ted called my attention to it. Kerouac died in '69—Ted was in Ann Arbor and I was visiting him from Iowa City. Anne Waldman called him while he was at work; he came back to the room where he lived, and I was staying, and collapsed, as they say, into my arms. This would be a newspaper clipping—I don't know why it would have turned up in England; I just can't remember. Yes, I knew it was going to be the last European edition. I didn't know for sure that it would be the last issue. This issue, again, should be seen in tandem with *The End of the Far West* by Frank O'Hara, the little booklet typed by Ted with covers by myself that accompanied it.

SA: I very much like your Art Institute essay in *Brilliant Corners* number 1. Were there other Chicago places in which you spent a fair amount of time? Any music venues?

AN: I really only went to the Art Institute, at least consistently. Everything else I attended was tied to poetry.

SA: Regarding European edition number 1: It seems to me like the interview is such a keystone for the issue. It really inflects, I think, the issue's curation—the discussion of groups (or the lack thereof) puts more emphasis on the single poets in the issue, perhaps. Of course, Oppen and Ginsberg together are an interesting overlay. Were you thinking of any of this as you were putting the issue together?

AN: I don't think "curate" or "curation" are at all the right words for editing *CHICAGO*. I edited it. I did soliciting of manuscripts, selecting of work, all correspondence, layout, typing, collating, mailing. "Curator" is a pukey word suggesting someone in an expensive suit with a chunky amber necklace; I think of myself in a state of late pregnancy in one of my two wearable garments nonetheless walking about the page-strewn room collating. Please PLEASE let me be

182   *Women in Independent Publishing*

the editor, you know like Harold Ross with the *New Yorker*. Look up "curator" in the dictionary; everything about it is awful.

I wasn't very interested in the idea of groups. Ted's idea of the New York School was that it was, essentially, a joke: You could join it if you gave him five dollars. "The Objectivists" was a kind of joke too, wasn't it? What a group of friend poets called themselves, in order to get Williams interested in them, before WWII blew them all out of the water. I myself am only interested in single poets . . . It's worth noting here that Allen Ginsberg was extremely interested in the poetry of Oppen's friend Reznikoff, a fellow New Yorker and noticer of concrete detail as the city displays it.

SA: A more general question: Do you remember any sense of your editorial intentions shifting as the magazine progressed, and as you moved from Chicago to England?

AN: Simply I was in contact with different single poets when the magazine moved, largely poets who spoke a different kind of English. The differences between American and British English cannot be overemphasized—the two poetries always sound more different than the page allows for, and I was fascinated by this. But the editing principle was always to find the poets and publish them.

SA: Some people I've been talking to here seem very excited about the possibility of exploring Chicago-based poetry as a way of combating what they see as the undue emphasis on the East and West Coasts in accounts of later-twentieth-century American poetry. Was any of this conversation happening at the time? It seems less likely, with so many people moving about. But was there an awareness of poetry "epicenters" or whatnot?

AN: Yes, there was a huge awareness of the poetry epicenter of New York, with the perhaps lesser one of the Bay Area. A lot of people hated New York for this reason. Ed Dorn was extremely hostile to NYC; Phil Whalen simply railed against the *New Yorker* magazine. Ted told young people who wanted to be poets that they had to go to New York. The advantage of New York lies partly in the way it's laid out—Manhattan, that is, creates the possibility of "community centers" easily gotten to by subway, if not walked to. San Francisco and

Chicago are by comparison much too spread out and divided up. Both cities are car-dependent even though there's relatively decent public transportation. The idea of an alternative Chicago-based poetry seems fanciful to me but very Chicago-like.

Figure 13. *Autumn Leaving* (2013) by Jaime Robles.

Jaime Robles

Coeditor, Five Trees Press (1973–1978, San Francisco)

OCTOBER 2014 TO JANUARY 2015, VIA E-MAIL, UPDATED JULY 2022

Stephanie Anderson: A Stanford University Special Collection roundup of "California Printers in the Fine Press Tradition" describes the press in the following:

> Three women founded Five Trees Press in a rented storefront in San Francisco's Noe Valley in 1973. Kathleen Walkup, Jaime Robles, and Cheryl Miller had become acquainted through Clifford Burke's Cranium Press, where Miller worked as an apprentice, and through Wesley Tanner at Arif Press in Berkeley. Each brought different skills and interests to the partnership, where they taught each other, working both independently and in mutually supportive ways. Most of the press's energy was devoted to printing, publishing and distributing small chapbooks of poetry written by women writers, some well-established, such as H. D. and Denise Levertov, and others whose work would not have been considered for publication by the predominantly male printing establishment. The press also published the work of cowboy poet Gino Clays Sky and the New England poet Paul Metcalf.

> Will you talk a little more about how you, Kathy, and Cheryl met? What kinds of "skills and interests" did you each have?

Jaime Robles: Five Trees Press was a publishing project within the larger collective of the Sanchez Street Press. Sanchez Street was five women: Kathleen Walkup, Cheryl Miller, and I who were Five Trees, and Cameron Bunker, who was studying bookbinding, and Eileen Callahan, who was also a significant partner in Turtle Island Press and ran her own imprint, Hipparchia Press. We worked out of a corner storefront at Sanchez and 26th Streets, San Francisco. We all met at Clifford Burke's press.

Clifford used to welcome people to Cranium Press on the weekends, inviting them to hang out, set type, and print broadsides. All these long-haired freaks would show up at Clifford's on the weekend to smoke dope, play basketball in the courtyard of the press, set type, print, and talk about books. This was the beginning of the seventies and the war in Vietnam had reached crisis levels. Many people took to the streets to protest, and printing political broadsides was an important part of the small press scene in San Francisco, especially at Cranium Press. Clifford also ran workshops on printing, and his wife, Diane, was a bookbinder. I think that's how Cheryl, Kathy, and Cameron arrived at the press; Cheryl also had an apprenticeship at Clifford's. Eileen knew Clifford because Turtle Island had hired him to print their Jaime de Angulo series. Eileen once showed up at Clifford's in a floor-length velvet cape. I had been pointed in Clifford's direction by a long chain of people that began with Kenneth Rexroth and included Tom Parkinson and Roger Levenson of Tamalpais Press in Berkeley.

It was revolutionary times. Just after the Free Speech Movement, new movements gripped the Bay Area. Civil rights, feminism, and Vietnam had made people, especially youth—and we were all very young at the time, most under thirty—restless and willing to challenge the establishment. The printing industry was primarily male run, just as writing and literary editing were male dominated. So, in the midst of that, what did five young women want to do? We wanted to create our own books in our own way. Kathy and Cheryl and I had larger ambitions of creating a press—one with a literary identity that created books that emphasized the beauty of the letterpress tradition but were also financially accessible. It was all very idealistic. Kathy had come from a political press in Boston, where she had worked with the collectives that produced the original *Our Bodies, Ourselves*. Kathy had strong offset-printing experience. Cheryl had arrived from the Midwest where she had been an active member in the feminist movement. She was interested in the traditional let-

terpress book that emphasized the beauty of the book's tactile qualities. I had studied poetry (with Kenneth Rexroth, Peter Whigham,
and Josephine Miles), English lit, and fine art. During college I had
puzzled over which path to follow, visual arts or writing. I had started
going over to Cranium Press while I was still at Cal in 1970. Making
ephemera and books addressed both visual and verbal arts; within
the printing format I could follow two practices I loved. I illustrated
most of the books at Five Trees.

SA: Will you describe the "predominantly male printing establishment"
of the Bay Area in 1973? What was it like to be a woman interested in
fine-press publishing?

JR: The letterpress community was different from the offset-printing
community, and I'll only describe the former because that's what
we worked in. There was only one real fine arts letterpress company, though—that is to say, a press printing letterpress editions for
bibliophiles and art collectors. The others were small presses using
letterpress to create a variety of radical and literary works. The Grabhorns, a pair of brothers, had run the fine press, along with the much
younger Andrew Hoyem, who took over the Grabhorn Press when the
brothers died. Hoyem, now retired, ran this press under the imprint
of Arion Press. Jane Grabhorn, Robert's wife who died in 1973, ran the
Colt and Jumbo Presses, very witty and satiric fine presses. She wrote
and designed her pieces but did not print them; nonetheless, it's a joy
to read the very wacky ephemera that she wrote and had printed in
black and red. The Grabhorn Press was in the tradition of the great
San Francisco printers like John Henry Nash. They printed for major
publishing houses and did many of the books for the Book Club of
California. Supporting organizations such as the Book Club of California and the Roxburghe Club did not allow women to be members,
or even come to functions except for once or twice a year. They were
just snooty men's clubs, like old British gentlemen's clubs. Needless to
say, book club organizations like that really got up our noses.

It was small press that really interested us. Much of the avant-
garde poetry that came out of the San Francisco Renaissance and the
Beats was printed letterpress, and the publisher-printers included

Auerhahn Press (Dave Haselwood), White Rabbit Press (Graham Mackintosh), Cranium Press (Clifford Burke), Zephyrus Image and Hermes Free Press (Holbrook Teter and Michael Myers), Tamalpais Press (Roger Levenson), Arif Press (Wesley Tanner and Alastair Johnston). These presses printed everyone from Robert Duncan and Jack Spicer to Ed Dorn and Ken Irby, plus a spectrum of political writing. Holbrook and Michael made a number of cryptic political items against the war and later calling for Nixon's impeachment. Though the men our age were more or less gracious about our interest in printing, there remained in our minds a barrier to be crossed. And I believe there was a barrier to be crossed in the minds of the men. It was with some heat that Cheryl would refer to Holbrook Teter's title for us: The Ladies. No one was entirely comfortable with us.

Though to be fair, the barriers had also to do with our being young and trying to secure our identities as artists and craftsmen. The misogyny that existed was the standard cultural one: that of women being ignored or discounted as less than serious. A problem we continue to suffer from. And of course, we were not being paid or recognized adequately. The latter, though, was something everyone suffered from, male and female; the difference was a matter of degree.

There were two other women interested in printing and small press publishing in the Bay Area at the time: Frances Butler and Betsy Davids. Frances, who was a designer, collaborated with Alastair Johnston at Poltroon Press. And Betsy, who was a writer, had Rebis Press with artist-photographer Jim Petrillo. Johanna Drucker was Betsy's student at California College of Arts and Crafts. Johanna has gone on to be a cultural critic of language and book arts, as well as a writer and artist. Frances, Betsy, and Johanna were located in the East Bay and we were in San Francisco, so we were not as close to them as we might have been. The small press world in the Bay Area was small, but there were divisions of locale, which were based in divisions of time and energy. Even so, everyone knew everyone else.

SA: Your *Eva Awakening* is very nicely done, and in a small-ish edition of 150. Was this one of the first Five Trees books? Who did the beautiful flower prints throughout the text?

JR: Thanks. *Eva* was our second book and my first book. The first press book was *Crocus/Sprouting*. I did all the work for *Eva Awakening*, including the drawings, except for pasting the book blocks into the cover, which was done by Cheryl's boyfriend Richie Berman, who at the time worked at Ferlinghetti's City Lights. The drawings were done in pen and ink, converted into zinc plates for letterpress, and tinted with linocuts. It's easier to reproduce artwork that's in pen and ink or tint blocks in letterpress. Halftones tend to be murkier. There were actually closer to 120 books made when all was sewn and pasted.

SA: I was recently able to look at a copy of *Crocus/Sprouting* in Special Collections. The cover is absolutely gorgeous—perfectly printed, with, I think, three colors/letterpress plates and then tinted? Your cover drawing is very elegant. What sparked your interest in, as you put it above, "books that addressed both visual and verbal arts"?

JR: That interest is part of my mission in life, I suppose. Both my parents were visual artists, and there are a number of artists on my father's side of the family. My uncle and his wife ran one of the more prominent art galleries in Los Angeles, Esther Robles Gallery, which was known for its support of women and California artists. So I grew up with lots of visual arts skills, and they have served me well keeping me employed. But along with that skill, visual art in my family was rife with ambivalence. My mother especially struggled with recognition and being validated as an artist. When I went to college, I became an English lit major. I loved poetry and have since an early age. I also wrote a fair amount of poetry as a kid. I was so bored in high school, I would stay home, playing hooky from school with a feigned illness, and write poetry. So, by the time I was a young adult, I had two skills that both rocked me: one, poetry, because I loved it, and two, art, because it was second nature to me. It was at university that the possibility of combining the two was presented to me, in an exhibition of the work from a letterpress-printing class run by art teacher Gary Brown and poet-translator Peter Whigham. I wasn't able to take the class, but I got a friend of mine to show me how to use the class's Vandercook press.

SA: How many books did the press do, total?

JR: Not that many really; maybe ten or so. The press only lasted a few years. The medium is slow and we were learning on the job. None of us had any money. We all needed to make a living, so we all had jobs as well. The press never paid for us; it was just something we were enthralled with. In the late seventies I traveled to Europe and stayed there over two years, which was great for me. It changed my life. But by the time I got back, the press was defunct.

SA: In 1975 Five Trees printed H. D.'s *The Poet & The Dancer*. I'm intrigued by this little book—I think (am I right?) that this is the press's one publication by an earlier modernist. Do you remember how that project came about? Were poetic lineage and women writer predecessors much discussed?

JR: Yes, we were all very aware of our lineage, not only that of the book world but of literature and women writers. The first few books we did were more or less spontaneous acquisitions. Then we began to think we needed a publishing policy, something that would direct our choices beyond making attractive and affordable books. We decided to publish in threes: one known woman writer, one unknown woman writer, one historically relevant woman writer. I'm not sure how we shoehorned in our first few books into that concept, but the H. D. was part of that policy. The acquisition of the text itself was interesting. It came from Eileen Callahan, who was part of the larger Sanchez Street collective. Eileen and her husband, Bob Callahan, ran Turtle Island Press and were very politically active and historically savvy. They had contacted H. D.'s executor Norman Holmes Pearson for a manuscript by H. D., and he had released that piece for publication. Pearson was known to be a difficult executor to deal with. Turtle Island decided not to do the book. I'm not certain why, but I think because it wasn't long enough for their publishing format.

The poem itself had not been republished since its earlier magazine publication in the 1930s. At that time, early seventies, H. D. had not quite undergone the validation that she has now; she was fairly unknown, lost in a way, and definitely not as secure within the literary canon as she currently is. I had studied her in college because I took a twentieth-century poetry class with an English poet and translator, Peter Whigham. He was rather grudging about her as a poet. Rather grudging about women writers in general, truth be told. In any event, we were all thrilled to be publishing the manuscript. It's a lovely poem. Kathy Walkup did the design; I did the illustration and the hardcover binding; and I think Kathy and Cheryl did the printing. It was handset, though I can't remember which of us did that; perhaps it was a joint effort. That was also part of our method: that we would all shift around design, typesetting, printing, and binding responsibilities.

SA: More generally, how did the press acquire manuscripts?

JR: That was easy. You open any kind of press, and you are immediately swamped with manuscripts. But most of the manuscripts came to us via friends. I think that remains the model for most presses: you print your friends. And there is some validity to that. After all, you know them and their work better than anyone else.

SA: Would you say that a community formed around the press? Was it always the five of you doing production, or did others occasionally help? Were there release parties for the books?

JR: The entire small press community was quite close-knit at the time. It was just the three of us, really, doing production for Five Trees. The only times that others joined in were the ones I've mentioned. We did consult with other printers. We would go over to Clifford's or Andy Hoyem's or Wesley's and ask how to do this or that. And a group of small press people helped us move equipment when it needed to be moved, which is a huge job. And there were lots of release parties. Great parties to which everyone would bring ephemera, broadsides, and booklets to be shared rather than bought. When Five Trees moved to the York Street studio with Cranium Press and Jungle Press, there was a huge party—over three hundred people showed up. Everyone in the small press community and many from the writing community showed up. Everyone brought friends. Even Valenti Angelo showed up. He had been an illustrator for a series of mainstream crossover fine-press books printed by the Grabhorns for Random House. He was a very formal and gentlemanly man. He was eighty-something when we had that party, and

192 *Women in Independent Publishing*

he showed up in his suit and tie to watch the wild children dance around the press. We cleared out an area for a dance floor, had a fabulous music tape, lots of food and drink, and everyone had a terrific time. Five Trees made pretty little dance cards for the party, printed in pink and green with silky tassels, and Alastair Johnston went around collecting the signatures of the artists he knew there. I'm not sure what happened, but in the eighties a lot of that communal closeness faded away. People moved out of the area, got jobs, found other interests, and, of course, competition eventually began to drive people apart. The communal joy sort of dissolved.

SA: What was, for you, the press's most memorable project?

JR: Well, there was no one project that was most memorable. I suppose, for me, *Eva Awakening*, because it was the first book that I made in its entirety. But the Denise Levertov book, *Modulations for Solo Voice*, was probably the most significant. I'm not even sure that the poetry in that book was ever published elsewhere. It was something she wanted published privately and in a limited edition. It was a series of love poems to a man she had had an affair with outside her marriage. There was a lot of emotion around it. Surely, by now, it's been republished.

SA: You mentioned, in opening, the "revolutionary times" of the early seventies and the protests against and broadsides about the war in Vietnam. How do you think that climate influenced your artistic development?

JR: I'm not sure it influenced my artistic development as much as my personality and my sense of social responsibility. I've been in Berkeley for the past two nights, and there have been ongoing demonstrations about the murders of African Americans by the police around the country, not just in Ferguson. Hordes of people out on the streets, helicopters overhead, police everywhere. The huge injustices of the world have not gone away. The United States has been at war in 225 years of the 243 years since 1776. We are currently engaged in 102 conflicts around the globe. That is just staggering. I don't go out and demonstrate at the moment, but I do write about it. I went back to protesting in the streets after Trump's 2016 election, though the pandemic has stopped that for many of us.

SA: Have you had difficulty finding a publisher? What do you think of the contemporary small press publishing scene?

JR: Well, I'm rather lazy when it comes to looking for a publisher for my work. I found myself so exhausted after my PhD work—the exhaustion was about changing countries so often in four years, even more than doing the degree—that I haven't been eager about publishing or seeking publication. It might be great never to look for publication again. That would be kind of refreshing. But when I've looked for a publisher, I have been able to find one. I'm working on another manuscript about fire; though it's not yet a completed book manuscript, I have published quite a few of the poems in journals and online. Someday it hopes to be a book. In the meantime I do continue to self-publish smaller series of poems I've written in microscopic editions.

The great thing about the contemporary small press scene is that there is so much of it, and it takes so many shapes; the current technology allows for a variety of publication, from books to online sites, and the publication can be done by anyone with the desire and energy to get texts and images out in the world. Technology allows for never-ending hybrids. I think that's great. Everyone should be able to express his or herself; there will always be an audience somewhere. And overlapping media—languages, images, still and moving, and music—encourages innovation in that expression. Though I'm not a big fan of the presses who won't publish the people they know, who are their friends, believing that that makes the press somehow more democratic or more objective and therefore somehow more politically correct or aesthetically true or fairer in some grand sense. That's kind of old-fashioned. It's like believing that the larger corporate publishing world has some more accurate authority about whose work merits publication and isn't run by connections. Art is always intensely subjective; that's what gives it its value, not the opposite. If you are going to take on the burden of publishing (and it is a burden because it's deeply detail oriented, requires a fairly sophisticated understanding of technology, and is costly), I recommend publishing the work you love by the people you love. Who else knows your work better than those who know you and what moves you? Make it a gift, or an

194   *Women in Independent Publishing*

act of love. And if someone likes your work well enough to publish it, then be nice to them. Respond to their generosity.

SA: What was your doctoral research on?

JR: My doctorate is in English literature, creative writing, from the University of Exeter, UK. My critical theory part of the dissertation was titled: *Dark Lyrics: Studying the Subterranean Impulses of Contemporary Poetry*. What I was looking at in the critical theory part of the thesis was the idea that poetry is generated from darker emotional states within the poet. This was tied into the idea that was the basis for the creative part of the thesis, which later became the collection *Hoard*. The poems use a buried treasure found in the UK as the central metaphor for how we treat our emotions. Like the precious objects buried by the Anglo Romans to secure and protect them, we bury our most precious emotions deep in the body and their interiority becomes our subconsciously fueled inspiration.

SA: What are some of your career highlights in the time since you worked on Five Trees, and what are you currently working on?

JR: My work since then has been diverse but also more divided, one skill from the other. I am working less as an editor, publisher, and book designer, but I've taken more care with my writing. The past two books I did—*Anime, Animus, Anima* and *Hoard*—were published in the UK by the excellent poetry house Shearsman Books; I really admire Tony Fraser's poetic expertise, so that's an honor. The books are kind of cross-cultural studies, really. The first about the world of Japanese anime, especially that which deals with the body, AI, and what it means to be conscious. The Shinto religion enables the culture to look at the material world as endowed with spirit: rocks, trees, the wind. That is a religious idea that I respond to more deeply than any other. There is also a lot of looking at the East looking at the West looking at the East in the book. *Hoard* takes its inspiration from a cache of Anglo-Roman jewelry buried in the English countryside, the Hoxne treasure, which was recovered in 1992 and is currently in the British Museum.

I'm now enjoying doing visual art and making large installations that mix poetry and imagery. Two of them used a beautiful

Victorian masonry wall on the University of Exeter campus—one, titled *Autumn Leaving*, is a selection of dried leaves that I printed with fragments of poems from a series called White Swan, which was published in *Hoard*, and the second installation, *The Wittgenstein Vector*, used poems and images that were responses to the *Tractatus* of Ludwig Wittgenstein. The latter I did with Mike Rose-Steel and Suzanne Steele in our collaborative identity as Exegesis. Another "jumping off the page" has been working with musicians. In 2014 I worked with Ann Callaway, who is a wonderful composer. We collaborated on a chamber opera, *Vladimir in Butterfly Country*, about Nabokov's love of butterflies. Today my musical adventures are less formal.

Most recently, I edited and produced a selection of the writings and artwork of the abstract-expressionist Sam Francis (*Cobalt Blue*, 2019) for the Sam Francis Foundation in the Los Angeles area. I worked for Sam during the latter half of the eighties, organizing the letterpress division of his publishing house, the Lapis Press, so the foundation asked me to do this project. I edited and selected the writing, designed the book, and managed the production. It was printed in China just before the onset of the pandemic. It's a gorgeous book, the printing is spectacular, the reproduction work of the highest quality now possible. Sam wasn't a bad poet, and it was kind of fun to read his many journals and revisit his thoughts and personality. I was able to choose, along with his former assistant Nancy Mozur, my favorite pieces among his monotypes and works on paper.

Currently, though, I'm working on a manuscript that started out as a series of poems about the cataclysmic fire of the global disaster of climate change. This fire that is becoming legendary is not only caused by climate change but also fuels it. There are also poems on sexual desire as a kind of fire, and poems about ritual celebrations using fire. The latter is also a cross-cultural series, emphasizing fire rituals in Asia.

SA: What was your favorite aspect of working for the press?

JR: I like making things.[1] That's my favorite thing of all things. It was then and it is now. Every day, if I'm not actually physically making things, I'm thinking about making them.

Figure 14. Barbara Barg and Rose Lesniak in their Bowery loft, 1978. Photo by Tim Milk.

Barbara Barg and Rose Lesniak

Coeditors, Out There (1973–1979, Chicago); Editor (Barg), Power Mad Press (1979–1981, New York); Producer (Lesniak), Out There Productions (1979–1988)

BARG: JANUARY 19, 2014, IN PERSON, CHICAGO
LESNIAK: APRIL 25, 2020, VIA FACETIME

Stephanie Anderson: [*recording begins mid-conversation*] So what was your press in New York?[1]

Barbara Barg: It was called Power Mad Press. We took the logo from Arm & Hammer Baking Soda, where it has the arm holding a hammer. Joseph Chassler, that was my boyfriend, he redrew it and made it look like the guy's hitting his shoulder with the hammer; it's kind of funny. It gave a certain ring to Power Mad. So yeah, we had this typesetting shop, Skeezo Typography. S-K-E-E-Z-O. I did these books—one of Bob Holman's, one of Eileen Myles's—because the thing was, back then, if you just had a chapbook, you couldn't really get it into the bookstores unless it had a spine.

SA: Right.

BB: So I decided I would start publishing books with a spine. I just couldn't deal with the administrative end of stuff, the forms and sending stuff out—that's why I never applied for grants or anything. I just would get them printed and I would say, "Okay, here, you distribute it." [*laughs*] And they would.

SA: What kind of technology did you have for the typesetting?

BB: Well, we had the first kind of machine that kind of made typesetting become more of a cottage industry. It was called the Compugraphic 7500. There's even a Facebook group on it because it kind of revolutionized the typesetting industry.

SA: Oh, cool.

BB: This was before computers. It looked about the size of a little spinet piano. It had a screen, and it had a keyboard, and it then had this thing here with all the chemicals where the paper would come through, and everything would come out in one long strip. In fact, I have a PDF on my website of this chapbook called *Obeying the Chemicals*, and the first poem in it, it just came out. It was four feet long; there were no breaks. But the screen itself looked more like DOS. I don't know if you remember DOS, before Windows?

SA: I do.

BB: It looked like that. And you'd see all the little instructions, coding and stuff. I think the most adventurous thing we typeset was a Hannah Weiner book, *Little Books / Indians*.[2] It had these parts in it where each letter would be like a stair step. So we typeset it, and Chassler would spend hours just pasting up each little letter in the exact spot. He was the paste-up guy.

SA: How involved were you with *Out There* when it was publishing?

BB: I don't know what the history of *Out There* was before Neil Hackman, but he was doing it, and then Rose took it over from him. I can't remember if Rose had already taken a class from Ted [Berrigan], or if we both started with Ted at the same time, but I offered to help with *Out There*. While I'm not good with filling out forms and stuff, I'm really good at typing and putting that kind of stuff together.

SA: Are you detail oriented like that?

BB: I'm just a fast typist. Well—when putting things together I'm detail oriented. Other stuff, not so much. But anyways we just sort of started doing it together and running the reading series. [Rose] was officially the head of it, but we pretty much did it a lot together. Because she moved in with me and Chassler, and she was like our kid sister. Although there were lots, *lots* of rumors about "what was actually going on with Chassler and Rose and Barbara." Everyone thought we were having some, I don't know—

SA: Polyamorous relationship?

BB: Yeah. So don't tell them—take away the [recorder]—naw, I don't care. Yeah, so we did that until we left Northeastern [Illinois University] and went to New York. She kept *Out There* going a little bit.

I don't know if the poetry magazine *Out There* survived as a North-eastern publication, but I think we might have done a couple of issues when we got to New York. That was before the typesetting machine.

SA: What year did you go to New York?

BB: '77. Rose has become this incredible dog trainer; she just sent me a video being interviewed on the news.

SA: Oh, wow.

BB: So she moved in with us when we lived in Chicago, and then we all moved to New York together. That little community also was together for something like, seven, eight, nine years? Something like that. Then things got kinda dark because of all the drugs and stuff. Rose left, and then Chassler and I split up, and then she went back and I hung out with Rose. And then she—I'm not sure what year, maybe '85, '84—she moved to Miami.

SA: Do you remember when Eileen Myles was doing *dodgems*? I think there was one in '77 and one in '79.

BB: Yeah, that was a great magazine.

SA: And then I hear there were these mythic collating parties for *Telephone*.

BB: Well, yeah, for just about anything. For the *Poetry Project Newsletter*, for anything that had to be collated that was, you know, there would be collating parties and people would get together and just have fun.

SA: Yeah. Do you feel like when the technology changed to offset and whatnot, there wasn't as much kind of community involvement?

BB: Well, people got mad at me because I offered to typeset the *Poetry Project Newsletter* for free, because I was really *into* technology. I was one of the first people to have a computer, and people would say, "I'm never getting a computer; I'm writing my poetry with a pen and ink." And I was really into that stuff. Like when the IBM self-correcting Selectric typewriter came out, I thought, "Oh my God, this is *amazing*. Self-correcting!" Even when Wite-Out was invented! That's how old I am. It was all carbon copies, but when Wite-Out was invented, it was like, "Oh my God, I can correct this?!" [*both laugh*]

SA: You weren't sad to see mimeo go?

BB: Well, I liked the idea of it, and I was very good at typing stencils with not many mistakes. But once I got that typesetting machine—that's what got me started into it. So yeah, I think things changed. One thing about Ted is he was really good at energizing a community and community activities, like hosting readings, putting out small press magazines, getting together and doing collaborations, hanging out—you know, living the life of a poet. So even though the collating parties didn't happen, there were so many other ways to be a community. One of the major things that changed the community in New York was economics, you know? When I went there, and even well into the nineties, you could get a waitressing job, or [get work at one of] the financial houses, and a lot of firms had *tons* of word-processing work. You know, like computer-related things. I did help desk, and computer training, and I had a job with this company that helped firms transfer from DOS to Windows, and trained the people, and stuff like that. There was *tons* of that kind of work that you could get. And you could really support yourself easily and get a *fairly* reasonable rent in the East Village or places like that. So everybody was able to live, and live in the same area. Because it was vertical instead of horizontal, we had a lot of energy packed into a small space, and I think that really was a major factor in fueling all of that. But as the place started getting more gentrified . . . I left before the crash, but, you know, the whole environment for supporting that kind of thing just wasn't there anymore. I lived in a six-story tenement—the East Village was mostly tenements—apartments in the front, apartments in the back, dingy little hallway, garbage cans off to the side in the hallway, you know. The landlady had several buildings, she lived down the block, and some really rich guy, after it became cool to live in the East Village, got an apartment there. I was paying my rent one day, and he's complaining about the condition of the hallways, and da da da da da—it's like he expected there to be a doorman or something? She was just looking at him, and she was looking at me, and I was looking at her. I said, "If that's what you want, you shouldn't have moved into an

East Village tenement." And he said, "Well, you may like to live in a shithole, but I don't!"

SA: Wow!

BB: But the rent was low, you know?

SA: Yeah. In some of the reminiscences I've read of that time it seems like people remember addresses, that those are major ways they kind of, like, organized their memory. "When I lived at this place, we were at this place, and so-and-so lived at this place . . ." Which is impressive because people seem to have moved around quite a lot too.

BB: Did you ever read that book, *Slaves of New York*? It was kind of about, if you were lovers with someone and the lease was in their name, you had to stay with them? Because it was harder to find an apartment . . . [*both laugh*] That's the sort of time when it was hard to find an apartment. But, yeah, there was a lot more mobility. And then there were people who were in rent-controlled apartments who wouldn't give up their apartments for anything; my last apartment I got was rent-controlled—it was two and-a-half rooms, but I just stayed there because I was paying under $700. I got there in 1986, and was paying $420, and by 2005 I was still under $700.

SA: That's great.

BB: Because they could only raise it a little. Rent-controlled is when it doesn't change at all but rent-stabilized it can go up a little bit. They can't kick you out unless you do something illegal. A new landlord bought the building, and he gave me thousands and thousands of dollars to give up my lease.

SA: Wow.

BB: I was about to turn sixty. That's when I decided—I don't know why—to move to Denver. I mean, I knew Maureen [Owen], and I knew some people at Boulder and stuff . . . I think I thought, oh, I'll live in the West, I've never lived in the West. But I moved there and immediately he started charging $2,500. He did a little cosmetic work, but. And, *and*, it was riddled with bedbugs! That's another reason I wanted to get out.

SA: Yeah, eeeee.

BB: I did a band all through the nineties and didn't do a lot of poetry. I'd go to readings and stuff, but I didn't stay abreast the way I had in the seventies and eighties. And then in the early part of the century, Chassler died, my mother died, the band broke up, and I was out of work for a while—I kind of just didn't think much about poetry—I lost touch with the poetry world. When I got to Denver I got back in touch with it somewhat; I'd go to readings.

SA: What was your band?

BB: Maggie Dubris was the guitar player. She and I started a poetry band. It was kind of a cult band in New York for about ten years.

SA: I remember Cassandra [Gillig] saying that she found you on . . . there's a video that she likes of Anne Waldman doing Plutonium?

BB: Well, Rose did those—that was Out There Productions. Rose started doing some video stuff, she did one of Ginsberg and Bob Holman and Anne. Oh God, I know, I've seen that on YouTube. That was pretty funny. When we were trying to think of a name for the band, because it was a poetry band, we were gonna be Homer—and then Senator Jesse Helms, that's when [there was] the whole Mapplethorpe controversy, and Jesse Helms was anti–homoerotic art, so we thought, oh, Homer Erotic. Just seemed to go so well.

SA: Where would you perform?

BB: Chris Kraus had a seminar with Baudrillard at a casino at the state line of Nevada. She brought us out there and we played this casino with Baudrillard and her and all these other wild things. And we went to a music festival in town. Mostly we played all over New York, all the clubs where bands played. We never, like, played a stadium or anything.

SA: Would the Poetry Project scene come out for those shows too?

BB: Oh, yeah, a lot of support. I started playing drums in the late seventies or eighties, because that was the real big Patti Smith–influenced time. So poets and visual artists, everyone just picked up an instrument and started banging away. Like Chassler the philosopher, he picked up a bass and started playing bass. I was playing drums, and he was playing bass, and then this guy named Mike Sappol who's a poet and an incredible guitar player, really skilled, we all started a band called Avant Squares, and we all wrote songs. So I was in a bunch of those little bands, and then Maggie and I had both been in bands and all our bands had broken up and we were at a poetry reading and [said], "God, I'd like to play music again," so we said, "Oh, yeah, let's start a band." So we did. All those scenes were kind of interwoven. Because again, I think—partly geography and the vertical nature of the city . . .

SA: Was it all women?

BB: Mmhmm. This woman here [*points to picture*], she was like this high [*gestures height*], she was the drummer, and we'd go into clubs and there'd be all these tough punk-looking guys around. She'd be driving her drums in this little thing and they'd go [*makes a skeptical face*], and they'd get up there and they'd play their music 4/4, and she'd get up there and she'd be playing all this exotic stuff—and they were like [*makes a surprised face*]. I loved that. And then Andrea—she was my next-door neighbor too—Andrea and Susie, we all lived in the same building. She was an incredible violinist. There's a song on here called "After Agriculture" that is just amazing. So that became my life for ten years. I did write some stuff, and I still taught some here and there, I just wasn't as involved in the poetry scene. Just because—at the time I'd met Ted through the eighties it was intense poetry all the time, 24/7. You were always at someone's house or at a reading or doing the magazine or doing this and that. And then Ted dying, too, left kind of a big hole in the East Village.

SA: Yeah.

BB: I don't know; I just got way into music the way I'd gotten into poetry, so I started going to hear all my friends—we shared practice spaces and stuff. I guess I'll have to find some kind of geriatric community now.

SA: [*chuckles*] What about other possibilities for performance?

BB: Actually, I was kind of known as a performance poet and I never even set out to be one; it's just kind of the way I did things? I don't know; maybe it's because my dad made me go to tapdancing school when I was young? I'd done plays in high school and stuff. I never paid that much attention to performance poetry. Sometimes I'd

204   *Women in Independent Publishing*

pretend to be a Southern preacher . . . My major in school was an-thropology; I didn't even major in English except to take Ted's class, and I never paid that much attention to [perceived genre boundaries]. I mean, I read theory, like Kristeva, and the French guys, and different people like that. Chassler was very deep into theory. But I never really thought, oh, this person is this [type of artist] . . . Like Eileen [Myles], sometimes they'd do a play, sometimes they'd do a performance, sometimes they'd read a poem. I never thought, "This is the kind of poet I am, and here is my theory for this and this." Every piece—depending on what you were doing—was just trying to find its own form. Does that make sense?

SA: Totally. It seems quite balanced. Did it take some of the pressure off publication?

BB: I never felt any pressure about publication. [*chuckles*] All my friends were published in magazines, but it never dawned on me to send anything to the *New Yorker*—though I did apply for one grant. It was in prose, and this guy really liked my thing. I didn't get the grant, but he submitted my story—I was like the first, or one of the first women fiction writers to ever be published in *Playboy*.

SA: [*laughs*] Wow!

BB: [When they published me] they had their first woman fiction editor, so maybe that's why women were just getting in. And my agent—through trying to get me published, he fell madly in love with this [editor]. A couple of years later a bunch of *Playboy* editors were killed in a plane crash, and she was one of them, and he was very upset.

SA: Oh, wow . . .

BB: But it was just like that; I'd write stuff and somehow it would be published somewhere. Or somebody would ask me for something. I don't know why I was like that; I mean, it's not like I don't want to be published. Even today I'll send a few things out, but I don't even know where to send stuff anymore. Chris Kraus published my book.[3] And my friend in Paris had to bring me over to Paris and literally beat me over the head every day to get it finished, because I kept being so late. I don't know what that is about. It's not that I don't want to be published . . . I don't know what it is.

SA: Do you like publishing with smaller presses?

BB: Yeah. I really think that strengthening regional stuff is more interesting to me now than positing everything in one or two scenes, like in New York and San Francisco. There was this group called the Committee for International Poetry that was Simon Petit and Ginsberg, Bob Rosenthal and some others, and [they] hired me to be the host of this radio show. They had different groups of poets from different countries—a night of Indian readings, a night of Haitian poets, and this and that. They would tape them and I would transcribe the tapes. Usually they'd read in their native language, and somebody would read the English. So I would transcribe the tapes and put together these little radio shows. I was also very political. I mean people like Amiri Baraka and the Nuyoricans were always very political, but somehow at St. Mark's people were always saying, "[You] shouldn't write about politics!" I can understand you shouldn't write something particularly didactic, or something. But I grew up the only Jewish kid in my class, in the Southern Belt in this really racist town during the Civil Rights era, and I was doing all that. So my heart was always there. Listening to all these different poets, like the Haitian poets and the Caribbean poets—the people in their countries knew who they were, you know? They had the hearts of their people, and they weren't at all didactic. They spoke from the heart of a community.

SA: Yeah.

BB: That's something I really, really like. I'm not *against* other poetry—it's not like if you like one thing you hate the other thing. It's just this is where my interest lies. I would like to see poetry strengthened in all the regions and have regional poets who speak from the heart of their community, and everybody not vying to be in the flash scene, or something like that.

SA: I feel like in some ways the Internet has made things more diffuse . . . Like I have a little chapbook press here in Chicago. And, granted, I don't devote a ton of time to it, but I feel like it's hard to distribute the chapbooks *here*, you know? It's easy to put them online and have people order them through PayPal, but it's harder to kind of make people aware of them *here*.

206 *Women in Independent Publishing*

BB: Give them to the poets; tell them to distribute them! Why should you do all the work? You're putting the book out! [*both laugh*]

SA: Fair enough!

BB: I don't know; I have a website that I do myself, and I know so little, I'm all baby-ish. I did manage to get it into HTML5 recently, but I have a page that's called "Acquire" instead of "Buy" or "Store." I have a bunch of old poems from earlier days, and I'm just gonna make little books in PDF form, and people can download them if they want to—it doesn't have to be in a bookstore—that'll be the archeological evidence of it. Like I say, it's not that I'm *against* [publishing books]; I'm not trying to say, "This is the way it should be." Everybody has to go their own path. It's just where my energy is. If someone said, "I want to do your book, can you put together a book?" I'd say, "Yeah, that'd be great." And then I'd take about five years to put together a book, you know? No, it wouldn't be that long. I'm older and things don't seem as urgent, or the career part of it doesn't seem as important. Although I never felt much differently when I was young, but . . . I don't know. I'm rambling and I have no idea what I'm saying.

SA: What was it like when the Language poets started coming on the scene at the Poetry Project?

BB: From the time I was there they were always at the readings and stuff. I always liked them, and I got published in one of their anthologies, and we were typesetting [their] books . . . I didn't understand for a long time that it was this whole separate movement going this way and that way. They were just other poets on the scene . . .

SA: Yeah, it seems bizarre that it has become above the "movement" so much.

BB: Yeah, and then people started saying, "Ahh, they're taking over academia, and this and that, and they have their own Poetry Project . . ." [*chuckles*] But I'm just so far removed from academia I just could give a shit. I worked with a lot of high school students in New York. I'll tell you a funny story about Pedro Pietri; have you heard of him? He was a Nuyorican poet and playwright. Great, great guy. I got along well with the Nuyoricans because—I guess we all grew up where there was a lot of sun, a lot of heat and humidity. And some places, even in the midst of the East Village, could be quite segregated, which astonished me! In the South, in a lot of the art scenes, it would be more integrated because there was only one little scene, or something. But I loved the Nuyoricans, I hung out there a lot. So the whole teaching thing, too, was an Out There endeavor that Rose worked on. Pedro and I were coteaching this class, and it was the first day of class, and I got there first, and he—he did alcohol, so he was late. So I go to class, and these guys are sitting there like this. And a lot of these guys are in gangs, or doing drugs—dealing drugs, because they could make a lot more money dealing drugs than they could flipping burgers. So I'm in there, and I'm talking about poetry, and they're sitting there like I'm not writing poetry, poetry's for sissies, and the girls are going [*makes a high pitched noise*]. So they're like that, and Pedro walks in. And I said, "Oh, this is our coteacher, Pedro Pietri. Pedro, introduce yourself." He drops his bookbag on the floor, he takes out a book of his poems, and he starts reading: "Fuck the police! Da da da da da da, fuck the police! Da da da da." And the next thing you know, they're all poets. The next day this guy, he comes to school—I don't know where he got this image—he comes to school, he's wearing these black-frame glasses, he's wearing an old corduroy blazer with the patches on the elbow like an old English professor, and he's got a sheaf full of poems this big, and he's going around helping people write their poems. He just became a poet—he was outed, he came out of the closet—overnight.

SA: Wow.

BB: And you'd see kids write the most amazing poems. Like this one kid could barely read or write, and he wrote, "We write poetry because the heart wants to speak but it has no mouth." Javier Rodriguez. We put it on a t-shirt; he was so proud. And they were listening to a lot of hip-hop and rap, so they were interested in language. Their language skills weren't that great—they were like ninth graders with, like, a third-grade reading level—but their verbal skills in that genre were incredible! They could do incredible rhymes, they could come

208 *Women in Independent Publishing*

up with them instantaneously, and they could rap it out rapid fire. And the thing is, the culture would say, "Stop talking that gangster stuff and start paying attention to—"

SA: Standard English.

BB: "—standard English, yeah. Don't think about that! Think about transitive and intransitive verbs and past and future participles." You know, and their eyes glaze over. If we could find a way to go in and reach them where their interests and imagination [are], [they're] really incredibly skilled at language, you know?

SA: Yeah.

BB: And for example, I have a theory about curse words. Because all the kids were "fucking this, and shit that, and fuck that." As a drummer, I think cursing adds a lot of percussion to the language, you know? *Shit*, that's like a high-hat. *Fuck fucking*, that's a drum, that's a snare drum. You know, if you say, like, "I'm going to the store," that's boring. But if you say, "Shit, man, I'm going to the fucking store," that has a rhythm. So I can see how it just naturally flows in the language if you have any rhythmic sense at all. So [Pedro] came in and he just turned around. That was so fun to teach there. I want to write poems like the people who have the heart of their community . . . I wish I could do that, and I wish I could do that without so much negative analysis, so to speak, of society.

SA: How do you think of your community now?

BB: My community? Well, I feel a little bit part of *a* Chicago poetry community. When I go to readings it's usually Red Rover or Myopic—of course, I can walk there. I have my old poetry friends, we're in touch by e-mail and stuff like that. Like Eileen will come down and they'll stay with me, or I'll see them. I have a ton of cousins; my parents were first cousins—I'm even cousin to my parents. I have a *ton* of cousins. These are some of my closest, that I live with here, but I have a whole cousin community in Chicago. My dad was from Chicago.

SA: Wow!

BB: That's a whole other community. And I've been volunteering down at the Plant, you know that place? It's an old meat-packing plant converted into an aquaponics farm and a business incubator. They're installing an anaerobic digester, so it will take all the waste from the businesses, and restaurants and stuff, and it will create a biogas that will create the energy for the building. We get tours there from all over the world. People are doing this all over the world! They're putting in aquaponics and hydroponics, all these college kids that are studying sustainability! *That* gives me hope, to see people who are focused in that direction, and so many teachers—we get high school kids coming out and working on sustainability and stuff. So that's a riff on community I've been getting involved in. I tell the students when I give a tour, I say, "Look. I'm depending on you to make this a better planet, so that when I reincarnate, I'll have a nicer place to come back to." [*both laugh*] At this point in my life, being in one community—it was great, being in the poetry and the musician community, and just doing that and being that—[but] now I'm certain I want to go back and teach in a Puerto Rican high school; that's an interesting community, and The Plant's an interesting community, and just experiencing different little communities that are trying to make a go of it in spite of all the obstacles, you know?

SA: Yeah.

BB: 'Cause there's hope there.

SA: I feel like that has been one of the hardest things about grad school, is not being able to be involved in anything else, really.

BB: Well, at a certain point, that's all you want to do and be, you know? Like I say, I'm older, so this isn't a this-is-what-you-should-do perspective; this is where-I-am-now perspective. Because sometimes I just lose all hope, and then when you lose all hope then it just doesn't matter if you eat a lot of Reese's Mini Peanut Butter Cups. [*crinkling as she opens the bag; SA laughing*] It's okay! I mean, I really cannot *believe* this country. Capitalism is just out of control, and they don't care about anybody. "You can't use our machine . . . you can die, we don't care. And we own everything, and you own nothing and it's 'cause God wants us to . . . God thinks that we deserve it." It's insane. And the military technology's so strong I don't see how people could revolt. And the ones who would revolt—the ones who have the guns—are the ones whose ideology I *really* disagree with. So I don't know. Keep it regional and small and it's easier to deal with.

SA: Yeah, yeah.

BB: So you can tell me about you, though. As Darryl F. Zanuck—the movie producer from the fifties—as he once said, "But enough about me, what did *you* think about my last movie?" [*both laugh*]

Stephanie Anderson: So you met Barb at Northeastern [Illinois Univer-

Figure 15. Rose Lesniak. Photo by Danijela Kandera and Yagil Rafaeli at Empowering Portraits.

sity]. In about 1975? A little before?

Rose Lesniak: '73. I met her through Neil Hackman. We were all in Ted [Berrigan]'s class at first. Neil was kind of in love with me and followed me around. He knew I was gay, but we always got along very well. He brought Barbara and I together. He was graduating, and he said, "I want you to take over the Apocalypse Poetry Project and *Out There* magazine." He told me Barbara was a great writer and that

the two of us would make a great team taking over what he was doing. At first, I thought, what the fuck. Barbara Barg? But as I got to
know her, I became very close to her, and I loved her. We took over
the readings in 1973.

SA: Okay. Tell me more about the readings.

RL: The Apocalypse Poetry Series was the series initiated by Neil Hackman. Barb wrote this about the readings in 1977:

> Apocalypse is certainly not an original name for a book. Bible fol-
> lowers know that the last book of the bible, Revelation, is often
> called Apocalypse. Apocalypse is a Greek word meaning a prophetic
> revelation. Quite assuredly, the staff of the Apocalypse is not nam-
> ing their magazine after the book in the Bible, rather for the Greek
> word depicting it. The Apocalypse staff puts out a poetry magazine
> in which Northeastern students and local poets try to get their po-
> ems published. They reveal their innermost thoughts as they com-
> ment on the world around them. Poetry readings are sponsored
> by the Apocalypse staff. At least once a month from somewhere in
> the United States, poets come to the creative writing center at 3307
> W. Bryn Mawr and perform and read their work.

> Ted was our advisor. Ted was always saying, "We're gonna bring in
> this person, and we're gonna fund them . . ." Really, it was my job to
> get the money.

SA: [*laughs*] Okay.

RL: I was very good at bureaucracy and sitting in front of the people who
had the money at Northeastern and increasing the budget. Barbara
would always say, "God damn! You got us like five thousand more
dollars; I don't know how you did it." But that's why Barg and I got
along so well—Barbara was very good at doing the magazines, selecting the poems and typing them up, and getting people to help
her, and I was really good at getting the money to help it happen.

SA: That makes sense; she talks about this too.

RL: When we took over the Apocalypse Poetry Reading Series, we had
great people, like Gwendolyn Brooks, Anne Waldman, Ed Sanders,

212   *Women in Independent Publishing*

John Giorno, and most of Ted's friends coming in. Anybody Ted said we had to have, we had to have. Ted: "Well you go back to those people and ask them for more money!" So I did, and it always worked. I was never involved with Power Mad Press—Barbara did that. Now I want to talk about when we went to New York. I'm going to be going ahead and back, intuitively . . .

SA: Great.

RL: It was June of 1977. We left the Apocalypse Series to follow Ted to New York City. I was already living in an apartment with Barb and Chass. We lived on Lawndale, in Chicago. Chass was a professor at the time. I moved in in '75, once Barbara and I became close. It was just, like, "Why don't you move in with us?" "Well, great! Okay, I will." And my mother was like, "Oh, no, you're not moving in with them." And I said, "Yes, I am." We had a great time on Lawndale. We'd make Beta series videos; it's very hard to find some of them. At that time Barbara's father had a lot of money. Anything that she wanted he gave her. So we got this Beta, the first video camera. We just sat around, and went to school, and did videos at certain times. There was one time, too, where somebody tried to rob us, I remember, coming in through the back window. And both Chass and I were sitting there, and we were actually doing one of the videos, and Chass just said, "Now, we don't have any money—look at the place we live in! Do you really want to come in here?" And the guy left. I'll never forget that. We did some incredible videos. We did one about Joseph and Mary and baby Jesus, and I was baby Jesus; we did one about the muse. Crazy videos, just making things up as we went along.

SA: Yeah.

RL: But we all lived together. We never had sex together—it was just that both of them, Barb and Chass, were like new teachers to me. They taught me a lot. That's why I came to live with them, and then eventually moved to New York City after we graduated. Chassler said, "I don't want to work over here anymore." In Barb's interview she said I left, but I didn't. She was put into rehab.

SA: Oh, okay.

RL: Barbara's father came, he flew in—he had a jet at that time—he put Barbara in the jet, and he took her to rehab. I stayed with Chassler after Barb broke up with him, and after rehab she moved on to 14th Street, into that little place. Living with Chassler just became so unmanageable, he was so heartbroken. And then I had the opportunity to buy that loft. I said, "You know what? The money's not worth it; I'm gonna die here if I stay." I left in '88, and before I left, I stayed with Chassler for a while. He was so dark, and his sadness about Barbara was just unbearable for me to watch. He kept doing heroin and coke, and I—I got a little bit involved in coke, but not much, and then I said, "I gotta get out of here. You know, Chass, if you want this place, you can make millions of dollars, fine, you can have it." And I just left. I went to Florida. I wanted you to know that.

SA: Yeah.

RL: Let's go back to *Out There* magazine. Like I said, Neil introduced us in the class, and we started in 1973. Ted was our advisor, and the budget was like $3,000. By the time that I left it was $20,000.

SA: Oh my god. That's amazing, Rose!

RL: Yeah. It was a lot for that time. People knew about *Out There* magazine because of Ted. He'd say, "Send all your stuff in!" We published a thousand copies through the university. We didn't have any donations; it was all funded through Northeastern. Over e-mail you asked why there was a year before we put out that postcard issue of *Out There*?

SA: Yeah.

RL: We just decided to keep publishing *Out There* magazine when I moved to New York—I kept the name, and that's when I created Out There Productions with Andrea Kirsch. I did performance and the poetry video project. I also funded a lot of different things—I would fund and try to get an advance for anyone with an interesting idea. I got grants and donations, and we were mixing poetry with other arts and forms with performances that we'd do in Times Square and in our loft.

SA: And it was your savviness and fundraising, too, that led to get the

214 *Women in Independent Publishing*

CCLM [Coordinating Council of Literary Magazines] grant and the New York State Arts Council grants for that postcard issue.

RL: I had a really good group of patrons. Glenn Close, Allen Ginsberg's friends . . . there were a lot of people who really liked us. It was a write-off for them; we had a nonprofit, so it was a donation to the arts. And things were really beautiful in the eighties—before the Republicans got in—people were donating. Every time I'd be out of money, suddenly a check would come. It was a wonderful time.

SA: Sure. I want to ask about the geographic range of *Out There* magazine. You were publishing people from across the country. Did Ted's connections pull people into the magazine who were outside the New York and Chicago spheres?

RL: Ted was just our advisor, but he was very proud of us and told other poets to send work to us. He loved Bob Dylan, he loved poetry . . . Allan Bates, a theater professor, was kind of in control of Ted. He would tell Ted how to get around, and how to get money, and what to do, and how to do things. And then they pushed us out of the university. They said, "These are people using marijuana, they're smoking, they're drinking . . ." So they gave us a spot at 3307 W. Bryn Mawr Ave., the theater and poetry area away from the university. Alan and Ted were the two teachers assigned to that center. All Ted wanted was to impart his knowledge of poetry and have a good time. And he did—his classes were huge. People loved him. You could get an A in his class if you brought him the right drugs.

SA: I'm wondering a little bit about Alice [Notley], who shows up in *Out There* magazine—whether she was around.

RL: Alice was right at Ted's side. But she stayed home and I never got close to her. I was very close to Ted. If I met Alice now, I would talk to her about what was going on, but at that time when I was in my twenties, I just didn't get it. I thought that she was oppressed by Ted. I thought she was his slave. She rarely ventured out; she was always stuck at home with the kids.

SA: Speaking of women poets, there's that amazing issue of *Out There*, issue 11, the one with the dedication to "women / dinner roles / douche bags / lipstick & clean work". . .

RL: That was the one we did in New York, when we went to New York. When we got there, we were a force! Barbara, myself, Eileen Myles . . . We went to poetry readings and heckled the men, who were talking like, "Oh, your breasts are so nice when I suck them . . ." and stuff like that. These guys! And the Iowa School, too, they weren't really talking about what was going on in the world! They were just out there dreaming in their sexist wonderhood. Our guys, the Beat poets, liked us because we were women who came into the scene who challenged them. They thought that was cute. And we were fun and fierce and serious about our poetry. We were a community of different individuals bonded together by poetry and the fun of it. We respected each other despite our diverse writing styles.

SA: Yeah, yeah.

RL: They didn't think, "Oh, power to them"; they thought, "Huh, these girls are pretty. We like them, they're pretty, they're tough, we like 'em!" Ginsberg, Giorno, even Ed Friedman, all of those people. They were like, "Oh, here they come! Be careful, Mark Strand, if you're gonna be reading poetry to these women about things that are bullshit, because they want to hear what you really have to say in the world." We would talk back. And Barbara and I really helped in that manner with the Poetry Project. When we first got there, they thought, "What the fuck." Though Ted was very positive about it. He said, "I like this, I like the strength that you have, I'm happy with that."

SA: Bernadette Mayer calls, I think, your group "the Feminists" in her letters—

RL: We were just women; we were like firecrackers. Yeah, we were the Young Feminists, we were the first to come in and say, "What the fuck are you saying in these poems?!" We would heckle them and make them very uncomfortable. And we were pleasurable! We'd all get high together, and we'd all drink together afterward,

216   *Women in Independent Publishing*

and we'd get to know each other—but we'd still be, "Okay, we're gonna . . ." [*slaps fist*] "You say something stupid and sexist, we're gonna ask you about it!" We weren't really anarchists, and we wouldn't hurt anybody—no. We wanted to ask you: "Why did you say that? Where'd that come from? Do you need therapy?" Ted found us very amusing, and Chassler was the lead feminist and Marxist to me.

SA: [*chuckles*] I love that. So it was you and Barb and Eileen Myles—who became head of the Poetry Project in '85, or so. Is there anyone else that I'm missing? I know that Barb talks about the other women in her band . . .

RL: I never really was a part of Barbara's band; that was her thing, and she wanted it that way. I came into Barbara's life because she had no spirituality; she was an atheist, and I always believed in God and the universe and nature. It wasn't until the end of Barbara's life that she started believing in Tai Chi, and the universe, and sound therapy, and stuff like that. At the beginning we had a real battle about that. My girlfriend Andrea Kirsch came in, and we formed Out There Productions and did the videos in New York. Barbara was involved in it, but she always had this attitude, like, "I don't understand your spirituality stuff." Which was okay to me, and I just did the things I wanted with other people.

SA: Yeah.

RL: That was always our first battle together, while Chassler would be talking about various philosophers and teaching me philosophy. Chassler taught me more about feminism than any teacher I had, and I had great teachers at Northeastern. I loved Barb and Chassler, and we were a family together. And because Barbara had a lot of money at the time we could afford these five-thousand-square-foot lofts, and we would have readings and parties. We had the best scene going on in the city, one of the most exciting scenes. Everyone wanted to come over. We were a big hit when we came to New York, because everybody thought we were loaded.

SA: Oh, yeah.

RL: We weren't really, but before Barbara's father went bankrupt, we had a lot of fun. We'd invite people over. Warhol came, John Giorno, Allen Ginsberg, a lot of different people . . . We had these things on Sunday where we'd read poetry, and there must have been at least seventy people in our loft.

SA: That's so fun!

RL: Once in a while we'd ask for donations, but mostly not. Once I got the nonprofit going, then we would ask for donations. Barbara was a real pig. She never cleaned; she wouldn't even clean her own dishes. This was part of my ongoing saga with her, and it always bothered me because we had these beautiful lofts. But she gave me so much that later anything she needed I would give to her—because when I was younger she would take care of everything. If I was hungry, she would go out and she would get me anything I wanted. If we couldn't come up with the rent, she would be there and pay it. So that was our life when we were in New York City at the beginning. I didn't have to worry about anything then; my basic needs were covered.

SA: Okay.

RL: I loved everything Barbara taught me, and everything we experienced together, but I couldn't stand having the loft be so dirty all the time, and I was constantly cleaning. I would tell her, and she didn't care. I felt in some way, too, that Barbara was kind of becoming a slave to drugs and to Chassler. So I was very upset about this. But I had lovers coming in, I had girlfriends, and Barb and Chass were always very open about it: "Okay, you're going to bring Andrea Kirsch in, okay, fine. You're going to bring Tone Blevins in, that's fine, you know. Oh, you like Deborah Thompson? Okay, that's fine." And Chassler would always be there for me. I'd be at a gay bar, and I'd say, "Chassler, I ran out of money . . ." He would be there in a minute. He'd take a cab, come in, give me money, and then leave. We always took care of each other.

SA: Yeah. Barb loved to talk about you. She talked about you doing a reading at the Ear Inn, and you dedicated a poem to Jim Brody, "the

218   *Women in Independent Publishing*

only man who ever gave me an orgasm!" And Barb thought that that
was so funny. She told me about how people would fall in love with
you at bars.

RL: Yeah, I wasn't really into men, but there were a few men—I always
loved Bob Holman, and I always loved . . . oh, what was his name.
It's like it's nothing to me, like Circe and her men. I liked men because I grew up with men; there were no girls around. I was always
free when I was young. I didn't have anybody watching over me, and
I grew up in an environment I wanted to leave.

SA: You're from Chicago?

RL: Yeah, I grew up in a middle-class home in Chicago. I loved my father; my mother had untreated bipolar depression. She had been
taken away from her family during the Depression and had spent
her early years in an orphanage with her brothers and sisters.

SA: Were most of the people who came to Northeastern from the area?
Was Barb kind of an outlier in that way?

RL: Yes. But there were a lot of people who came in from foreign countries too. It was good for me, because I had never met even a Black
person in my life, being in my middle-class area. Meeting all types
of people when I got to Northeastern was eye-opening, and it was
very important.

SA: Yeah. What about the neighborhood on Lawndale?

RL: It was a mix of all types of people, young and old, different types.
I don't even think I even cared about the neighborhood! I cared
about what we had happening inside our house—the love going
on. Barbara had her cousin Ellen living upstairs, so she would
come down too. It was a family that I always wanted to have, that
I never had.

SA: Was it ever tough to do the magazine? Being a woman, was it
ever—

RL: It was fun. I loved being a woman. I always loved being gay. I never
had a problem with it; it was always an asset.

SA: It was all fun?

RL: Yeah, any challenge that was came up was not a challenge to me.

I looked at it like, "Oh, this is fun." I didn't really care that I was a woman; I was just a person who was doing a magazine; Barbara and I enjoyed it, and everybody else did. We had a blast! It was only one thousand copies. I never really had a struggle in my life in anything. When I came out: "Okay, so what." If I was gay in the sixties, nobody cared. If I was heckling at a poetry reading, nobody really cared. It was just like, "Oh, that's Rose, okay, fine." My challenges had to do with my wanting to go out in the world and being raped, or being kidnapped, or stuff like that . . . Those were my challenges I had to deal with emotionally. It all happened to me early; I had a lot of trauma early in my life. Everything else seemed so minimal after that that I could care less. It made me a strong person.

SA: You know, I think about how tough you had to be to kind of make your way—

RL: I don't even think it's toughness. I think at that point I'd experienced so much horrible things in my childhood that this was freedom to me! I could say what I wanted because I had been so abused in my childhood. You know, the Catholic Church, the nuns, the Hell's Angels, being raped, being heckled all the time because I was pretty . . . Those are the things that really made me crazy. By the time I got to New York I was like, "Wow, this is great! People listen to me!" It was different in New York than in Chicago.

SA: How was it different?

RL: People understood. Like in Chicago, for example, if you walked by and there were construction workers heckling, and you said, "Hey, fuck you," they'd maybe hit you with a pipe. But in New York they looked at you and they laughed. It was a different environment and a different feeling in New York City. I felt like, "Okay, let me be honest then." And people are saying, "What are you, crazy?" And I'd say, "Yeah, maybe I am . . ." But Chicago was very dangerous when I was growing up. My mother wasn't around much in my early childhood and my grandmother took care of me the best

220 *Women in Independent Publishing*

she could. She was a bookie and a gambler, so there were always people coming over to the house, which didn't make it safe for me, being pretty and little.

SA: I also went from Chicago to New York when I was young, and I felt people were just mixing more geographically, and there was maybe more of a tolerance for difference.

RL: Right. Good point; I agree.

SA: Let me look and see what we haven't covered. I'm curious about—oh, go ahead.

RL: The death of Ted. When Ted died, there was a hole in New York. I can't even remember when it was, but I was heartbroken.

SA: I think it was '83? Bernadette Mayer has this line in one of her letters to Clark Coolidge at the time, something like, "Ted's absence is too much a presence."

RL: Yeah, a great line. It was true.

SA: How did things change in the longer term after Ted died?

RL: Everybody did their own thing. There was a lot of branching out— that's when I formed Out There Productions and started doing performance art. Barbara started Power Mad Press. We were together, but it wasn't as though we had our leader. Even though he was a weak leader, he was still our leader.

SA: Yeah.

RL: What else?

SA: I'm curious to go back this postcard edition of *Out There*, issue 14. Were those postcards actually meant to be mailed?

RL: We wanted people to cut them out and mail them. I think I should put that out again, because it would be a great thing; who sends postcards to anybody now? It would be great to put out that edition again, just because our world's not like that anymore.

SA: I think you should!

RL: Well, I would do it, but you know I have little desire to do it unless somebody approaches me. I would rather concentrate on my dog training and my poems about dog training—and still go out in the light. Poetry is a solitary process. There's too much isolation in the

SA: What other kinds of things did Out There Productions do? You did the videos . . .

RL: We did the videos, we did the Poetry Learning Project in the schools that Barbara talks about. Laura Vural—a teacher at the Fashion Institute, teaching media and technology—took over that aspect of it. When I left New York I kind of left Out There in limbo; I just wanted to get out and do something different. I said, "You know, I'm going to go to Florida, I'm going to do investigative work, that's what I want to do." I had a lot of training in poetry and children, so I got a job and began doing what I had to do with regard to investigation work. Because I really wanted to help children.

SA: Yeah.

RL: I came here to Miami in '88, and I immediately got involved in child welfare and began to do investigative work, and then the Miami Beach Police hired me. Then I said, "This is boring and my heart is breaking," and went on to study dog training for a couple years.

SA: So how long has the dog training been going on?

RL: Since 2003.

SA: Barbara was very excited to show me the clip—back in our 2014 conversation—of you on the news talking about how to help a dog adjust to a new baby.

RL: Well, Barg was a genius. She was the most interesting person I have ever met in my life. Probably my favorite piece she ever wrote was called "Walks in New York City." I don't want to put any videos out; I want to help people, and I don't want to be defined by any videos that I have out. I mean, I have these poems that we did early in life; I hate them. In 2020 I want to be anonymous. My business is good; I will go to people's houses and do my work and that's all I want to do 'til I die. You know? And write some poems.

SA: So you're still writing poems?

RL: Yes.

SA: Do you have an audience of friends that you share them with?

RL: Most of my friends have nothing to do with my poems. A lot of them,

222 *Women in Independent Publishing*

my clients, have no idea I write poetry, and that's fine.

SA: Do you ever miss the publishing aspect of things?

RL: No.

SA: Barb didn't much either. She kind of said that's not really where my energy is anymore, that's not where I'm interested in thinking about poetry.

RL: I put all my poems on my website. It's called Rambling Rose, if you Google me my poems will come up, and if you want to read them, you read them. Somebody said, "Oh, can I publish your book?" Alright, but my goal is to help people with animals; that's what I really want to do right now. All of the work that I've done, all of the things that I've done . . . Barbara certainly was my inspiration to get to this point. If I died tomorrow, I'd be happy because I've accomplished everything I want to. Really, if I could continue to help people communicate with their animals, that's what I want to do.

SA: That's amazing, Rose. To have found ways of finding fulfillment in different kinds of work—at least from the vantage of my generation, I think it's getting increasingly hard; it's wonderful.

RL: You've gotta love what you do. Everything I did I loved! And when I didn't love it anymore, I got rid of it: "Time to move on!"

SA: That's a great thing about having a job that really feels like a separate job, is that you can both love it and be invested in it, but also know when to move on because it's a job, right?

RL: Right. And obviously it's important to have people like you because I could give two shits about the history. But this feminist piece at the Poetry Project is *very* important! It changed the whole course of the Poetry Project. It really did. All of us, there, had never been there before, and no energy like that had ever been felt in New York City at that time. And the guys—the Beats were like, you know, "We're number one, but this is interesting shit . . ."

Figure 16. Kelsey Street Press Book Table at the Association of Writers and Writing Programs' Annual Conference Bookfair. Photo by Rena Rosenwasser.

Rena Rosenwasser and Patricia Dienstfrey

Coeditors and Copublishers, Kelsey Street Press (1974–present, Berkeley)

NOVEMBER 2019 TO APRIL 2020, VIA E-MAIL,
UPDATED SEPTEMBER 2022

Stephanie Anderson: Rena, in your piece on Kelsey Street Press for *Chain*'s "Editorial Forum" (1994), you talk about how the press grew out of a women's reading group and write, "Co-founding a press to publish new writing by women was a means of questioning the centrality of the male figure in writing." Will you and Patricia talk a little bit about the Bay Area poetry scene in 1974?[1]

Rena Rosenwasser and Patricia Dienstfrey: We and the four other founding members of Kelsey Street—Karen Brodine, Marina LaPalma, Laura Moriarty, and Kit Duane—met in the Berkeley Poet's Co-op, a workshop held in a home open to any poet off the street. People who showed up were about equally divided between men and women, and there was an egalitarian feeling to the gatherings. At the same time, we began to notice that poems women thought were strong men saw as weak. For the most part, their subjects were outside the "literary canon." We felt a need for a smaller, all-female reading group to give ourselves room to write apart from this critical voice. For one thing, it allowed us to engage in a more embodied poetics. And commenting on each other's work allowed us to explore a much larger space for poetry.

It was the seventies and feminist issues were being examined. It was a time of immense energy channeled into consciousness-raising groups, woman-run businesses, and new feminist cultural forums. The Feminist Institute, in which several press members

226   *Women in Independent Publishing*

were involved, was one. There were a number of salons set up during that decade, meetings in homes for discussion of feminist politics and culture. One sought to bridge class and economic differences and lasted little more than a year. The Bacchanal Bar, a lesbian bar, opened in 1972. One of the two owners, Joanna Griffin, was a poet. Readings and art exhibits took place there. Many Kelsey Street Press members participated. Rena remembers an early performance where Ntosake Shange read from her play *For Colored Girls Who Have Considered Suicide/When the Rainbow Is Enuf*. It was in an early stage of development and Ntozake's performance astonished everyone. Kelsey Street writers also read in women's bookstores on both sides of the Bay, including one called Mama Bears in Oakland furnished with comfortable chairs in a homey atmosphere. Some bookstores didn't allow men inside. I believe we decided to hold readings in these venues while, at the same time, we disagreed with their position.

As for feminist publishing ventures, there was a book called *The Passionate Perils of Publishing* with a purple cover written to help women self-publish their work. There was shameless hussy press run by Alta, books typewritten and reproduced by mimeograph with stapled spines. Alta published the first edition of Ntozake Shange's *For Colored Girls* and many other fine writers. Five Trees was the name of a local women's collective that published poetry in letterpress editions, which started around the same time KSP did. They did very fine work. We helped each other out from time to time. But there wasn't much exchange, probably because we were both intently involved in finding our ways in new territory—our values, aesthetics, and poetics. But we contributed to an exploratory and committed collective atmosphere that sustained us.

Bay Area readings at that time were all over the place, from the Beat/Jazz-influenced venues in San Francisco to coffeehouses that supported local, emerging writers. Sometimes, at open-mic readings, you had a mix. It could be wild.

SA: Why the name Kelsey Street Press?

RR and PD: The press was located at 2824 Kelsey Street in the basement of Patricia's home. In our early publicity, we played with the domestic setting for a press we saw as following in the footsteps of famous women-run presses of the early twentieth century—Winifred Bryher and Robert McAlmon's Black Sun Press, the Hours Press run by Nancy Cunard. We were standing on tall shoulders. These presses and others brought out writers who were experimental at the time and later entered the canon—James Joyce, Ernest Hemingway. Gertrude Stein came to occupy a niche of her own. We wanted to bend the social construct that a woman's place is in the home and the place of art belongs to the public sphere. We wanted to change the narratives around where art comes from and who is an artist. We wanted to go back to the roots of "the artist, she" and bring her into the present. This is true, also, now, of "the artist, they."

SA: Thinking more about the press name: As you know, Kelsey is also a famous manufacturing company of tabletop letterpresses. Was this a delightful coincidence?

PD: My first press, before the Vandercook, was a little tabletop Kelsey. I had fun taking it to schools, usually my kids' classrooms, sometimes to college book-making classes, and to printing demonstrations at small press publishing events like a Bay Area–wide Ink Slingers weekend in the eighties—great name, and it swarmed with publishers, printers, writers.

We held brainstorming sessions to come up with an interesting press name—one I remember was "Tender Benches." We settled on Kelsey St. because nothing better came up, because it was the press's address, and because it represented a combination of its domestic setting and urban avant-garde models. The name began as Kelsey St. But we changed it to Kelsey Street in the 2000s because people consistently mistook us for a religious press.

SA: It's great that even the name of the press involves "play[ing] with the domestic setting for a press," which, as you note, has such important historical continuities. That address is still the address for the press, right? Was there ever discussion of moving it?

PD: The press has moved at least four times—from the "domestic setting" in my house in the seventies, to an unrented housing unit in Berkeley in the eighties, then to a space near Rena's house in the nineties, then back to Kelsey Street in the early 2000s. During this time, the office space needed to run the press changed. In the seventies, Kelsey Street in my basement was a matter of two letter-presses—a Vandercook and a Chandler & Price, a more automatic press that turned out pages faster—book papers, several type cases, etc. Now the press downstairs fits into a space just large enough to hold a computer, a printer, shelf space for books and materials for fulfillment tucked in between two bedrooms—added as my family grew—and a laundry room. As for the "domestic" narrative, that went out in the eighties as survival required we pay attention to the business end of publishing. We went from a collective model to being a press in which members had defined functions—marketing, publicity, promotion. Rena became director and ran the office, and I became manuscripts editor, overseeing this aspect of press life. As a whole, we continued to select manuscripts by consensus and to rotate work on book production.

A little bit more on change: KSP is a press with a long historical arc that has changed pretty much from decade to decade. For example, changes in the character of the meetings: In the seventies they were held over meals when press members shared what was going on in their lives and work. This practice stopped in the eighties when the collective and social values of the women's movement gave way to developing the business side. Also, the eighties poetry scene was heavily influenced by the Language poets, a different atmosphere from the feminist seventies. Then, in the early 2000s we enjoyed a sudden infusion of poets, all of them friends and members of the same writing group. The dinner meetings began again and have continued to the present. By that time the poetry community was more integrated and included writers from a wide range of age, racial, ethnic groups, and aesthetic practices, often working in small collectives.

Our almost continual turnover in membership has been a survival factor for KSP from the beginning. (Have I said that the press has always been an all-volunteer organization?) For a long time, I thought of us as a press that works in the twenty-fifth hour. Now it's the twenty-sixth or twenty-seventh—it's this much harder. Membership took on a new aspect in the nineties when we needed to bring in young members, often graduates from college creative-writing programs, to help Rena make the transition in the office to digital technology. For a time, as Rena was continually training new young members, she was being trained by them.

Notable fact: For a few years in the 2010s the press membership included women in their thirties, forties, fifties, sixties, and seventies.

Numbers of members have varied from two to nine.

SA: What about the printing press itself and the early years using it?

RR and PD: Kelsey Street's first press was a 1936 Vandercook proof press. We assembled the books ourselves, even hand-stitching the spine. Our first title, *Neurosuite*, included poems of the Italian author Margherita Guidacci. Marina La Palma, one of the original members of the press, translated the poems and worked with Patricia on producing the book. The second title, *Making the Park*, was a collection of poems by the founding members. Patricia printed on the Vandercook and Rena set the type. We were definitely into it. For one thing, we worked under the influence of the famous photo of Virginia Woolf setting type for the first printing of *Ulysses* at Hogarth Press. Also, we both had fallen in love with the look of the letterpress imprinted page, with working with fine papers, mixing colored inks; in brief, with all the sensuous pleasures involved. If there were setbacks, it came from Patricia's perfectionist tendencies and ridiculously time-consuming make-ready sessions (when one uses fine paper to correct unevenness in the impression of letters on the page). But Rena had some, enough, of those tendencies too. Also, Patricia had three young children at a time that fell between the postwar fifties, when mothers were expected to stay at home, and the early nineties when working mothers and two-income families were more the norm. Trying to "do it all" periodically took its toll. But the experience, as a whole—the chance to bring out work by women, poetry we loved in beautifully designed books—felt like a privilege. It was truly a joy.

SA: What were some of your favorite books to print during those years?

PD: First, I should say that, although KSP began as a collective, the "we" I use refers to Rena and myself. We were the closest in our aesthetics and passion for book design, a constant through all the change, one that has definitely been a factor in the press's longevity.

I'm going to answer another question, a misreading of the one you sent, which I read as: "What were some of the favorite books you were reading during those years?" I was excited by it because it was fundamental to KSP's beginning. Yes, we were driven to erase the absence of women in the poetry world. But we were also deeply involved in our readings of innovative poets and work published by the literary small presses of the late nineteenth and early twentieth centuries, a line of influence in which literary innovation and small presses were inseparable. We were steeping ourselves in the French experimentalists—Stéphane Mallarmé, Pierre Reverdy, René Char, Paul Claudel. We read V. Woolf's essays and fiction; the early lesbian writers, Radclyffe Hall and Djuna Barnes; and the writers in the overlapping circles of Pound's and Gertrude Stein's Paris now ensconced in the twentieth-century literary canon. We were interested in collaborations between writers and visual artists—Virginia Woolf and Vanessa Stephens Bell, Juan Gris and Reverdy. These were models that excited us and were a profound inspiration.

Now to the question you wrote: What were some of your favorite books to print during those years?

Easily, the book I loved working on the most was that first book, *Neurosuite*. We were reading writing in translation and our interests moved easily between women writers in Europe and the US who shared a history of neglect and erasure. I produced this book with Marina La Palma, a member of the original collective. Marina could be taking part in a dizzying number of works-in-progress at one time, involving poetry, translation, music, dance, visual arts, book design. Born in Italy, her first language was Italian. She had recently translated Guidacci's poems written from the poet's experience of confinement to a mental institution, sent there by male doctors who mistook her emotions for madness. It is a collection of biting, bright, short poems.

Marina and I had taken a letterpress printing class from the wonderful fine printer Clifford Burke, and I had bought the Vandercook and installed its over-a-ton bulk in my basement, hauling it on rollers over flagstones and removing a door to get it inside. In this, I had the help of Clive Matson, a letterpress printer, poet, and publisher. The model for the book's cover design were Gallimard publications, the press that had brought out so many of the French writers Rena and I loved. We admired the simplicity of the covers that played with just a few design elements—ruled borders, typography, and colored inks, mostly red and black.

Marina and I chose Italian Old Style and Centaur typefaces. We included a frontispiece because we were interested in crossovers between poetry and visual art. This image by Xenia Lisanevich was one of my favorites to print—an ink drawing of a bird with a velvety black head and wings in a network of fine-webbed lines. I experimented with impression; for this first work I made it light, the letters just visible on the back of the page. Minimal. No spine, handsewn by press members at a dining room table. I loved all this, but I can't say I enjoyed printing the book—I was too nervous that I didn't know what I was doing, and I suffered from perfectionist angst. Even when Clive took me around to show the finished book to other literary publishers/letterpress printers, when they expressed their appreciation, I felt embarrassed. But now I can see that it came out well and I love seeing it when we display our books.

The next book, *Hair-Raising*, was a collaboration between visual artists who were members of an LA Arts collective, and LA and Bay Area poets, a project Rena curated. Because of the artwork, this book was reproduced by offset photolithography. We applied the minimalist Gallimard aesthetic to the cover design, which was simply the title on a plain white matte finish. Which makes this the book that taught us that matte white covers look striking as long as no one handles them.

SA: Were there release parties for the books?

PD: We were into release parties. We viewed the publication of a book as a cause for celebration with food and wine. We were also into food. And wine. Press meetings, during the first decade, were usually held over dinner or dessert that included interesting dishes—Rena was the most involved in these experiments. One memorable release party was for *Hair-Raising*, held in a dance studio in Berkeley's industrial area, a costume party; the theme, hair. We had also learned that book launches sell books. In the case of poets who didn't live in the area, we sent money for them to organize release parties in their areas.

SA: I love the inclusion of visual artists in the "Six Southern California Artists" portfolio section of *Hair-Raising*. KSP has been such an important bridge between literature and visual art; were those connections already there? How easy have they been to maintain?

RR: In 1972 the seminal exhibition Womanhouse, a feminist art installation, took place in Los Angeles. Miriam Schapiro and Judy Chicago began the Feminist Art Program at Cal Arts (FAP) and Womanhouse was their premier project. My brother Robert Rosenwasser was attending Cal Arts at the time. Wandering through the rooms in the house with him I met a number of the artists. Nancy Buchanan was one. Later I would meet the performance artist Rachel Rosenthal. In 1976 these associations helped shape the photos of performance art in *Hair-Raising*.

My memory is a bit cloudy. I believe Marina LaPalma had the initial idea of doing a book of hair poems. Marina also had a keen sense of the Los Angeles art world. The two of us together decided on the artists.

A love of fine art, especially contemporary art, was as formative in my evolution as my love of literature. Growing up in New York City, my brother Robert and I hung out at MOMA.

When the feminist movement of the seventies was in full swing, I turned my attention to the woman artists that had long been ignored. After the press ceased printing on letterpress, Robert designed many of our titles. In the nineties Lory Poulson of Poulson Gluck Design was a press member. She designed the books, other than our collaborations. Since 2007 Jeff Clark of Crisis Design has taken over as designer.

In the mid-eighties Kelsey Street began a series of collaborations with contemporary artists. I initiated these projects with artists and poets that I knew. Working closely with a local printer, West Coast Print Center (Keith Whitaker and Marian O'Brien), we were able to produce some striking books. The press's mission has always been to bring out publications affordable to poets. We kept costs down by offering limited editions of signed and altered books. These alterations were in the form of signed drawings and/or prints that were included with the book. Selling these collector items helped subsidize the production. This allowed us to keep the regular edition prices reasonable. Visual artists we worked with were Cecilia Vicuña, Kiki Smith, Alison Saar, Richard Tuttle, Laurie Reid, Jennifer Macdonald, June Felter, Anne Dunn, and Kate Delos. Robert worked closely with the artists designing many of our collaborations. Two of our authors, Cecilia Vicuña and Etel Adnan, are poets as well as visual artists.

SA: One book of artist-poet collaborations that I find particularly stunning is Rosmarie Waldrop and Jennifer Macdonald's *Particular Motions*, with its translucent "s/kins." What was the process of making that book like?

RR: When I first read Rosmarie Waldrop's manuscript *Peculiar Motions* I immediately thought of a close artist friend. Jennifer Macdonald's conceptual approach seemed ripe for engagement with Waldrop's imagery. My reasons were numerous, some simple and some complex. Her conceptual work as part of the artist team, Leone and Macdonald, probed linguistic codes, as well as codes of gender. She was that rare artist who had a poet for a parent and was a close reader of poetry. She studied at Brown, was well versed in semiotics, and knew of the Waldrops's Burning Deck Press. Burning Deck, like Kelsey Street, emphasized experimental writing. The one difference is that we were devoted to writing by women. Recently we moved to also including trans and genderqueer authors.

For *Peculiar Motions* Jennifer Macdonald created "s/kins" made as vellum overlays for the poems. Rosmarie and I were equally astonished by the overlays. This remains one of the collaborations that surprises me each time I open the book.

SA: When did you move away from letterpress?

PD: After *Neurosuite* and *Hair-Raising*, we printed one more letterpress book, *Making the Park* in 1977, an anthology of the press's five poets—white cover (not matte), black rule, green ink. I had three very young children in short school sessions, and, like every woman writer I knew, was in a constant state of deprivation regarding time to write. I was sinking precious hours into a time-consuming production process. Also, the press had become interested in possibilities offset printing offered for playing with images and colors. Finally, we saw that browsers at bookfairs went right past the simple designs to the colorful covers. In our last letterpress book, *The Celebrated Running Horse Messenger* by Frances Phillips, I used more impression, experimented with a more three-dimensional page. Frances showed us a marvelous photo of a horse and rider and we decided to use it on the cover.

SA: Both the typesetting and cover image of *The Celebrated Horse Messenger* are gorgeous, and I appreciate your description of "a more three-dimensional page." It makes me think of the physicality of the printing process; it seems apt somehow for the book, which is so much about embodiment. (The copy I saw even has some very faint ink smudges on one of the pages, bringing to mind the hands printing the work.) Was this aesthetic exploration inspired by the book, or was it a natural extension of your printing work up until that point?

PD: (Yikes! Ink smudges!) I'm glad you asked about that book. It's the last one I printed on letterpress, a work I feel a deep affection for looking at it now, but that got lost in the many changes going on in the press at the end of the seventies—the change to offset; the need to sell the presses and type cases. Also, we were adapting to the changes in the poetry community and in Kelsey Street's organization that I mentioned earlier. This said, I enjoyed printing this book. The design is the result of a desire to experiment with the sculptural possibility of the letterpress page. I really bore down on the type. For the cover, as I said, Frances offered us the wonderful image of the gleaming horse with cropped tail and four white socks and its perfectly seated rider. Otherwise, I would probably have stayed with the rule and typography of earlier books. Instead, for the first time, we printed a cover centered on an image using brown inks on a creamy tan paper, a nod to the sepia atmosphere of the photograph. In this case, the old-fashioned air was complicated by Frances's gift for colloquial language and the hip, contemporary sound of her poems. It makes me wonder, writing this now, what Kelsey Street books might have looked like if we had continued printing books this way. But the poetry would always have been the first design consideration.

SA: Regarding the "search for a useful business model," the changes to which you summarized above—will you talk about the process of selecting manuscripts by consensus?

PD: This simply means that we choose the books collectively. Everyone in the press, whether we number three or eight, has read and supports every book we produce. The exceptions to this process have been the collaborations Rena has curated; the Frances Jaffer First Book Awards series, which I produced (these books were chosen by judges); and the second first book series, Firsts!, also chosen by judges.

SA: Going back to something you mentioned earlier—limited time, so often a theme of work that blurs the domestic. (I've had two children since beginning these interviews.) Do you have advice for those of us balancing publishing projects with a myriad of other demanding aspects of life? I guess another way of asking this question is, how do you stay excited about publishing over a long duration, like that of Kelsey Street?

PD: Balancing demands on one's life as a mother and writer. It's been a while since I've had to worry about this, but I remember! I don't think it's changed that mothers are assigned the primary responsibility for taking care of the house and children at the same time that most now are working in salaried jobs. I used to feel almost defeated by trying to balance both: I saw each as, by their nature, a full-time commitment. I could feel split right down the middle.

In the nineties I collaborated with others having the same

236 *Women in Independent Publishing*

struggles—with whom I shared a sense of community, exploration, and experiment—to put on three conferences on the subject of motherhood, writing, and making art. The last was held in New College in 1996, a two-day symposium planned by poet Brenda Hillman, visual artist Amy Trachtenburg, and myself. A few things I remember: Some women talked about integrating home life into their subject matter, one coining the term "table-top poetics." One talked about incorporating interruption into her form. There was the pragmatic "Dear Eloise" kind of advice such as Brenda's "Floss at red lights." Fanny Howe talked about making the time to write by getting up an hour earlier than her children. The tone in those conferences was of women taking their work seriously enough to persevere and of being creative about integrating the two creative aspects of their lives. I love that C. D. Wright and Erica Hunt observed, in an anthology Brenda and I edited later—*The Grand Permission: New Writings on Poetics and Motherhood*—that being mothers had empowered rather than disempowered them as poets, that they were better writers because of being mothers, not in spite of this. Finally, I want to add what maybe, alas, I didn't acknowledge then—that I, personally, don't think I could have managed without an unreservedly supportive partner.

How to stay excited about publishing over a long period of time? For me, three women interviewed in this book—Hettie Jones, Margaret Randall, Maureen Owen—state the case: Passion for what one is doing is built into the small press publisher's love-driven world. People feed off each other's excitement for this book, that poet, that look on the page or cover. And off the experience of working with a new writer or artist or of attending a reading and hearing new work you'd love to publish. The pleasures pervade your life and help you get through the times when you're tired, when your table at a bookfair is stuck back in a corner, and when you're up against the "poetry doesn't sell" aspects of the business.

SA: Additionally (and impressively), you were also both making time to write and then publish your own work! What was the publication process like for books like Patricia's *Small Salvations* and Rena's *Elephants & Angels*? Did you ask each other for editorial input?

PD: On the production of *Small Salvations*, I don't remember the editing process, whether Rena and I were still habitually reading each other's poems. I do want to say that the design, which I had nothing to do with, was a collaboration between Rena and the artist Kate Delos. Which led, later, in the early eighties, to a book entitled *Simulacra* that became the first in a series of collaborations between poets and visual artists that took Kelsey Street's book list into new territory. These editions were brought out by complex processes that involved the poet, artist, book designer, book printer, and Rena as the producer. They reside now in library, museum, and private collections. *Simulacra*'s subject was Roman portraiture. The cover of *Small Salvations* features a portrait from this series, in profile, and repeats it as a cutout made of translucent paper tipped in at the front of the book, through which one reads the title page. I think it's wonderful. The surprise still holds up.

SA: So the reception of *Simulacra* led to other books in the series?

RR: When Barbara Guest saw the finished book, she assumed that our press was devoted to collaborations. My esteem for Barbara, as one of the great luminaries of twentieth-century verse, led to my susceptibility to anything proposed by her. And propose she did. Barbara wanted to collaborate with her painter friend June Felter. June was born the year before Barbara and was part of the Bay Area figurative school. The two grand dames went on driving trips through Sonoma County. June did watercolors of the hills and Barbara wrote the spacious poem *Musicality*. With the publication of their book the press decided to return to our letterpress roots, though this time we hired the printer Peter Rutledge Koch of Magnolia Press. I set the type. Peter rolled the presses and *Musicality* was pressed on the page.

Through *Musicality* and Barbara's desire for me to hand the volume to the poet Mei-mei Berssenbrugge, our next collaborations were set in motion. As was also Kelsey Street's longstanding history of publishing Mei-mei's books. Mei-mei and her husband, Richard Tuttle, remain among my closest friends.

SA: Is there another poet–visual artist collaboration that you remember especially as an example of this "complex process"? Or one whose distribution ("library, museum, and private collections") ended up being especially surprising?

PD: For me, as an outsider looking on, I was immensely impressed by the collaborative process that became *Endocrinology* by Mei-mei Berssenbrugge and Kiki Smith. In its first edition, it was published by the United Limited Artists' Editions (ULAE), well-known in the arts world for its stunning lithographs and limited-edition books by contemporary artists. This book was 21 1/4 inches by 21 inches, printed on handmade papers in hand-mixed inks and sold for $7,000. Our facsimile was 18 inches by 18 inches and priced at $23. Its production required reproducing the translucency of the pages of the original while maintaining clarity of Kiki's images. To achieve this involved pulling repeated page proofs, continual consultations among Mei-mei, Kiki, Robert Rosenwasser (book designer), and Keith Whitaker and Marian O'Brien (book printers Rena has mentioned). I wish we had been able to document this five-way creative process. But just getting the book out was all we could do. Another notable thing about this collaboration: The signed limited editions, priced at $142, sold out immediately to private art-book collectors. Our response: "Wow! This is different!" The regular edition sold out, as well.

RR: Singling out one of our collaborations over another is not easy. Each one, when held in my hand, brings back a reservoir of memories. Even now the tactile quality of our collaborations as I turn pages induces pleasure.

For *Sphericity*, a poetry book of Mei-mei Berssenbrugge's, Richard Tuttle created the image for the cover as well as the interior drawings. Lifting up the book today the metallic in the inking continues to shimmer. I remember proofing the cover with Richard at West Coast Print Center. It was 1993 and Richard flew to Berkeley for the printing. Keith Whitaker of West Coast Print Center was pulling proofs off the press. Richard kept commenting as proof after proof was pulled. Some metallic was added to the silver, a little more, a little less. When Richard had his "ah hah" moment we knew we had it right.

Kiki Smith and Mei-mei made several collaborations with the press: *Endocrinology* in 1997 and *Concordance* in 2006. I had known Kiki since the mideighties. Patricia already described the production of *Endocrinology*. It is impossible not to cite both these works as among the most challenging to produce and the most rewarding to read. Circling around both artists for all these decades has been a source of inspiration for me and pride for the press.

Symbiosis, a collaboration between Barbara Guest and Laurie Reid, was released in 2000. By the nineties Barbara, long known as a New York School poet, relocated to Berkeley, California. Helen Frankenthaler, one of her NY artist colleagues, had done the image for one of Barbara's earliest books, *The Blue Stairs*. Whenever I visited Guest's house, I would see the original Frankenthaler drawing on the wall. After Barbara was fully settled into her cottage on Milvia Street I introduced her to the Bay Area artist Laurie Reid. Laurie lived near Barbara, and they shared a love of French poetry, especially Mallarmé. If ever there was a symbiosis it could be categorized by the two of them bonding together. Laurie, whose work involves adding pigment to watercolor, created a long, narrow drawing. The height of the drawing was 7.5 inches, and the length was 330 inches, beginning on the front cover, traveling through the interior pages, and ending on the back. The stained pigment drawing carried all the way through. It was one continuous drawing and Barbara's poem also stretched uninterrupted for the duration of the book. Each page contained a few lines or stanzas. The drawing was printed by West Coast Print Center on offset and the type on letterpress by Peter Rutledge Koch. Just recently I was reminiscing with Laurie about coming up with the color for the cover typography. It was risky using vivid turquoise, but looking at the cover now, I love the impression of this ink on the Proterra Antique Stucco cover stock. When we brought the cover with the turquoise impressions to Barbara to view, we were relieved when she was also pleased with it. This was the last book I handset for Kelsey Street. Setting the type letter by letter, I thought of the seventies when I set the type and Patricia rolled the presses. Almost thirty years have gone by since those early books. For the book's dedication

240   *Women in Independent Publishing*

Barbara wrote, "A writer and an artist working together establish a Symbiosis, as in Nature, where dissimilar organisms productively live together."

SA: So in the eighties you were doing some offset, like Opal Palmer Adisa's *Bake-Face and Other Guava Stories* (1986), at the same time as these collaborations, right? How did producing and distributing offset have its own challenges and advantages?

PD: I can only think of the practical advantages of the offset printing process for us. It was much less time-consuming than letterpress. It opened up possibilities for interesting cover designs, a chance to bring in art by well- and lesser-known women artists. It made possible the complex processes that have produced our collaborations. Also, it brought us to our long relationship with the ever-inventive Jeff Clark, the designer Rena mentioned previously.

SA: What are some of your recent favorite books and why?

PD: This question reminds me of being asked which is my favorite child. But it's different. There are circumstances that have set certain books apart for me. First, there are a few books that, when first reading them in manuscript form, just a few pages in, I have thought: If KSP doesn't publish this, I'll do it myself. I felt this way when I first read *recombinant* by Ching-In Chen. Their poems introduced a voice that was new to me, an old voice that draws a line and speaks through cultural groups and artifacts. The poems resonated with a power that can't be appropriated, colonized, or denied their worth.

Another book that has moved me in a special way is Andrea Abi-Karam's *EXTRATRANSMISSION*. It required time for me to understand and respect the poetry as deeply as I do now, the way Andrea writes of pain and trauma. In conversations I found out that poets in the community had been waiting for this book: It was on classroom syllabi before it came out. It's a special feeling when you are shown situations in the current society you didn't know about and that are important to you. I am eighty and many of the books we are publishing are written by authors in their thirties. There's half a century between us. It gives me insight into where poetry goes to be relevant. Also, Andrea performs their work. I've enjoyed the flows in their readings that move from Andrea through the audience, from page to performance through their body and their words.

RR: Poets often are given to declare that their most recent work is their favorite. My sentiments are a bit like that regarding the books I helped to produce. Forty years after our early forays into bookmaking I undertook producing *Cecilia Vicuña: New and Selected Poems (1966–2015)*, edited by Rosa Alcalá. This book is one of the most ambitious the press has undertaken. It was our first bilingual production and included images of Vicuña's performances, drawings, as well as poems. A Literary Translation Fellowship from the NEA allowed Rosa Alcalá to translate Cecilia's poems from Spanish and Quechua to English. Her translations were crucial. Also, without the help of press member Anna Morrison assisting me this complex project would not have been possible.

SA: What parts of the publication process have been particularly challenging?

PD: Keeping going, basically. Bringing in and training members. Fundraising. Constantly. We live from year to year with the truth of the saying, "Poetry doesn't sell," which has come up in this interview before.

SA: What challenges/opportunities were introduced to KSP (and, I presume, with which you continue to grapple) by technological shifts in the 2000s?

PD: Personally, I remain nonconversant in the way of websites and social media. But I've appreciated the platforms and information networks the Internet opened up for us in the nineties. Using it involved a steep learning curve, as I think I've said. A graduate from Brown's creative writing program, Tanya Erzen, set up our website domain, www.kelseyst.com. For months we researched other presses' web pages to get design ideas for ours. We put out calls for generous tech-savvy people willing to work pro bono. Then we took on more members to keep the calendar, newsletter, and blog current, a task now a fundamental part of press life.

SA: In four years KSP will turn fifty! Did you imagine, when setting out, that the press would have such longevity?

PD: Not even close! We began in response to a void in this society where women writers were missing. Having decided to form, we had to learn everything. For years we simply put one foot ahead of the other. And, in publishing, everything is always changing—technology, poetics, social issues, and the poetry community. It was only sometime in the midnineties, when Rena and I were having breakfast one morning, that we realized that people in NYC and in other parts of the country, people whose work we loved and respected, knew who we were, and that people at bookfairs now recognized our name and knew our books. That was a moment!

RR: At this juncture, Patricia Dienstfrey and I are turning the press over to the younger press members—Mg Dufresne, Ching-In Chen, Carla Hall, and Erin Wilson. They have formed an Emerging Group that will, in the future, choose and produce the books and run the press. Patricia and I remain involved as mentors and available to assist, but our hope is that this next generation continues the press's historic run.

SA: Some time has passed between our initial interview; have there been any major changes in the press?

PD: One day, a former press member, Hazel White, asked me if I had ever heard the term "Founders' Syndrome." I hadn't. Subsequently, the four younger press members met with Frances Phillips, a board member and skilled group facilitator. After a single session, of the four younger members with Frances Phillips, a new Kelsey Street Press emerged.

It had been bewildering to Rena and me that, in a press organization that was nonhierarchical and in which each member was free to propose projects and changes, another dynamic had been at work. Frances Phillips, with Hazel White's encouragement, was key to this next phase of the press. It had been forty-five-plus years since Rena and I were involved in founding the press. As of 2020 we are a press under the Emerging Group's leadership. We continue to be a completely volunteer organization committed, one and all, to collective principles. Rena and I take care of certain tasks, attend alternate press meetings, and are on hand to lend press decisions an ineffable quality that has to do with continuity, which we all value.

SA: What advice do you have for women hoping to start a small press?

PD: If you want to start a press, do it. You'll get more out of it than you put in. Don't be afraid to try new things.

Figure 17. Bolinas Hearsay News (Wednesday Edition, March 29, 2017). Photo of Joanne Kyger and cover by Steve Heilig.

Joanne Kyger

Wednesday Editor, Bolinas Hearsay News *(1974–present, Bolinas, CA)*

DECEMBER 2013 TO MAY 2014, VIA E-MAIL

Stephanie Anderson: How did the *Bolinas Hearsay News* begin? Were you involved in its founding?[1]

Joanne Kyger: Before the *Bolinas Hearsay News* started publication in 1974, there were three small, irregularly published papers, the *Bolinas Hit*—Bill Beckman publisher—*Beaulines*, and the *Paper*. I remember the first copies of the *Hearsay* being written on paper plates down at Scowley's, one of the two local eateries. Greg Hewlett had organized fundraisers earlier to buy the town a press. Through spaghetti dinners and donations a multilith was purchased and housed in a garage on the mesa. It was later moved to Mickey Cummings's house a few blocks away and he was the first official printer of the "Mesa Press." Bill Berkson published some of his early Big Sky books on it. While still housed there, the first *Hearsays* came out. They would often be collated downtown at Scowley's and then distributed locally, as they are now, at three or four downtown businesses and in a mailbox outside the *Hearsay* office. The *Hearsay* was offered a space in the building behind the Bolinas Public Utilities office in the middle seventies and remains there to this day.

I helped the Wednesday editor, Nancy Whitefield, with the paper for several years before it moved to the BCPUD [Bolinas Community Public Utility District] office, when it was at Bill Johnson's house. He was a talented and playful graphic artist and the mornings were long with coffee, brandy, and long pauses for inspiration when no articles were handed in. But the paper was always delivered to the printer by noon. A calendar of events is still the main front-page feature, with birthdays listed in another column. It was a way for the

246   *Women in Independent Publishing*

town to find out what was going on, and remains a mainstay of information about musical events, happenings at the community center, meetings, etc.

I became the Wednesday editor on my own in 1984, and usually asked someone to be an "assistant" editor in order to bring other elements of news and events into the paper. Bolinas is an unincorporated town, but we have three elected bodies that represent us to the county: the Bolinas-Stinson School, the Fire Department, and the Bolinas Public Utilities District—the latter acts as a public forum for any issues that concern the town, which are brought up at the beginning of its monthly meetings. The *Hearsay* published all the minutes for these meetings, plus those of the Bolinas Community Center, which owns the main building downtown where different town events take place.

All articles accepted by the *Hearsay*, which are dropped off during the mornings when the paper is laid out or dropped in the mail slot in the door, must be signed. I think that is the only editorial requirement.

SA: Could you say more about the genre of the *Hearsay News*? It seems a bit like a free-for-all, in terms of content. What distinguished it from the three small papers published before it?

JK: The fact that it was reliably published three times a week and had a calendar of events.

SA: Sometimes it's difficult—or impossible—to find a "masthead," then or now, for the *Hearsay News*. Was anonymity something prized, or did the community simply know everyone involved in production?

JK: Mastheads were various; editors could use whatever they wanted, as long as they remembered to notate the date and day of the week.

SA: One thing that strikes me in the first issues of the *Hearsay* from 1974 is the little pieces of art and poetry (including a *Hearsay* limerick contest!) tucked away among the lost and found notices, etc. Were those items filler, or were they meant to have the same import as more "practical" news? Did the *Hearsay News* ever publish items by those visiting (or residing) poets and artists?

JK: The *Hearsay* editors could publish anything they wanted to fill up the paper. I always liked using poems from visiting poets. The graphics often came from visitors also. When I was editor, I relied on Donald Guravich frequently for drawings and covers. The copy machine we used as a vital part of our layout design could reduce or enlarge drawings. Local pieces from contributors came first before reprints of other articles, even though they were about Bolinas. All this was laid out during morning office hours 9–12, and then the printer came in and ran off the copies and took them downtown by at least 3 or 4 that afternoon.

SA: When you say, "Local pieces from contributors came first before reprints of other articles, even though they were about Bolinas," does that mean that work by residents always came first, regardless of content? What kind of reprints would you consider?

JK: Articles about Bolinas printed in the *San Francisco Chronicle*, magazines, other newspapers, etc. There were always lots of pieces about Bolinas tearing down the road sign on Highway 1 that said with an arrow BOLINAS 2. Like it was a town that never wanted to be found by the causal driver, tourist. They made local bumper stickers that said BOLINAS 2 and people would drive all over California with them. It actually was a mysterious advertisement.

SA: How many copies were printed?

JK: When I first moved here in 1969 there were about five hundred people who lived here full time. Now there are about 1,500. People share copies of the paper, and there is always a copy at the downtown library. There are anywhere from 100 to 250 copies printed, depending on whether there are big election issues in which everyone wants a voice. Now that it is online I'm not sure how many copies are printed. I stopped being the Wednesday editor about a year ago.

SA: In the age of instant information and global news, what are some of the benefits and challenges of the *Hearsay*'s localism—of publishing for and about such a specific community?

JK: It certainly keeps a community glued together. Birth announcements, weddings, deaths; announcements concerning roads, water usage, the fire department, the school, etc.; and agendas for

248   *Women in Independent Publishing*

meetings for all pertinent organizations, including the community center. Also the minutes taken at these meetings are published. It makes the "government" here much more transparent. The paper works as a community bulletin board in which everyone is a "reporter"—the only requirement being that you sign your name. The display ads and classified ads are local and very useful in moving goods and services around.

SA: Your phrase "everyone is a 'reporter'" reminds me of the idea that the typewriter makes it possible for everyone to be a "publisher." What technological changes did you witness at the *Hearsay* over your thirty-plus years of editing? And did you publish poems in the *Hearsay*?

JK: Not everyone had a typewriter or printer. Many pieces were, and still are, written out by hand. We tried to aim for a 3 ½-inch column width. So one could be a publisher if you had machine that could make multiple pages. I never published any of my own poems, but Steve Heilig, who became an alternate Wednesday editor, published some of my work. I never heard anyone mention what they thought about my writing. I tried to keep a fairly translucent role as editor, publishing whatever was turned in, and with a back-up of articles relevant to the community to use as filler when needed. One of the editors, StuArt Chapman, made some official-looking laminated *Hearsay News* press passes, which some "reporters" have used to gain access to things like the Democratic Convention here in the eighties, and various theater events.

SA: Did working on the *Hearsay* change your ideas about publishing and/or how you approach your creative work?

JK: I found out how easy it was to layout a page (8 ½ by 17, legal size), what designs and space worked best. Actually, I found out how easy it was to publish something once the "right" set-up is there and have it on the street on the same day.

We did a few publications on the press, called it Evergreen Road Press, and published a few issues of a small magazine called *GATE* with Stefan Hyner, who then published it on a bigger scale in Germany where he lived.

SA: You've published some e-books; do you feel like the immediacy of the Internet is similar to the oft-lauded immediacy of mimeo publication?

JK: I'm not aware of any e-books I've published. What are they? The Internet is quickly accessible, but unless you print out what you're reading, it isn't as easily available for a return read—which one wants to do with magazines and poetry.

SA: I found the e-books on your EPC author page.

JK: Found the two e-books; forgot about them. Coyote Books's *Distressed Look* was also in a small edition form. *Permission by the Horns* was eventually unsatisfactory since it wasn't in a paper form.

SA: What do you think makes poetry or magazines something you want to see in print, to "return read" as you say?

JK: I think poetry is something you need to read more than once—unlike headlines in a newspaper.

SA: What was your favorite aspect of being Wednesday editor?

JK: I liked being able to "produce" a publication/newspaper in one day. Very gratifying to see it all distributed at the various stores downtown and at the library. For some years there was home delivery by a crew of young kids on bikes. And also I liked meeting other members of the community who came to the office with articles or questions or to place a classified ad. One could get a feel for what the ephemeral but personal sense of what makes up "the news" in a small community.

SA: Why did you stop being Wednesday editor?

JK: I thought I would take a break from the paper for a while, and that while kept getting longer. New editors eventually stepped in, reflecting another side of Bolinas. One has to watch a tendency as editor to write articles advertising oneself.

SA: What's special and/or ordinary about Bolinas, a place that I feel has become almost mythological for poets and artists? You've lived abroad; why Bolinas for the last thirty-plus years?

JK: Bolinas is very beautifully situated in front of the coast range, on a lagoon and a mesa. Surrounded by protected parkland. I bought my house and land here in 1972 when it was still very inexpensive. I found for a while I had to save up to be able to get out of town,

250 *Women in Independent Publishing*

which is always useful for perspective. It's very easy to live here, but one needs to make an hour's drive over the coast range to larger towns to do any extensive shopping for groceries, hardware, clothes, etc.

SA: Sounds like a lovely and insular community. Did that make the arrival of visiting poets and artists especially important for the community? (I'm thinking of Joe Brainard's *Bolinas Journal* and all the different people he mentions meeting.)

JK: For the poets it was always wonderful to have visiting poets. I'm not sure what the rest of the community thought.

SA: Apart from the *Hearsay News*, what were the other kinds of publishing ventures with which you were involved (as editor, helper, etc.)? (I'm thinking of the *Turkey Buzzard Review* and *Wild Dog*—would you talk about those? Were there others?)

JK: The *Turkey Buzzard Review* was a loose gathering of friends, mostly women, who got together and drank coffee and brandy and decided what to publish. Dotty le Mieux was the most ambitious, so we decided she would be editor. We gave several "theatrical" *Turkey Buzzard* readings for the community. It was always fun and barely serious. Some years before I helped edit *Wild Dog*, which moved from Idaho to San Francisco in 1965 to 1966, when I was living there.

SA: The 1971 oil spill had a galvanizing effect on the Bolinas community. Do you think that that event influenced the literary-publishing scene? (And if so, how?)

JK: Kevin Opstedal does a good and accurate job of talking about Bolinas "literary" history in *Dreaming as One*, the title of which he has since changed to *All This Everyday*. It still hasn't been published outside of being online and a few Xerox copies, one of which is at the library. He covers the oil spill accurately, which does give a picture of the "rest" of the community, the nonpoet and very active participants. It did start a very active political participation in the town's problems, and subsequent participation on the Bolinas Community Public Utility board, elected offices. Lewis MacAdams's *News from Niman Farm* is a great reflection of that time. He was an elected member of the board, and the only poet.

SA: Opstedal calls the *Hearsay News* a "community forum" and "ongoing biography of the town, a true and immediate diary of community consciousness." Is this an apt description?

JK: Kevin is right on with his comments about the *Hearsay News*.

Figure 18. Basil and Martha King. Photo by Sanjay Agnihotri.

Martha King

Coeditor, Two and Two Press (with Susan Sherman, 1975, New York),
and Editor, Giants Play Well in the Drizzle *(1983–1992, New York)*

NOVEMBER 2019 TO MAY 2020, VIA E-MAIL

Stephanie Anderson: Will you talk a bit about how you came to edit Two and Two chapbooks with Susan Sherman in the late seventies? Do you remember how you and Susan met?

Martha King: When did we meet? The dawn of time . . . fifty-five years ago, around the time we moved to Second Avenue, probably through Harry Lewis, with whom Baz [Basil King] and David Glotzer started *Mulch* magazine. We were part of a loose crew of art types, several of whom also lived at 57–59 Second Avenue, corner of 4th Street. Paul Pines, e.g., Matt Umanov—he started his guitar shop a few years later. Many others nearby. Fee [Fielding] Dawson (Baz's first-year roommate from Black Mountain), Gil Sorrentino, LeRoi and Hettie Jones, A. B. Spellman, Hubert Selby Jr. (Cubby), Dianne DiPrima . . . and more. It was quite a neighborhood.

What is it about 4th Street! We now live on it in Brooklyn. QUITE different.

SA: Taking off from that statement, was Two and Two Press a "Manhattan" project (despite being printed in Brooklyn) and *Drizzle* a "Brooklyn" project (despite being often put together at work—in Manhattan, right?), somehow?

MK: Let's see: Two 4th Streets: Well, it's just an accident that we lived on the LES [Lower East Side] on 2nd Avenue at 4th Street and moved in 1969 to Brooklyn's 4th Street. But it really didn't have an effect on my projects. It was mostly a matter of school for the kids. They'd had a wonderful time at the old Church of All Nations Day Care Center on 2nd Avenue but the public school there was a major nightmare.

254 *Women in Independent Publishing*

We were deeply opposed to private schools—still are. This part of Brooklyn even then had okay neighborhood P.S.'s and that's why we ended up here. (Helped no end by a nice windfall, which I've written about.[1])

SA: Where did the name Two and Two Press come from?

MK: Susan and I went round and round looking for a name. I wanted something simple, as simple as 2+2 I said at one point, and that's what we finally chose. Susan handled design and production almost single handedly. Did beautiful design work. We agreed that the appeal of a short chapbook would depend on good visuals—at that time there were so many Xeroxed and copy-shopped materials kind of thrown together. Plus a widespread penchant for collage that we both found distracting, and hard to see as well as making the text hard to read.

SA: All three chapbooks incorporate visual art, though the illustrations for your book *Women & Children First* (1975) are "found." Was incorporating visual art one of the goals of Two and Two?

MK: Our stance was low cost, very cheap, easy to produce—that does not mean cluttered or ugly. Restraint. Conscious of visual impact. We both wanted to show that text could be respected with visual art as a partner. We also wanted a quick output. Something written in March could be a little chapbook by April or May.

SA: What do you recall about your role in editing and making the chapbooks? The press seems to have had a fairly short run—was it meant to be a limited project at its inception? Was it founded to circulate specific work? Also, I love the last line of the last poem, the almost-sonnet, "Autobiography," in *Women & Children First*: "no unused spaces."

MK: I'm not sure what our long-distance plans were . . . I think mostly they weren't. Those were careless times.

I was supposed to do promotion. Ahem. Which is why I still have a stash of *Women & Children First* in my basement. Susan did much better, especially in the day when the whole country was covered with independent feminist bookshops. Ah, long lost now. She

Martha King   255

got many readings and sold or gave away her copies . . . I wrote less and less. The struggle to get and keep jobs plus kids and living with a dear but very complicated mate who was having his share of artistic woes . . . Oh, well. "No unused spaces" indeed. That was an ideal, not to be personally realized by me for years. I did/do love looking at an egg. What a design marvel.

SA: Turning to *Giants Play Well in the Drizzle*, do you think you realized this "ideal" of "no unused spaces" in your editing of *GPWITD*? In your memoir you call the publication a "zine," and it does have an aesthetic of immediacy, like a newsletter. It usually doesn't leave poems haloed by white space.

MK: Space was always a guiding editorial principal for *GPWITD* as I didn't want to exceed what could go for one first-class stamp. Plus seeking a balance among pieces for an issue and my strong feeling that what one reads is very influenced by what is before it, facing it, or opposite it. Visual art is very strongly affected by this. I'm always very aware of how a museum or gallery hangs or places art stuff. I can't say "no unused spaces" in the *Drizzle* because I was often left with "overs"—texts I had planned to include but couldn't make work in the ensemble. I didn't ever want to cram . . . The pages were intended to flow and to set off some resonances from one work to another. Counterpoint? Contrast? Dissonance??

There was a response to this as contributors began, over time, to send me short and shorter poems and prose. It could so easily become a formula. For me and for them. DANG. So yes, I did consciously disrupt patterns. I think I wrote in my memoir that Robert Frost said every collection of ten poems is the eleventh poem, and while I am rarely crazy about his work this does nail it.

SA: I know you cover this in the memoir,[2] but for readers who haven't yet read that book, would you summarize again how so much of *GPWITD* was assembled during your nine-to-five job? Were its aesthetics at all influenced by its production content?

MK: As reported in my memoir, I was being urged to leave my job via a standard corporate move: I was given less and less to do and was cut out of planning meetings and other timewasters. It was meant to break down morale and confidence but I (😁) closed the door and got on with it. PULEEZE don't throw me in that briar patch! Brer Rabbit's scams were as familiar to me as Tom Sawyer's fence-painting con. That happened in 1983. I'd been hired a little over a year earlier at Memorial Sloan-Kettering Cancer Center (MSK) for the publications and public relations department—minus any credentials in science or science writing—by a lovely guy who told me he'd picked me because I was the best writer of all the applicants; he then gave me a couple of seminal books and encouraged me to attend grand rounds and read reports, and learn by doing what reporters do—asking questions, etc. During that period I was WAY too busy to steal any time, but he was kicked out by the Center's head boss (he got a very lush settlement) so a dedicated sycophant could be installed in his place. The MSK job had catapulted our family into the middle class the year before, which was just as our oldest child was ready for college. Change of boss in 1983 meant I had to cling to that job like a limpet. I didn't have enough under my belt to seek another science-writing job. Keeping busy with the *Drizzle* was an important survival tactic besides being a wonderful opportunity for me to work with words and be in touch with interesting writers on my own terms. Eventually, the situation changed, but by then I was able to finesse some regular days when I worked from home.

At first I did all the Xeroxing in the office after hours . . . Later my mailing list was too large, so I got it done at modest cost from a local copy shop out here in Brooklyn. Much, much later I found out that Allen at the copy shop was Barbara Henning's beloved and the boy who was often hanging around riding his skateboard in front of the shop was their son.

By the way, the *Drizzle* period ('83–'92) also covered the transformation of office equipment everywhere . . . from typewriter to clunky word processor to portable personal computer as you might notice from the changes in typography.

SA: The notes say that *GPWITD* is published "periodically," or "irregularly for the pleasure of setting things in motion," and so forth. It seems to me that it came out two or three times per year. Did that coincide with having filled the pages? Or were there other things determining the irregular schedule?

MK: I'm not sure why the publication was so irregular. I regret that. But I was also writing poetry, and my husband and I were shepherding two young women, one born 1963, the other 1964, through all those early adult transitions, first love affairs, college choices, etc., including our younger daughter's disastrous decision to marry the wrong man. He was so wrong, and his family was so awful; we threw a great, big wedding event at our house and at the Brooklyn Botanic Japanese garden. We had to stake our claim as it were. The young man and his family wanted total possession of her, and it was a long time before she recognized what was happening.

Midway through the *Drizzle*'s span (1988) we also hosted a huge party at Basil's big studio on 39th Street, Brooklyn . . . invited everyone I'd published to that point for a long afternoon's reading. And people came from all over. New England, California, Ohio . . . Hung some of Basil's large paintings (portraits of David Rattray, Paul Metcalf, and Nancy) and his surreal takes on the playing cards (The King Eats at Six, etc.). It was quite a production. I had the audio guy from St. Mark's record the lot and I have the cassettes somewhere in our cellar . . . It was both a great success—the loft was packed—and a disaster, as Basil's work did not go over well. Too long a story to tell. But it is part of what occupied time and energy during that time.

SA: I love the story of naming *GPWITD*, "a headline from a tabloid sports page, deciphered from my upside-down view as I hung on a swinging metal subway handle on my way to the early morning office." Did anyone ever "catch" (sorry) on to the title?

MK: A few English correspondents asked about that, sorting out British football, US baseball, who plays in the rain, etc. No American

258   *Women in Independent Publishing*

ever asked. But I have told the story and New Yorkers always get the business of reading other people's newspaper headlines. I do miss the tabloids. Now faces are buried in cell phones—BUT books are making a comeback at least on the trains in NYC.

SA: In the memoir you talk about your time in Grand Haven and your writing there, saying, "I wanted to use Olson's conception that the resonance of a place is revelatory and that out of a jumble of information—personal stories, devices, connections, extensions—could come *form*." Is editing also about discovering form in the jumble, or does the editor create a new jumble?

MK: I'm not a devotee of Cage, but a great deal of what happens seems to start with chance. Does the editor discover form in the jumble or create a new jumble? Well, both. Both order and disorder are actually quite sneaky. I think it's wonderful that special computer programs have to be devised to generate *truly* random numbers. Otherwise, random numbers tend to contain patterns and rare people with special facilities can even tune in and predict them.

SA: About editing, you write, "Then as now my editorial acumen lived in the pit of my stomach." You expand on it more in the book, saying that you were "looking for an essential energy, the jazz of conversation"—will you talk a bit about how that worked? Also, a circulation of eight hundred (in 1990) is pretty good by contemporary small press poetry standards. Some of the copies I received on interlibrary loan had been addressed to Allen Ginsberg, and others to John Ashbery. What were some of the surprising connections that resulted from the magazine's circulation?

MK: I asked people to send me work for the *Drizzle*, but increasingly people sent stuff I would never have found otherwise. Complete and strange surprises in submissions from:

Arnold Falleder
David Rattray (Well, I knew he wrote but I was knocked out by his riff on "In Nomine," which he learned to play on the piano, fairly well . . .)

Elizabeth Robinson
Gerald Burns
Laurel Speer
Miriam Sagan
Todd Moore (Oh, actually, Paul Metcalf told me to look him up. He turned me on to Lucia Berlin too.)

Looking at the full list today, I'm again hit by my thought (hits a lot of people who teach adult and other poetry classes outside academic programs) that among otherwise dull and cliché-ridden ordinary work, a piece pops up, coheres! I think almost anyone might write a wonderful poem once or twice . . . but you don't want all their output! Some of the people I published were truly marginal, under the influence of mental disorders, whatever. That's a whole 'nother subject, isn't it? It doesn't frighten me, but it is—they are—recognizably different, off. We do need the alien. The *Drizzle*, I'm happy to brag, presented this work without explanation or label and in concert with other writings. My contribution was to create pages on which poems could resonate and vibrate with each other. An anthology of the soul. Sounds WAY too flossy . . . thank goodness the *Drizzle* was short!

SA: I'm also curious about whether you were working to include women in the magazine. That there are more men than women is not surprising, given the time and the scene—but I noticed that there's usually at least one women included, and they're usually different people, not simply the same person in issue after issue. Was that something you were thinking about while putting the magazine together? Did your thinking on this topic change over the years?

MK: I'm a bit of an apostate about gender issues. Aware that "more men than women" write. Or have done so publicly. But angry that women writers are so often confined to a gender ghetto. Black writers have a similar problem. HATE anthologies designed to shine a light on this or that aspect. Women writers have always

260 *Women in Independent Publishing*

been in my world because of what they write . . . not their sex.
H. D. Susan Howe. Stevie Smith. Denise Levertov. Zora Neal
Hurston. And on and on. Is there a "woman's voice"? I SO doubt
it. "A"? "a voice"??? Gender (and experience) are much more fluid
than that. Does ethnicity influence writing? You bet. So does history, both personal, geographical, and national. Maybe you better
not quote me; I don't want a swarm of angry folks chiding me.
My thinking on this formed in my late teens. I grew up in a liter-
ary household where both my mother and my father strongly and
sincerely believed in female inferiority as far as art is concerned.
(And my father was a book editor whose clients included Eudora
Welty, Katherine Anne Porter, and Jean Stafford. Go figure.) And
I was then influenced by Black Mountain College MEN—Olson,
Creeley, Duncan, etc. Go figure again!

SA: Regarding the technology changing while *GPWITD* was being produced—did you have a favorite form of production? Or a particular
part of the process that you liked?

MK: I was a stubborn late adapter! Still am. When the office at MSK first
brought in word processors I threatened to never finish a writing
assignment again. But it came to me slowly . . . Ease of adjust-
ment. Design possibilities. Type changes. You can see a bit of it in
the *Drizzle* formats. I very slowly came to love the technology which
was developing at speed when I was trying to master it! I first had a
word processor with no "gooey interface"—the mouse and all that.
Everything had to be handled via typed-in commands of various
sorts. No wonder I was so opposed!

Now I can hardly imagine working without it. Would be like
going back to the goose quills. Plus—the Internet came along. If
I'd continued to publish *GPWITD* I think I would have plunged into
electronic distribution—and tried to tackle the problems involved
in reading seriously with this speedy, ephemeral, unquiet, and profoundly distracting technology. It's still a daily battle—and I find
myself longing for print, compliant and passive. But today I wouldn't
give this up!

SA: Anything else?

MK: I think (I hope) I've answered much of what you asked. The only other comment I do need to make is that I am not as sure now as I was when younger that my personal anarchy served me well. I wish I had been more cooperative. Created more alliances. Involved other people in my editorial and distribution processes. Not been so wary. (Growing up in my family taught me swift lessons in self-protection.) Going it alone and doing everything my own way made me love the *Drizzle* dearly. But, but, ah, but.

Figure 19. Patricia Spears Jones. Photo by Marcia Wilson.

Patricia Spears Jones

Editor, W. B. (1975, New York); Coeditor, Ordinary Women *(1978, New York); Editorial Staffer for the Heresies Collective (1976–1993)*

JULY TO AUGUST 2015, VIA E-MAIL

Stephanie Anderson: Your mimeo mag, *W. B.*, came out in 1975, and the title page thanks the Poetry Project "for the use of their facilities." Will you talk a little bit about the magazine's context and why you started it?[1]

Patricia Spears Jones: I was going to workshops and hanging out at the Poetry Project. It was the mimeo magazine time, and Maureen Owen and others urged me to develop a journal. I am proud of it. Lee Breuer, who is one of the founders of Mabou Mines, contributed, as did Levi Frazier Jr., one of my college classmates, who also happens to be a Black American. Indeed, as with many of my projects, race and gender diversity were very much in the midst. I think I was multicultural in my focus long before it became a convention.

SA: Did you have any models, at the Project or elsewhere, for this kind of multicultural endeavor? What were some of the challenges to diversity in 1970s New York art scenes?

PSJ: I think I was basically the start of that in many ways—the Project was for the most part white and male. So anybody who was not white or male was a diversity. Ha! Downtown was much smaller and there was a lot of mixing it up on the loft jazz scene, in some experimental theater, but for the most part, then as now, New York City was hypersegregated. Because I was not a native New Yorker, I pretty much talked to everybody: Jews, Puerto Ricans, Asians, etc. And because of the rise in cultural feminism, there were many opportunities to work with poets-artists involved: June Jordan rounded many of us up for a protest against the *American*

Poetry Review (*APR*); the "Sisterhood," which was for Black women writers, met on the Upper West Side and in Brooklyn. The Basement Workshop was the closest to having a multicultural ethos even though it was located in Chinatown and was actively engaged in improvements for its citizens. Fay Chiang, who later coedited *Ordinary Women*, started the Basement Workshop. And of course, almost anyone with a hankering to showcase their talents (whether they had any or not) could check out the Nuyorican Poets Café. The remnants of the Umbra workshop were seen in Ishmael Reed, Steve Cannon, and Joe Johnson's Reed, Cannon & Johnson imprint, which CUNY grad center folk are documenting with the help of David Henderson, one of the poets still active in New York City. Sometimes these various groups came together, but mostly not. Of course, we were all so very young.

SA: What was the protest against *APR*, and how was it important to you?

PSJ: June Jordan, who wrote columns for *APR*, pointed out that she and Alice Walker and other poets of color never had their actual poems published in *APR*, and at that time most of the poets published were white and male. It was fascinating to participate in a protest run by poets who were successful and who still faced serious discrimination. The irony was that one of the younger poets who I asked to send work to *APR* and who was published by the magazine was white and male!

SA: What is the significance of the mimeo mag's title *W. B.*? And the subtitle, *(short works)*?

PSJ: I can't remember why I called it *W. B.* but it was some kind of talisman—those two members of the alphabet. *(short works)* was just that: The pieces were not long. Remember I had to type out each of those darn pages and then run them off and then get friends (yeah) to help me collate and bind them. The mimeo scene was full of fun, camaraderie, and support. But it still cost more than I could do, despite all the volunteer efforts, so I only did one issue.

SA: Did you produce them at the Poetry Project?

PSJ: Yes. And it was fun.

SA: *Ordinary Women* is obviously a fairly different endeavor from *W. B.*—

OW is an anthology, offset printed, perfect-bound. How did the idea for this collection come about?

PSJ: It came about from conversations with other young women poets writing and working in New York City who wanted to see our work presented. We wanted an anthology that was intentionally diverse because most of the women's anthologies were mostly white with token writers of color. We had heard of the *Third World Women* anthology from the West Coast, and we wanted something that came close to that. Sara Miles and I asked Fay Chiang and Sandra Maria Esteves to join us, and we did outreach to white, Black, Asian, and Latina poets. Cynthia Kramen and Lois Elaine Griffith, who is an artist and a poet, were also extremely important to the success of the anthology. Adrienne Rich was a supporter and granted us funds for the publication, and she wrote a wonderful introduction. We wanted to show that NYC women poets were like all the other the other young women in the city—making our way in our world the same way that actors or designers or political activists were making their way. Ultimately, I think we found a way to show autonomous women poets with varied life experiences who walked these sometimes mean, sometimes wonderful streets.

SA: How long did it take to put *OW* together? The introduction describes an intensive manuscript solicitation: "We solicited manuscripts through notices in women's papers, poetry newsletters, community centers, friends . . ." How did selection and production work, and what were some of the hurdles?

PSJ: About a year from outreach to production. As with any collection, we had the usual issues: Some women poets objected to a gender-based anthology; our desire for diversity was paramount, but many felt like it might be tokenism; there were aesthetic differences among the editors. But in the end, we were satisfied with our list and the poems that we selected.

SA: What was your favorite part of making the anthology?

PSJ: Getting that wonderful range of poets in print; many have gone on to produce books, develop new organizations, teach, etc. We did not request permission to do this. We did not ask for grants.

266 *Women in Independent Publishing*

It was our limited funds, our ideas, our time on the line. I feel like we gave women poets a great model for how to not use tokenism. There were criticisms, as there should be. But we cast a wide and cleverly made net across this city and came back with some interesting young women poets and their work. And I am sure others took that as a sign to do something similar—at least I hope so. And I am grateful that as of this writing, Sara, Fay, Sandy, and I are still breathing and still making great work in different ways. We all respect the ability of women to make a world we want to live in, and we continue to try and make that world.[2]

SA: What was the reception of the anthology like? How did you respond to the critique that, as Eileen Myles wrote in a mixed review for the *Poetry Project Newsletter*, that "the gathering of these poems seems to have sprung from a sociological impulse, not an aesthetic one"?

PSJ: Eileen Myles was doing the usual "poetics" versus agitprop line. They were roundly denounced for that petty review. But this was the kind of mindset that allowed white poets to question the "quality" of the work of poets of color, even the most formal and conventional, because said poets might use words to describe the skin tones of Black people. Racism can be blunt or subtle, simply the status quo. And patriarchal notions, even from those with serious rage against the patriarchy, show up—it's part of our cultural DNA. Again, there were many women who did not want to be part of gender-based projects. It has always seemed to me that these kinds of critiques are part of America's difficulty with marrying very public issues with private concerns in art—and it is a kind of fallout from McCarthyism. That is, political poetry and art were suspect because they dealt with those public concerns—the antiwar poets of the 1960s received similar critiques. I would suggest that Myles has changed their tune given their work with AIDS activism and the LGBT community. But this criticism matters little because the work aesthetically and politically continues to shine.

SA: In the introduction to *Ordinary Women*, Adrienne Rich writes, "The jazz poetry movement, the mass antiwar readings of the 1960s, the grassroots cultural centers where music and poetry come together,

Patricia Spears Jones 267

and above all the surge of women's poetry readings, have created a new oral style, an almost tribal awareness, the poem not as artifact of solitude but as cry of recognition, outreach, accusation, celebration. And so, this is often a poetry meant to be spoken and heard." Almost forty years later, do you agree with this assessment of the rise of orality in poetry? Do you think it continues?

PSJ: Yes, I do. That is why slam poetry and open mics all work. That is why the Poetry Project's series are still amazing. That is why there are collective programs from Black Poets Speak Out to One Million Poets. While there will always be poets who veer towards monasticism, solitude, the carefully tended garden, there will be others who will speak to, speak of, and speak out about specific communities. The trick is to create work that can do that and reach farther than one's own tribe.

SA: When did you start working with the Heresies Collective?

PSJ: 1980.

SA: You were on the editorial staff of issue 17, the "Acting Up!" issue (1984). Will you talk a little bit about your experiences with the Heresies Collective and with the collective publishing model of the magazine?

PSJ: Working at Heresies was complicated. Coming to consensus on anything is difficult, and the range of personalities, ideas, agendas often brought up unexpected conflicts, and there was never enough money. That said, these women were fierce in their artmaking and their commitment to a feminist ideal. The conversations were powerful: Lucy Lippard, Sabra Moore, Sue Heinemann—they gave younger women like me great models of women's creativity and intellectual rigor. The "Acting Up!" issue was my first foray into that kind of intellectual rigor. We really identified many of the people and trends that would reshape or shape theater and performance— I am pleased with our capture of a feminist moment in that issue.

SA: "Acting Up!" contains excerpts from your collaborative theater piece "Women in Research" (with Cindy Carr and Lenora Champagne). Was it difficult to move between the media of the stage and the page? Or to translate performance to the page?

268   *Women in Independent Publishing*

PSJ: Actually, I think our excerpt works on the page because the writing was really good. If the writing is strong, then the themes and concerns in the piece will be conveyed, no matter the medium.

SA: So many of the concerns that motivated your involvement in small press publishing—issues of representation and privilege, and the elision of voices of writers of color—are currently being discussed in the poetry world. In your experience, what are some of the similarities and differences between the discussions as they currently play out versus when you were editing *Ordinary Women* in the late seventies?

PSJ: It is simply larger—the numbers of people involved in these conversations—and more theory driven. Words like "intersectionality" or "ally" are simple ways in which people are trying to define themselves and others. And there are always "others," whether we like it or not. The main difference is that whites are now having to confront their whiteness as whiteness. It has taken decades for Black Americans, for instance, to explore a range of ways of being Black, with some seeing this in opposition to whiteness and others who see assimilation into more mainstream culture as key to success. Now the mainstream is shrinking—whites will no longer be in the majority soon and, well, not one group on this planet has ever given up power with grace. Not one and this nation has a very nasty racist history. But while the violence and anger and missteps taking place now—which spill into the art world—are awful to experience, it also feels like a birth of a different, more complicated, and, yes, shared culture. A culture where Blacks can lead without racist framing or whites can lead without presumptions of superiority or mixed-race people are allowed to explore all of their heritages. And finally, privilege is at issue for the children of the upper middle class and super wealthy, and they can be any color. How do they "intersect" with the rest of us? Will they support work that does not mirror their own backgrounds? The poets of the 1960s and 1970s could explore their ideas, leave behind bourgeois convention because the economics was not so damning. Now, that is pretty much impossible. A culture based in lives of privilege is often formal, often static, or overly technological and static. Class privilege can support a new vision or damage one.

SA: What's next for you?

PSJ: I am pleased to have four decades of my work published in *A Lucent Fire: New and Selected Poems*. I feel like I have and will continue to make important work that will make readers think and feel and inspire them to do their work.

SA: What advice would you give a young woman now who wants to publish a magazine or anthology?

PSJ: My only advice to anyone is to try and do what you want to do to the best of your ability, and to find and keep good friends who give you advice, hugs, and support your dreams. And be honest with yourself and with others. The more people "game" the system, the worse the work is. Go for excellence; that is what lasts.

Figure 20. C. D. Wright. Photo by Forrest Gander.

C. D. Wright

Editor and Publisher, Lost Roads Press (1976–present, Fayetteville, AK; San Francisco; and Providence, RI)

NOVEMBER 2013 TO DECEMBER 2014, VIA E-MAIL

Stephanie Anderson: Was *Room Rented by a Single Woman* Lost Roads's first book? As author, how much input did you have into the publication process?[1]

C. D. Wright: *Room Rented . . .* did end up being LRP's first book. Frank [Stanford] had printed a few titles and then scrapped them because he was dissatisfied with the printing job. He redid them, and mine was included in that lot of six titles—he put the sequence together. In truth they came out pretty simultaneously.

SA: Do you recall Frank's aspirations for the press?

CDW: It was Frank's press until his death. Frank wanted to publish poets who were not part of a larger sphere, who did not have that kind of access (himself included). He was aware of how removed we were from a publishing center. This was something valuable he passed onto me—start where you are. The truffles are right under your nose.

SA: Do you know how the name of the press came to be Lost Roads?

CDW: The title Lost Roads Publishers comes from a Lorca poem. Frank's version of it appears in *YOU*, published posthumously. He titled it "Circle of Lorca" and it was spun out of Lorca's "Little Infinite Poem."

SA: What were your motivations for continuing the press?

CDW: How could I not continue it: he had published six titles, he had six more titles on the docket that were in progress. We had the equipment in the rental house we shared, and an appointment set up with the binder in Tulsa, and as it happened, an NEA had been awarded and was to be withdrawn because of his death, but Professor James

272 *Women in Independent Publishing*

Whitehead intervened, and the award went through under my aegis. A year later I moved to California. By that time I had the publishing bug. I enjoyed it. I only brought out one title while I was in California, *Trouble in Paradise*, a collection of pencil drawings by Zuleyka Benitez. I had had the books shipped to California, general delivery, since I had no San Francisco address. I stored half the inventory in Fayetteville, Arkansas, in the basement of the *Grapevine*, an independent community newspaper, a weekly. The day before I came back to Fayetteville to recover the inventory, a flood ruined most of it, including more than half of the copies of *The Battlefield Where the Moon Says I Love You*. So an edition of I think 1,500 was reduced by half at least. This poem had been printed two-up and was 542 pages long. It was a huge loss.

SA: *The Battlefield* is an epic in every way, including length. What was the process of printing and assembling it like? Did you have assistance?

CDW: Before Frank died, *The Battlefield* was printed in Bentonville, Arkansas, by Overstreet Printing, a printing business he had used for other titles. As I said, it was printed two-up, and that is a lot of plates. When the flats came back to the house we rented on Jackson Drive in Fayetteville, Frank organized a sorting party (this was weeks before he died). Some women came over and we sorted the pages into stacks we could take to the binders. We drove the flats to the binder in Tulsa, a family of really large folks who worked their way around their warehouse set-up to bind books. I picked the books up after his death. He never saw it bound.

    We had a printer helping us with the press; we had a Verityper which we operated ourselves, an unbelievably archaic way to set type, and a vertical Agfa Gevaert camera, a handmade light table to strip up the negatives, an old carbon-arc burner we used to burn the plates, a rebuilt 1850 multilith, a stash of paper in the garage . . . It was a dedicated amateur operation, and we did not know how to use any of the equipment except by trial and error.

    (If you have an original copy of *The Battlefield*, hang onto it. I probably have three.)

SA: Will you say a little more about the Verityper and the multilith? I feel like that equipment is difficult for us now to envision, and "Verityper" certainly doesn't turn up helpful hits on Google.

CDW: Verityper was a pretty primitive way to set type. I shipped the machine back to Irv Broughton after Frank's death as Irv kept insisting he wanted it back. Irv was Frank's first publisher, Mill Mountain Press. The Verityper set the letters proportionally, one deep peck at a time. Then we switched to an IBM typewriter that had proportional spacing. Cumbersome, but at least it plugged in. The AM Multilith was a common printer. We could only print two-up.

SA: Was Frank envisioning each of the first six books as being a discrete set? Were these "truffles" all by writers within a certain geographical range?

CDW: Frank envisioned the books as a series of six at a time and had selected and committed to the second six at the time of his death, as well as to printing *The Battlefield* in conjunction with Mill Mountain, but it was finally all taken on by Lost Roads.

SA: What do you think Frank would have thought about the current incarnation of the press?

CDW: I don't speculate about Frank. I knew him in his twenties, which he resolved not to outlive. I cannot project him forward.

SA: *Room Rented by a Single Woman* opens with a Dickinson quote, "But you must go to bed. I who sleep always, need no bed." It, and some of the voices in that book, invokes the sprawling and shifting dreamscapes of *The Battlefield*. Then and later on, did the process of physically building books influence your creative work?

CDW: I am still physically building books; that is how it feels to write.

SA: After Frank died, how did you market and distribute the books?

CDW: Marketing was nominal. Small Press Distribution handled the books. Not so differently than they do now: listing them in their catalog, stocking a small number and restocking if enough orders came in to warrant it. Occasional ads were placed in whatever sources we knew to place them and could afford it. Review copies were sent out, and a list cultivated of potential reviewers. It was like that, nothing exceptional but time intensive. A sequence of small tasks.

SA: What was the publishing community in Fayetteville like? How did it

CDW: There was no publishing community as such in Fayetteville. Frank was publishing, for the most part, poets who had finished their degrees and moved away. The other independent publisher was the *Grapevine*, a weekly newspaper, and it was read by virtually anyone engaged with the times. As with us, assembling the paper was very manual and required volunteerism. That spirit ran through the artistic and political community of Fayetteville. For Lost Roads, the printer and binders were paid. Frank and I did the rest.

SA: How did the mission of the press evolve while you were editing? How did the production of the books change?

CDW: The mission was to publish books I liked. I published one title in San Francisco. The first twelve books were books Frank had already selected and begun readying. The flats of *The Battlefield* had already been printed. When I moved to San Francisco I published the Benitez pencil drawings, as I mentioned. The next round of books began to include California poets, while still publishing poets and fiction writers I had known in Arkansas. Frances Mayes, Stan Rice, Honor Johnson I met in San Francisco. After moving to Mexico briefly with Forrest Gander and then to Arkansas briefly and then to Rhode Island, we began to publish writers we met in Providence. A micropress. It commonly works in such a way. Contests break that up, but rarely for the good of the press. A kind of cohesiveness that begins with geographical proximity, kindred literary intentions, and friendship is built into the small press. For that matter, so is a New York publishing house, which as Forrest said of the entire city, is like someone's apartment.

The production of the books improved once Forrest and I hired an outside designer. Forrest coedited as we came to share the tasks. We both had a taste for it, and didn't mind the detail, but we knew the books would look better if someone else took on the design. We were still setting them on an IBM Selectric.

Covers were almost always by artists we knew. The cover of Franz Wright's translations of René Char's *No Siege Is Absolute* was by

H. Lane Smith, a Providence artist, RISD professor on the cusp of retirement when we met him. Denny Moers, a Providence photographer, did the cover for Besmilr Brigham's *Run Through Rock* (as well as several of mine and of Forrest's from our own respective publishers). The look of the books improved dramatically when we hired Peter Armitage (a Providence-based RISD graduate) to design them. I think he started with *Trench Town Rock* by Kamau Brathwaite with a cover by Deborah Luster, a friend from Arkansas then living in North Carolina. We were still publishing writers we knew, but our sense of the local expanded because of being at a university where any number of writers filtered through; because we were both more in touch with writers by mail and travel, the press took on a somewhat broader character.

SA: Will you talk about the publishing and writing culture you found in Providence?

CDW: There were a couple more active presses in Providence, especially Burning Deck. There was also Copper Beech Press. Moyer Bell was based in Newport for a time. A letterpress called Paragraph is in East Providence. As long as I have been in Providence, there have been fine writers about—living and teaching and studying here, running presses, running reading series. Bookstores have closed, but there are still two excellent used bookstores in town, Cellar Stories and Paper Nautilus, and a very small but choice store largely committed to poetry, Ava Books, and a store with an interesting selection of theory, art, literature, graphic books, etc., Symposium. Brown runs a general bookstore, and they are very accommodating about ordering what they do not carry. This is a viable town for writers, among the few I would say.

SA: Did you have a favorite part of the publishing process?

CDW: I liked most of it—the mail, the selection, the layout (which we still did in Rhode Island for quite a while). I liked working with Forrest. We often had a student intern, someone likewise interested in what we were doing, usually a young writer. It made me feel useful. Actually selling the books was not my forte. Nor is it of most small press editors. Distribution is limited to the outfits designed to serve

276 *Women in Independent Publishing*

the small literary press and we did not publish enough titles for the ones who actually had reps. To make a go of it you have to be very ambitious. We just liked doing it, and once our son was born, it became harder and harder to find the time.

SA: It sounds like Forrest joined the process pretty seamlessly. Was it ever difficult to edit with someone else?

CDW: He took to it and our tastes have always been compatible. His appetite for "discovery" outstripped mine, but I could still net someone out of the way and wondrous.

SA: What was your favorite book to work on?

CDW: I don't know. My favorite was the one at hand. Your attention shifts with the focus required of the title you are intent on bringing into being.

Many of the titles I return to: Frances Mayes *HOURS* and *Ex Voto*, Franz Wright's translations of René Char's *No Siege Is Absolute*, Arthur Sze's *River River*, Phillip Foss's *The Composition of Glass*, John Taggart's *Standing Wave*, Besmilr Brigham's *Run Through Rock*, Kamau Brathwaite's *Trench Town Rock*. Stanford's *The Battlefield Where the Moon Says I Love You. The Book of Seeing with One's Own Eyes*, stories by Sharon Doubiago, and Steve Stern's *Isaac and the Undertaker's Daughter*, his first collection of stories; Alison Bundy's *A Bad Business* and Mary Caponegro's *Tales from the Next Village*. We were amateur publishers, but we published some terrific books. I don't even have the list with me, so I won't go on.

SA: And then did you step back from the press because of the time constraints you mentioned? How did you decide what would be next for the press?

CDW: Time puts its vise on you once job, child, job, child, writing, animal, child, bills work their way in. The press under those constraints was the one dispensable concern. Mind you, we just had the one child. Many people accomplish a great deal with multiples. We were stretched with one.

SA: In some of the books, the NEA is credited with helping to support the press. How else did you get enough money?

CDW: We were able to get grants with some regularity from the NEA and more modest ones from the state arts agency. The titles generated enough money to pay for the next one or two. We kicked in. It was not exciting monetarily.

SA: Yeah, it seems rarely to be. I'm thinking about the voices in and title of your first book—you've been interested in the status and independence of women more generally. Did you have strong feelings about being a woman editor?

CDW: It seemed a good thing, to be a woman, to be an editor. I ran a very small press. When I think of the work Jill Schoolman (Archipelago) has produced, I think of a professional. Or Barbara Epler (New Directions). Or Rosmarie Waldrop (Burning Deck), who also edits (with Keith Waldrop) a small press, but one with so many titles, and such longevity . . . Rena Rosenwasser, Patricia Dienstfrey, and co. (Kelsey Street). Now there are many—Rusty Morrison (Omnidawn), Janet Holmes (Ahsahta), Rebecca Wolff (Fence), Carmen Giménez (Noemi Press, who later turned it over to Evan Lavender-Smith), E. Tracy Grinnell (*Aufgabe* the magazine and Litmus Press), Lost Roads Publishers (Susan Scarlata), and on and on.

SA: What would you say to a young woman interested in starting a micropress?

CDW: Give your press a good name. Give books a good name. Befriend a young graphic designer. Choose each title very, very carefully. "Enlarge the temple," as Merwin said. Books are increasingly worthless, but this means they are also increasingly precious. I will miss them when I'm gone.

Figure 21. dodgems Issue 1 (1977). Cover by Eileen Myles.

Eileen Myles

Editor and Publisher, dodgems *(1977–1979, New York)*

FEBRUARY TO OCTOBER 2014, VIA E-MAIL

Stephanie Anderson: Why the name *dodgems?*

Eileen Myles: I grew up with the name. It was my favorite ride in the amusement park in Revere Beach, Mass. I loved riding in those cars, deliberately smashing into other kids. It was a total vehicle for tomboy rage. The cover was a bunch of nuns riding them in Chicago. I think it's an Irish word too. Lots of places just call them bumper cars. Boston's tipped toward the Irish language-wise. *dodgems* signified a refusal to pick a particular aesthetic in poetry at that time. I can't emphasize how much people, especially men to a female poet, were always pressuring you to sign up. Other magazines like *Roof* used to be this swarm but then it increasingly meant this not that and not everyone could come. Language [poetry] was like that, having a particular conversation. If I have any aesthetic, it's the awareness of being in a multiple. There were so many poetries at the time and I liked the collision. That's what I came to New York for. I wanted to be in it. Wanted *dodgems* to say that.

SA: You've said in several places that you don't like mimeograph. How were you trying to differentiate *dodgems* (in form or content or whatever) from magazines that preceded it or were contemporaneous with it? What kind of production value did you want the magazine to have?

EM: I thought mimeo just looked cheap and poor. I went to Catholic schools in Boston and we always had the cheapest materials and everything was Rexographed, which was like mimeograph, which was depressing. I worked in the library of the American Stock Exchange in the late seventies and I loved how their annual reports looked.

280   *Women in Independent Publishing*

Clean, very bold. In terms of the font, well, the art world at the time was all Helvetica, sort of minimalist and Scandinavian looking. And I loved comic books, magazines, anything with color and flash. The poetry magazine look to me was thoughtless. I never had any sentimental attachment to its scarcity aesthetic. I already *was* there, being both poor in the moment and from the working class. So I guess my irony was a movement away.

SA: How did the production of the magazine happen?

EM: I worked at a place called Prisoners Legal Services down, like, near the World Trade Center. I had keys so I'd go late at night ripped on speed and Xerox my ass and type up *dodgems*'s poems on their IBM Selectrics. There was a print business on the first floor of the building that made corporate annual reports which were often plastic ring–bound like *dodgems* was. I wanted it to look state of the art. To be kind of a faux corporation was my joke. Fido. So I did some labor and then I paid a bunch of money to do a run of five hundred. I borrowed the money from a friend and paid it back much later. It took years, I think. One issue cost $750 and the other was $900. I considered it my luxury and my drug.

SA: Where did the covers come from?

EM: Well, for the first issue I did research, which meant I went to a photo archive. The Bettmann Archive, and I just looked up amusement parks. I really needed actual dodgem cars for the cover of the first issue and was so amazed that what I came up with had nuns in it. I'm not really into nun comedy. That kitsch. You know if you actually studied with nuns you don't get the humor. It's like, duh. But there they were. The second issue with all the cans on the cover I just tore out of some magazine. It had some national advertising council message accompanying it, like, without advertising you don't know what you're getting but how much better to have a poetry magazine saying that. Like what the fuck is this.

SA: How did you choose work for the magazine? How did you choose your own work?

EM: Stuff I liked. I liked a mix of poetry and prose. I liked including documents since it was such a conceptual art moment in Soho where

I was living. I put in my own best work and also work by people I wanted to be in conversation with. Including my own best poem made me more excited about distributing *dodgems* widely, me to be in such great company. You know, with only a few exceptions it was the absolute beginning of getting published. Next to Alice [Notley], John Ashbery, and Lilly Tomlin!

SA: I like how you put reviews alongside poems, instead of in their own section.

EM: Did I? Oh, of course it would be about it all swarming together. I don't like the sectioning thing. It seems spoon feeding. Here, kids, now we're going over here.

SA: Mixing everything together reminds me of a moment in *Inferno*, when you write:

> I had a magazine, I called it *dodgems*. My concept was all these styles colliding like an amusement park ride. I didn't have to decide. I love the corrupt part of anybody's art. I put my ideas in a magazine. You had to do it; it was like being in a band. And people were doing that too. The Teds and the Alices kept saying painter painter, wanting to get us in relation to the art world, but we all liked bands. Those were our friends. [. . .] It was really different if you were in bands.

> Can you talk more about publishing a magazine in relation to bands and the music world? Or more about how these worlds overlapped?

EM: Well, it was our collective art form. It was our naming experience. I don't call my aesthetic the secretaries or sonic youth. I called it *dodgems*. It was a circus tent. I loved music and it was the driving art form in the seventies and eighties. You know older poets were pushing us toward the art world but it wasn't what was surrounding us. We were essentially eating in the same restaurants—Veselka's, Kiev, etc.—that everyone in bands were eating in and we were going to hear them, the bands, and yet you really conducted yourself as if they weren't hearing you. It didn't matter, though; in the eighties lots of people, many poets, did start bands. Mostly shitty ones but

282 *Women in Independent Publishing*

people were trying. When I got a CAPS grant—a NY state grant; my first grant in 1980—I bought a bass guitar and had lessons—well, like, one from my friend Mark Breeding, who was in a band with Tom Carey. I was very excited about it and then I sold it. I couldn't really stick to anything but poetry. I knew I had it going so why dilute your point.

SA: What were your favorite bands? Did you go to a lot of shows?

EM: A lot. Mostly whichever you could get in free to. Talking Heads, Patti Smith, Bruce Springsteen, Television, Replacements, Bow-wow-wow, everything for years. Plus all the eighties noise bands that Sonic Youth sprang from . . .

SA: What do you mean when you say, "You really conducted yourself as if they weren't hearing you"?

EM: Oh, I think we all knew that we were going to their shows, etc., but there seemed to be no buzz for people in bands coming to our readings. I mean, certain people like Richard Hell and I don't know who else had a relationship to the poetry world, but, really, he wasn't hanging out and hearing us either. But I guess what I'm trying to say is we weren't slavishly devoted to making them hear us. They were informing the time and we were, too, just more quietly, in a more insular way recording it and listening and altering and being part of the same moment. I mean something dignified, nice. And later on you learned that more people heard you than you knew. There was a nice thing of not trying hard but still feeling connected.

SA: Do you have a favorite memory of a show?

EM: The last show Television gave at the Bottom Line was like a religious experience. They were so quietly formidable and elegant. It was heartbreakingly beautiful. It was just red. And I remember waiting in the street for hours to get into Bruce Springsteen in 1975 almost more than the show; the wait on the street was so charged. Even the line was hot. But the show was one of the best, most charismatic, like, um, music filling every crack in the room. His early rock was incredible. Again, weirdly at the Bottom Line. Patti Smith at the Hotel Diplomat, 1974. I've written about it already. Her self-consciousness was so much of the art. Her kind of brash innocence and utter presence. She was poetry in her very existence right in front of us. But you know we're not talking about an antediluvian time.

SA: Were shows discussed in the same way readings were?

EM: I don't think either were really "discussed." You just went, you shared records and books, you let each other know what you shouldn't miss. I think people acted more than talked, or that was my prejudice. I went to a reading at St. Mark's about a year ago and a guy I like a lot opened for a woman I'm close to and he read for like forty-five to fifty minutes. He read first. It was appalling. I've seen men do this a million times. They do it to me. There was a lot of talk about how fucked up that was but I don't think anyone talked to *him*. I kept thinking I should; in fact, people even asked me to but I'm so tired of being feminist-conscience Eileen. Other people know him. I think in the seventies or eighties we would've hooted him. Friend or not. We would have said shut up. It would not have passed uncommunicated.

SA: In both issues of the magazine, the number of men outnumbers that of women by more than two-to-one. Were there more men writers around than women writers? When you say, about the reading last year, that the fact that the man read too long "would not have passed uncommunicated," did the audience in the seventies and eighties have to be more assertive about creating space for women writers because the number of them was fewer? When editing *dodgems*, did you think about the gender ratio?

EM: That was totally reflecting the scene. I actually did really well in my gender parity. Oh, we were very loud at a certain point if someone was being a total dickhead, which was often the case. I think the seventies and early eighties was simply more outspoken. It wasn't compensating for anything. It was celebrating that there were, by then, enough of us at a reading to notice. Brashness made it be an event. *dodgems* 3, which sadly didn't see print, was I think fifty-fifty, but, of course, I can't prove it. I, by then, was having sex with women and was even more committed to publishing women's work.

SA: Going back to the music—do you think the music influenced your poetry? (In terms of content or formal qualities like rhythm?)

EM: I think music is why I've never had anything against the idea of lyric. Lyric to me just always means song. What's not to like about song. I've always been influenced by everyone's good lyrics, the simplicity of them and how they get in and sure the stripped-down power quality of good music. Attitude too. Being around and young at the explosion of punk allowed one to be obnoxious, outspoken, bratty. I've always listened to a lot of music so living in this neighborhood then it was just more and newer and more local and you could see the style on the street then too. I did always feel like I was writing songs for a band.

The major art form at the time was punk and it informed all the art forms once that occurred. It influenced how you heard all the music around it before it. I mean, I loved acid rock in high school and blues. I was lucky I grew up near Cambridge and Boston, which, because of all the schools, always had great music and film. My culture was always much more sophisticated than I was.

SA: When do you think you caught up to your culture?

EM: In New York. In Boston I was a kid living at home. I didn't have a life, per se. In New York I was living a celebration of having a life in which I could do what I wanted. What people in the suburbs didn't get then because of the lack of the Internet was proximity. I realized everyone around me actually was an artist and that was part of the meaning of what we were doing. The nearness produced something. A shared confidence. The person *was* making art. It wasn't out there. It was right in here with us. I suspect that intimacy might be getting lost again.

SA: Is the Internet responsible for that suspected loss of intimacy?

EM: Totally. I mean, I love science fiction and that's what we've swapped for it and people will ardently seek intimacy, I think, for a long time, but it used to just be in the room. You just had to walk over there. You know what it's like. When I heard a loud bang when I was alone in the country with my dog and we'd look in each other's eyes. Now, like, if you're out w[ith] people and you don't have some information, you can get it right away. Previously you'd have to either make shit up or stick with not knowing. That's a bond. Like a shared disconnect.

SA: I've heard about how Patti Smith hung out at the Poetry Project, but how else was the Project a nexus for the scene, including music?

EM: Was she really hanging out at the Project. I'm not sure I ever really heard that. I guess she was like an open reading person and then she had her big moment. And then she was gone. For, like, years. The Project was always expert at inviting it in, or attracting artists from a wide range of walks because of, like, a genuine rootedness in New writing, Beat writing, New York school, Language, Sound poetry, performance art, and music. In the early days there really were very few venues for performance art. So the Project always attracted and welcomed it all. When the church had a big fire in '78 (which I have to say was the best thing. It was so great to stand there and watch that church burn. The older poets were all weep weep.) there was a big benefit at CBGB's that included everyone from Elvis Costello to Andrei Voznesensky . . . I have to go online cause almost all I remember are male names and undoubtedly there were some girls. Richard was in it and Anne was and myself, which was an amazing honor to be on stage with all of those heroes. The point being that the project sort of functioned like a kind of wheel of art. Okay, here's a list. I still would kill for a fire benefit t-shirt. Never got one! It was Allen Ginsberg, Lou Reed, John Giorno, Elvis Costello, The Erasers, John Ashbery, Stimulators, Peter Orlovsky, Richard Hell and the Voidoids, Anne Waldman, Ted Berrigan, Ron Padgett, Nervus Rex, the Tom Carey Band, The Student Teachers, Rudies, The B Girls, Maureen Owen, and others. I was "others." There were all these poet bands; Susie Timmons had a band, Tom Carey from the above list, brother of poet Steve Carey, and Barbara Barg had a band. She was more connected to the noise band people. A lot depended on who had a van, who had typesetting equipment and a loft (Barbara Barg had both), and their van shuttled bands around, and the typesetting helped people make a living. Economy. Very common flow, even when people were just moving together rather than knowing each other.

SA: Speaking of flow, the issues of *dodgems* aren't dated; was that a con-

286 *Women in Independent Publishing*

scious choice?

EM: Time isn't always important. 1977 seemed radiant then. It looked good.

SA: And on the title page, *dodgems* is called "a subsidiary of fido productions"—what was that?

EM: fido productions was to be my company that did everything—books (there was one), videos (there was one), and one day there would be films.

SA: What was the book? And the video?

EM: A book called *I Like You* by Richard Nassau, which was a pseudonym for a guy named Richard Bandanza, who was a really great poet; still is, I think. But, of course, it was his only book so no one ever knew it was him. I used a pile of *I Like You*s once as an installation in an art show. Last line of the text: "the poet remains obscure." The video was "Laundromat," which was a bunch of poets reading in a laundromat on Thompson Street in Soho. It wound up being sillier than the avant-garde spectacle I imagined but pretty cool. I wasn't much of a director. More of a fuck up but a conceptual artist still! Bob Holman helped me pull it together.

SA: How do those and the magazine look to you now?

EM: I love how they look. I'm very proud of them. It's raw. Well, the magazine was more of a mix of raw and high production. It was what I meant.

SA: What kind of films would fido productions start to make?

EM: I'd like to write little puppet films and just shoot them. I want to make a film of my opera "Hell." *Chelsea Girls* needs to be a movie. I wouldn't mind having something to do with that. Great for fido to be a producer.

SA: Maybe we could talk a little more about the specifics of the magazines. I love "A Good Neighbor" in the bumper car nuns issue; it describes such a truism of city living and feels like it could have been written last week. What was the deal with that piece?

EM: Well, this is so weird. There was an actor, David Clennon, who lived under me. And I was often drunk and coming in late and wore clogs. And I do, in fact, walk very heavily. I have fights with my current downstairs neighbor and always have to be contrite with Carl because these New York apartments make us very dependent on each other for our peace of mind. So that was an actual note I received from David. The conceptual art movement of the seventies was all about documents so I thought to publish that was cool. I've erratically followed this guy's career ever since. He was in *Being There* and just the other night I was watching *House of Cards* in bed and there was David, kind of old and being a sort of sensitive and cagey senator. And he is the father now in *Gone Girl*. Actually, there's a very strange Lily Tomlin connection now too. I wrote her and asked for a poem and I got that funny form letter from Omnipotence Inc. Well, she is in an upcoming film called *Grandma* about a lesbian poet who is helping her granddaughter get an abortion. She needs to raise some money and she's selling her first editions of poetry. Anyway, in the film it's my books she's selling. The movie even opens w[ith] a quote from *Chelsea Girls*. I am always convinced of the poetry and prophecy connection so same goes for editing. Same flow. At some point Lily even goes: "That reminds me of an Eileen Myles poem."

SA: I also love your long-ish poem in the shopper issue, "Romantic Pain." It's so New York and broke and desperate and sad and funny. Is there a special reason you picked that poem for the issue?

EM: I thought it was my best and it was long. I wanted to get it right out there and was delighted I had that power.

SA: Were there release parties for the two issues?

EM: I think there must have been and I think they would have been very drunken. I really can't remember but I would not have done it without a party.

SA: What happened to issue 3?

EM: Well, I put it together and it was great and the cover was Mae West, like, posing as the statue of liberty. It was the political issue and that meant women mainly. But I had a lump of money to do it. I got a grant from CCLM [Coordinating Council of Literary Magazines] and I had my first girlfriend who I was sort of inseparable from and I was given some money to go to Naropa and she wanted to go too

288 *Women in Independent Publishing*

so I spent the *dodgems* money on two Grey Rabbit, the worst hippie bus, tickets to Naropa and our beer money too, I guess.

Once I decided it was more important to bring my girlfriend to Naropa I then felt (and this was the stupid part) that I had to "take control" of the situation so I decided to kill *dodgems* before I took the trip so I sent everyone's work back with a form letter declaring the death of *dodgems*. Again, a conceptual piece! But, sadly, so much of that work was just lost because of the chaos of so many people's lives, etc., and also I could have done that issue later, like now. That would be amazing. I still think about doing *dodgems* 3. But back then I wanted to be "complete" in some way, meaning, I guess, affirming my own failure to produce another issue.

SA: A little bird (Cassandra Gillig) told me that each issue has a theme. Is that true?

EM: Yes. The first one was very conscious cause I meant for *dodgems* to mean the pure collision of styles I was encountering when I arrived in the poetry scene, both the one I was in and things I liked that had nothing to do with it. It seemed to do a magazine was to hold them all together. The second one I think was more statement, like people were making real or fake statements about themselves. Pithy or bragging. Something autobiographical. Oh, and now I'm also remembering there was this embarrassing thing about *dodgems* 3, which was that all these men gave me poems either dedicated to me or about me and then they wanted me to publish it. I thought, I'm either going to look like a huge narcissist or offend them by not publishing it. It was definitely not something they would put on a man. Like my magazine would be filled by all these little China dolls of me.

SA: Do you have any favorite magazines now? What would you say to someone thinking about starting a magazine?

EM: Every time I see an issue of *Big Bell* I think that's the coolest cause it's so retro in design. He's like a music geek. His magazines [are] like record albums. I like a magazine with a style. Most poetry magazines should kill themselves, they're so ugly. Re: liking . . . likewise the one Robbie Dewhurst did, *Satellite*, something that was mimeo.

Small and felt really good and thick. I loved *LTTR*, which is a while ago, because every issue they did was an event. It really capitalized on the fact that people make things now to have places to go. *LTTR* was a meeting place. I totally missed Renee Gladman's magazine cause I think I was living in Provincetown then. Ariel Goldberg was giving a presentation at the NYPL and I thought this has to come back. I think the magazine I love doesn't exist. I'd like one that people would show up with their poem or essay or picture and everyone would put it together and there'd be that many issues and it would go away when the night was over. Yeah, I'm inventing the past. I think a poetry magazine is a bad idea but a magazine is always a great idea, but you really have to invite the world in so poetry can bob around in a real place. I think the only reason people give a shit about having a poem in the *New Yorker* is that it's a mixed purpose thing that's many genres and listings, etc. Your poem goes among things instead of positioning itself within a poetry movement. Why not just stay home if you're going to do that.

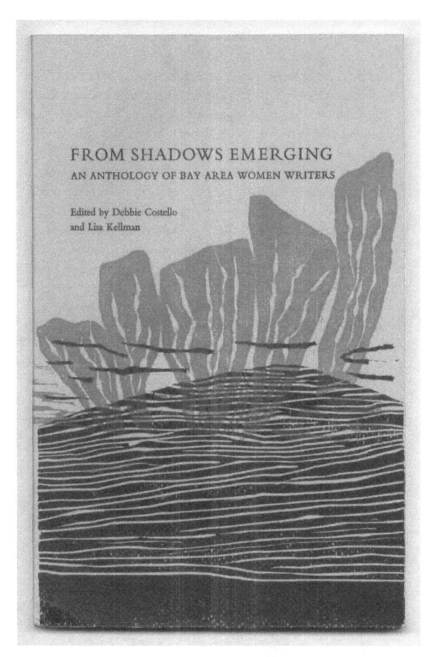

Figure 22. From Shadows Emerging: An Anthology of Bay Area Women Writers (1981). Designed and printed by Lisa Kellman and Deborah Costello.

Deborah Costello and Lisa Kellman

Editors and Publishers, Black Oyster Press (1981–1984, Berkeley and Chicago)

FEBRUARY TO APRIL 2020, VIA E-MAIL

Stephanie Anderson: You were each separately at the Woman's Building in LA before you met, as you say, through a friend in San Francisco in 1978. Will you talk a little bit about your experiences there and the importance of that space and the Feminist Studio Workshop to your subsequent desire to start a press?

Deborah Costello: I was working in a dead-end job, licensing trucks for a container-leasing company and spending a lot of time in women's poetry workshops and at readings in San Francisco. I took a workshop with a woman who had gone to the summer art program at the Woman's Building in LA. What she said about the program excited me.

Spending time at the Woman's Building felt meaningful. I was part of a passionate, committed community of women writers and artists primarily from the US and Canada. I felt that our voices were catalysts for a much bigger movement. I had some wonderful mentors in Linda Norlen and Sheila de Bretteville and I met women visitors that I had admired, such as Kate Millett and Andrea Dworkin. I learned to print on letterpress and published a book of my poems with woodcut illustrations, *Looking In*.

When I came back to SF, I felt both charged up and somewhat aimless. Lisa Kellman and I met through a mutual friend and decided to work together on a book about women writers making changes in their lives. Working together felt like a next step in taking some of the experience from the summer at the Woman's Building forward.

Lisa Kellman: Forming Black Oyster Press represented a merging of two strands of my life's interests and viewpoints at a particular time of my life. One was an interest in design and the beauty of hand-crafted objects that took me from studying calligraphy to hand bookbinding to letterpress printing. The other was partially a result of being a child of the sixties, with an awareness of the injustices of the world and a strong desire to work against them. In my time in LA, I majored in women's history at UCLA and participated in an activist group that fought against images of violence against women. Both led me to the Woman's Building in LA, where I learned how to print on letterpress and printed my first book, *Beluga & Blue-birds* by Lorie Dechar.

The opportunity to meld these interests by working with Debbie to print a book of women's writing brought these two worlds together in an exciting process.

SA: Lisa, will you talk a little bit about your work at Arion Press?

LK: Getting the job at Arion Press felt like quite a privilege given the esteem with which Andrew Hoyem and Arion Press were held. My job consisted of working on the binding of a beautiful edition of *Moby Dick*. It was educational to be in a professional environment of that caliber in the book arts world, but I also was disappointed not to have the opportunity to further my printing knowledge.

SA: Why the name Black Oyster Press?

DC: We brainstormed a number of names. We liked the idea of a marine mollusk that was irregular in shape, rough on the outside, and had a mysterious, smooth black pearl inside. We responded more to the visual abstraction of "Black Oyster" than to its literal meaning but we did connect to the idea of a mysterious, iridescent pearl emerging from the oyster.

SA: The cover of Black Oyster's influential first book, *From Shadows Emerging: An Anthology of Bay Area Women Writers* (1981), is a gorgeous, organic print on textured red paper. It's reminiscent of both landscape and plants in water. How did the cover come about?

DC: There must have been a metaphorical connection to the similarity of "from shadows emerging" and the pearl emerging from an oyster.

SA: What was the process like for soliciting and editing the contents of *From Shadows Emerging*?

DC: Difficult—when we decided to do the project, we were looking at the whole project, the book. We had never done any of it before, soliciting manuscripts, editing, designing, printing, publishing, marketing. We also hardly knew each other but must have trusted we could collaborate and pull this off. We reached out to small press journals, feminist literature professors, women's bookstores, and bulletin boards in women's coffeehouses for manuscripts. We were very focused on looking for writers who had strong, inspiring work that showed women making changes in their lives. We looked for both well-known writers and new writers, young and old writers, writers from different classes and races. In reaching out to feminist writing teachers, we got pieces from teachers as well as from their students. There were several instances where we rejected a well-known writer because their work did not fit the theme. We agonized over each choice, and we were determined to stick to our theme.

SA: The introduction to the anthology begins, "In putting together this anthology, we looked for works that show women making changes in their lives." You go on to specify this as the "transformative energy of change." Will you talk a little bit more about the importance of focusing on change at this particular moment in history, and about the tradition to which you were reacting? How did you balance the desire for diverse voices—for "differing points of view," as you put it—with the broader concept of women united as a category, looking to make change?

LK: After my move to SF in 1978, I became a staff person at the Women's Building in SF. The organization was run collectively, and we had copious meetings where we discussed many issues relating to women's rights, including disparities in the women's movement between white women and women of color. We advocated for changes in the society at large. As a woman in her twenties, I benefited from the experience and wisdom of the diverse women (age and race) who were involved there. It was also a time that I was coming out as a lesbian. All these factors contributed to an expansion of my world-

294   *Women in Independent Publishing*

view and a commitment to activism.

DC and LK: In partnering on *From Shadows Emerging*, we were committed to having diversity be a focus. As mentioned above when we discuss the solicitation process, we rejected some well-known writers, even writers that we had solicited, in order to have room for diverse writers.

SA: Do you remember if the women you rejected were understanding about your reasoning and your vision for the book?

DC and LK: I don't think we got much response from the women we rejected. We sent letters to each one of them and paid special attention to those that were well known or we had connections to. We felt terrible. I don't think we ever heard from those we rejected.

SA: I love the care that the volume suggests, and how the fact that you "agonized over each choice" supports that care. This must have been difficult for two people who also "hardly knew each other," as you say. What was the process of becoming friends and collaborators like?

DC and LK: At that point in our lives, we had a close friend in common, we had both spent time at the Women's Building in LA, and we traveled in similar circles in the women's and progressive circles in SF. These commonalities meant a great deal to us. We expected to like each other, and we did. If we had not clicked, this ambitious project would have fallen apart quickly. We were excited that we had found each other. We collaborated on the process of the book, and we shared what we thought and what we each were dealing with in our lives. My hunch is that part of the reason this was so easy to do was because we were in our twenties.

SA: The book does, indeed, contain a very interesting mix of poets, many of whom, like Nellie Wong and Rena Rosenwasser, have had long careers in literature, performance, and publishing. Did (or do) you have the sense that your call for submissions was unique in the literary landscape of the time?

DC and LK: We were very committed to our mission, but I would not say that we realized how unique we thought the book would be. We just thought it was the right thing to do! Later, the uniqueness became clearer.

SA: How long did it take to put together the book?

DC and LK: The book took about six months to produce. The prework took several additional months.

SA: How did the production of the book work? Did you divide up various responsibilities? (The print run, of six hundred, is still a pretty large one to do by hand!)

DC and LK: There was much overlap between the two of us but some sorting out because of individual strengths.

Debbie did more of the manuscript review since she had a literary background. Lisa was a more experienced printer and handled more of the printing while Debbie set type. Decision-making about the final choice of writers, the book design, contacting writers—we were very collaborative.

SA: Was there a release party for *From Shadows Emerging* (or the other two books, Susan Dambroff's *Memory in Bone* or Judith Small's *From the Island*)?

DC and LK: There was a release party for *From Shadows Emerging*. We held it in the Women's Building in San Francisco.

Figure 23. Contributors to *Home Girls* at a benefit for Kitchen Table Press, November 19, 1983, in New York City. Standing, left to right: Jewelle Gomez, Audre Lorde, Michelle Cliff, Cheryl Clarke, Barbara Smith, Shirley Steele, and Akasha (Gloria T.) Hull; *kneeling, left to right*: Raymina Y. Mays, Donna Allegra, and Linda C. Powell. Photo by Colleen McKay.

Barbara Smith

Editor and Publisher, Kitchen Table: Women of Color Press (1981–1995, Boston, New York, and Albany)

AUGUST 6, 2023, OVER ZOOM

Stephanie Anderson: We were just talking informally about mimeograph. I have such a tendency to romanticize mimeo and other modes of production, but they were very slow and difficult compared to current technologies; I was thinking about this when I was reading a description of editing and production time-intensive labor in "A Press of Our Own."[1] So maybe you could start by setting the stage for us a little bit. What kinds of labor and activities were you doing when you were running the press at the beginning?

Barbara Smith[2]: By the time we were involved in publishing, the process had moved from hot type to whatever that next thing was. But it still required that we deal with printed galleys and then with page proofs. We did not do our book production using computers because they weren't available at that point. We were founded in 1981; we started talking about doing a press and having a press in 1980. So there was no desktop publishing or anything like that in those days. You had to have somebody who was a graphic artist, who could lay out the pages. It was a physical product—it definitely was not on a screen—and easy to correct in that way. During the time that the press existed, desktop publishing began to come into existence, but we never did a book that used that computer technology.

One of the things that I like about the old-school methodologies is that they required a level of precision and an ability to catch mistakes, to know grammar, to know capitalization, to know spelling—all the kinds of things that people generally pay no attention to now because they are communicating via text. And e-mails, of

298   *Women in Independent Publishing*

course, are old school now; only older people use e-mails. From what I understand, younger people don't care for them because an e-mail is text heavy, like two sentences versus a word or an emoji—good grief. I really feel like something is lost as far as print culture is concerned, although, obviously, wonderful literary works and other kinds of books are still being produced. But as far as the culture into which those books arrive—I think it's quite different. I've done archival research looking at letters of individuals, and one of the things that struck me is that people who dropped out of high school or who were high school graduates in the 1920s, 1930s, 1940s were better writers than my college students, because they had been taught how to express themselves in writing at a time that there was no Internet. When I'm having this conversation about technology, I talk about how there used to be only three ways that you could communicate with somebody across a distance. One was telephone—long-distance telephone calls were expensive. So, letters, telephone calls, and if it's an emergency, a telegram. That was it. And I guess newspapers had teletypes, but that's not anything anybody would have access to as a regular person. So, as I said, I feel that the way that I was introduced to writing, reading, literature, etc., has stood me in good stead because I actually know what's wrong when I look at something. As you know, I'm very politically active, have been for my entire life starting as teenager, and I'm still politically active. And one of the things I find myself doing is correcting things that groups I'm a part of are putting out in print. It's like, "Yeah, I can fix that!"

SA: You're still editing!

BS: It tickles me. It's not high-level editing, per se, because most of the people I'm dealing with are decently good—and even very good—writers. It's just what I know versus what people who've not been in the field, so to speak, know. For example, you write a press release. You're supposed to put three number or pound signs, they're the same thing, at the end. And the reason you do that is so that the person who's reading the physical copy knows that that's it, there's nothing else. Pages may or may not be numbered; they should be. But the [pound signs are] the absolute sign that this is the end of this press release or this whatever it is you're handing out. Of course, you don't do that with a manuscript; you might write "the end," but that gets taken care of in production. But, as I said, it's these little things.

Somebody gave me a manuscript—and people do that. You say I'm still editing? Yeah, because people who are friends of mine sometimes ask me to look at their manuscripts. In some cases, they're asking me what I think of it overall, as opposed to can you correct [it]. But I can't help but to correct some things because who knows if they'll be caught. The last one that I read was single spaced, and it was like, "What?!" [*chuckles*] But see, that's all this arcane—or seemingly arcane—knowledge from being my age and just loving everything about print and literature and reading and writing—I love everything about it. I often say I never forgot a single thing that a teacher said about writing. For example, if you're talking about something being the result of something, you don't say "due to." Now you can read that in the *New York Times*, "due to," d-u-e t-o, "due to," as opposed to, "as a result of" or "because of." And one of the common errors that people make is the difference between *renown*—a person of great renown—and a person who is *renowned*, with an "ed" on the end. And most people don't know that. I'm sorry, you got me on a hobby horse, which will happen.

SA: Great.

BS: How you spell a *foreword* to a book, as opposed to going *forward* in a car, or walking—it's two different words. But, as I said, I'm from the old school; some of this knowledge will die with me. [*chuckles*] I mean, people used to say—this is back when we were learning about writing longhand—they would say, "You should make your signature unreadable or difficult to . . ." What's that word? Like, copy, or . . .

SA: Forge?

BS: Forge, that's the word. So it would be difficult to forge. Now, of course, you don't have to sign anything in order for money to change hands. But my perspective is when I get one of those signatures on, like, a business letter—not that anybody sends business

300   *Women in Independent Publishing*

letters anymore—but when I get something like that and can't read it, I'm always thinking about the historical record. So my signature is perfectly clear, and it always has been, and it always will be, because when somebody picks up a piece of paper with my handwritten signature on it, I want them to know whose it was, simple as that. Anyway, enough of that.

So we were doing physical production; we were doing copyediting and proofreading. The most challenging proofreading was books that we did by two Japanese American authors, Hisaye Yamamoto and Mitsuye Yamada—and particularly in Hisaye's books, there were transliterations of Japanese words. We didn't know what it said in Japanese. If it had been in Japanese characters, of course we wouldn't know, and we also didn't know if it was spelled accurately using our familiar alphabet. The only way to check between the manuscript and the galleys was to read it out loud, because that was easier than going back and forth and back and forth and back and forth.

SA: Yeah.

BS: One of my dearest friends was an intern at Kitchen Table in the late 1980s. Her name is Sheilah Sable. I just talked to her this morning because we are lifetime friends. [*chuckles*] She was just over here yesterday, and I could go on and on about the wonderfulness of this lifetime friendship. But she likes to talk about how, when we were editing and working on those books, we were reading aloud; she was looking at one version, and I was reading from the other version. I don't know who held the manuscript and who held the galleys, but that's how we did it. We had to spell it out, because there's no way we'd know right or wrong except to consult the original manuscript. It was much easier to do it that way . . . I could have done it by myself—it would have taken twice as long and probably would not have been quite as accurate. It would have been very tedious. So, old school.

SA: *Cuentos: Stories by Latinas* was also bilingual, and I was thinking about that book because it's very long and must have entailed an intense proofreading process.

BS: Right. But that was published early in the press's life, and there were Latinas involved with the press who read and spoke Spanish. I think we had somebody who read and spoke Portuguese as well. I didn't have to be involved in the accuracy at all. What I was involved in—and approved of, as did everybody involved with the press at the time—[was] that this book was not translated. People have had real issues with the fact that it's not a translated book—that whatever language the person submitted their work in, that was the language it was published in. I was involved in selling and displaying the book, like at the American Booksellers Association Convention—which is now called Book Expo, I believe, and there would be attitudes from, in this case, Anglo women: "Why isn't this book translated?" And we would explain, "It's because we see a Latina or Latino reader as primary readers for this book." In other words, somebody who speaks English or Spanish—they're people who are Latina and Latino. I don't use Latinx because I've been told that's not what people call themselves, but I know why that term exists—to get rid of the assumed gender identifications. But in any event, there are people who are Latina or Latino and don't read Spanish, so it's not just excluding white people. But what was interesting to me was the kind of white arrogance that came through when people were disturbed that it wasn't fully translated.

SA: That they weren't the audience, necessarily.

BS: Right, yeah! That decision shows one of the political perspectives of Kitchen Table, which is: Who are the books for? Who are we publishing for? How do we define our authorship? How do we define our audience and our readership? We decided, through very thoughtful conversations early in the press's life, that we would define a woman of color as any woman who identified with indigenous people of her locality—of her place of residence, of where she immigrated to. One of the reasons that we talked about that is because there were and are Spanish-speaking people of European heritage in Latin America—I'm thinking particularly of Argentina but undoubtedly in other places too. In other words, people who don't have indigenous heritage living in Spanish-speaking countries. The question was: Would we publish their work? And our an-

302   *Women in Independent Publishing*

swer was: Yes, we would, and we did. Race and identity and all those things are incredibly complex and contested to this day, and that was a decision that we made. And actually, I've thought of some examples of how that definition would not stand in good stead. Like, for example, a person who had *no* Native American heritage living in the United States who claimed that they did and therefore should be published by Kitchen Table. I don't remember ever getting into that kind of challenging situation, but I think we had a shared understanding of it. In other words, we were not asking people to send us a photograph of what they looked like. We were not basing who we saw as our potential contributors and authors based upon physical appearance, history of immigration, where they came from—you know, it was more complex than that. That was a very thoughtful and even sophisticated decision at a time when most people weren't thinking that way. The other decision that we made [was] that we were a press for all women of color. And people to this day describe Kitchen Table as a Black women's press because of the fact that I became the most visible person associated with it. But it was never a Black women's press, and it never was intended to be. And that was a political decision as well.

SA: Yeah, the publications show that not to be true very obviously.

BS: Right, but they are basing it on me. [*laughs*] It's Barbara's press, and maybe they're thinking about Audre [Lorde], who was not involved actively with Kitchen Table for most of the years of its existence— although she was always supportive of the Kitchen Table, and that's clear through seeing her work published. That last pamphlet that we did was *Need: A Chorale for Black Women Voices*. And she was always supportive; she was a major source of support for me, who continued to carry the ball of the press.

While we talk about politics, I want to talk about the politics of the press, too, in general. Kitchen Table was a press that had high literary standards and also a political consciousness and political commitment. We saw ourselves as a movement press, and that was for more than one movement. And at that time, before the Internet, we functioned as kind of a clearing house for women of color—really around the world. It was exciting to get the mail, and to see—because I'm a secret stamp collector, I love stamps. Don't do very much mailing at all these days, sadly, because I have succumbed to the easier way of communicating. But anyway, it was always exciting to get the mail—to see the foreign postmarks and stamps, to see where people were reading us. Particularly exciting when they came from Asian countries.

SA: I'll send you something from China for your collection.

BS: Oh, nice! [*laughs*] Well, I don't really have a collection anymore—I guess some people were into having a stamp collection, which my sister and I did when we were growing up. But the reason I'm so into it is because it's another aspect of writing and communication. And also in some cases, when you're creating physical correspondence, there's an aesthetic part of it too.

SA: Yeah, I find that deeply satisfying too.

BS: Yeah, and then there's also the fact that when you get a letter from someone who's important to you and/or dear to you, you know they touched it. And that's just delightful. It's delightful to know that they took time to write to you, to write something down, etc. I still send greeting cards on occasion.

SA: Referring again to "A Press of Our Own," you write, "Kitchen Table's work is international in scope, both because of our foreign distribution and because the issues addressed in our publications make connections with and are inspired by the global movement of Third World women." And I was thinking about how embracing that sort of distribution is a big project, and how such an incredible number of copies of *Home Girls* and the anthologies especially were distributed. To look at it now the print runs for *Conditions: Five* and *Home Girls* are sort of staggering to me. It was ten thousand of *Conditions: Five*. And part of why you were inspired to do *Home Girls* was because you wanted to make *Conditions: Five* more available, and they didn't have funds to do a third run, right?

BS: Yes.

SA: I was wondering if you could talk a little bit about that distribution, and about how these two projects related to each other.

BS: Well, the thing is, they were never going to do a third printing of

Conditions because they were a periodical. It became a back issue, and so I wanted to turn it into a book to preserve it. Rutgers University Press, which has published *Home Girls* since 2000, is bringing out a fortieth anniversary edition this fall, for which I have written a new preface. They insisted on that. I'll say it on tape, you know, for posterity: I hate writing. It's just so odious. It wasn't always, but it has become so in recent years. But whenever I say that, people [are] like, "Really?" Because there's evidence to the contrary.

But be that as it may, yes, I wanted *Home Girls* to become a book, which meant that it could have—I didn't know it'd have a shelf life of forty years, but apparently that worked. And as far as overseas distribution, we had a distributor in the United Kingdom. I don't remember having a distributor in any other country, but we did hear from people from those other countries, including African nations and also India. One of the things that I grew to understand is that wherever English was spoken our books had the possibility of going and being read. That's a lot, because the British Empire did a lot of imperialism and colonization. And English, of course, is a dominant world language because of those same kinds of factors, and that includes the role of the United States in the global political economy. So there are a lot of English-speaking audiences in various places that were able to find our books.

We also participated in more than one international bookfair, because there used to be these international women's bookfairs around Europe, and there was one in the United States. The last one I think we participated in was in Montreal—actually not in the United States. I participated a couple of times in the international bookfair— I feel like it was twice—in London, in the United Kingdom, and I think there were ones in other places that we would send our books to. And then, you know, presses of that time—independent presses, independent women's presses—we would meet each other in different contexts or even correspond with each other. There was no such thing as what we're doing today, which is meeting via Zoom. But sometimes we would have our books displayed at an international bookfair where we ourselves were not physically able to be. In New

York City, there was an annual Asian American bookfair. We went out of our way to get our books into contexts of people of color. We were thorough. I got the idea of putting the number of books that had already been sold on the book's cover to drum up credibility and excitement and interest, and I think the last printing of *Home Girls* that Kitchen Table did had 27,500 on its cover. And so that meant that that last printing probably took it to thirty thousand, but we never did another printing. At least thirty thousand, because we usually did printings of three thousand, five thousand. People are really amazed at the amount of books that we sold. *This Bridge Called My Back* was near a hundred thousand.

SA: Wow.

BS: Yeah, and that's for a tiny press with no money and little staff to speak of.

SA: One of the things you've said was that there are certain genres that are more available to Black women writers. I'm thinking about how you were looking for specific genres when you were editing for *Home Girls*, and you switched the submission method. There was an open call for *Conditions: Five*, but for *Home Girls*, you wanted to fill gaps in the anthology. And I was thinking about the way in which *Home Girls* is structured and how wonderful it is to read a mix of genres within each category. I was wondering if you could say a little bit more about that.

BS: Frankly, I hardly remember. The genre that I was thinking of most when I wrote that, or said that, is long-form fiction and fiction generally. I think that poetry . . . A lot of people think they're writing poetry; they think that poetry is something short written on a page, something that rhymes, perhaps. They don't necessarily know that there's a lot more to it than that. People in literature, like myself, generally think that poetry is the most difficult literary form. And I would tend to agree, because there are a lot of elements that you don't necessarily have to take into account when you're writing prose. For example, having your poem scan. Now, it doesn't have to scan. But the thing is, if you're trying to do it like something that rhymes, or something like that, those lines need to even out, you

306   *Women in Independent Publishing*

know? [*chuckles*] I mean, you can do free verse. I'm not a big poetry person, but because my field is African American literature, there's no way that you can teach African American literature and not be well versed in poetry. My favorite genre is fiction, and the reality is that writing novels takes time. It takes practically full-time. I mean, Toni Morrison was going to work at Random House and creating masterpieces at the end of the day, as well as raising—I think it was two sons? Very few people could do that and get the results that she got, you know?!

SA: Yeah, I'm a poet who always wants to write more fiction, and it's like where would I find the time?

BS: Exactly! So that's what I saw was missing. I think because there was a collection that existed, I could see gaps in a way that one couldn't have if there was nothing there before. And just to be clear, *Conditions: Five* was the first widely distributed collection of writing by Black feminists and lesbians ever published in the United States.

SA: That's amazing.

BS: It's not that there was no other work by Black lesbians, but this is the one that went far. In the 1970s Ann Allen Shockley's groundbreaking book *Loving Her* came out, but the difference is that it was one book by one author. The critical mass of having all these voices in one collection—that was unique, and it was very powerful because in those days they wanted to pretend that there were no good Black women writers, no decent Black women writers. That Black women writers were an exception, and that there weren't that many of us, and blah blah blah blah blah. Let alone that there were Black lesbian writers and that writing by Black lesbians was credible! Nobody agreed to any of those things that I just mentioned. In fact, they were totally hostile. And yet here's this beautiful publication, done with great care, that just basically poked holes in all of the assumptions. And then, good grief, it sold out the first printing within a matter of weeks. Is there an audience for this, perhaps? [*laughs*]

SA: Another aspect of that great care is the way in which the visuals were curated for the press. Will you talk a little bit about that?

BS: Yes, I will, and this gets into my two favorite parts of publishing.

My two favorite parts of being a publisher were graphic design and publicity and promotion, including marketing. Those are the things that I loved. My first business card for Kitchen Table, before we had ever published a book, said: "Barbara Smith, publicity and promotion." That's what it said underneath because that's what I wanted to do. To me, editing is too much like grading papers. It was a necessary evil. In order to get books to design, and books to promote, I had to edit. [*chuckles*] But many of the books that we did—the writers were so good they didn't really need a lot of editing.

So, the design: We were fortunate to have a wonderful graphic designer in our early days whose name was Ann Cammett, who became an attorney. She was just brilliant. Oh, my Lord. And funny, just so much fun to work with. We had hilarious conversations. Just brilliant, brilliant, and so nice, and great ideas. I learned a huge amount about graphic design from Ann. The look of Kitchen Table books and catalogs, she had a lot to do with them.

Now, *Home Girls* was originally going to be a book published by Persephone Press. I write about the design of that book in the new preface to *Home Girls*. I had a huge amount of input into what that book ended up looking like; the first edition had a dark-blue-and-white print design in the background and then yellow type. I didn't choose a yellow type, but that was a great idea. We kept the design when it became a Kitchen Table book. Persephone never published the book, of course, and what I told them is that I wanted it to look like the book by Alain Locke, *The New Negro*. I went and Xeroxed pages of the book from a copy at the Boston Public Library, and I gave it to them, and I told them, "I want my book to look like this." And in the preface, I explain why I wanted the book to look like that. I wanted to have the African visual kind of language. In each piece in *Home Girls* there's a graphic, a black-and-white graphic. There's a publisher called Dover Publications; I don't know if you're familiar with them.

SA: Yeah, yeah.

BS: This is, again, before everything was on a screen. Dover Publications did—they still do—these black-and-white, very inexpensive books, really interesting books. Some of them, nothing but graphic

308 *Women in Independent Publishing*

designs that people were allowed to use for no cost. So, if you used ten or fewer different graphic designs from a Dover publication you did not have to pay anything for that, and you did an acknowledgment. You will see that at the beginning of *Cuentos*; you'll see it at the beginning of *Home Girls*. Those graphics for *Cuentos*—that really nice border that's along the left side of the front cover—that's from Dover as well.

SA: Oh, I see that now that you say it.

BS: Yeah. The logo for Kitchen Table was a Dover graphic that we found. I want to say that it was Indigenous because it looks like a woven basket, but I can't really say—I just know it was a Dover image. So we were integrating those authentic graphics from different cultures into our visual look. And Annie was really good at type and choosing type. On that erstwhile platform that was a great people's forum, which was Twitter, sometimes there'll be a picture of *Home Girls*—and I can tell just from looking at the picture, I'll say, "Well, you know, this is the first printing. This is a first printing, because the first cover . . ." As I said, it had been designed by Persephone. And when I was starting to work with Ann, Ann suggested putting a hairline blue, the same blue as the background, to put a hairline around that big type to make it, as she said, "pop." Of course, I thought "pop" was something she thought of; now I know that "pop" is a design term. But I thought she thought of it because that's how brilliant I thought she was, and she was.

SA: [*laughs*] Let's credit her anyway.

BS: So we need to make it pop, you know. I can look at a picture, and I can say, "That's this printing," or "You have a first printing—first edition, first printing." How do I know? Because it doesn't have that hairline around the type. You can see how much I love this stuff! And also the pamphlets, the Freedom Organizing Pamphlet series— Annie designed those solely. They included those wonderful graphics from Dover, and she chose the typeface, which I love. She would do the direction for the internal design as well, although it was being typeset by someone else. That was like a wonderful, wonderful collaboration, and I learned more and more about design. Now, besides having a great appreciation for visual art and having seen huge amounts of art in my lifetime, I also know how to sew. In high school and college, I used to sew very well, because I don't do things that I only can do in an average or medium way . . . It's either do it well or don't do it. That's called being a neurotic perfectionist—or a person who doesn't like to waste their time. [*both laugh*] I prefer to think of it as I don't have time to waste! I'm not going to buy this pattern, this material, spend all this time, and then come out with something that doesn't look right!

SA: It's powerful, doing something well.

BS: Yeah, but the reason I connect sewing to book design is that you have to be able to visualize something that doesn't exist in your mind before it exists and/or have an idea about it—I had an early experience of looking at something that was two-dimensional; namely, a picture of something I wanted to make, and the other two-dimensional thing was a fabric, because even though it's actually three-dimensional, the depth of it might as well be two-dimensional. Like a piece of paper is considered to be two-dimensional, even though it actually has like a tiny, tiny height to it. So I had the experience of looking at something—colors, designs—and being able to put it together in my head. I really loved doing it.

I loved working on the catalogs too, and deciding what I wanted them to look like. There was a magazine that came out in the 1980s called *Lear's*, started by Norman Lear's wife, and it was for women fifty and older or forty and older; it was for people above a certain age. It had beautiful design, and one of the first issues had this dusty rose, I would call it—grayed-down rose. Not bright pink, not Barbie pink, but grayed-down rose. I cut out the page, and I said, "I want this for my next catalog." With the Pantone system, easy enough to match, so I got that color onto a catalog. Another favorite was the first handout announcing the Freedom Organizing Pamphlet series. In the days when you read print, the *Guardian* newspaper— that is, the US *Guardian*—was still publishing, and *Gay Community News* was publishing, and they were actual newspapers. So what I did in the leadup to doing this design idea that I had for the Freedom Or-

310 *Women in Independent Publishing*

ganizing Pamphlets is that I would cut out headlines and put them in a folder. And then we used the headlines—the actual headlines—and arrayed them on the cover, which was like 8 1/2 by 14 piece of paper. Folded in half so there were four sides, and the cover was these headlines about things that were going on. The things that we chose were eclectic. It wasn't feminist this and lesbian gay that, it was everything that was going at this time, with about ten headlines. I got this beautiful terracotta paper, and I loved it. I mean, that was my favorite of all the ones that I did because I thought I was clever to think of cutting out the headlines. [*laughs*] I really liked the politics of it: this is introducing the Freedom Organizing Pamphlet series, and these are the kinds of issues that we are thinking about as political people.

SA: I love this idea that you have an idea, and you conceptualize it and it's there—because in some ways it's opposed to writing, right? Which is often a very messy process in which you try and try again and try again. This is giving me a new way to think about the visual component. Being able to see the whole thing is really cool.

BS: Well, you also have to try and try again, because there are covers that we had to have redone. One of the books—I think it was *Camp Notes* by Mitsuye Yamada—we were doing a second edition of it and working with a graphic artist who was as horrible as Ann was wonderful. She was a good graphic artist, but she was a terrible person, just terrible, and it was really, really hard to work with her. I think probably because she and her colleagues were white and racist. I'd seen some work that she had done—she was local—that I liked, and I thought, let's call them up and see if they can do something. They did a couple of things for us, but it was really terrible working with her. But be that as it may, for some reason, the cover of that book came back, and the color of the cover, as I described it, was Campbell's tomato soup orange, which I never wanted. I was appalled, and I don't know how that happened. We rejected that cover, I believe, and chose a nice wine red for the cover, and we redesigned the cover.

The original cover for *A Comrade Is as Precious as a Rice Seedling* [by Mila D. Aguilar]—that's the only nonprofessional cover that we ever did, because I was not involved with that cover. It was done by

Barbara Smith 311

other people involved with the press at the time, and it was just not up to standards, and so I was not happy with the cover. Because a book cover—that's an important thing! I mean the type, the graphics. Do you have pictures? Do you have drawings? That's really important. And there are some books that attract people on the basis of their beautiful covers, or their dynamic covers, or their interesting covers.

SA: For sure.

BS: And I was not happy, as I said, with that one. But then Mila Aguilar was released from prison—she was in the first group of prisoners that Corazon Aquino released; Corazon Aquino became president of the Philippines following the horrific Marcos regime. And we did then a second edition of *A Comrade Is as Precious as a Rice Seedling*. That's a beautiful cover to me. There's a picture of Mila on the front of it, but the picture was processed in such a way it wasn't from the camera to the book. There were things done to that picture to make it a little more dramatic and a little more poetic. And then on the back is a picture of her as she gets released from prison. There's a religious sister who is embracing her, and we put a—people used to recognize something as a photograph if you put that border around it that looked like it was film, with the sprockets and the holes. As it happened, this is her getting out of prison, that date, that minute. So we put that around it. And I think I worked with Ann on that. So, as you can tell, the way I talk about this many years later, you can see how much we put into that. We had two covers for *Seventeen Syllables* [by Hisaye Yamamoto]. The first one was Japanese writing, and I think the writing might have said "seventeen syllables," I'm not sure, but it was beautiful, and red type. Another thing I did is, for the books by Mitsuye and Hisaye, is that I'd seen fly leaves, or whatever you call them, where the first page of a book was a different color from the rest of the book. Like Hisaye's had red type on the cover, red and black stuff on the cover, and then her—I call them fly leaves, that may not be right term.

SA: It might be end papers?

BS: End papers, that's it. The end papers were red for that book and for Mitsuye's book they were a peach color. That was just elegant. It's like, oh, these books are being produced by people with no money?

And the thing is some of the things I'm telling you about—they did not greatly increase the cost of these books! It was being clever. Another thing I like—that we never did—is on a paperback book having a fold-over flap with the information, like you would if it was a hardback with a book cover. I love that.

SA: Yeah, I like those too; they're nice.

BS: I love that; it's so clever. And what does it cost? Virtually nothing, in comparison to just doing the regular trim of a cover. Then some of Hisaye's short stories were made into a film for PBS. And I said, we're going to redesign this cover and we're going to use a still from the movie. All of the stills that we got were black and white—and that terrible graphic artist that I told you about, who's a terrible person but a really good graphic artist—figured out how to make it look like an old-fashioned tinted photograph. It's gorgeous, oh my God. We won a design award in New York City where all the major publishers as well as independent publishers compete! We got the top prize for a paperback for that cover. I loved it. And you may have seen the poster of Audre Lorde?

SA: Yeah.

BS: Ann Cammett designed that poster. That was a black-and-white photograph. She worked with it using a computer to get it to color at a time when it wasn't as easy to do all that. Enough about design! Moving to publicity and promotion. Any way I could get word about the books out I did. I got reviews of the two books I just described. They were *Desert Run*, which was short stories and poetry by Mitsuye—Mitsuyue introduced me to Hisaye—and then *Seventeen Syllables*. I wanted them to be reviewed in *Publisher's Weekly*, and Mitsuye had given me a set of postcards by a very long-ago, centuries-old Japanese artist named Hiroshige. Have you ever heard of him?

SA: Yeah.

BS: Beautiful, very classic. She'd given me these postcards, and I would write handwritten notes to the person at *Publisher's Weekly*, like about every two weeks or so. I would talk about the books and there was one point when I included half covers of the books that we would use for publicity and promotion purposes. With a half cover, you can make it into a postcard and mail it; if there's a book event or book party or whatever, you can use it for your invitation or for your announcement. I sent about three different communications to the person at *Publisher's Weekly*. In my handwriting, I would say something intriguing about the book, the books, like: This is a Hiroshige print, one of the stories in *Seventeen Syllables* is about a writer who enters a contest where the prize was a Hiroshige print—whatever I said! Whatever I did, it worked.

SA: Wow!

BS: There was a wonderful stationery store in downtown Albany, where I'd gotten some beautiful different color envelopes and different kinds of paper. They were not card-size envelopes; they were like manila-size envelopes, but they were beautiful colors and beautiful paper. And that's how I would send my correspondence. So, immediately, even before you open it: Oh! This is different, you know, this is not a manila envelope. Wonder what's in it? It's hand addressed. And then the stamps! I was always very careful about stamps. I told people whenever they would go to the post office—of course we used a lot of postage—and I said, "Don't ever bring any flag stamps back here. Ask for commemoratives." "What's a commemorative?" I would explain.

Our mail looked good. Our stationery . . . This is a decision that we made. Back in the day when women of color started to organize and do things, one of the things we did was to start using different shades of tan and beige and paper that wasn't white. So, Audre [Lorde] had stationery, I think that was, like, cream color with brown type—stationery that she had printed. I had stationery that I ran off at a copy shop that had a nice tan paper. We had regular white envelopes for Kitchen Table, but we also had really high-quality, beautiful café au lait—I don't drink coffee—but like coffee with cream in it and with brown type, and those were for our special correspondence. I could go on and on! I need to stop talking about design. I am really good at publicity, distribution, sales, promotion, whatever. I think I haven't gone into as much detail about that as I did about the design stuff, because I just went off, clearly. But you may not have talked to another publisher who had as much of an affinity for that as I did.

SA: Well, and it's true that a lot of the women who I've talked to loathed distribution or didn't look forward to it at all and left it to the authors.

BS: Oh, no, you can't do that. [*laughs*] Oh, no! Oh, that's why we sold so many books! No, I always wondered, like, when I would meet—and of course, I was meeting writers all the time, and some of them had self-published a book, usually a book of poetry. And I would ask, "How many did you print?" "Five hundred." I said, "Oh, so how many are left?" "Oh, well, they're mostly, you know . . . I think I might have gotten rid of a hundred." I'm thinking, okay. Not to be a snob, but the thing is that I used to say the root word of publishing is *public*. Making something public. I don't know what the *Oxford English Dictionary* says about that, but let's face it: publication, publishing. It says to me, you're getting work out, and getting work out to a broad public, and that's exactly what I wished to do. Because I saw the books as political vehicles, I wanted the word to get out. I didn't care if the person read the book; I just wanted them to buy the book—not because of the money but because that meant it went home with them.

SA: And then someone else picks it up at home.

BS: Yes, exactly. *Home Girls* goes home with someone who we sold it to at an academic conference. Their niece or nephew comes over—their kid, their neighbor, their sister, brother, whoever, sees the book and says, "Oh, what's that?" You see what I'm saying? You never know, and I talked about how books have legs—that had both positive and negative meanings. When I said they had legs, I was often talking about people taking them, stealing them when we were doing public events. And they did. So, I said, just remember, books have legs; we have to keep them where they belong.

SA: Speaking of family, I love the photographs in "A Home Girls' Album" in *Home Girls*. What was the inspiration for this section?

BS: I wanted those photographs because people, to this day, maintain that Black lesbians, Black gay, Black queer people, Black trans people, Black nonbinary people, two-spirited people—although two-spirited people in traditional Indigenous contexts are more

Barbara Smith   315

embraced, I think, but there's definitely homophobia in Indigenous contexts as well. And I wanted there to be photographs of us when we were kids so they could look at us and explain how we were not Black. We came from somewhere. The name of the book is *Home Girls*. I was making points in the introduction, and by the title, that we're part of this community.

SA: The *Home Girls*'s introduction is astonishing in its range.

BS: It's insane. It shows how much energy I had as a young, Black, passionate thinker, writer, and political person. That introduction represents a huge amount of passion, a huge amount of commitment. I knew people would be reading stuff they'd never read before. There was nowhere else to read that. And *Home Girls* was the first book that had, on the cover, "Black Feminist." I write about it in the new preface, that there was no ambiguity about what was in this book. For *But Some of Us Are Brave*, that was the first book ever published that had "Black Women's Studies" on it. I was really passionate about all those things, and I had the energy and the skills to try to follow through.

You know, from having read about this, and in probably more than one place, that the press began as a conversation between Audre Lorde and me. She was coming to Boston for a Black women's poetry reading on Halloween with several other women from New York City who were also going to be reading. And she said in this conversation, "We really need to do something about publishing," and I immediately agreed. Somebody recently did some interview or some something, and they talked about how Audre had to persuade or explain that to me. And I let them know; I said, "No, that's not what happened. It was a conversation. She said it; I agreed." I immediately understood what she was saying, because we had been around the block more than once with the challenges of being parts of special issues, working with editors who were not conscious and antiracist. The editors of *Conditions* were totally conscious, and it's not by accident that *Conditions* played such an important role in my early writing individual things and also projects—that was where "Toward a Black Feminist Criticism" appeared, in the second issue.[3] So we had a meeting at my house in Roxbury that weekend and that's how Kitchen Table began.

316 *Women in Independent Publishing*

The work of keeping Kitchen Table alive was arduous—there's no other word for it. The constant worries about money, financing—and by that, I mean my own making a living because I obviously was not making a living from running the press. So anyway, that was the hard part. I remember being at the main post office in Albany that was open late on Christmas Eve, sending out fundraising letters. That was Kitchen Table. It was a labor of love. And even though we did not last as long as I had wished and hoped, it made an impact. People are so interested in knowing what were our perspectives and what did we do? Every time I hear about a young writer of color who is often also a part of the LGBTQIA+ community getting a book contract for their first book with a mainstream publisher—I see that as Kitchen Table's work. We opened the way. Nobody was interested in those kinds of writers back in the early 1980s or before. No one. And we proved that you could do it and that those books could sell and that there was an audience for it. Political movements also contributed to those recent book contracts because had we not built the movements—I'm speaking specifically of the women's movement and of the LGBTQIA+ movement—there would also have been no audience and no contracts for those authors. But, very specifically, Kitchen Table laid the groundwork for those subsequent successes.

SA: And what an amazing groundwork. Are there any release readings or events that you think of as especially memorable?

BS: I just saw a picture on Twitter—I will continue to call it Twitter. I just saw a picture on Twitter a few days ago of the event that we did in New York City to launch *Home Girls*, and I think probably almost everybody who read that evening is in the picture. All so young, me with black hair, go figure. [*chuckles*] I'm lucky to have any hair at this point. But be that as it may, that was one of the most memorable events for me because it was for my book. It was in New York City, at a public school where we used to have a lot of events. I think Grace Paley lived on the same street that the school was on, in the West Village, and I got to be friends with her. She was totally supportive of Kitchen Table, and, in fact, when I moved to Albany and Kitchen Table was still in New York, guess whose keys I had to their apartment? Grace Paley's. She was a genius, as we know, one of the best writers who has ever lived, and just so down-to-earth. She used to make fun of me because of how I said the word "Paris." She had a distinct New York City accent, from my point of view, because I'm from Cleveland, the Midwest, right? And the thing is that, she said, "Oh," she said, the way I said it was "so Midwest." [*both laugh*]. I said, "I don't hear it. I don't get it!"

SA: I can't even imagine what the difference would be.

BS: She heard something! She heard something that she could hear because of where she was from. I mean, that just captures the quality of our relationship. Just a wonderful person, oh my God. But, as I said, I think the school was on the same street that she lived on in the West Village. But yeah, I like that event, and I like the picture too.

SA: Great.

BS: Let's see. There's a point when at the American Booksellers Association we had been exhibiting with feminist women's presses, gay presses, lesbian presses. The smaller presses, independent presses, form consortiums, and if you did a block of a booth, then you got to create an aisle or a half of an aisle. And that was a good marketing. So although none of us could afford what the mainstream publishers were doing, together we could have signage decoration, things above the booth that would unify us, and so we did that with the women's and lesbian and gay presses for a while. And then there was a point when I was so tired of their ignorance and their racism and just not knowing how to be nice people in some cases, just basic, you know, how were you raised?

But at a certain point in those days, we also had started a Black publishers' consortium called the Black Press Association or something like that. We would have meetings; I would go down to Baltimore, to Philadelphia for meetings and was a welcome part of that. Of course, our press was the only women's press in that group, and certainly the only lesbian or gay press. And yet I was much more comfortable working with them than I had been with the white presses that supposedly I had something in common with. And by that time, we were doing the work. Doing the work has such impact on how people think about you and see you, because we were all engaged in the same challenges, being Black publishers, publishers of color, in an inhospitable publishing environment. We knew what it took to get a book out; we knew what the financial strains and stresses were; we shared strategies; we created a bookmark with all of our presses listed on it. The white women—and I don't know about the gay presses—but the white lesbian publishers, they were like, "Oh, really?" They were not pleased, I think, with my decision. I did not make it for them. In the book *Ain't Gonna Let Nobody Turn Me Around* there's a dialogue amongst feminists of color publishers, and we get out a lot of our challenges in that.[4]

SA: Will you talk a bit more about press friendships?

BS: The friendships with Lu—Lucretia Diggs—and with Sheilah Sable.[5] Well, Lu died in the late 1990s, but that was a lifetime friendship, and with Sheilah, it's ongoing. It's so delightful, that we would have known each other so long ago. And Sheilah considers herself really lucky as a white Jewish American woman and a lesbian to have had the experience of working at Kitchen Table and having her eyes opened in a way that never would have happened otherwise. One of our delights to this day is I love to share cultural things with all of my friends, but with Sheilah it can be as silly as I actually am because she appreciates that; she sends me TikToks all the time. You may see a watermelon behind me, up on my bookshelf? That's actually a cutting board. I collect watermelons, I've had them for years, representations of watermelons, and I do love it, although you know there's such racist stereotyping associated with it. Why wouldn't you love something that's as delicious as anything could possibly be? It is delicious, you know, what's wrong with you people?! Well, they're racist, that's what's wrong with them. But be that as it may, we were talking, Sheilah and I were talking about watermelon a couple of weeks ago, and I was talking about how hard it is to find a good one, because ever since they went seedless they don't taste as good.

SA: It's true.

BS: I was saying how I was really surprised to see that they still sell watermelons with seeds, but I was saying, I don't know how I would get one home because it's so big, and I said, "Well, I guess I could use that cart that you gave to me." So the week before last, Sheilah bought a watermelon—we share food with each other on occasion. Both of us really like to cook, and she brought me part of a watermelon that she thought was really good. And I told her how my dear aunt, who raised my sister and me after our mother died, told us that when we would have watermelon, she said, "Well, you know this is a letter from home." A letter from home. So that's another term for watermelon. Before I sent it to Sheilah, I looked it up, and it's an expression that's used by people of various backgrounds, not just African Americans; it generally refers to a food or an experience that reminds you of your home country or where you lived. And people referred to the South as the old country, you know. Sometimes, when Black people were joking, they would call it the old country, like European Americans called Europe the old country. So anyway, we love sharing these things, and one of the things that I love, too, is that there is an infinite amount of Black culture to share. [*chuckles*]

I have devoted my life to reading about, teaching, writing about Black culture, Black literature, etc. And yet practically on a daily basis there's something new and something wonderful. That's really nice, particularly since certain people want to erase the whole thing. You know. How dare you teach that accurate African American history? How dare you? You know, it might make the little white children feel sad. Well, how sad did I feel every day? [*laughs*] I mean, and I got a great education. There were some terrible public schools in Cleveland; but I was lucky to go to some of the best because my family moved to a neighborhood where they could afford to buy a house and where they also had really good schools. But sometimes we were sad in our classrooms. We were sad about the stereotypes of Africans and of Black people. We were sad about the fact that there were no Black people in our books. But it's okay for Black and other children of color to be sad, and for poor children to be sad. It's just that you can't have white children be sad by telling the truth about history, and on that crazy note . . . [*laughs*]

Figure 24. Aché 5, no. 2 (Summer 1993). Artwork by Jackie Hill.

Lisbet Tellefsen

Editor and Publisher, Aché: A Journal for
Lesbians of African Descent *(1989–1995, New York)*

AUGUST 3, 2023, OVER ZOOM

Stephanie Anderson: I'm really excited to talk about *Aché*.[1] It was such
a wonderful experience going through the publication all at once
chronologically and leaping between the issues, because you could
really see how much it changed in an incredibly rapid time. And
I was struck by the fact that on the Beinecke Library's website, in
their online exhibition about *Aché*, they feature an archival draft
questionnaire, in which the brainstorming name for the publication
is *Changes*. So I wanted to start there, because that "changes" is such
a good alternative title or a background title for *Aché*.

Lisbet Tellefsen: The genesis of *Aché* is: I met Pippa [Fleming] somewhere in 1988. I was doing percussion workshops at my flat in
San Francisco, and she came through one day and spied my tennis racket. We began playing tennis together, and at that time our
schedules were such that we had a lot of free time during the day, so
we started hanging out almost every morning. We'd go down to the
Brick Hut, the local lesbian cafe, to have breakfast and brainstorm.
So as Pippa and I are having these conversations, they start to veer
toward creating something like a calendar of events and/or newsletter for the lesbian-of-color community. And, as fate would have it,
at the time I actually owned a printing press and knew how run it.

This was also the era when desktop publishing was becoming
a thing, and I was falling in love with my Mac computer. My most
recent ex at the time was a poet-artist named Storme Webber, and
when we were together I'd spent a lot of time trying to help her put
out her first chapbook, so publishing was already on my mind. I've

222 *Women in Independent Publishing*

always had a thing about publishing and my first endeavor was back in middle school when some friends and I used the school's mimeograph machine to put out a zine called the *Phony Express*.

SA: [*chuckles*] That's pretty good.

LT: Pippa is also very creative, and she was the perfect brainstorm partner to bounce things off of. I think those notes you saw are probably in her handwriting. We had a lot of different ideas about what it could be called . . . I think *Sister Insider* was on it, as was *Changes*. I had come out of a chapter of being immersed for years in Afro-Cuban culture. The Orisha tradition was a significant part of that, and though that's not my spiritual path, it was Pippa's. So I think she came up with the name *Ashe*, and because *Aché* is the Cuban derivative we chose that. The name fit well in what we were trying to do as what we were dreaming up crossed a lot of borders.

The generation before us was very butch-femme, very firm in their ideas around identities and roles, and we were not. Our generation was androgynous, dreadlocked, and nose-ringed, and many older women didn't know what to make of us. I think the journal's pages reflected that we were inclusive; we didn't see any contradictions in publishing the work of men, for example. In the earlier issues we spoke to the changes we were going through on an almost monthly basis.

SA: I love the fact that all of these things are tied together: the production, the ways in which the magazine—I keep calling it a magazine in my head—it starts out as being a newsletter, right? One of the things I was interested in was the fact that in that archive questionnaire I mentioned at the beginning, there's not any mention of poetry and art, but that's such an integral part of *Aché* so quickly, and you talked about poetry when you talked about the context of the publication.

LT: Our initial conversations were around building an events calendar since I had been doing a similar thing for the local public radio station. I had also just spent the previous year immersed in typing up poetry and helping my ex publish her art and poetry chapbook "Diaspora." Her words were fire, and she had a really strong visual aesthetic, so as we began thinking about laying out a calendar it occurred to me that it would be great to have something more visual and creative to break it up. I ended up asking Storme if we could feature her in the first issue and that set the tone.

SA: Yeah.

LT: The first issue has a profile on A Woman's Place bookstore, a piece on the second Black Gay and Lesbian Conference, then our calendar, which was so big it required a separate insert page on red paper. We also posed a topic question and featured some responses that Pippa had gone out and gathered, and then poetry and artwork.

These past couple years the *Aché* archives, which are among my personal papers at Yale's Beinecke Library, have been getting a lot of use. There was actually a seminar at Yale on Black lesbian aesthetics that included two class visits to my papers. That led to an aha moment for me when I realized that the act of featuring a different artist every month served to accelerate the development of a Black lesbian aesthetic. Whereas before you might have some art in an anthology, like *Conditions: Five: The Black Women's Issue* or *Home Girls*,[2] that kind of specific content was few and far between. With the exceptions of some early journals, like the *Black Lesbian Newsletter* (later *Onyx*) published in early eighties—which featured the artwork of a single artist, Sarita Johnson—that was it. And then *Aché* came along and began to feature really strong Black lesbian–centric imagery month after month after month. It's like bam! Bam! Bam! That didn't happen very often before us. I would say also, in terms of poetry and writing, there were not a lot of vehicles for beginners to hone their craft. You had journals like *Sinister Wisdom*, where you probably had to already consider yourself a writer to take the leap to submit something. *Aché* was clearly outside of that. We struggled to even call it a journal, because that made it sound like a scholarly endeavor. I still call it a "grassroots publishing project" because that's a better descriptor.

SA: Yeah, totally.

LT: It was almost as if every issue was the sum of its parts—and could be completely different than the issue before it. Some of that was because in the early days we were coaxing out content from everyone

324   *Women in Independent Publishing*

we could. And as a vehicle *Aché* was helping those in the community who had writing impulses to put their work out there and evolve.

SA: I think the themes of each issue really help with that. The fact that quickly—I think somewhere in the first year—there's a recognition that the themes are pulling people in and almost serving as writerly prompts, right? So there's an effort made to get the themes out a little bit further in advance so that the community can really respond.

LT: Themed issues came about due to a major shift that happened during the journal's second year. While I was the publisher throughout *Aché*'s entire run, I was only editor for the first year or so. Sometime in 1990 Pippa told me she was moving to London. And this happened at a point where I was already drowning. When we started *Aché* I wasn't aware that she was dyslexic and couldn't really help with anything on the production side. So the division of labor became that she was the face of *Aché* in the community while the editing and physical production of the journal was my realm. She would be writing poetry and statements, doing interviews, handling outreach and distribution. I would be doing all the editing—which included a lot of back-and-forth with young writers—layout, production, and getting it printed. Which included funding it.

While initially I thought I'd be able to print it myself, the first issue taught me I didn't have the skills to do so. The process became that I would create the layouts at home on my computer, then save it to a floppy drive and take it to the local copy shop for printing. However, the minute I popped that disc into their computers, it would completely scramble all the fonts and layouts, so literally I would spend hours re-creating the documents and hoping I fixed everything before sending to print. I began getting resentful that I was doing that all by myself.

SA: Yeah.

LT: At some point I told Pippa, "Even if you aren't able to help with computer stuff or production, at least be there so it feels like we're going through this together." She agreed. And the very first time she shows up with a date—and I'm like, unclear on the concept. But her date was this woman named Skye Ward who *immediately* grokked it—she's like, "Got it; I know what you need."

So Pippa went off to London while Skye got a key to my house and pretty much moved in on day one. The ball started rolling with regards to putting together a team that could help manage this growing thing. One of the first things we did was to create a team to deal with the journal, people with editorial experience. Matter of fact, the woman, Janet [Wallace], who'd done the layout for *Onyx: Black Lesbian Newsletter* back in the eighties volunteered to do our layout. A woman who had experience as an editor, DeeAnne [Davis], came on as editor and that's when themed issues really took hold. Now, what that meant is that a lot of the organic nature that was part of the early magic—that shifted. There began to be more of a focus on writers who were writers, artists who considered themselves artists, things like that. But it also created some much-needed infrastructure that meant we were able to last for twenty-seven issues, which was really a coup. I don't know many dedicated Black lesbian publications that had that type of longevity.

SA: Yeah, this is really evident in the table of contents, as you just sort of flip through them—the different categories start to stand out more. I like that you mentioned Sarita Johnson, because I love her quote about her own practice in one of the early issues.[3] There's an opportunity for the artists to reflect on what they were doing, and so there was already this kind of criticality, or this kind of thinking about the aesthetics embedded within practice, which is also really interesting.

LT: Within the journal committee, roles were broken down even further: We got an art editor—the first one was Amana Johnson—who made it her mission to ensure that there was an artist's statement. We had a poetry editor, among others. It became much more organized in that people were responsible for certain aspects and made sure that no beats were missed. Whereas the first year I'd been [*juggles frantically*].

SA: That first year is astonishing in some ways. I was thinking, too, about the fact that as these changes happen, they're happening

326 *Women in Independent Publishing*

fairly quickly, or at least they appear to be. A year is a lot longer when you're under a certain age, right? But the committee turns over a couple of times after you are no longer editor. So maybe part of learning about collaboration or learning about how to make this thing was about preventing burnout by rotating roles more quickly?

LT: So, the genesis of the editorial team of the journal . . . after the initial journal committee was instituted, we quickly decided that themed issues were helpful. We would announce the themes ahead of time and we began having rotating editors who could be working on an upcoming theme over months. There was essentially arranged turnover of editors. I don't know if we called them guest editors or whatnot. I know the first editor after me was DeeAnne Davis and subsequent editors included Blake Aarens, Natalie Devora, and maybe some others. The poetry editor was Dawn Lundy Martin and Aya de Leon, and art editors included Amana Johnson and Dawn Rudd.

There may have been some turnover due to burnout, but I think there was also frustration with bottleneck on my part. With regards to journal production, I had gone from doing everything myself to then having people show up asking, "What do you want me to do?" And that required, in the midst of keeping everything going, to be able to also find time to effectively download and train, which I wasn't always successful at. There were certain things that I was able to immediately hand over, but there was also always a sense of . . . me just . . . burning.

And at that point *Aché* had become more than the journal. When it became impractical to self-fund, we started doing fund-raising events and I became the main event producer. Then it became clear that—in addition to the journal, which had become a virtual lifeline—once we started to have physical events, it was clear we *needed* to be in community with each other physically. There was a completely different kind of power in that. So now we're not just producing a monthly journal; we're producing one or two monthly events in addition, which become critical because they're also bringing in money. There was this snowball effect *very* quickly, where the need and the hunger for this sort of community was just a palpable, living, thirsty thing. I'll say one thing about being in your twenties: you can drive yourself really hard and somehow survive on only caffeine and toast. You know?

SA: [*laughs*] That's true.

LT: What you can't do is stop and think you'll be able to go right back to where you left off. There's an amping-up period and it can keep going as long as you keep going. But once you stop it's very hard to get back there. I think of *Aché* as that chapter in my life, when we came together to burn intensely. At the end of the day, I feel there's a lot of us that have such pride in that work—and we have something wonderful to show for it.

SA: One of the things I like about the events is that in the juxtaposition of the calendar and the accounts from events, *Aché* is creating the community and documenting the community at the same time. But it does seem very intense. I mean, the calendar has events happening every day, right? I wanted to ask about some of the events: film screenings, the Drag King events . . . What events were most important? And later on in the run of the publication—when you're no longer editor—one of the subsequent editors writes in the notes that the events usually come up twenty dollars short, and that the events are really about building community.

LT: Yeah.

SA: I'm just thinking about what an important aspect this is to the publication.

LT: It's funny; in my head these live as a chapter, because the journal can't be separated from the events, which can't be separated from the community they engendered. It was a moment. This moment was also larger than *Aché*. I think we started in '89. We limped into '95. I think '94 was really our end date, so we had a five-year run. But the significance of that era in Black queer culture globally was huge. When Marlon Riggs dropped his documentary *Tongues Untied*, it landed like an earthquake and kicked off this explosion in Black queer cultural production. Isaac Julian and Pratibha Parmar were

328　*Women in Independent Publishing*

doing their thing in London. Joseph Beam, the Black gay publisher and editor, drops his anthology *In the Life*[4] and his magazine the *Real Read*. And then AIDS began decimating the Black gay community and what should have been the most productive chapter of many of these giants' lives were cut short.

One thing about history is that you don't know it when you're making it. History is something you recognize in retrospect. To look back and realize that *Aché*'s pages were a time capsule where we were documenting a significant moment in Black LGBT history.

SA: Yeah.

LT: There were so many takeaways, and this is non sequitur, but the last exhibit that Yale did that included the papers, *We Are Everywhere: Lesbians in the Archive*.[5] I was speaking to the curator, and she told me the genesis of that exhibit was that she went into Yale's holdings, and in the search engine typed in "lesbian." That meant that previous generations of lesbians, whose lives were lived "in code," wouldn't show up in a search engine. The fact that we put "A Black Lesbian Journal" in our title would bring us up to the forefront in the present era of SEO.[6] I found that so interesting.

SA: There's an early issue, too—I think it's number 7—that's full of erotica. It's wonderful.

LT: Yeah, we had woman who did safe-sex work in the community approach us to add a sex column. We were constantly saying: if there's something you want to see in the journal, let us know—or better yet, create it!

SA: In your essay "Celebrating the Legacy of *Aché* Magazine" in *History Happens*, the newsletter of GLBT Historical Society (San Francisco), you say, "The years we were active were in many ways to Black gay culture what the Harlem Renaissance was to African American culture." And so, thinking about this historical moment again as being so fomenting.

LT: When I think of the Harlem Renaissance, I think of a significant historical moment where Black culture thrived—and there were also a lot of Black queer moments in the Harlem Renaissance, right? But during the time of *Aché*, the fact that AIDS was blowing

Lisbet Tellefsen   329

through the Black gay community—it meant that you had these bright, shining supernovas, like poet Essex Hemphill, that were just gone at the height of their powers. Just as cancer was taking folks like Audre Lorde and Pat Parker. It was a moment that can't really be replicated. In the midst of all the tragedy it felt like we were in a moment of something special and sacred. I don't have any other way to say it. And in this midst of all this is an explosion in openly overt Black queer culture. No longer in code or in the shadows, but in your face. For those of us who were there and caught up in the whirlpool, it felt like something important and divine was playing out.

SA: How did these years and this work on *Aché* shape your work afterward?

LT: Well, first of all, it gave me some incredible stamina. You don't know what you're capable of until you really get tested, and it tested me in a lot of ways. I think I'm a natural introvert who is probably most comfortable in my own cocoon. And, whereas in the beginning of *Aché* Pippa allowed me to stay in that lane—where I could be in my own little world—when she was gone there was a moment of "Oh, shit, what have I gotten myself into?"

But there were so many life lessons and skills developing during the *Aché* chapter that are integral to who I am today. For starters, I found my tribe. I also consider myself somewhat techie in that part of me believes that if I just get the right tool and learn how to use it well enough, I can be omnipotent, right? [*chuckles*] And to have seen what can be done with the rudimentary tools that existed back then—I dream of what the next chapter of creative output could be. In many ways I've been iterating creatively ever since then. *Aché* was an excellent chapter, yet I would say that some of the things that I've done since then have been equally as life-changing for me.

SA: Yeah, as a scholar who mostly looks at stuff in the in the sixties, seventies, looking at an *Aché* is like, "Whoa! Computers! No wonder!" It feels like a big aesthetic, technological shift. And it still looks so good!

LT: Thank you. First of all, I hear that, and thank you. But one of my big-

330   *Women in Independent Publishing*

gest regrets is that we existed in the era of bitmap printing. [*chuck-les*] Within a couple of years you have color laser printers and Photoshop and all of that, but *Aché* was created during a fairly primitive era. And somebody young looking at our old issues today, they don't recognize this. They may just see a black-and-white Xeroxed zine with pixelated graphics. Natalie Devora, one of the former editors, and I are always threatening to do a best of—some sort of retrospective—and I'd try to pop a little color in somewhere.

But when I look at how the seeds of *Aché* played out . . . Roxanne Gay was on our mailing list! A couple of years ago I sent her e-mail, asking, "Are you the same Roxanne Gay that subscribed to *Aché* back in the day?" She's like, "Yes, I was!" Too bad she didn't submit anything back then; that would have been something.

SA: Being able to look at some of the poetry by Dawn Lundy Martin is pretty amazing.

LT: That's my biggest source of pride, that *Aché* had a hand in the development of so many folks who would go on to do big things: writers, poets, artists, and organizers.

SA: Maybe we could end with a question about current publications, or forums, or other places and modes—whatever you want to call them—that you consider to be the legacy of *Aché*.

LT: Because I spend so much [time] in archives and collections, these days in terms of publishing—I seem to be moving backward. Currently, I'm still in the nineties or early 2000s—like I just discovered *Whirlwind* magazine by Lamont Steptoe. I feel now that Black lesbians have a really robust footprint in book publishing; look at Alexis Pauline Gumbs, for example. It feels like BIPOC LGBTQ+ folks are in the mainstream now. I don't know that magazine publishing or publishing is even a thing anymore; I feel like the Internet provided alternative publishing forums that destroyed much of physical print culture. You don't go to a bookstore and see these type of zines and things like that anymore.

In some ways I feel like the communal aspect of *Aché* has been replaced with social media. For physical communing we seem to have reverted. Once again, the folks that do book readings, they're at the bookstores; people who do clubs, they're at the clubs; people who like art, they're at the galleries or museums. I think one of the most beautiful things about *Aché* was that it was one of those rare spaces where you could go and, soup to nuts, see the entirety of your community, from the fresh-out baby dyke to the ninety-something with her partner. We were all in the same room together. That may be what I miss the most.

Figure 25. Summer Writing Program, Jack Kerouac School of Disembodied Poetics, Naropa University. *From left to right*: Lorenzo Thomas, Joanne Kyger, Bobbie Louise Hawkins, Allen Ginsberg, Anne Waldman, Michael McClure, Diane di Prima, David Life, Jack Collom, Hal Willner, Steven Taylor, and, sitting on ground at right, Lee Ann Brown as a "spy in the audience," to quote Rosmarie Waldrop. Photo by Liza Matthews.

Lee Ann Brown

Editor and Publisher, Tender Buttons Press (1989–present, New York)

FEBRUARY 2016 TO JULY 2022, VIA E-MAIL[1]

Maybe I can ride the music in the air and write you more about Tender Buttons.
I was pretty obsessed with poetry already—since high school
especially—no, really since second grade!
I'm writing to you from the back lounge of a club called Elsewhere in Brooklyn where
I just arrived with my almost seventeen-year-old Emrys to hear one of their favorite
bands, Chastity Belt.

And was really yearning for an experimental,
experiential approach to poetry (I remember clutching my orange
poet's notebook in my interview in the ornately carved admissions
offices at Brown and being convinced that talking about my poetry
helped me get into the school).
Obaa hands me torn out pages of her handwritten address book—
all my past ones since leaving home
It makes sense to me to try and do this during a concert since, if I think about the early
days of Tender Buttons, it was definitely a night time / between time thing to do.
I had recurrent dreams of Utopian
communities of free-floating ideas and interchange, always a
different landscape.
Not to be overly sentimental, but poetry is like wildflowers—you have to know
where to look
and found and helped create these at Brown,
at Naropa, in SF briefly at New College, and finally in New York,
based at the Poetry Project.
The eternal NYC conversation
Insert writing about Allen's house
About Sonic Youth

334   *Women in Independent Publishing*

> Our party where who came
>> R Hell
>> Evelyn McDonnell and her magazine *Resister*

Poets scene
> Will Patton story

>> Freshman year at Brown I studied with Michael Harper who introduced me to a lot of traditional forms as well as blues / ballads of Robert Hayden and Sterling Brown, as well as the writing of Gayl Jones, and later with Carolyn Beard Whitlow, whose intensely musical blues poem about Nina Simone and her crown of sonnets on the history of slavery impressed me immensely—one reason was that I could see what Michael Harper had taught her and how she made it her own—her first book *Wild Meat* was published by C. D. Wright and Forrest Gander at Lost Roads Press and I began to see how the book is what makes the poet.

So many times excitement
> Small
>> Stay small

First was
/ party is over poem

The opening band Stranger Ranger just started playing. A nice mix of uplifting indie pop. I am holding my kid's coat and making myself scarce so they can feel free to dance with their pal Shiloh. It's freezing out. I've only been here once before, and the weather was even worse, freezing rain and slush industrial wasteland trek—it was to hear Thurston Moore and his ensemble of wild guitars.

>> I became involved in an intense group of women friends congregating around the Sarah Doyle Women's Center—we were very interested in poetry and feminist theory and how they might fit together. I was on the editorial board of *Clerestory* (an undergrad lit and art journal) and had poems there as well as *Issue* and in more independent magazines we started like *Cleavage* and *Positions*, which was our take on feminist-produced porn, which was a hot topic after years of "pc" repression, and came out the year I was away from Brown

to much controversy. The editors went on *The Phil Donahue Show*
to defend their position, and there was a media tie-in to another
group of women on campus who had become sex workers who
we didn't even know. We were exploring how the personal and
political intersected: we had a very emotional and fiery "speak-out"
on the frat quad which surrounded the dining hall where many of
us detailed our harrowing experiences with rapes and harassment
so far in our lives of nineteen, twenty, twenty-one years old.

Women in our circle

Included people like Miven Booth (psychoanalyst and writer),
Jennifer Callahan (documentary filmmaker), Heather Findlay
(psychoanalyst, feminist theorist, editor), Sharon Marcus (scholar
of French lit and theory who now teaches at Columbia), Catherine
Saalfield (filmmaker and activist), Claire Cavanah (went on to
be owner of sex-positive store and collective Toys in Babeland),
Cecilie Surasky (peace activist, videographer), and many others
who impacted my coming to be a serious artist and producer of
poetry and community like Julie Regan, Stacy Doris, Caroline
Crumpacker, and Melissa Smedley . . . the list goes on.

The sound of the word *publishing* usually reminds me of "making public"—as in "publi-
cating," which also feels like it includes doing poetry readings in a way—a way to make
work "public"—and in a way the reading is intimately tied to my publishing practice of
my own work since it is a lot more efficient time- and space-wise in a way because you
actually SEE and FEEL the energy of the people receiving it and it's harder to know
who actually reads it when it's printed.

We were exploring our sexuality as well as connections between
our artistic, intellectual, social, and life pursuits.

It takes a lot of time

To really get it right

Not that I was over employed

My rent was $250 / month to start and I thought that was a lot

Then $500 or so then a sublet for $800 something then $1,000

twenty years later

thirty years later   it's a different story

437 East 12th Street—the "Poets Building"

336 *Women in Independent Publishing*

M Scholnick Allen Ginsberg Peter Orlovsky
Greg Masters Larry Fagin Simon Pettet Richard Hell
Lorna Smedman
John Godfrey
Harry Smith recorded my entire going-away party
He left the tape recorder on the floor
To "get the sound of the creaking floorboards"
Heard a guy ask as I passed through the crowd, So it's a band with *all girls?*
Miven Booth was
one of these friends—the first person I knew who owned her own
Macintosh computer (that really dates me!). My senior year was
the first year I typed papers at the computer lab—and that
liberation of putting writing into print that way and changing
margins and typefaces probably greatly enabled the possibility of
making books—the year after graduation, typing every one of
Bernadette Mayer's *Sonnets* into the computer at Allen Ginsberg's
office—embedding them in memory,
"public-cating" as in making public or sharing, making available to others. I remember making the decision to print books with companies such as McNaughton & Gunn
instead of fancy letterpress in order to make easy multiples and "get the poetry out
there." Now I feel torn between wanting the book, any book, in mine and others'
hands versus "free" on the Internet. Maybe both somehow?
As well as Mei Mei Berssenbrugge's *Empathy*, which
had just come out from Station Hill.
The Sites include
437 E. 12th
172 E. 4th (Bernadette's house, address and phone number notated in
the acknowledgments page of her free book, *Utopia*)
working at the Poetry Project
Jim Brodey coming by and someone calling to ask if
Moondog was still around
Six jobs:
Bridge Bookshop, as archivist for Jackson Mac Low
Finally poetry workshops without grades
BERNADETTE'S EXPERIMENT LIST

Yes, it's boring only talking about myself—though I love to share all the amazing stuff I run into! I guess that's a lot of why I do the press, now that I think of it!

I remember reading a copy of the *Poetry Project Newsletter* in my room senior year (1987) at Brown and just knowing that was what I should do next—where I should go to work after I graduated. I had already made connections with New York poets of that "scene" by going to Naropa the summer of the year I took off between my junior and senior years at Brown (1985). C. D. Wright was a new professor then—I remember her giving her first reading at Brown in her red high-top sneakers in the Crystal Room—her translations of the *Gospel Back into Tongues* and her torque into SF experimentalism a great intertwining contrast of influence. I had bought the books from her course on the New Long Poem and discovered Bernadette Mayer's *Midwinter Day* that way.

Then moved to
52 East Manning Apt, inhabited by years of poets:
Peter Gizzi   Sawako Nakayasu Jennifer Moxley   Steve Evans across the street
Elizabeth Willis Prageeta Sharma Kevin Young Tom Ellis Major Jackson
The Dark Room Collective forming over in Cambridge
visits from Tom Raworth   Rod Smith
Stephen Rodefer
forays to C. D. and Forrest's refigured schoolhouse home for a poetry
back to NYC and Hannah Weiner seeing words on my arm
J
Max Fish photos
me and Piero Heliczer and Euphrosyne Bloom and her mom
Rosy Sky!
Washington Heights   Audoban Ballroomland
2nd St
3rd St
Providence
Boulder
NYC again
lived briefly in the Autonomedia loft in Williamsburg

338   *Women in Independent Publishing*

then sublet Fiona Templeton's on St Mark's Place
Ludlow Street in a tenement named Esmerelda
On other floors:
Tara Jane O'Neil and   Cynthia Nelson
Will Oldham briefly appearing with silver painted toenails
Met poet girl bands with Karla Schickele and
Ida Pearle   Anna Padgett   Joined Fort Necessity Writing group briefly with
them and Maggie Nelson and Lily Mazella
Only went a few times
I just saw a very, very tiny baby in a carriage at Chelsea Market and am having flash-backs to having one to hold.

I, too, am in the throes of wondering what form the book takes for me at Tender Buttons Press and in my own work, praying that I won't be overwhelmed into inaction by the possibilities.
Louise Landes Levi's micropress and cassette label, Il Bagatto, produced wherever she happens to be.
Carolee Schneemann as body poet, her interior scroll.
Julie
Patton's long-term, potentially massive project "B" would be could be "broadcast" as in seed sowing on any number of media platforms and is necessarily so because of her multiplicitous permutational and permit-atonal poetry which morphs in performance—but I desire to publish a baseline book to "anchor" her predictive in the poetry word world "first" or at least at the center of a vortex of sound drawings / typographical marks on bound page.
On the 14th Street bus now going to the farmers market at Union Square in hopes of scoring some duck confit for Tony to cook for a benefit dinner for the workshop of *La Pucelle, or Joan of Arc*, a play by John Reed.
Did I talk about the morphology of the word
"broadcast" as seed sower?
Talk about Harry Smith
alter nation with Naropa
Gregory C story photos

Sparrow
Movie stills
Hal Willner recording Wm Burroughs's "Thanksgiving Prayer"
Marianne Faithfull's "Broken English" and "The Eyes of Lucy Jordan"
Allen G's *The Lion for Real*
Williamsburg
Torns
NC : NYC
Interest in the southern:
How the folk and the avant-garde are not that different
old-time psychedelic
Back to Providence for grad school
lived in the Waldrops' house while they were away
slept in K and R's bed mattress tilted into the middle
every room surrounded by books
a whole room for poetry
with Keith's collage flat files in the middle
a Wunderkammer in the dining room
Wastepaper poets theater at the RISD museum
letterpress in the basement
the translation connection
I set out to read all the poetry beginning with Zukofsky
I woke this morning to a fearful continuing flare up of eczema on my hands—
between my fingers—I hope I can get to a place to continue working, but for now I
am getting in a soothing bath to listen to Tennessee Williams read Hart Crane's "The
Bridge" on YouTube—
That's a rich metaphor and probably
the root word anyway for the word from the farmer sowing a large
field by flinging out the seeds to grow in the rich cultural fields!
There's also this great book by Octavia Butler with poetry inside
called *The Sower*—have you read it?
A "true poets'" morning ritual—late start—yesterday was the first anniversary of
Tony's father's death—we went into the forest to light a candle—the forest on the
mountainside right before the Tanbark Ridge Tunnel was alive and green quivering

340 *Women in Independent Publishing*

with rain and red and brown mushrooms everywhere and tiny white pip-
sissewa flowers in bloom.

      Erin O'Neal

           Lynn Martin

                  All these names

        All the little stories she never tells

                         They need photos

By the way, I just saw a great draft of a poetic doc by my friend Melody
which has an outrageous sketch of Creeley's attitudes toward whichever
"wife at the time" he had wanting to be a writer too—forbidden! He said
something to the effect of all of the poets' wives want to be writers too (and
that includes Joanne Kyger who was with Gary Snyder!) and if they were
writers, they already would have been, and if he suspected Bobbie of writing done in the barn, she would return to the house to find him sitting, and
pouring a big glass of whisky . . . (stewing into abuse)

                            And the environment is rare

                Once was everywhere

                  Sowing poetry on all kinds of soil

            In all kinds of wavelengths

                      Janie Geiser

           Stan Brakhage

      Lewis Klahr

           When Bernadette had her cerebral hemorrhage

                          Photos from SF

          Buffalo Park

          Don Yorty

I was trying to conjure the "scene" and think about how central music (the
punk / Rimbaud contingent) is / was to NYC poetry and all the rest of the
other related, hidden, and oppositional . . .

          Laynie Browne telling me about Liz Phair

                    and how she's playing *right now*

         And we ran to CBGBs

Miraculously opened door and there she was
"I saw it coming
            I saw it coming
and now it's gone"

Afterword

MC HYLAND

Dear Stephanie,

I hope you don't mind that I've chosen the format of a letter to you, my oldest micropress friend, for the afterword to this book of conversations between women editors. The two things I've always found most exciting about this interview project have been, first, the way it understands conversation as a site of meaning making and, second, the way it allows me to better see, through your discussions with other editors, the work through which you and I built our friendship and built our lives in poetry. In this afterword I want to think about contemporary micropress publishing through the window of our practices: the wheres, whos, and hows of your and my writer-driven publishing over the last decade and a half.

I started DoubleCross Press in 2008, the same year that you and Sam began publishing chapbooks as Projective Industries.[1] We'd arrived at the publishing genre of the poetry chapbook via different routes. You and Sam had both had chapbooks published around the time you graduated from the MFA program at Columbia—yours by New Michigan Press and Sam's by Octopus, and you wanted to give your own writer-friends the care and attention that you'd received from those editors.[2] I knew that I loved poems, and that I wanted to make things, and that I'd assembled a skillset I could use to turn poems I read on screens into physical objects in the world.

After I wrote a first draft of this introduction, we talked a bit about what the chapbook meant to you, more generally, at that time. Because students or recent graduates of the Columbia MFA program regularly won the Poetry Society of America's New York Chapbook Fellowship, you understood chapbooks—or at least certain chapbook contests—as presenting a "step-

344   *Women in Independent Publishing*

ping stone into becoming a poet with a capital P."[3] These books made clear the connections between the institutions of a certain well-resourced New York poetry world—in particular, between Columbia and the Poetry Society of America—and demonstrated how these institutions, among others, formed a gatekeeping network. But, at the same time, your own books had been produced outside New York, by peers or near-peers, and working with those presses made you want to take the process of publishing into your own hands. You were getting interested in how small presses could be a counteracting force to gatekeeping networks.

As for me, the training that led me to publishing was informed not by contemporary (or, for that matter, historical) poetry publishing but, instead, by the fine press tradition.[4] Fine press publishing has its own lineages and its own scholarship.[5] My teacher, Steve Miller, was a student of Walter Hamady, the prolific Wisconsin book artist and teacher who, among his other achievements, popularized the practice of fine printing on the Vandercook cylinder press. That this fact was one of the first things I learned about Hamady—and that the use of a cylinder proof press instead of a more labor-intensive (and more antique/old-fashioned) iron handpress represented a kind of rebellion—speaks to the centrality of craft in the fine press world.

By the time you and I met, I'd learned some book-making hand skills. I'd also learned how fine press publishers operate: by selling small runs of books to book collectors and special collections libraries, often through the intermediary of one of a small number of artist book dealers. The kinds of books my classmates and professors made could fetch prices in the hundreds or thousands of dollars, because their makers not only worked with high-end materials in labor-intensive ways but also carefully accounted for the hours they spent on each book, paying themselves an hourly wage appropriate to each task, and to the training and the skill level that task required.[6] A friend in my book arts graduate program once told me that I should carefully choose whom I published because of the prices I would need to charge to pay myself for my labor. It would be easier, he said, to sell a book by a well-known elder poet, rather than by a young writer who had perhaps just published a few poems in the online mags where the most interesting work was coming out. He believed that the people who were used to spending money on expensive handmade books would be familiar with poets a generation or two above me, but not with poets of my own generation.

Against this training, I wanted to publish the work of peers. When you and I met, I was figuring out what it meant to do so: how to connect readers with books and how to make a publishing practice sustainable. I'm not sure either of these questions can ever have a permanent answer, though occasionally I find something that works for a while, until conditions change.

But let's talk about 2009, when you and I met. Already, like some of your interview subjects remembering work they did decades earlier, I'm finding that I have some trouble recalling the scene around our early friendship with clarity. Here's my best attempt to piece together what the world that birthed both of our publishing practices looked like, who was there, and how it functioned.

You and I met at the 2009 Associated Writing Programs (AWP) conference in Chicago, where we'd both asked Matt and Katy Henriksen if we could share a bookfair table with their handmade magazine and chapbook press, *Cannibal* / Cannibal Books. You and I had both made piles of hand-sewn poetry chapbooks and needed a place to sell them, and the conference, which that year was attended by 8,500 writers, was the place to do so.[7]

You and Sam knew Katy and Matt from New York, where they'd run the Burning Chair reading series in the mid-aughts, as well as published handmade books and magazines out of their Greenpoint apartment. You'd come to New York to attend the Columbia creative writing MFA program, but you also, in the years you were in the city, met other young poets at readings, and at bars and parties after readings. Though I wasn't there at the time, the impression I have (especially now, after the outpouring of testimonials about Matt's influence after his sudden death in March 2022) is that Matt and Katy were a nexus for poetry activity among the young, mostly white crowd of poets who were either in creative writing MFA programs or, like Matt, recently graduated from one.

I'd met Katy and Matt at the 2006 AWP conference in Austin, Texas, where we'd all been in the sparse audience for a panel on contemporary small press publishing and, later the same night, ended up in the large backyard of the same bar.[8] I wish Matt was still around to help me remember who else was in the audience at that panel—he and I used to joke that there were just fifteen or twenty people in that room, but all of them went on to start presses or magazines in the next few years.

At any rate, Matt and Katy started *Cannibal* and Cannibal Books in 2006, and by 2009, they were regularly buying a bookfair table in the AWP conference to sell their handmade books. It wasn't unusual for them, and other small-scale publishers, to split table costs with friends, so that two, three, or even four micropresses might share one table. Sharing not only made the long days in the bookfair more fun but also made it easier to swing the exorbitant table fees.[9] You and I both asked to join them at their table that year, and that's where I met not just you but so many of my first poet-friends from outside my MFA program. Sitting at that table, I met Farrah Field and Jared White, who would later open Berl's Brooklyn Poetry Shop. I met Nate Slawson, who was either already running or soon to start Cinematheque Press. I met my other closest micropress friend, Brian Teare, who was trading copies of Albion Books chapbooks from a backpack.

The centrality of MFA programs and the AWP conference to this whole story isn't an accident—our generation of small-scale poet-publishers came out of the explosive growth of creative writing graduate programs in the early 2000s. While we understood the work we did as publishers as a DIY labor of love, it came from, and made the most sense within, this institutional context. Over the twenty-year period between the midnineties and the mid-twenty-teens, the number of MFA programs in the United States more than tripled.[10] As members of this generation of freshly minted professional poets, *of course* we and several of our peers wanted to create more ways for writing to be not only shared but also, quite possibly, credentialed.

We both attended MFA programs at the confluence of two trends that maybe made our generation of DIY publishers inevitable. On the one hand, there was an enormous increase in MFA students and graduates. On the other hand, especially after 2008, there was a decline in stable, full-time university employment—the very jobs for which MFA programs understood themselves to prepare their graduates—as administrations turned more and more positions, especially in the humanities, into part-time adjunct lines.[11]

Afterword   347

You and I have talked for years about the relationship between writing, labor, and social class—and still I'm not sure I can do justice to the complexity of these issues in this brief afterword. Among my peers from the Alabama MFA program, many ended up teaching at the college level as adjuncts, lecturers, or (usually a few years down the road) on the tenure track. This trajectory was possible because we'd already taught so much by the time we graduated: Students in the program were fully funded, but, in exchange, taught two courses per semester for three to four years. It helped that we were already living in, or willing to move to, inexpensive parts of the country, where you might just be able to cover your bills with the lower-paying teaching jobs that tended to be available to us. For your Columbia classmates, who'd often accrued significant graduate-school loan debt while living in the most expensive city in the US, the situation was more complex. Sometimes the choice to stay in New York and adjunct was only available to writers with independent sources of financial support.

Generationally, we were shaped by universities but also forced into marginal positions in (or outside) those institutions. We and our peers wanted a kind of publishing that resembled our worldview, which was institutionally shaped but also in a fraught relationship with those institutions. We also wanted more dispersed networks, and we wanted aesthetic objects that spoke to the ways we saw ourselves as outside the university's systems of power. I also wanted (and I think you did too) books that spoke, both in their content and their form, to what had been cool for us as teenagers in the nineties: the antisellout inscrutability of indie rock and the anticapitalist independence of zine culture. The first time I walked around an AWP bookfair, at that 2006 conference in Austin, I remember looking for books that telegraphed their countercultural commitments through their form (hand-sewn, hand-printed, ISBN-less), and seeing relatively few. Just five years later, DoubleCross and Projective Industries shared a table with two other micropresses (Friedrich Kerksieck's Small Fires Press and Tom Hummel's handheld editions) at a twenty-table bookfair aisle called Table X, composed of thirty-six small presses.[12]

The systems of evaluation in the twenty-first-century university are tied to research productivity, and in the field of writing, this means full-length books published by presses whose reputations have reached the people in

348 *Women in Independent Publishing*

charge of hiring, or of promotion. This was part of what made chapbook publishing seem rebellious and countercultural. The ephemerality of the chapbook, and its persona-non-grata status within many university metrics, made it feel like a way to circulate the work of peers in a context that was personal rather than professional.

There was a lot that was joyful about chapbook publishing, I think for both of us, in the late aughts and early-to-mid teens. In addition to helping other people's writing find new audiences, we made friends—with each other and with so many other writers. We traveled to read in independent reading series. We gossiped and road-tripped and threw book-sewing parties. You and Sam came to Minneapolis less than six months after we'd met, and we all made a magazine together, which we hand-sewed copies of for three years.[13]

But our world as publishers also was fraught with tensions that are more visible now than they were then. Independent publishing was rocked particularly hard by #MeToo scandals, with several presses shut down by complaints about their male founders and editors. The informal sociability of the micropress social world offered cover for a number of inappropriate and exploitative behaviors, many of which were hard to see unless or until a friend directly confided in us. The pressures of maintaining a belief in community endeavor, and of not burning bridges within a small scene, short-circuited the mechanisms of complaint that might otherwise have brought problems to light sooner. That our small press world was dominated by heterosexual men and couples only exacerbated this problem. I know that, as someone who was often with a male partner in social situations, there was a lot of my friends' behavior that I wasn't privy to, and this could include behavior that undermined other friends' safety.[13] Above and beyond issues of sex, power, and coercion, it is worth noting that queer and genderqueer people were, in the small press world we moved in, underrepresented as editors of small presses, and this underrepresentation meant a paucity of perspectives on gender and sexuality.

Worse, those same pressures of maintaining a belief in community endeavor made it difficult, for a long time, to talk and think about the whiteness of the literary small press world. It wasn't until after the 2014 publication of Junot Diaz's *New Yorker* essay "MFA vs. POC" that the default whiteness of the MFA program, and the harmfulness of this environment for nonwhite writers, became a topic of conversation *outside* of communities of BIPOC writers. As a publisher who understands her practice in relation to these institutional spaces, I need to think carefully and ongoingly about the ways my own practice has assumed whiteness as normative, and to actively shift beliefs and behaviors tied to that assumption.

I find a great deal of inspiration in the new genre of pedagogical books like Matthew Salesses's *Craft in the Real World* and Felicia Rose Chavez's *The Anti-Racist Writing Workshop*. Both of these books describe and offer suggestions for deconstructing the white supremacy of the MFA system. Though programs and publishers have worked in the intervening years to address these imbalances, the chapbook's refusal of professionalism has made it an especially fraught field for the struggle against white supremacy in poetry. After all, what's the power of a format that poets have gravitated to *because* of its nonprofessionalism?

So: What might a book like *Women in Independent Publishing* look like for our contemporary moment? Such a book would need to respond to developing ideas of gender by highlighting not just cis-femme but trans, genderqueer, and nonbinary editors, asking how and whether these editors understand their role as cultural practitioners as shaped by their experiences of gender. It would need to think about BIPOC projects that understand self-publishing as a sovereignty practice, like Demian DinéYahzi's *Survivance* zines and Jennifer Tamayo's recent, self-published artist book *Bruise Bruise Break*. It might consider the expansion of publishing practices within the worlds of activism, visual art, and social media, and the ways these worlds overlap and inform each other.

Stephanie, we've talked about these issues over the last decade-plus, and I know we'll continue to talk about poetry, publishing, and politics for many years to come. What I appreciate most about our shared time in poetry (and now in scholarship and teaching) is that it creates occasions for our ongoing conversation—a conversation that the historical study you've undertaken in this book has infinitely enriched. Thank you for this work, through which I have been able to better understand our publishing, and our peers', as part of a longer lineage.

xx,

MC

RESOURCES

Additional Selected Women Editors and Publishers

The interviews in this book focus on a limited number of editors and publishers. This section provides some additional starting points for other scenes—including some established by and centered on women of color—that emerged in relation to presses and publications in the years between the 1950s and 1980s. The brief entries that follow are not meant to be exhaustive regarding editors-publishers, publications, or the scenes. Instead, they might suggest some paths and resources for further vital research and inquiry. As with the interviews, the listing is chronological by publication/press founding year, and not the years of the editors-publishers' involvement.

LITA HORNICK, EDITOR AND PUBLISHER, *KULCHER* AND KULCHUR PRESS / KULCHUR FOUNDATION (1960–2000, NEW YORK)

Lita Hornick took over *Kulchur* magazine from its founder, Marc Schleifer, in February 1961, and became its publisher after the second issue.[1] She also founded Kulchur Press in 1961. She was not involved in the editorial work for issues 3 to 5 but concentrated on the business end of the magazine.[2] *Kulchur*'s focus changed from a political to literary orientation starting from its fourth issue, and Hornick brought significant subsequent changes to the magazine as an editor, publisher, and art collector.[3] In 1970 the organization's name changed officially from Kulchur Press to the Kulchur Foundation, emphasizing its role as a "cultural foundation."[4] The editorial team that worked with Hornick from the seventh to the twelfth issue included Gilbert Sorrentino, Joel Oppenheimer, LeRoi Jones, Frank O'Hara, Joe LeSueur, and Bill Berkson. While "the core of the magazine" had been poems and poetry reviews, issues 7 to 11 presented a diversity of genres by including jazz review sections, drama (issue 9), and essays on music.[5] After twenty issues, Hornick

354 Additional Selected Women Editors and Publishers

decided to change the focus from criticism to publishing poetry. She explains the "abrupt" change in her memoir: "Little-magazine editors have never been known for their reasonableness."[6] *Kulchur* ceased publication in 1981, and the foundation work continued until Hornick passed away in 2000.[7]—Yilin Xu

DIANE DI PRIMA, COEDITOR AND PUBLISHER, POETS PRESS (1963–1969, NEW YORK) AND *THE FLOATING BEAR* (1961–1969 AND 1971, NEW YORK AND SAN FRANCISCO), AMONG OTHERS

Diane di Prima founded Poets Press with her first husband, Alan Marlowe, in 1963. She had gained publishing knowledge and experience when assisting Amiri Baraka (then LeRoi Jones) and Hettie Jones with *Yugen* and Totem Press books.[8] As a feminist Beat poet, she was devoted to publishing for its "democratizing and radical" potential regarding sexuality, feminism, and class.[9] Allen Ginsberg praised her for breaking "barriers of race-class identity,"[10] and Robert Creeley commented that she never settled for "static investment or solution[s]."[11] Similarly, Jolie Braun referred to the press as an "intersection" for many major underground literary movements in the mid-twentieth century.[12] Di Prima was also a contributing editor to *Yugen* and *Kulchur*, coeditor of *The Floating Bear* (with Baraka), cofounder of the New York Poets Theatre, and founder of Eidolon Editions.[13] Both Poets Press and Eidolon Editions focused on avant-garde poets' works.—Yilin Xu

GLENNA LUSCHEI, EDITOR AND PUBLISHER, SOLO PRESS (1966–PRESENT, CALIFORNIA)

Glenna Luschei (Glenna Berry-Horton) has been dedicated to publishing poetry since 1966. As the founder and publisher of Solo Press, she believes that "we always publish the known with the unknown and the local with the universal."[14] Poet, essayist, and small press publisher Harry Smith praises Luschei for her "passionate clarity and earthy universality."[15] Solo Press released its first magazine, "the ground-breaking" *Café Solo*, in 1969 and has launched three more literary magazine series since then: *Solo, Solo Café,* and *Solo Novo*.[16] As the editor of *Solo*, David Oliveira recalls, after years of *Café Solo*'s consistent publication, that Luschei wanted "a fresh look" instead of "a singular voice," in her words.[17] Therefore, Luschei invited Oliveira and Jackson Wheeler to be the first editors of a new journal called *Solo*, which produced seven issues over eight years.[18] Wheeler describes Luschei's own work as "ecstatic" and *Solo* as "not in the sense of alone, but singular."[19]—Yilin Xu

ANNE WALDMAN, COEDITOR, *ANGEL HAIR* (1966–1969, NEW YORK AND BOLINAS, CA) AND EDITOR, *THE WORLD* (1967–2002, NEW YORK)

The magazine *The World* emerged from the Poetry Project at St. Mark's Church in-the-Bowery. Joel Sloman, the assistant of the project, proposed the magazine's establishment and edited its first issues in 1967.[20] At that time, Anne Waldman was the secretarial assistant to Sloman and the Project's first artistic director, Joel Oppenheimer.[21] After Sloman left the project, Waldman took over his editorial work and served as second director from 1968 to 1978. Waldman edited three anthologies of Poetry Project–related writing: *The World Anthology: Poems from the St. Mark's Poetry Project* in 1969, *Another World* in 1971, and *Out of This World: An Anthology of the St. Mark's Poetry Project, 1966–91* in 1991.[22] The last issue of *The World*, number 58, was published in 2002. According to Waldman, the magazine filled the gap when some influencing little magazines ceased publication or were in decline. In an interview, Waldman recalls that *The World* evolved along with other activities in the Poetry Project, consistently publishing works and reviews of some writers who she had followed for ten years, as well as some newcomers.[23] Waldman also edited the magazine *Angel Hair* with Lewis Warsh. The name *Angel Hair* comes from a line of a Jonathan Cott poem.[24] After six issues, Warsh and Waldman separated and stopped publishing the magazine. When asked how she felt working as an editor, a project director, and a writer at the same time, she states that she considers such experiences "little miracles."[25]—Yilin Xu

CAROLYN RODGERS, EDITOR AND PUBLISHER, THIRD WORLD PRESS (1967–2015 AND 2015–PRESENT AS THIRD WORLD PRESS FOUNDATION, CHICAGO)

In addition to "establish[ing] herself as a major influence on the direction of Black poetry early on in her writing career,"[26] Carolyn Rodgers was also a founder of Third World Press, one of the oldest and largest Black presses in the United States. With the mission "to always honor Black writers and artists and to celebrate artists of all cultures,"[27] Third Word Press provided "an unprecedented documentation of Black American literature and social justice" for over sixty years.[28] Rodgers passed away in 2010; in 2015, Third World Press became the nonprofit Third World Press Foundation. Despite the changes to the organization's structure, when discussing the mission of the foundation, publisher Haki R. Madhubuti states, "Our mission is the same. We continue to play an activist role in supplying literature to our community."[29]—Siyuan Wang

JUDY GRAHN, EDITOR AND PUBLISHER, THE WOMEN'S PRESS COLLECTIVE (1969–1979, OAKLAND)

Judy Grahn and Wendy Cadden founded the Women's Press Collective in Oakland, California, in 1969.[30] Grahn was also involved in founding the West Coast New Lesbian Feminist Movement.[31] She used her poetry to advocate for economic and social justice, antiracism, and an end to violence against women.[32] Grahn was radicalized by her dismissal from the air force on charges of homosexuality in 1961.[33] In 1965 she picketed with the Mattachine Society for Gay Rights and afterward began to write and publish pro-lesbian works.[34] The Women's Press Collective worked to "redefine poetic language and to draw out the political potential of a collective lesbian identity," and Grahn and her peers believed that feminist poetry was a political tactic important for revolutionary struggle.[35] The years following the founding of the press saw twenty-four books of poetry, memoir, prose fiction, political essays, and a gun ownership manual published.[36]—Sydney Brown

ALTA, EDITOR AND PUBLISHER, SHAMELESS HUSSY PRESS (1969–1989, OAKLAND)

Shameless Hussy Press was founded by Alta Gerrey, a feminist poet, in 1969 as the first feminist press in the United States. Alta printed and published *Remember Our Fire*, a collection of ten poems by women writers, which then became the *Shameless Hussy Review*. Her book *Freedom's in Sight*, printed in a first edition of 250 with John Oliver Simon's Noh Directions Press, sold out in six months. Many women writers began submitting to Shameless Hussy Press, including Susan Griffith, Pat Parker, and Ntozake Shange. As submissions increased, so did readership, and the press's audience grew. Alta chose to end the press in 1989. It is archived in the Special Collections

Additional Selected Women Editors and Publishers   357

department of UC Santa Cruz's University Library as part of the UC/Stanford US History and Women's Studies Consortium California Feminist Presses Project.[37]—Sadey Dong

JANICE MIRIKITANI, EDITOR, *AION* (1970–1971, SAN FRANCISCO) AND VARIOUS ANTHOLOGIES AND PUBLICATIONS

Janice Mirikitani was the cofounder and editor of the first Asian American literary magazine, *Aion*, which published two issues. The editing of the first issue significantly addressed the oppressed reality of Asian Americans and other third world people and proposed to reconstruct a culture of community, resisting imposed racial values and standards.[38] After college, Mirikitani was based in San Francisco, where she and a group of San Francisco writers and artists cofounded Third World Communications (TWC). In this publishing group she participated in editing "the first women of color anthology," *Third World Women* (1972), as well as *Time to Greez! Incantations from the Third World* (1975), published by Glide Publications.[39] Her interest in feminism, especially that of women of color, is deeply related to her childhood experience of sexual abuse and her search for a voice encompassing Asian American identity.[40] Her activist work intersected with her editing work in publications like *I Have Something to Say about this Big Trouble* (1989) and *Watch Out! We're Talking: Speaking Out about Incest and Abuse* (1993). She also coedited the groundbreaking book *Ayumi: A Japanese American Anthology* (1980), which includes literary pieces and visual arts by Japanese Americans "focused on wartime imprisonment and postwar settlement."[41]—Xiaomeng Yan

FAY CHIANG, DIRECTOR, BASEMENT WORKSHOP (1970–1986, NEW YORK)

Fay Chiang, an artist and poet, became the director of Basement Workshop, a seminal Asian American multidisciplinary arts initiative, in 1975. Basement Workshop left a lasting imprint on Asian American arts and culture in the East Coast and beyond.[42] It began after a group of graduate students involved in Danny Yung's 1969 Chinatown study recognized the need to preserve their research and rented a basement on 54 Elizabeth Street (later 22 Catherine Street). Inspired by the activism happening in the neighborhood, the same group started gathering regularly to talk about identity, politics,

358 Additional Selected Women Editors and Publishers

and art.[43] By 1974 Basement Workshop had grown into a large volunteer group with many projects, including publishing magazines of literature, archiving Asian American history, producing and introducing the public to art, and offering education to both high school students and adults. Around 1974 and 1975 Basement Workshop was forced to give up half of its spaces, and a few years later it faltered both financially and organizationally. Members decided that the work of Basement was complete and closed in 1986. Two important print legacies of Basement Workshop are the journals *Yellow Pearl* and *Bridge*.[44]—Sadey Dong

JUNE ARNOLD, EDITOR AND PUBLISHER, DAUGHTERS INC. (1972–1978, NEW YORK)

Like the other editors of Daughters Inc., June Arnold always "dream[ed] of building a feminist literature in which the power of women's words can reshape both language and culture."[45] Based in New York, the press's publications primarily revolved around gender and lesbian experiences and featured works by several notable feminist authors to create a "women's world."[46] In 1973 Arnold published the novel *The Cook and the Carpenter* under a pseudonym with the press, and in 1975 she published a second novel, *Sister Gin*.[47] According to a 1977 *New York Times* article, the women of Daughters sought "to build the working models for the critical next stage of feminism: full independence from the control and influence of 'male-dominated' institutions—the news media, the health, education and legal systems, the art, theater and literary worlds, the hanks."[48]—Siyuan Wang

NAOMI LONG MADGETT, EDITOR AND PUBLISHER, LOTUS PRESS (1972–2015 AND 2015–PRESENT AS BROADSIDE LOTUS PRESS, DETROIT)

Naomi Long Madgett was a talented poet and started writing poetry at an early age. After college she continued writing and publishing while teaching African American literature courses in public schools and universities. In 1972 she established Lotus Press to publish her fourth book, *Pink Ladies in the Afternoon*, because "much of the poetry by African Americans at that time was characterized by anger and rage, but Madgett's poems were quiet and subtle and she was unable to find a publisher who would accept it."[49] At first she did not intend to publish additional books, but in the classroom she

Additional Selected Women Editors and Publishers   359

found that texts representing the diversity and richness of Black poetry were absent from the curriculum. She subsequently published a poetry portfolio of living Black authors and later some works of her students. In the early stages of the press, she managed the printing process by herself and stapled all the books by hand. In 1980 Lotus Press was recognized as a 501(c)(3) organization, eligible for donations and grants.[50] However, Madgett remained the main funder of the press, as well as the editor and publisher, and "never paid herself a penny for her services,"[51] referring to her publishing work as "a labor of love."[52] In 1993 the Naomi Long Madgett Poetry Award was launched to provide African American poets more publishing opportunities.[53] Many authors first published by Lotus later published with larger presses, and Madgett saw herself as "a ladder upon whom authors may climb to better opportunities."[54] She worked until age ninety-two as publisher-editor for Lotus Press, at which point it merged with Broadside Press and began to operate as Broadside Lotus Press.[55]—Xiaomeng Yan

ELLEN MARIE BISSERT, EDITOR AND PUBLISHER, *13TH MOON*
(1973–2009, NEW YORK)

13th Moon, a feminist literary magazine, was founded in 1973 by Ellen Marie Bissert. The magazine was supported by the Writing Organization for Women at the City University of New York. It published short fiction, essays, and reviews by female authors, aiming to put women's work at the center of both traditional and "innovative modes of writing."[56] Bissert edited the magazine from 1973 to 1982, corresponding extensively with readers and editors of other publications during her editorial tenure.[57] The magazine sponsored poetry projects and did special projects about early American female poets.[58] Marilyn Hacker took over the editorial work after Bissert and edited volumes 7 and 8. Other editors included Judith Fetterley, Hollis Seamon, and Judith Johnson.—Yilin Xu

LYN HEJINIAN, EDITOR AND PUBLISHER, TUUMBA PRESS
(1976–1984 AND 2001–PRESENT, WILLITS, CA, AND BERKELEY)

As Lyn Hejinian notes in *A Secret Location on the Lower East Side*, originally she was "looking to various modes of 'experimental,' 'innovative,' or 'avant-garde' writing for information; the subsequent chapbooks represent a

360   Additional Selected Women Editors and Publishers

commitment to a particular community—the group of writers who came to be associated with 'Language Writing.'"[59] She founded Tuumba in 1976, calling it a "solo venture"; however, the venture "was not a private or solitary one."[60] In additional to publishing fifty pamphlets, Tuumba released broadsides and ephemera.[61] The press also published several books by Hejinian, including *A Thought is the Bride of What Thinking*, which appeared in 1976, and *Gesualdo*, which came out in 1978. After a hiatus, in the early 2000s it began publishing full-length books again.—Siyuan Wang

JOAN GIBBS, COEDITOR, *AZALEA: A MAGAZINE BY AND FOR THIRD WORLD LESBIANS* (1977–1983, NEW YORK CITY)

Joan Gibbs, along with Linda Brown and Robin Christian, was coeditor for *Azalea: A Magazine by and for Third World Lesbians*.[62] The magazine was published by the Salsa Soul Sisters, a collective of Black and Latina lesbians who sought to create a community for lesbians of color.[63] The Salsa Soul Sisters (originally the Black Lesbian Caucus) was a part of the Gay Activists Alliance founded after the Stonewall Riots in 1969.[64] The pages of *Azalea* contained an assortment of poetry, short stories, interviews, journal entries, and visual art.[65] The editors of *Azalea* made it a point to not edit any of the material included in each issue to allow lesbians to say whatever they needed to without censoring their messages.[66] The first issue was centered on seven writers in the United States and over the years the magazine expanded to include thirty artists from multiple continents.[67]—Sydney Brown

NORMA ALARCÓN, FOUNDER, THIRD WOMAN PRESS (1979–2004 AND 2011–PRESENT, BLOOMINGTON, IN, AND BERKELEY)

Norma Alarcón, inspired by the Midwest Latina Writer's Workshop at Indiana University, founded Third Woman Press (TWP) in 1979.[68] Rapidly becoming a significant platform for LGBTQIA+ and BIPOC dialogs, TWP championed decolonial feminist and queer perspectives. Alarcón described TWP as "a forum for self-definition and self-invention . . . The title 'Third Woman' mirrors the enduring realities women face."[69] However, financial challenges led to a temporary halt in 2004. With determination and the support of Christina L. Gutiérrez and Sara A. Ramírez, Alarcón revitalized TWP in 2011.[70] This revival aimed to honor and perpetuate the legacy of women of

Additional Selected Women Editors and Publishers   361

color in publishing. Among TWP's enduring publications is *This Bridge Called My Back*, first introduced in 1981 and reissued in 2002. Additionally, TWP has published vital works including Gloria Anzaldúa's *Living Chicana Theory* (1998), Cherrie Moraga's *The Sexuality of Latinas* (1993), and Carla Trujillo's *Chicana Lesbians: The Girls Our Mothers Warned Us About* (1991).—Flora Xu

SUSAN CLARK, COEDITOR, *RADDLE MOON* (1983–2003, VANCOUVER)

Susan Clark abhors the "hyper-patriarchal job title 'editor-in-chief,'"[71] and *Raddle Moon*, a journal renowned for its attention to innovative writing by women, turned toward a multi-editor model after its initial issues (published from the University of Victoria and then, after issue 13, by the Kootenay School of Writing Collective). Other editors during the journal's twenty issues include Kathryn MacLeod, Pasquale Verdicchio, Jeff Derksen, Steve Forth, Hilary Clark, Lisa Robertson, Catriona Strang, Norma Cole, Nicole Brossard, and Erin Mouré. Clark reports that she felt the magazine "came into its own when I re-shaped it," shifting to its distinctive black-and-white cover and 6 1/3 by 8–inch format with volume 13 (1994). Her steadfast editorial presence makes *Raddle Moon*, as Ted Byrne says in a 2003 talk, "both a vast collaboration and [her] singular project."[72] *Raddle Moon* became a vital venue for discussions about Language poetry, theory, translation, and feminism.[73]—Stephanie Anderson

KATHLEEN FRASER, EDITOR AND PUBLISHER, *HOW(EVER)* (1983–1992, SAN FRANCISCO) AND *HOW2* (1999–2004, SAN FRANCISCO)

When teaching the course Feminist Poetics at San Francisco State University, Fraser realized that many great women modernists had been overlooked in textbooks, and she decided to start a journal for women poets.[74] In 1983 she founded the journal *HOW(ever)*, aiming to create a space for modernist women's poetry. The journal's name is from Marianne Moore's line about poetry: "I, too, dislike it. / However, there is a place for it."[75] Believing that learning about the poets' writing process is essential for readers to understand their poems, Fraser envisioned *HOW(ever)* as a "process-oriented" journal that would include poets' editing notes and "informal" "studies" of scholars and critics.[76] During its seven years of publication, the journal developed into an essential site for women poets to discuss and publish their examination of the

362 Additional Selected Women Editors and Publishers

connection between language and gender.[77] The journal is Fraser's gesture to counter the "prospect of submission to the high-powered," male-dominated mainstream and avant-garde publications in the sixties.[78] In 1999 Fraser began *HOW2*, which published online until 2004.—Yilin Xu

SANDRA KAY MARTZ, EDITOR AND PUBLISHER, PAPIER-MACHE PRESS (1984– 2000, CALIFORNIA)

Sandra Kay Martz founded Papier-Mache Press in 1984 under the influence of 1970s second wave feminist publishers.[79] This press "was known for publishing accessible books," presenting "important social issues through enduring works of beauty, grace, and strength, and creat[ing] a bridge of understanding between the mainstream audience and those who might not otherwise be heard."[80] In the United States more than 1.6 million copies of the underground anthology *When I Am an Old Woman I Shall Wear Purple* were sold, and it became one of the first books for a general audiences about women and aging written by older women themselves,[81] "challeng[ing] stereotypes and confront[ing] the invisibility of older women in America."[82] Fourteen years after its founding, Papier-Mache Press had published an impressive sixty titles.—Siyuan Wang

IRENE RETI, EDITOR AND PUBLISHER, HERBOOKS FEMINIST PRESS (1984– 2002, SANTA CRUZ, CA)

Irene Reti never intended to start a press. Instead she wanted to publish local anthologies and had put out *Lesbian Words: A Santa Cruz Anthology* (1984) and its sequel, *Lesbian Words : Photographs and Writing* (1985). To gain wider distribution outside of Santa Cruz, in 1984 she got a business license. Her-Books was a small, all-volunteer press, running on low overhead and publishing pioneering radical feminist titles. The press's publications have included a variety of subjects, including feminist, lesbian, political, and cultural volumes; some publications include *Childless by Choice: A Feminist Anthology* (1992) and *Remember the Fire: Lesbian Sadomasochism in a Post-Nazi Holocaust World* (1986).[83] HerBooks is now archived at Special Collections, UC Santa Cruz Library, which also features an oral history interview with Reti.[84]—Sadey Dong

JENNIFER MOYER, DIRECTOR, MOYER BELL
(1984–PRESENT, WICKFORD, RI)

In 1984 Jennifer Moyer and her husband, Britt Bell, founded Moyer Bell, their own publishing house, which specializes in art books and literature and is known for its diverse list. Later they also added Asphodel Press (a nonprofit imprint) for poetry, essays, and translations.[85] Moyer Bell received five reviews in the *New York Times Book Review* in 1998 and reissued many well-selling books.[86] However, as it became increasingly challenging for independent booksellers to survive, Moyer Bell struggled with sales despite dedicated publicity work. Eventually, the press became an imprint of Beaufort Books, and Moyer Bell's titles began to be restocked, saving them from endangered novels lists.[87]—Sadey Dong

List of Selected Small Presses and Publications with Women and Nonbinary Editors and Publishers, 1950s–1980s

This list is not complete and is meant to provide some jumping-off points. It includes publications that involved women and nonbinary editors and publishers, though not necessarily throughout the duration of the press's or publication's existence.

Presses

Folder Editions (1959–2001, New York)
Secret Books Press (1960s–1970s, London)
Burning Deck Press (1961–2017, Michigan and Rhode Island)
Poets Press (1963–1969, New York)
Angel Hair Books (1966–1969, New York and Bolinas, CA)
Solo Press (1966–present, Carpinteria, CA)
Third World Press (1967–2015, Chicago)
The Women's Press Collective (1969–1977, Oakland, CA)
Shameless Hussy Press (1969–1989, Oakland, CA)
Telephone Books (1969–2003, New York, Connecticut, and Denver)
Basement Workshop (1970–1986)
Feminist Press (1970–present, Baltimore, MD, and New York)
Lotus Press (1972–2015, Detroit)
Five Trees Press (1973–1978, San Francisco)
Helaine Victoria Press (1973–1990, Los Angeles and Bloomington, IN)
Kelsey Street Press (1974–present, Berkeley)
Two and Two Chapbooks (1975, New York)
Metis Press (1975–1984, Evanston, IL)
Heresies Collective (1976–1984, New York)
Eidolon Editions (1976–2006, San Francisco)
Lost Roads Press (1976–present; Fayetteville, AK; San Francisco; Providence, RI)
Vehicle Editions (1976–present, New York)
United Artists Books (1977–present, New York)
Power Mad Press (1979–1981, New York)

365

366   List of Selected Small Presses and Publications

Third Woman Press (1979–present, Bloomington, IN, and Berkeley)
Kitchen Table: Women of Color Press (1980, Boston; 1981–1992, New York)
Cleis Press (1980–present, Minneapolis)
Black Oyster Press (1981–1984, Berkeley and Chicago)
Aunt Lute Books (1982–present, San Francisco)
Spinsters Ink (1982–present, Upstate New York and Tallahassee)
Awede Press (circa 1980–1985, Vermont)
Papier-Mache Press (1984–2000, California)
HerBooks Feminist Press (1984–2002, Santa Cruz, CA)
Moyer Bell (1984–present, Wickford, RI)
Second Story Press (1988–present, Toronto)
Tender Buttons Press (1989–present, New York)

Magazines

Folder (1954–1956, New York)
Yugen (1958–1962, New York)
Two Cities (1959–1964, Paris)
Amazing Grace Poetry Magazine (1960s–1970s, London)
TISH (1961–1969, Vancouver)
The Floating Bear (1961–1969 and 1971, New York and San Francisco)
El Corno Emplumado / The Plumed Horn (1962–1969, Mexico City)
Hardware Poets Occasional (1964, New York)
Io (1965–1977; Amherst, MA; Ann Arbor, MI; Cape Elizabeth, ME; Plainfield, VT;
        Berkeley, CA; Bar Harbor, ME)
Angel Hair (1966–1969, New York and Bolinas, CA)
0 TO 9 (1967–1969, New York)
IKON (1967–1969 and 1982–1994, New York)
The World (1967–2002, New York)
Telephone (1969–1983, New York, Connecticut, and Denver)
Café Solo (1969–1996, Carpinteria, CA), *Solo* (1996–2011, Carpinteria), *Solo Café, Solo
        Novo* (2011–present, Carpinteria)
Center (1970–1984, Woodstock, NY, and Santa Fe, NM)
Oink! (1971–1985, Chicago)
Bridge: An Asian American Perspective (1971–1986, New York)
CHICAGO (1972–1974, Chicago and the UK)
The Capilano Review (1972–present, Vancouver)
13th Moon (1973–1984, New York)
W. B. (1975, New York)
Out There (1975–1979, Chicago)
Conditions (1976–1990, New York)
Calyx: A Journal of Art and Literature by Women (1976–present, Corvallis, OR)

List of Selected Small Presses and Publications 367

Lilith (1976–present, New York)
Sinister Wisdom (1976–present, Berkeley)
Dodgems (1977–1979, New York)
Periodics (1977–1981, Vancouver)
Azalea: A Magazine by Third World Lesbians (1977–1983, New York)
United Artists (1977–1983, Lenox, MA, and New York)
Heresies: A Feminist Publication on Art and Politics (1977–1993, New York)
Top Stories (1978–1991, Buffalo, NY, and New York)
Third Woman (1981–1989, Bloomington, IN)
How(ever) (1983–1991, San Francisco)
Giants Play Well in the Drizzle (1983–1992, New York)
Raddle Moon (1983–2003, Vancouver)
Tessera (1984–2005, Quebec)
Bolinas Hearsay News (1984–present, Bolinas, CA)
M/E/A/N/I/N/G (1986–2016, New York)
New American Writing (1986–present, San Francisco)

Anthologies

A New Folder (Folder Editions, 1959)
Third World Women (Third World Communications, 1972)
Yellow Pearl (Basement Workshop, 1972)
Time to Greez!: Incantations from the Third World (Glide Publications, 1975)
Ordinary Women: An Anthology of New York City Women (Ordinary Women Books, 1978)
Ayumi: A Japanese American Anthology (Japanese American Anthology Committee, 1980)
From Shadows Emerging: An Anthology of Bay Area Women Writers (Black Oyster Press, 1981)
This Bridge Called My Back: Writings by Radical Women of Color (Persephone Press, 1981; Kitchen Table, 1983; Third Woman Press, 2002)
Home Girls: A Black Feminist Anthology (Kitchen Table, 1983)
Shadow on a Tightrope: Writings by Women on Fat Oppression (Aunt Lute Books, 1983)
Lesbian Words: A Santa Cruz Anthology (HerBooks Feminist Press, 1984)
The World Between Women: An Anthology (HerBooks Feminist Press, 1986)
Between the Lines: An Anthology by Pacific / Asian Lesbians of Santa Cruz, California (Dancing Bird Press, 1987)
Bubbe Meisehs by Shayneh Maidelehs: An Anthology of Poetry by Jewish Granddaughters about Our Grandmothers (HerBooks Feminist Press,[1] 1989)

Notes

Introduction

1. Allen, ed., *The New American Poetry, 1945–1960*.

2. For a sense of the importance of Allen's anthology, see, among others: Delbos, *The New American Poetry and Cold war Nationalism*; Woznicki, ed., *The New American Poetry*; Golding, "'The New American Poetry' Revisited, Again." For Aldan's importance to Allen, see Delbos, 48.

3. In order to emphasize woman and nonbinary editors-publishers' sense of agency, this book uses "independent" and "small press" interchangeably, despite the fact that in the scholarship the latter is usually seen as a subcategory of the former or they are seen as overlapping spheres.

4. Notley, *Doctor Williams' Heiresses*, n.p. Notley, well-known as a poet, has also been involved in all aspects of book publication as an editor of little magazines. *Doctor Williams' Heiresses* itself was printed and distributed as a pamphlet in July 1980 by writer and editor Lyn Hejinian at Tuumba Press.

5. This interview formed the basis for a paper presented at the Chicago Poetry Symposium at the University of Chicago Special Collections and was later published in Jed Birmingham and Kyle Schlesinger's vital periodical *Mimeo Mimeo*. I am especially grateful to symposium organizer David Pavelich for guiding me toward *CHICAGO* and other objects of study, as well as being a model small press publisher himself.

6. Notley's questions reverberated, and after my ensuing presentation on *CHICAGO*, the curator Nancy Kuhl suggested that I pursue a series of interviews with women small press publishers, a suggestion that led to the larger interview project *Women in Independent Publishing*.

7. In addition to Aldan receiving awards for her writing and translating, the Donnell Library Center hosted an exhibit about Folder Editions in October–November 1989, followed by an exhibit at the Small Press Center in November 1990. Daisy Aldan Papers, boxes 6 and 9, Yale Collection.

8. Rasula, *The American Poetry Wax Museum*, 223–47.

9. In the chronology of Aldan's life included in her *Collected Poems*, for instance, the dates for *Folder* are listed as 1953–1959, implicitly including *A New Folder* in the magazine's chronology (viii).

10. Rifkin and Dewey, eds., *Among Friends*, 4.

370   Notes

11. Woolf's lecture was published in 1929 by her and Leonard Woolf's Hogarth Press. For a "small press" publication, *A Room of Own's Own* enjoyed huge sales: more than 22,000 copies in the United States and England in the first six months (Willis, *Leonard and Virginia Woolf as Publishers*, 154). In fact, it was partly the financial success of Hogarth Press and of this particular book that allowed Woolf to realize, in both senses of the word, the material resources necessary for a woman writer to be able to pursue her writing work (Walker, "A Press of One's Own").

12. See, among many others, Keller and Miller, "Gender and Avant-Garde Editing"; Marek, *Women Editing Modernism*; Dennison, *Alternative Literary Publishing*; Morrisson, *The Public Face of Modernism*.

13. For an introduction to the Mimeograph Revolution, see the groundbreaking Clay and Phillips, *A Secret Location on the Lower East Side*. While the companion website (https://fromasecretlocation.com/updates/) provides additional resources about publications written and edited by women, men still dominate and often write accounts of presses even when they were coediting with women. In his introduction to the recent Little Magazines cluster at *Post45*, Nick Sturm discusses the relative lack of scholarly attention to post-1960 little magazines ("Introduction: Deep Immersion").

14. Osman and Spahr, eds., "Editorial Forum"; "Page Mothers Conference Recordings."

15. In Anderson and Kinzie, eds., *The Little Magazine in America*, just four chapters of interviews, reminiscences, and essays are by or with women (one is a discussion between Anne Waldman and Larry Fagin, and one is an interview with Daisy Aldan) out of forty-one. *Against the Grain* (ed. Dana) contains just one interview with a woman out of nine, and the same year (1986) *Green Isle in the Sea* (eds. Kruchkow and Johnson), which includes both interviews and written reminiscences, contains three entries focused on women editors out of twenty-four. Recently, Morris and Diaz, eds., *The Little Magazine in Contemporary America* includes eight accounts by women out of twenty-one, and Schlesinger's *A Poetics of the Press* includes seven out of eighteen (two are joint interviews with men).

16. Anderson and Kinzie, *Little Magazine in America*, 268, 275.

17. Keller and Miller, "Gender and Avant-Garde Editing," n.p.

18. Mirikitani generously agreed to an interview, but illness prevented us from completing it before her passing.

19. Rifkin and Dewey, *Among Friends*, 5.

20. And prior to that a child star of the radio program *Let's Pretend*.

21. Malanga, "Daisy Aldan, Poet."

22. Roberts, On Daisy Aldan.

23. Harms, ed., *Celebration!*, 66.

24. *Folder Magazine*; Riva Castleman, "Floriano Vecchi and the Tiber Press"; Hennessey, "On Daisy Aldan"; Patterson, "New York Poets." Paterson's article reproduces two *Folder* covers.

25. Aldan Interviewed by Dorothy Friedman, Daisy Aldan Papers, box 31, Yale Collection.

Notes   371

26. It's worth noting that Aldan herself de-emphasizes New York as the point of commonality, stating, "What brought us together was *Folder*" (Aldan, "Daisy Aldan: An Interview on Folder," 273). Thanks to Nick Sturm for reminding me of this moment in the interview.

27. Seita, *Provisional Avant-Gardes*, 5, 11.

28. Patterson, "New York Poets," 985; "The Folder Poets."

29. Aldan Interviewed by Dorothy Friedman.

30. Hennessey, "On Daisy Aldan."

31. Delbos, *The New American Poetry and Cold War Nationalism*, 48.

32. Ibid., 62.

33. Daisy Aldan Papers, box 3, folder 5, Harry Ransom Center.

34. Delbos, *The New American Poetry and Cold War Nationalism*, 61.

35. Zahn, "An Inch of Culture." This review employs sexist language as insult.

36. Aldan, "Daisy Aldan to James Boyer," September 23, 1960, James Boyer May (Amsberry-May) Papers.

37. Ibid.

38. Delbos, *The New American Poetry and Cold War Nationalism*, 60.

39. Daisy Aldan Papers, box 3, folder 5, Harry Ransom Center.

40. "The Folder Poets," 73.

41. Daisy Aldan Papers, box 4, Yale Collection.

42. Aldan Interviewed by Dorothy Friedman.

43. "Vanity, n.," in OED Online.

44. "Google Ngram Viewer." It is worth noting that this period overlaps with the usage of vanity as a piece of furniture associated with women. The OED's first example of a vanity as a table at which a someone might attend to a beauty routine dates to 1937, and the first example given of a vanity unit is from 1967.

45. I assume this is a typo for Kelsey.

46. Additionally, type brought together Aldan and Anaïs Nin, who wrote to ask if Aldan had purchased her old type. Anderson and Kinzie, *Little Magazine in America*, 268, 275.

47. For more on the history of gender and letterpress printing, see Battershill's *Women and Letterpress Printing*: "Well into the twentieth and twenty-first centuries, the printing industry continued to be impacted by what it inherited: exclusionary trade unions, factory acts that legislated restrictions on female participation in industrial labor, and cultures of misogyny and gender essentialism" (29).

48. Harms, *Celebration!*, 71.

49. For more on women and printing, see Fanni, Flodmark, and Kaaman, eds., *Natural Enemies of Books*.

50. Please note that from here forward, "Jones" refers to Hettie Jones and "Spears Jones" refers to Patricia Spears Jones.

51. Kittler, *Gramophone, Film, Typewriter*, 216.

52. For more on the 1880s gender shift in secretarial work, see Ibid., 184.

53. Mottram, "The Mimeograph Revolution."

372   Notes

54. Myles, "Mimeo Opus"; Mayer, "Mimeo Argument."

55. Aldan Interviewed by Dorothy Friedman.

56. Daisy Aldan Papers, box 3, folder 5, Harry Ransom Center.

57. Harms, *Celebration!*, 70.

58. Daisy Aldan Papers, box 100, Yale Collection.

59. Daisy Aldan Interviewed by Dorothy Friedman.

60. Daisy Aldan Papers, box 3, folder 4, Harry Ransom Center.

61. Including, among others, Richard Eberhart, James Merrill, M. C. Richards, Larry Eigner, Madeline Gleason, and Storm De Hirsch.

62. Delbos, *The New American Poetry and Cold War Nationalism*, 60.

63. Daisy Aldan Papers, box 3, folder 4, Harry Ransom Center.

64. Daisy Aldan Papers, box 4, Yale Collection.

65. Daisy Aldan Papers, box 3, folder 4, Harry Ransom Center.

66. Daisy Aldan Papers, box 4, Yale Collection.

67. Ibid.

68. Cran, "Space Occupied," 501.

69. Daisy Aldan Interviewed by Dorothy Friedman.

70. In an interview about *M/E/A/N/I/N/G* (1986–2016), an art magazine edited by Mira Schor and Susan Bee, Schor uses the image of "spies" to describe the material editorial process: "Because our studios were close-by, we'd meet at the corner of Canal and West Broadway and exchange envelopes, manila envelopes, like we were spies. 'Here's the document.'" Schor and Bee, "Mira Schor and Susan Bee Discuss the Many Meanings of Art Writing."

71. "Never not singing" was inspired by a phrase ("but I am singing") used by Lee Ann Brown in email correspondence, and I use it here with gratitude.

72. The other points of the hexagon are Frank O'Hara, Edward Field, John Ashbery, Denise Levertov, and Kenneth Koch, with Michael McClure in the middle.

73. Daisy Aldan Papers, box 25, Yale Collection.

74. Daisy Aldan Papers, box 3, folder 4, Harry Ransom Center.

75. King says in her interview, "Both order and disorder are actually quite sneaky."

76. Harms, *Celebration!*, 72.

77. In these instances, men have often told the stories of the presses. The tensions of coediting, especially with a male partner, are largely elided, though Randall discusses how the editorial notes are a place where you can see her and Sergio Mondragon headed in different directions. Chernoff says, "We always had a tacit agreement that, okay, if one of us feels strongly enough about something, then it's in."

78. Aldan, "Daisy Aldan: An Interview on Folder," 269.

Hettie Jones

1. As a reminder, interviews are ordered by the founding year of the earliest

press-publication project with which the interviewee was involved, regardless of the year when the interviewee became the editor-publisher.

Margaret Randall

1. Mexican poet Sergio Mondragón was, with Randall, cofounder and coeditor of *El Corno Emplumado*. Randall and Mondragon were married for eight years in the 1960s.
2. Ehrenberg passed away in 2017.

Lindy Hough

1. Grossinger and Hough, *Io Anthology*, xvii–lxiii.

Bernadette Mayer

1. Halloween decorations strung up on the porch, visible from the window of the "winter study," where the interview took place.
2. Cofounder of *0 TO 9*.
3. To the reprint by Ugly Duckling Presse.
4. Cofounder and coeditor of both Angel Hair and United Artists.
5. Friend of Mayer's.
6. See Mayer and Coolidge, *The Cave*.
7. Poet and friend of Mayer's.
8. Poet and Bernadette's partner.
9. Poet and friend of Mayer's.
10. At the time of the interview, Bernadette had a broken arm and it was difficult for her to read lying down. So before bed she was reading just the right-hand pages of books.
11. See Tapson, "Joint Experiments."

Susan Sherman

1. This source is no longer available, but Sherman's essay on *IKON*'s history will appear in *Sinister Wisdom*, Spring 2024. The Complete *IKON* Series 2 archive is now at https://www.lesbianpoetryarchive.org/IKON.
2. See Sherman, *America's Child*.

Renee Tajima-Peña

1. Tajima-Peña served as editor from 1981 to 1983.
2. See Tajima-Peña, "Toward a Third Wave" and "Moving the Image."

374 Notes

3. See Cheang and Tomes, "Shu Lea Cheang," 4.

4. See Jeung, Umemoto, Dong, Mar, Tsuchitani, and Pan, *Mountain Movers*. The website links to the book project and is also a digital archive of videos, documents, and more. See also Singh, "Asian American Little Magazines."

5. "Bridge Magazine–Basement Workshop."

6. Tajima-Peña, "Moving the Image," 13.

Maxine Chernoff

1. Chernoff served as coeditor of *New American Writing* from 1987 to 2014 (issue 32).

2. Hölderlin, *Selected Poems*.

3. See VIDA: Women in Literary Arts. Beginning in 2009 this organization has been doing an annual count of women in "the journals, publications, and press outlets."

4. Here Chernoff is referring to a hypothetical magazine, not Notley's magazine of the same title.

Jaime Robles

1. See also Davids, Colby, and Robles's 2016 exhibition catalog, *Sisters of Invention*.

Barbara Barg and Rose Lesniak

1. Barg's Power Mad Press began in 1979; in 1975, she and Lesniak became associate editor and editor, respectively, of *Out There* with issue 8.

2. Published by Roof Books in 1980.

3. *The Origin of THE Species*.

Rena Rosenwasser and Patricia Dienstfrey

1. Rossenwasser and Dienstfrey coedited and copublished Kellsey Street Press from 1974 to 2022.

Joanne Kyger

1. Kyger served as an editor from 1984 to 2013.

Martha King

1. See King, *Outside/Inside*.

2. Ibid.

Patricia Spears Jones

1. Spears Jones edited *W. B.* in 1975. Her work as an editorial staffer for the Heresies Collective took place from 1980 to 1984; she was also the office manager for the collective from 1981 to 1983.

2. Fay Chiang passed away in 2017; please see the resources section for more information about her.

C. D. Wright

1. Wright began as editor of Lost Roads in 1976 and was coeditor from 1980 to 2009.

Barbara Smith

1. Smith, "A Press of Our Own," 11–13.

2. For additional interviews with Smith about Kitchen Table, see Smith, *Ain't Gonna Let Nobody Turn Me Around*, sec. 5.

3. Smith, "Toward a Black Feminist Criticism."

4. See "Packing Boxes and Editing Manuscripts" in Smith, *Ain't Gonna Let Nobody Turn Me Around*.

5. See "A Rose" in Smith, *The Truth that Never Hurts*.

Lisbet Tellefsen

1. Tellefsen was editor from 1989 to 1991; publisher from 1991 to 1995.

2. See the interview with editor Barbara Smith earlier in this book.

3. "The creative work of untrained African-Americans has often been discredited as 'decorative' and 'non-art.' Yet it has always held the cultural relevance, values, and visuals specifically vital to African-Americans. In the art I do, and in my perceptions of what is 'art,' I strive to give meaning to that tradition." *Aché* 1, no. 9, n.p.

4. See Beam, *In the Life*.

5. See Colangelo, ed., *We Are Everywhere*.

6. SEO stands for Search Engine Optimization.

Lee Ann Brown

1. Text by LAB, arrangement by SA and LAB.

Afterword

1. In these endnotes, I (MC) will try to address a more general audience, filling

376 Notes

in information that you, Stephanie, are already aware of. I was the sole editor of DoubleCross Press in its first year. Jeff Peterson joined in 2009 and took on much of the book cover design, and Anna Gurton-Wachter joined as a second editor, working with authors on manuscripts, in 2013; all three of us also work together to make the press's books. Meanwhile, Stephanie Anderson and Sam Amadon started Projective Industries in 2008; Sam left as a coeditor in 2010 (later founding *Oversound* and Oversound Books with his wife, Liz Countryman); Kate McIntyre (and, eventually, Karen Lepri) later came on as Projective Industries coeditors. DoubleCross Press is still running as of this writing, while Projective Industries ceased publishing chapbooks in 2018, around the time Stephanie permanently relocated to East Asia (China, then Singapore, then China again).

2. Given the focus of *Women in Independent Publishing*, it seems worth noting that Octopus, like many of the influential small poet-run presses of the mid-to-late oughts, was run by white men: Matthias Svalina and Zachary Schomburg. Similarly, although New Michigan has always had a larger volunteer staff, Ander Monson has been editor-in-chief since its founding. (Incidentally, Ander graduated a few years before me from the creative writing and book arts MFAs at the University of Alabama.) This prevalence of white hetero and cis male editors or editors-in-chief at many of the small presses publishing more experimental work in the late oughts and early twenty-teens, as I'll discuss later, could sometimes make this scene less than hospitable for women, nonbinary writers, and writers of color. Off the top of my head I can think of, in addition to New Michigan/*DIAGRAM* and Octopus, the following presses and online magazines that were run by one or more white men: H_NGM_N, Spork, *The Canary* / Canarium Books, Birds LLC, Coconut Books, *Typo*, Greying Ghost, Letter Machine Editions, Minutes Books, Magic Helicopter Press / *Nöo*, and *Forklift, Ohio*. Many of these men are or have been my friends and publishers—but that doesn't mean that gender and racial dynamics don't bear closer scrutiny (or that the community was not rocked by #MeToo, in response to which at least two presses closed). I've always understood your project, in *Women in Independent Publishing*, as an attempt to redress the gender—and, in your interviews with Barbara Smith, Lisbet Tellefsen, Patrica Spears Jones, and Renee Tajima-Peña, racial—imbalance of that publishing scene.

3. As of this writing (in October 2022), the Poetry Society Chapbook Fellowship no longer awards two New York Fellowships and two national ones, nor recognizes, in past years' winners, a distinction between New York and national contest winners. Quotation from personal conversation with Stephanie Anderson, October 11, 2022.

4. I studied in the Book Arts MFA at the University of Alabama between 2004 and 2008, though I didn't finish my master's thesis in book arts until 2011. My teachers in Alabama were Anna Embree, who'd trained in bookbinding at the University of Iowa, and Steve Miller. I also learned about bookmaking at the Center for Book Arts, New York (first through a summer internship in 2005, and later as an artist affiliated with the center) and at the Minnesota Center for Book Arts, where I joined the artist co-op in 2008 and the administrative staff from 2009 to 2012. Both book art centers are heavily invested in letterpress technology and hand-bookbinding, and both centers collect

communities of artists who come to those centers for access to those tools. MCBA's facilities also accommodate papermaking and screen printing. One way of tracking patterns of influence in artist bookmaking is through who shared what studios at what time—my way of making books is profoundly shaped by the other artists I've worked alongside in these spaces. That is, however, a story for another book.

5. See, for a start, Drucker, *The Century of Artist's Books*; Bright, *No Longer Innocent*.

6. For example, during my master's program, a speaker on professional development showed us a project budget for a book he'd recently completed. In this budget he billed his typesetting labor at about ten dollars less an hour than his printing labor.

7. See "2009 AWP Conference & Bookfair."

8. The panel was called "Accidental Dominance: The State of Small Press Publishing," and the speakers were Rebecca Wolff (*Fence* was by that time an establishment, founded in 1998), James Meetze (an author who had, at the time, published with three small poet-run presses: Cy Press, Tougher Disguises, and Sea.Lamb.Press), Kazim Ali (who launched Nightboat in the previous year), Anna Moschovakis (representing Ugly Duckling Presse, another late-nineties small press institution), and Joyelle McSweeney (who had launched Action Books with Johannes Göransson the previous year).

9. The first year I paid for a bookfair table, 2010, the "early bird" table fee was $450; for the 2023 AWP it's $650—more than DoubleCross makes selling books at AWP in a good year (not to mention the cost of transportation and lodging, which drives up conference costs out of the price range of many nonlocal writers and small presses).

10. A November 2014 report published by the Association and Writers and Writing Programs shows this startling growth: there were 64 creative writing MFA programs in 1994, 109 in 2004, 156 in 2008, and more than 200 by 2012 (Falcon, "2013–2014 Report").

11. The adjunctification of higher education has been noticed and discussed not just within the field of higher education itself but also in mainstream media and even at the level of government. When I was looking for statistics on the growing rates of adjunct faculty in the first decade of the 2000s, I found a 2014 congressional report called "The Just-In-Time Professor" (see House Committee on Education). This report summarized responses to a congressional eForum about adjunct working conditions. This report states the scale of the problem: "In 1970, adjuncts made up 20 percent of all higher education faculty. Today, they represent half" (1).

12. Ugly Duckling Presse Organized this table from 2009 to 2013; for more about this project, see Yankelevich, "The New Normal." A list of participating presses at the 2011 AWP can be found on the UDP website ("Table-X at AWP").

13. This magazine was called *We Are So Happy To Know Something*.

Additional Selected Women Editors and Publishers

1. As with the interview section, date ranges in this section refer to the years that a magazine or press was operational, not to the timespan of a particular editor-publisher's involvement.

2. Hornick, "Kulchur: A Memoir," 281.

3. Ibid., 282.
4. Kulchur Foundation, "Kulchur Foundation Records."
5. Hornick, "Kulchur: A Memoir," 285–90.
6. Ibid., 297.
7. Kulchur Foundation, "Kulchur Foundation Records."
8. Braun, "A History of Diane di Prima's Poets Press," 3.
9. Ibid., 11.
10. "Diane Di Prima," Academy of American Poets.
11. "Poets Press."
12. Braun, "A History of Diane Di Prima's Poets Press," 3–22, 7, 163, 166.
13. "Diane Di Prima," Poetry Foundation.
14. Linn, "Glenna Luschei."
15. Raz et al., "A Prairie Schooner Portfolio."
16. Ibid.
17. Linn, "Glenna Luschei"; Raz et al., "A Prairie Schooner Portfolio," 45–92, 77.
18. Linn, "Glenna Luschei."
19. Raz et al., "A Prairie Schooner Portfolio," 74, 80.
20. Champion, "Insane Podium."
21. Waldman, "Oral History Project."
22. Champion, "Insane Podium."
23. Waldman and Fagin, "Discussion of Little Magazines," 496, 510–11.
24. Waldman and Warsh, eds., *Angel Hair Sleeps*.
25. Waldman and Fagin, "Discussion of Little Magazines," 497.
26. Peart, "Introduction."
27. Third World Press Foundation, "About."
28. Reid, "Third World Press's 50 Years."
29. Ibid.
30. Kelly, "The Women's Press Collective."
31. "Judy Grahn," Poetry Foundation.
32. "Poet, Activist, Scholar," Judy Grahn Official Site.
33. Ibid.; "Judy Grahn."
34. "Poet, Activist, Scholar," Judy Grahn Official Site.
35. Kelly, "The Women's Press Collective."
36. Ibid.
37. Alta, *Alta and the History of Shameless Hussy Press*.
38. Singh, "Asian American Little Magazines."
39. Murguia, "Poetry and Solidarity in the Mission."
40. Cheung, *Words Matter*.
41. Google Books description.
42. Chinese-American Planning Council, "In Memory of Fay Chiang."
43. Wong, "Basement Workshop," 35, and Yung, "Brief Summary of Basement Workshop Early Years."
44. Chinese-American Planning Council, "In Memory of Fay Chiang."

45. Gould, "Creating a Women's World."

46. See publications by Daughters Inc. in the Lesbian Poetry Archive; Gould, "Creating a Woman's World."

47. Cottrell, "Arnold, June Fairfax Davis."

48. Gould, "Creating a Woman's World."

49. "Brief History of Lotus Press, Inc."

50. Ibid.

51. Zurek, "Publishing Profiles: Dr. Naomi Long Madgett."

52. Ibid.

53. Ibid.

54. "Brief History of Lotus Press, Inc."

55. "Naomi Long Madgett & Lotus Press."

56. 13th Moon Press, "About."

57. 13th Moon Records.

58. Ibid.

59. Tuumba Press, From a Secret Location.

60. Ibid.

61. Ibid.

62. Sachs, "Sexuality and Three Third Worlds in *Azalea*."

63. "Salsa Soul Sisters."

64. Ibid.

65. Sachs, "Sexuality and Three Third Worlds in *Azalea*."

66. Ibid.

67. Ibid.

68. "About TWP."

69. Ibid.

70. Ibid.

71. Clark, e-mail to Anderson, "Re: Raddle Moon."

72. Byrne, "A Talk on the Occasion of the (Belated) Launch." The editor list is reproduced from this talk.

73. See also Seita, "The Politics of the Forum."

74. Fraser, "The Tradition of Marginality," 25.

75. Ibid., 26.

76. Hogue, "An Interview with Kathleen Fraser," 2.

77. Ibid., 2.

78. Ibid., 17

79. Martz and Reti, *Sandra Kay Martz*.

80. Ibid.

81. Ibid.

82. Ibid.

83. Reti, *Irene Reti and HerBooks Feminist Press*.

84. Ibid.

85. *New York Times*, "Jennifer Moyer."

380 Notes

86. McEvoy, "Moyer Bell."
87. "Moyer Bell and Its Subsidiaries."

List of Selected Small Presses and Publications with Women and Nonbinary Editors and Publishers, 1950s–1980s

1. For more anthologies by HerBooks, see https://oac.cdlib.org/findaid/ark:/13030/ft7v19p04b/admin/.

Bibliography

The following categories are meant to assist readers who are exploring sources. However, it is necessarily incomplete and imperfect, and some texts are applicable in several categories. Though gender could have served as a category itself, it weaves throughout many sources, and readers are especially encouraged to look further into the history of feminist and LGBTQIA+ publishing. Readers locating a specific citation's source might find it helpful to search across categories.

Library Archives Cited

Aldan, Daisy. Daisy Aldan Interviewed by Dorothy Friedman at the Living Theater. Interview by Dorothy Friedman, March 3, 1991. Daisy Aldan Papers, box 35. Yale Collection of American Literature, Beinecke Rare Book and Manuscript Library.

———. Daisy Aldan Papers. Harry Ransom Center, The University of Texas at Austin.

———. Daisy Aldan Papers. Yale Collection of American Literature, Beinecke Rare Book and Manuscript Library.

———. "Daisy Aldan to James Boyer," September 23, 1960. James Boyer May (Amsberry-May) Papers, SC.87. California State University, Fullerton. University Archives and Special Collections.

Digital Archives

Eclipse Archive. Accessed November 3, 2023. http://eclipsearchive.org/.

Hearsay News Archives. Accessed November 6, 2023. http://hearsaynews.org/archives. html.

IKON Second Series Archives. Lesbian Poetry Archive. Accessed September 9, 2024. https://www.lesbianpoetryarchive.org/IKON.

Independent Voices. Accessed November 6, 2023. https://about.jstor.org/revealdigital/independent-voices/.

Lesbian Herstory Archives Exhibition Collections. Accessed November 5, 2023. https://lhaexhibits.omeka.net/.

Lesbian Poetry Archive. Accessed November 5, 2023. http://www. lesbianpoetryarchive.org/.

382   Bibliography

Modernist Journals Project. Accessed November 3, 2023. http://modjourn.org/.
Modernist Magazines Project. Accessed November 3, 2023. http://modmags.dmu.
    ac.uk/home.html.
Modernist Magazines Project. Accessed November 2, 2023. http://modernistmaga-
    zines.com/.
Open Door Archive. Accessed August 7, 2015. http://opendoor.northwestern.edu/archive/.
Reissues | *Jacket2*. Accessed November 3, 2023. http://jacket2.org/reissues.
Singh, Amardeep. "Asian American Little Magazines 1968–1974." Accessed April 19,
    2022. https://scalar.lehigh.edu/asian-american-little-magazines/index.
Sturm, Nick. "Alice Notley's Magazines: A Digital Publishing Project." Accessed
    November 3, 2023. https://www.nicksturm.com/digital-publishing-project.

Memoirs by Women Editors and Publishers

Hornick, Lita. *The Green Fuse: A Memoir*. New York; Berkeley: Giorno Poetry Systems,
    1989.
———. "Kulchur: A Memoir." TriQuarterly 43, (Fall 1978): 281.
Jones, Hettie. *How I Became Hettie Jones*. New York: Grove, 1996.
———. *Love, H: The Letters of Helene Dorn and Hettie Jones*. Durham, NC: Duke University
    Press, 2016.
King, Martha. *Outside/Inside: Just Outside the Art World's Inside*. Buffalo, NY: BlazeVOX,
    2018.
Madgett, Naomi Long. *Pilgrim Journey*. Detroit: Broadside Lotus, 2006.
Prima, Diane di. *Recollections of My Life as a Woman: The New York Years*. New York:
    Viking, 2001.
Randall, Margaret. *I Never Left Home: Poet, Feminist, Revolutionary*. Durham, NC: Duke
    University Press, 2020.
———. *To Change the World: My Years in Cuba*. New Brunswick, NJ: Rutgers University
    Press, 2009.
Sherman, Susan. *America's Child: A Woman's Journey Through the Radical Sixties*. Willi-
    mantic, CT: Curbstone Books, 2007.

Interview Collections

Anderson, Elliott, and Mary Kinzie, eds. *The Little Magazine in America: A Modern Docu-
    mentary History*. Yonkers, NY: Pushcart, 1979.
Brandt, Kate. *Happy Endings: Lesbian Writers Talk About Their Lives and Work*. Tallahas-
    see, FL: Naiad, 1993.
Cheung, King-Kok. *Words Matter: Conversations with Asian American Writers*. Intersec-
    tions: Asian and Pacific American Transcultural Studies, 26. Honolulu: Univer-
    sity of Hawaii Press, 2000.
Courtney, Cathy. *Speaking of Book Art: Interviews with British & American Book Artists*. Los
    Altos Hills, CA: Anderson Lovelace, 1999.

Bibliography 383

Dana, Robert, ed. *Against the Grain: Interviews with Maverick American Publishers*. Iowa City: University of Iowa Press, 1986.

Kruchkow, Diane, and Curt Johnson, eds. *Green Isle in the Sea: An Informal History of the Alternative Press, 1960-85*. Highland Park and Chicago: December, 1986.

Morris, Ian, and Joanne Diaz, eds. *The Little Magazine in Contemporary America*. Chicago and London: University of Chicago Press, 2015.

Schlesinger, Kyle, ed. *A Poetics of the Press: Interviews with Poets, Printers, & Publishers*. Brooklyn: Ugly Duckling, 2021.

Cited Small Press Publications

For the magazines and anthologies that are the subject of many of these interviews, see the list on pages 366–367.

Acconci, Vito, and Bernadette Mayer. *0 to 9: The Complete Magazine: 1967–1969*. Brooklyn: Ugly Duckling, 2006.

Aldan, Daisy. *Collected Poems of Daisy Aldan*. Troy, MI: Sky Blue, 2002.

Allen, Donald, ed. *The New American Poetry, 1945–1960*. Berkeley: University of California Press, 1999.

Barb, Barbara. *The Origin of THE Species*. Los Angeles: Semiotext(e), 1994.

Beam, Joseph. *In the Life: A Black Gay Anthology*. New York: Alyson Books, 1986.

Folder Magazine. Accessed December 21, 2021. http://www.foldermagazine.com.

Grossinger, Richard, and Lindy Hough, eds. *Io Anthology: Literature, Interviews, and Art from the Seminal Interdisciplinary Journal, 1965–1993*. Illustrated edition. Berkeley: North Atlantic Books, 2015.

Hölderlin, Friedrich. *Selected Poems of Friedrich Hölderlin*. Translated by Maxine Chernoff and Paul Hoover. Richmond, CA: Omnidawn, 2019.

Hough, Lindy. *Wild Horses, Wild Dreams: New and Selected Poems, 1971–2010*. Berkeley: North Atlantic Books, 2011.

Jones, Patricia Spears. *A Lucent Fire: New and Selected Poems*. Buffalo: White Pine Press, 2015.

Mayer, Bernadette, and Clark Coolidge. *The Cave*. New York: Adventures in Poetry, 2008.

Notley, Alice. *Doctor Williams' Heiresses: A Lecture*. Vol. 28. Berkeley: Tuumba, 1980.

Randall, Margaret. *Selections from El Corno Emplumado / The Plumed Horn, 1962–1964*. Center for the Humanities, the Graduate Center, The City University of New York, 2011.

Smith, Barbara, ed. *Home Girls: A Black Feminist Anthology*. 40th anniversary ed. New Brunswick, NJ: Rutgers University Press, 2023.

Waldman, Anne. *Out of This World: An Anthology of the St. Mark's Poetry Project, 1966–1991*. New York: Crown, 1991.

Waldman, Anne, and Lewis Warsh, eds. *Angel Hair Sleeps with a Boy in My Head: The Angel Hair Anthology*. New York: Granary Books, 2001.

Wright, C. D. *Room Rented by a Single Woman*. Fayetteville, AR: Lost Roads, 1977.

384   Bibliography

Scholarship and Sources about Small Presses, Magazines, and Editors

13th Moon Records, Manuscripts and Archives Division. The New York Public Library. https://archives.nypl.org/mss/1#bioghist.

13th Moon Press. "About." Accessed May 22, 2022. http://13thmoon.net/html/about.html.

"About TWP." Third Woman Press | Queer and Feminist of Color Publishing. Accessed October 22, 2023. http://www.thirdwomanpress.com/.

Aldan, Daisy. "Daisy Aldan: An Interview on Folder." In *The Little Magazine in America: A Modern Documentary History*, 262–79. Yonkers, NY: Pushcart, 1978.

Alta. *Alta and the History of Shameless Hussy Press, 1969–1989*. Interview by Irene Reti. University of California, Santa Cruz, University Library. August 2000 and February 2001. Accessed May 25, 2022. https://library.ucsc.edu/reg-hist/alta.

Among the Neighbors. Pamphlet series. Buffalo: University at Buffalo, 2016–present.

Anderson, Stephanie. Personal communication with MC Hyland. October 11, 2022.

———. "Shiny Collisions: Editing as Serious Humor in *dodgems*." *Women's Studies* 51 no. 8 (2023): 925–944.

Bergé, Carol. "An Informal Timetable of Coffee-House Activities in New York." *Magazine* 2 (1965): 21–25.

Biggs, Mary. "From Harriet Monroe to AQ: Selected Women's Literary Journals, 1912–1972." *13th Moon* 8, no. 1–2 (1984): 183.

———. "Women's Literary Journals." *The Library Quarterly* (Chicago) 53, no. 1 (1983): 1–25.

Braun, Jolie. "A History of Diane di Prima's Poets Press." *Journal of Beat Studies* 6 (2018): 3–22.

"Bridge Magazine—Basement Workshop." Accessed April 19, 2022. https://artsandculture.google.com/asset/bridge-magazine-basement-workshop/-wHJcLubN-wNUPQ.

"Brief History of Lotus Press, Inc." Broadside Lotus Press official website. Accessed November 4, 2023. http://broadsidelotuspress.org/About%20Us.htm.

Byrne, Ted. "A Talk on the Occasion of the (Belated) Launch of Issues 19 and 20 of Raddle Moon." Kootenay School of Writing, Vancouver, July 25, 2003.

Castleman, Riva. "Floriano Vecchi and the Tiber Press." *Print Quarterly* 21, no. 2 (2004): 127–45.

Champion, Miles. "Insane Podium: A Short History THE POETRY PROJECT, 1966–2012." The Poetry Project Blog. Accessed August 4, 2022. https://www.2009-2019.poetryproject.org/about/history/.

Chinese-American Planning Council. "In Memory of Fay Chiang," October 26, 2017. https://www.cpc-nyc.org/news/1325/memory-fay-chiang.

Clark, Susan. E-mail to Stephanie Anderson. "Re: Raddle Moon," March 14, 2020.

Clay, Stephen, and Rodney Phillips. *A Secret Location on the Lower East Side: Adventures in Writing, 1960–1980: A Sourcebook of Information*. New York: New York Public Library and Granary Books, 1998. See also the From a Secret Location website: https://fromasecretlocation.com/.

Colangelo, Gabrielle, ed. *We Are Everywhere: Lesbians in the Archive*. Yale University

Library Online Exhibitions. Accessed November 6, 2023. https://onlineexhibits.library.yale.edu/s/we-are-everywhere/page/welcome.

Cottrell, D. Mauldin. "Arnold, June Fairfax Davis." TSHAonline.org. Accessed August 4, 2022. https://www.tshaonline.org/handbook/entries/arnold-june-fairfax-davis.

Cran, Rona. "Space Occupied: Women Poet-Editors and the Mimeograph Revolution in Mid-Century New York City." *Journal of American Studies* 55, no. 2 (May 2021): 474–501.

Davids, Betsy, Sas Colby, and Jaime Robles. *Sisters of Invention: Forty-Five Years of Book Art by Sas Colby, Betsy Davids, and Jaime Robles*. San Francisco: San Francisco Center for the Book, 2016.

Dennison, Sally. *Alternative Literary Publishing: Five Modern Histories*. Iowa City: University of Iowa Press, 1984.

"Diane Di Prima." Academy of American Poets. Accessed June 30, 2022. https://poets.org/poet/diane-di-prima.

"Diane Di Prima." Poetry Foundation. Accessed June 30, 2022. https://www.poetryfoundation.org/poets/diane-di-prima.

Diaz, Junot. "MFA vs. POC." *New Yorker*, April 30, 2014. Accessed October 8, 2022. https://www.newyorker.com/books/page-turner/mfa-vs-poc.

DuPlessis, Rachel Blau. "Anne Waldman: Standing Corporeally in One's Own Time." In *Don't Ever Get Famous: Essays on New York Writing after the New York School*, edited by Daniel Kane, 173–94. Champaign, IL: Dalkey Archive, 2006.

Durand, Marcella. "Publishing a Community: Women Publishers at the Poetry Project." Outlet, 1999.

"Eileen Myles–Bio/Cv, Pics." Accessed May 1, 2022. https://www.eileenmyles.com/bio/.

"The Folder Poets." *Mademoiselle*, January 1960, 72–73.

Gould, Lois. "Creating a Woman's World." *New York Times*, January 2, 1977. https://www.nytimes.com/1977/01/02/archives/creating-a-womens-world-the-feminists-behind-daughters-inc-a.html.

Grant, Jaime M. "Building Community-Based Coalitions from Academe: The Union Institute and the Kitchen Table: Women of Color Press Transition Coalition." *Signs: Journal of Women in Culture and Society* 21, no. 4 (July 1996): 1024–33.

Grossinger, Richard. "A History of Io, 1964–1976." *TriQuarterly*, Fall 1978, 482–95.

Harms, Valerie, ed. *Celebration! With Anaïs Nin*. Riverside, CT: Magic Circle Press, 1973.

Harter, Christopher. *An Author Index to Little Magazines of the Mimeograph Revolution, 1958–1980*. Lanham, MD: Scarecrow Press, 2008.

Hejinian, Lyn, and Andrew Schelling. "An Exchange." *Jimmy & Lucy's House of "K"* 6 (May 1986): 1–17.

Hennessey, Michael S. "On Daisy Aldan, 'A New Folder.'" *Jacket2*. Poetry in 1960, a Symposium. University of Pennsylvania: 2011. Accessed November 3, 2023. https://jacket2.org/article/daisy-aldan-new-folder.

Hogue, Cynthia. "An Interview with Kathleen Fraser." *Contemporary Literature* 39, no. 1 (Spring 1998): 1–26.

386 Bibliography

Jaussen, Paul. "The New Broadside Lotus Press." *Jacket2*, https://jacket2.org/commentary/new-broadside-lotus-press.

Jeung, Russell, Karen Umemoto, Harvey Dong, Eric Mar, Lisa Hirai Tsuchitani, and Arnold Pan, eds. *Mountain Movers: Student Activism and the Emergence of Asian American Studies*. Accessed April 19, 2022. https://www.aasc.ucla.edu/aascpress/mm/.

"Judy Grahn." Poetry Foundation. Accessed November 1, 2023. https://www.poetryfoundation.org/poets/judy-grahn.

Kane, Daniel. *All Poets Welcome: The Lower East Side Poetry Scene in the 1960s*. Berkeley: University of California Press, 2003.

———. "Angel Hair Magazine, The Second-Generation New York School, and the Poetics of Sociability." In *Don't Ever Get Famous*, edited by Daniel Kane, 90–121. Champaign, IL: Dalkey Archive, 2006.

Keller, Lynn, and Cristianne Miller. "Gender and Avant-Garde Editing: Comparing the 1920s with the 1990s." *HOW2* 1, no. 2 (1999). Accessed November 27, 2013. http://www.asu.edu/pipercwcenter/how2journal/archive/online_archive/v1_2_1999/current/readings/keller-miller.html.

Kelly, Catherine. "The Women's Press Collective, 1969–1977." *Chicago Review* 66, nos. 3–4 (2023): 107–16.

Kranich, Kimberly. "A Bibliography of Periodicals by and about Women of Color." *Feminist Teacher* 5, no. 1 (1990): 26–41.

Kruchkow, Diane, and Curt Johnson, eds. *Green Isle in the Sea: An Informal History of the Alternative Press, 1960–85*. Highland Park, IL, and Chicago: December Press, 1986.

Kulchur Foundation. "Kulchur Foundation Records, 1936–1994 Bulk 1969–1989." Accessed June 13, 2024. https://findingaids.library.columbia.edu/ead/nnc-rb/ldpd_4078552.

Kurowski, Travis, ed. *Paper Dreams: Writers and Editors on the American Literary Magazine*. Fountain Hills, AZ: Atticus Books, 2013.

Lamott, Kenneth. "'Poetry Here, Hot off the Press!'" *New York Times*, August 29, 1976. http://www.nytimes.com/1976/08/29/archives/poetry-here-hot-off-the-press.html.

Linn, Sarah. "Glenna Luschei: Poet, Publisher, Patron of the Literary Arts." KCET, December 17, 2012. https://www.kcet.org/shows/artbound/glenna-luschei-poet-publisher-patron-of-the-literary-arts.

Lost & Found: The CUNY Poetics Document Initiative. Pamphlet series. New York: CUNY, 2010–present.

Lyons, Kimberly. "The Itineraries of Anticipation (Women & the Poetry Project)." Lecture presented at the conference Where Lyric Tradition Meets Language Poetry: Innovation in Contemporary American Poetry by Women. April 1999, New York City, Barnard College, Columbia University.

Malanga, Gerard. "Daisy Aldan, Poet." Excerpt from unpublished memoir. November 10, 2021.

Marek, Jayne E. *Women Editing Modernism: "Little" Magazines & Literary History*. Lexington: University Press of Kentucky, 1995.

Martz, Sandra, and Irene Reti. *Sandra Kay Martz: Papier-Mache Press & the Gentle Art of Consciousness Raising 1984–1999*. 2001. Retrieved from https://escholarship.org/uc/item/86j5779n.

McEvoy, Dermot. "Moyer Bell: 22 Years A-Growing." *Publisher's Weekly* 253, no. 44 (November 3, 2006). https://www.publishersweekly.com/pw/print/20061106/15607-moyer-bell-22-years-a-growing.html.

Morrisson, Mark S. *The Public Face of Modernism: Little Magazines, Audiences and Reception, 1905–1920*. Madison: University of Wisconsin Press, 2000.

Mottram, Eric N. W. "The Mimeograph Revolution." *Times Literary Supplement*, August 6, 1964.

"Moyer Bell and Its Subsidiaries." Accessed November 6, 2023. https://www.midpointtrade.com/publisher.php?id=930.

Murguia, Alejandro. "Poetry and Solidarity in the Mission." Found SF: The San Francisco Digital History Archive. Accessed November 3, 2023. https://www.foundsf.org/index.php?title=Poetry_and_Solidarity_in_the_Mission.

"Naomi Long Madgett & Lotus Press." Broadside Lotus Press official website. Accessed November 3, 2023. http://www.broadsidelotuspress.org/aboutlotus.

New York Times. "Jennifer Moyer." Obituary, June 19, 2001: 21.

Notley, Alice. E-mail to Stephanie Anderson. "Symposium Talk," April 18, 2010.

Osman, Jena, and Juliana Spahr, eds. "Editorial Forum." *Chain* 1, no. 1 (Spring–Summer 1994): 5–118.

Patterson, Ian. "New York Poets: Folder (1953–56); Neon (1954–60); and Yugen (1958–62)." In *The Oxford Critical and Cultural History of Modernist Magazines*, 2: 983–1025. Oxford: Oxford University Press, 2013.

Peart, Andrew. "Introduction" to the Carolyn Marie Rodgers Portfolio. Poetry Foundation website. Accessed October 12, 2022. https://www.poetryfoundation.org/articles/158590/introduction-6317717fcfb30.

"Poet, Activist, Scholar." Judy Grahn Official Site. Accessed November 1, 2023. https://judygrahn.org/the-author/#more-11.

"Poets Press." From A Secret Location. Accessed September 8, 2016. https://fromasecretlocation.com/poets-press/.

Post45 Little Magazines Cluster. Accessed November 3, 2023. https://post45.org/2023/06/introduction-deep-immersion-in-the-little-mags/.

Raz, Hilda, Ted Kooser, Harry Smith, Maxine Kumin, James Bertolino, John Brandi, Anita Segalman, et al. "A Prairie Schooner Portfolio: Glenna Luschei." *Prairie Schooner* 78, no. 4 (2004): 45–92.

Reid, Calvin. "Third World Press's 50 Years of Black Literature and Politics." *Publishers Weekly*. September 29, 2017.

Reti, Irene. *Irene Reti and HerBooks Feminist Press*. December 5, 2001. https://escholarship.org/uc/item/4wn4458v.

Rifkin, Libbie. "'My Little World Goes On St. Mark's Place': Anne Waldman, Bernadette Mayer and the Gender of an Avant-Garde Institution." *Jacket* 2 (1999). http://jacketmagazine.com/07/rifkin07.html.

388 Bibliography

Roberts, Renee M. On Daisy Aldan. Interview by Stephanie Anderson. Phone, November 17, 2021.

Rubin, Lena. "Women of the Mimeo Revolution: Diane DiPrima & Anne Waldman." Off the Grid: Village Preservation Blog. Accessed November 3, 2023. https://www.villagepreservation.org/2021/03/05/women-of-the-mimeo-revolution-diane-diprima-anne-waldman/.

Russo, Linda. "The 'F' Word in the Age of Mechanical Reproduction: An Account of Women-Edited Small Presses and Journals." *Talisman* 23–26 (2002): 243–84.

———. "On Seeing Poetic Production: The Case of Hettie Jones." *Open Letter* 11, no. 1 (2001): 7–15.

Sachs, Miriam. "Sexuality and Three Third Worlds in Azalea: A Magazine by and for Third World Lesbians." *Medium*, January 31, 2018. https://medium.com/@artemis.usc/sexuality-and-three-third-worlds-in-azalea-a-magazine-by-and-for-third-world-lesbians-d1a8e4087817.

"Salsa Soul Sisters." National Museum of African American History and Culture. Accessed September 4, 2024. https://nmaahc.si.edu/lgbtq/salsa-soul-sisters.

Schor, Mira and Susan Bee. "Mira Schor and Susan Bee Discuss the Many Meanings of Art Writing." *Hyperallergic*, April 15, 2018. https://hyperallergic.com/435959/mira-schor-susan-bee-meaning/.

Seita, Sophie. "The Politics of the Forum in Feminist Avant-Garde Magazines After 1980." *Journal of Modern Literature* 42, no. 1 (2018): 163–82. https://doi.org/10.2979/jmodelite.42.1.11.

———. *Provisional Avant-Gardes: Little Magazine Communities from Dada to Digital*. Stanford, CA: Stanford University Press, 2019.

Sherman, Susan. "Creativity and Change: IKON, the Second Series." Forthcoming in *Sinister Wisdom* (2024).

Singh, Amardeep. "Asian American Little Magazines 1968–1974." Accessed April 19, 2022. https://scalar.lehigh.edu/asian-american-little-magazines/index.

Smith, Barbara. *Ain't Gonna Let Nobody Turn Me Around: Forty Years of Movement Building with Barbara Smith*. Edited by Alethia Jones and Virginia Eubanks. Albany: SUNY Press, 2014.

———. "A Press of Our Own Kitchen Table: Women of Color Press." *Frontiers: A Journal of Women Studies* 10, no. 3 (1989): 11–13. https://doi.org/10.2307/3346433.

———. "Toward a Black Feminist Criticism." *Conditions* 1 no. 2 (October 1977): 25–44.

———. *The Truth That Never Hurts: Writings on Race, Gender, and Freedom*. New Brunswick, NJ: Rutgers University Press, 1998.

Sturm, Nick. "Alice Notley's Magazines: A Digital Publishing Project." Accessed November 3, 2023. https://www.nicksturm.com/digital-publishing-project.

Tajima-Peña, Renee. "Moving the Image: Asian American Independent Filmmaking 1970–1990." *Moving the Image: Independent Asian Pacific American Media Arts*, edited by Russell Leong, 10–32. Los Angeles: UCLA Asian American Studies Center Press, 1992.

———. "Toward a Third Wave: Why Media Matters in Asian American Studies."

Journal of Asian American Studies 17, no. 1 (2014): 94–99. https://doi.org/10.1353/jaas.2014.0013.

Tapson, Kristen. "Joint Experiments: Clark Coolidge, Bernadette Mayer, and the Coproduction of Knowledge." PhD diss., New York University, 2017.

Third World Press Foundation. "About." Accessed November 6, 2023. https://third-worldpressfoundation.org/pages/about.

Tuumba Press. From a Secret Location website. Accessed August 4, 2022. https://fromasecretlocation.com/tuumba-press/.

Waldman, Anne. "Oral History Project." By Stacy Szymaszek and Nicole Wallace, Poetry Project at St. Mark's Church, New York. January 7, 2012. Accessed November 6, 2023. https://www.poetryproject.org/library/recordings/oral-history-project/anne-waldman.

Waldman, Anne, and Larry Fagin. "Discussion of Little Magazines and Related Topics." *TriQuarterly* 43 (Fall 1978): 496–513.

Walker, Scott. "A Press of One's Own: Leonard and Virginia Woolf as Publishers: The Hogarth Press, 1917–41, by J. H. Willis Jr." *Los Angeles Times*, January 10, 1993. https://www.latimes.com/archives/la-xpm-1993-01-10-bk-1234-story.html.

Willis, John H. *Leonard and Virginia Woolf as Publishers: The Hogarth Press, 1917–41*. Charlottesville: University of Virginia Press, 1992.

Woolf, Virginia. *A Room of One's Own*. 9th ed. London: Grafton, 1977.

Zahn, Curtis. "An Inch of Culture: The 'New' 'Poets'—1945–1960 As Defined by Evergreen." *Trace*, October 1960, 40–44.

Zurek, Katherine. "Publishing Profiles: Dr. Naomi Long Madgett of Lotus Press, Inc." *Independent Publisher*. http://www.independentpublisher.com/article.php?page=1761.

Scholarship and Sources about Small Press Publishing and Print Cultures

"2009 AWP Conference & Bookfair." Associated Writing Programs, Conference Archives and Photo Albums. Accessed November 6, 2023. https://www.awp-writer.org/awp_conference/archive/2009/overview.

Allen, Gwen. *Artists' Magazines: An Alternative Space for Art*. Cambridge, MA: MIT Press, 2011.

Aptheker, Bettina. *Tapestries of Life: Women's Work, Women's Consciousness, and the Meaning of Daily Experience*. Amherst: University of Massachusetts Press, 1989.

Baker, Cathleen A., and Rebecca M. Chung, eds. *Making Impressions: Women in Printing and Publishing*. Ann Arbor, MI: Legacy, 2020.

Battershill, Claire. *Women and Letterpress Printing 1920–2020: Gendered Impressions*. Elements in Publishing and Book Culture. Cambridge: Cambridge University Press, 2022.

Biggs, Mary. *A Gift That Cannot Be Refused: The Writing and Publishing of Contemporary American Poetry*. New York: Praeger, 1990.

390 Bibliography

Bright, Betty. *No Longer Innocent: Book Art in America, 1960–1980*. New York: Granary Books, 2005.

Bryan, Sharon, ed. *Where We Stand: Women Poets on Literary Tradition*. New York and London: W. W. Norton, 1994.

Chaitas, Lilian. *The Anthology Wars of the 1950s and 1960s: How New Is the New American Poetry?* Paderborn, Germany: Brill Schöningh, 2017.

Cheang, Shu Lea, and Kimberly SaRee Tomes. "Shu Lea Cheang: Hi-Tech Aborigine." *Wide Angle* 18, no. 1 (1996): 4.

Clay, Stephen, and Rodney Phillips. *A Secret Location on the Lower East Side: Adventures in Writing, 1960–1980: A Sourcebook of Information*. New York: New York Public Library and Granary Books, 1998. See also the From a Secret Location website: https://fromasecretlocation.com/

Clover, Joshua. "The Genealogical Avant-Garde." *Lana Turner*, no. 7 (2014).

De Loach, Allen, ed. *The East Side Scene: American Poetry, 1960–1965*. New York: Anchor, 1972.

Delbos, Stephan. *The New American Poetry and Cold War Nationalism*. London: Palgrave Macmillan, 2021.

Dewey, Anne. "Gendered Muses and the Representation of Social Space in Robert Duncan's Poetry." *Contemporary Literature* 50, no. 2 (2009): 299–331.

Drucker, Johanna. *The Century of Artists' Books*. New York: Granary, 1995.

Duncombe, Stephen. *Notes from Underground: Zines and the Politics of Alternative Culture*. 2nd ed. Bloomington, IN: Microcosm, 2008.

Dworkin, Craig, Simon Morris, and Nick Thurston. *Do or DIY*. Northern England: Information as Material, 2012.

Eichhorn, Kate. *Adjusted Margin: Xerography, Art, and Activism in the Late Twentieth Century*. London and Cambridge, MA: MIT Press, 2016.

Falcon, Susan. "The 2013–14 Report on the Academic Job Market: Adjunct Unions, Administrative Bloat, & Reform of Student Loans." Association of Writers and Writing Programs, November 2014. Accessed October 8, 2022. https://www.awpwriter.org/careers/career_advice_view/3604/the_2013-14_report_on_the_academic_job_market_adjunct_unions_administrative_bloat_reform_of_student_loans.

Fanni, Maryam, Matilda Flodmark, and Sara Kaaman, eds. *Natural Enemies of Books: A Messy History of Women in Printing and Typography*. London: Occasional Papers, 2019.

Fraser, Kathleen. "The Tradition of Marginality." *Frontiers: A Journal of Women Studies* 10, no. 3 (1989): 22–27. https://doi.org/10.2307/3346436.

Frost, Elisabeth A. *The Feminist Avant-Garde in American Poetry*. Iowa City: University of Iowa Press, 2005.

Fulton, Len, Alta, et al., eds. *Small Press Review: Women, Poetry, and the Small Presses*, 3, no. 3 (1972).

Golding, Alan. "'The New American Poetry' Revisited, Again." *Contemporary Literature* 39, no. 2 (1998): 180–211

"Google Ngram Viewer." Accessed June 9, 2018. https://books.google.com/ngrams/gra

ph?content=transcription&year_start=1900&year_end=2000&corpus=15&smo
othing=3&share=&direct_url=t1%3B%2Ctranscription%3B%2Cc0.

Harker, Jaime, and Cecilia Konchar Farr, eds. *This Book Is an Action: Feminist Print Culture and Activist Aesthetics*. Urbana: University of Illinois Press, 2015.

Hogan, Kristen. *The Feminist Bookstore Movement: Lesbian Antiracism and Feminist Accountability*. Durham, NC: Duke University Press, 2016.

House Committee on Education and the Workforce Democratic Staff. "The Just-In-Time Professor: A Staff Report Summarizing eForum Responses on the Working Conditions of Contingent Faculty in Higher Education." 114th Congress, 2014. Accessed October 8, 2022. https://democrats-edworkforce.house.gov/download/the-just-in-time-professor.

Jeung, Russell, Karen Umemoto, Harvey Dong, Eric Mar, Lisa Hirai Tsuchitani, and Arnold Pan, eds. *Mountain Movers: Student Activism and the Emergence of Asian American Studies*. Accessed April 19, 2022. https://www.aasc.ucla.edu/aascpress/mm/.

Johnson, Pauline. *Creative Bookbinding*. New York: Dover, 1990.

Kane, Daniel. *All Poets Welcome: The Lower East Side Poetry Scene in the 1960s*. Berkeley: University of California Press, 2003.

———, ed. *Don't Ever Get Famous: Essays on New York Writing After the New York School*. Champaign, IL: Dalkey Archive, 2007.

Keller, Lynn, and Cristianne Miller. "Gender and Avant-Garde Editing." *HOW2* 1, no. 2 (1999). Accessed November 27, 2013. http://www.asu.edu/pipercwcenter/how2journal/archive/online_archive/v1_2_1999/current/readings/keller-miller.html.

Killian, Kevin. "Bad Conscience: At the Page Mother's Conference." *Tripwire: A Journal of Poetics* 3 (Summer 1999): 97–107.

Kittler, Friedrich A. *Gramophone, Film, Typewriter*. Stanford: Stanford University Press, 1999.

Lundquist, Sara. "The Fifth Point of a Star: Barbara Guest and the New York 'School' of Poets." *Women's Studies* 30, no. 1 (March 2001): 11.

Lyons, Joan, ed. *Artists' Books: A Critical Anthology and Sourcebook*. Layton, UT: Gibbs Smith, 1987.

Marek, Jayne E. *Women Editing Modernism: "Little" Magazines & Literary History*. Lexington: University Press of Kentucky, 1995.

Mayer, Bernadette. "Mimeo Argument." *Poetry Project Newsletter*, April 1982.

McMillian, John Campbell. *Smoking Typewriters: The Sixties Underground Press and the Rise of Alternative Media in America*. New York: Oxford University Press, 2011.

Morrisson, Mark S. *The Public Face of Modernism: Little Magazines, Audiences and Reception, 1905–1920*. Madison: University of Wisconsin Press, 2000.

Myles, Eileen. "Mimeo Opus." *Poetry Project Newsletter*, March 1982.

Page Mothers Conference. Recordings. n.d. https://oac.cdlib.org/findaid/ark:/13030/kt509nb0hf/entire_text./

Radway, Janice. "Zines, Half-Lives, and Afterlives: On the Temporalities of Social and Political Change." *PMLA* 126, no. 1 (2011): 140–50.

392 Bibliography

Rambsy, Howard. *The Black Arts Enterprise and the Production of African American Poetry*. Ann Arbor: University of Michigan Press, 2011.

Rasula, Jed. *The American Poetry Wax Museum: Reality Effects, 1940–1990*. Urbana, IL: National Council of Teachers of English, 1996.

Rifkin, Libby, and Anne Dewey, eds. *Among Friends: Engendering the Social Site of Poetry*. Iowa City: University of Iowa Press, 2013.

Rosenbaum, Susan. "The 'Do It Yourself' Avant-Garde: American Women Poets and Experiment." *A History of Twentieth-Century American Women's Poetry*, edited by Linda A. Kinnahan, 323–38. Cambridge: Cambridge University Press, 2016.

Seita, Sophie. *Provisional Avant-Gardes: Little Magazine Communities from Dada to Digital*. Stanford, CA: Stanford University Press, 2019.

Shaw, Susan M., and Audre Lorde. "Poetry Is Not a Luxury." *Women's Voices, Feminist Visions: Classic and Contemporary Readings*, edited by Janet Lee, 371–73. New York: McGraw-Hill Education, 2015.

Sturm, Nick. "Introduction: Deep Immersion in the Little Mags." *Post45*. From *Little Magazines* Cluster. Accessed November 3, 2023. https://post45.org/2023/06/introduction-deep-immersion-in-the-little-mags/.

Sullivan, James D. *On the Walls and in the Streets: American Poetry Broadsides from the 1960s*. Urbana: University of Illinois Press, 1997.

"Table-X at AWP." Ugly Duckling Presse website. Accessed November 6, 2023. https://uglyducklingpresse.org/events/table-x-at-awp/.

Uchmanowicz, Pauline. "A Brief History of CCLM/CLMP." *Massachusetts Review* 44, no. 1–2 (2003): 70–87.

"Vanity, n." OED Online. Oxford University Press. Accessed December 22, 2021. http://www.oed.com/view/Entry/221396.

Vickery, Ann. *Leaving Lines of Gender: A Feminist Genealogy of Language Writing*. Middletown, CT: Wesleyan University Press, 2000.

VIDA: Women in Literary Arts. "VIDA Count • VIDA: Women in Literary Arts." Accessed November 3, 2023. https://en.wikipedia.org/wiki/VIDA:_Women_in_Literary_Arts

West, Celeste, and Valerie Wheat. *The Passionate Perils of Publishing*. San Francisco: Booklegger Press, 1978.

Wong, Ryan Lee. "Basement Workshop and Asian American Resistance Culture." *Signal* 6 (February 2018): 29–48.

Woznicki, John R., ed. *The New American Poetry: Fifty Years Later*. Bethlehem, PA: Lehigh University Press, 2015.

Yankelevich, Matvei. "The New Normal: How We Gave Up the Small Press." Harriet, 17 Feb. 2020, Poetry Foundation. Accessed September 10, 2024. https://www.poetryfoundation.org/featured-blogger/83635/the-new-normal-how-we-gave-up-the-small-press.

Yung, Eleanor. "Brief Summary of the Basement Workshop Early Years." Asian American Arts Centre. Accessed June 13, 2024. http://www.artspiral.org/basementworkshop.php.

Contributors

Stephanie Anderson (she/they) is the author of several poetry books and chapbooks, including *If You Love Error So Love Zero* (Trembling Pillow Press, 2018) and *Bearings* (*DIAGRAM*/New Michigan Press, 2024), as well as the coeditor of *All This Thinking: The Correspondence of Bernadette Mayer and Clark Coolidge* (University of New Mexico Press, 2022). Her poetry and prose have recently appeared or are forthcoming in *Fence Steaming, Gulf Coast, Post45, Typo, Textual Practice, Women's Studies*, and elsewhere. She is an assistant professor of literature and creative writing at Duke Kunshan University and lives in Suzhou, China.

Barbara Barg was a pre-Socratic/post postmodern/pre-Apocalyptic poet and through those lenses explored writing, music, performance, teaching, the ground, the sky, and life in general. She was raised in Eastern Arkansas near the Mississippi Delta and—after many wanderings—moved to New York City where she became a several-times-recognized-in-a-coffee-shop poet-musician on that throbbing scene. She edited and published with Power Mad Press and, with Rose Lesniak, *Out There* magazine; her own books include *The Origin of THE Species* and *Obeying the Chemicals*. She moved to Chicago in 2008 and passed away in 2018.

Lee Ann Brown is a poet who uses collage methods and song forms in her multiplicitous works, which recently include *Other Archer* (published in French as *Autre Auchère*, in translation by Stéphane Bouquet). She edits for the independent Tender Buttons Press and cocreates poetry happenings such as the Plays on Words at the Ontological Hysteric Theater Incubator Series and the Polyphonic Poetry Festival at the University of Cambridge, where she was the Judith E. Wilson Poetry Fellow, and through her home salon, Torn Page in Chelsea, New York City. She teaches poetry at St. John's

394 List of Contributors

University in Queens, New York City, and lives part time in Marshall, North Carolina.

Maxine Chernoff is the author of nineteen books of poems and six works of fiction. Her most recent book is *Light and Clay: New and Selected Poems* (2023), and her book of stories *Signs of Devotion* was a 1993 New York Times Notable Book of the Year. A special issue of the *Denver Quarterly* (57:4) was recently devoted to her work, and a book about her work is forthcoming from Mad-Hat Press in 2025. She is the recipient of a 2013 NEA in poetry and the 2009 PEN Translation Award for the work of Hölderlin, cotranslated with Paul Hoover. In 2024 she was the keynote poet at the Louisville Conference, and in 2016 she was a visiting writer at the American Academy in Rome. She also was a lecturer in poetry at Exeter University in England in 2013. She has read from her work in Brazil, Scotland, England, China, the Czech Republic, and Russia. Professor Emerita of Creative Writing at SFSU, she edited *Oink!* and then *New American Writing* until 2013; the latter continues under editor Paul Hoover and is published by MadHat Press.

Deborah Costello grew up in Hanover, New Hampshire, the second of five sisters. An American literature graduate of Middlebury College, she also studied at the University of California and the Art Institute of Chicago. In 1977 she attended the innovative feminist art program at the Woman's Building in Los Angeles, where she learned letterpress printing. After experiencing the empowerment of women's culture and feminist art in Los Angeles, she met Lisa Kellman in San Francisco. They started Black Oyster Press and collaborated on the outreach, editing, and publishing of *From Shadows Emerging: An Anthology of Bay Area Women Writers*, about women making changes in their lives, as well as several additional titles by women. Deborah has continued to work to build women's empowerment in projects including editing and managing *Women, Power, and Politics*, a technology-based exhibition available online at the International Women's Museum. She also developed educational career content for tribal teenage girls in Northern Thailand whose family career experience was farming. She is presently helping Afghan refugee women and girls assimilate into a foreign culture in Northern Vermont.

List of Contributors   395

Patricia Elliot Dienstfrey's publications include *The Woman Without Experiences* (Kelsey Street, 1995), winner of the America Award for Fiction (1996); *Love and Illustration* (a+bend press, 2000); and *The Grand Permission: New Writings on Poetics and Motherhood* (Wesleyan, 2003), which she coedited with Brenda Hillman. Her work has also appeared in *Moving Borders: Three Decades of Innovative Writing by Women*, edited by Mary Margaret Sloan (Talisman House, 1997), and *The Addison Street Anthology: Berkeley's Poetry Walk*, edited by Robert Hass and Jessica Fisher (Heyday Books, 2004). She is currently at work on a manuscript long in the making titled *One Writing / Autobiography on the Planes of Consciousness*. A cofounder of Kelsey Street Press, she lives with her husband, Ted, in Berkeley, California.

Lindy Hough was born in 1944 in Denver, Colorado. She graduated from Smith College and earned an MFA from Goddard College. A journalist and dance critic, she taught writing and literature in colleges and universities in Michigan, Maine, Vermont, and California. She cofounded the literary magazine *Io* and the publishing company North Atlantic Books in Berkeley with Richard Grossinger in 1974 and was copublisher and editorial director of NAB for many years. She coedited the anthologies *Nuclear Strategy and the Code of the Warrior: Faces of Mars and Shiva in the Crisis of Human Survival* and *The Io Anthology* and edited herself *Wondrous Child: The Joys and Challenges of Grandparenting* in 2012. Hough is the author of seven books of poetry, including *Changing Woman, Psyche, The Sun in Cancer, Outlands & Inlands,* and *Wild Horses, Wild Dreams: New and Selected Poems 1971—2010*. She lives in Portland, Maine, and Bar Harbor, Maine. She is presently working on *Wild Horse Mesa*, a novel about the love affair between a New Mexico burlesque stripper and a Denver collage artist in the early 1950s during the uranium boom in the Four Corners. More at www.lindyhough.com.

MC Hyland (she/they) is the founding editor of DoubleCross Press, a poetry micropress, and the author of more than a dozen poetry chapbooks/artist books and two full-length books of poems: *THE END* (Sidebrow, 2019) and *Neveragainland* (Lowbrow Press, 2010). MC's third book, a collection of very short essays called *The Dead and the Living and the Bridge*, is forthcoming from Meekling Press in 2025.

List of Contributors

Best known for *How I Became Hettie Jones*, her memoir of the Beat scene of the fifties and sixties, **Hettie Jones** authored twenty-four books for children and adults, including the award-winning *Big Star Fallin' Mama (Five Women in Black Music)* and *Drive*, the first of her three poetry collections, which won the Poetry Society of America's Norma Farber Award. In addition to her own work, Jones also wrote *No Woman No Cry* for Rita Marley, *Grace the Table* for the chef Alexander Smalls, and coauthored *From Midnight to Dawn, the Last Tracks of the Underground Railroad*. Her short fiction appeared in various literary journals such as *Ploughshares* and *Fence*, and she published reviews, articles, and stories in the *Washington Post* and the *Village Voice*, among others. She passed away in 2024.

Patricia Spears Jones is a poet, playwright, educator, cultural activist, and anthologist. In 2023 she was named New York State Poet, and in 2017 she received the Jackson Poetry Prize. She is author of five full-length collections and five chapbooks, including *A Lucent Fire: New and Selected Poems* (White Pine, 2015) and, most recently, *The Beloved Community* (Copper Canyon, 2023). She coedited the groundbreaking anthology *Ordinary Women: An Anthology of New York City Women* (1978) and organized and edited *THINK: Poems for Aretha Franklin's Inauguration Day Hat* (2009). Her poems are widely anthologized, most recently in *African American Poetry: 250 Years of Struggle and Song* and *Why to These Rocks: 50 Years of Poems from the Community of Writers*, and her poems, essays, and interviews have appeared in many books and journals, including the *New Yorker*, *Bomb*, www.tribes.org, the *Writer's Chronicle*, the *Poetry Project Newsletter*, *Pangyrus*, *Cutthroat Journal*, and many more. Mabou Mines commissioned and produced two plays with music. Additionally, she has curated programs at the Poetry Project of St. Mark's Church (New York City), Center for Book Arts, and created WORDS Sunday series in Brooklyn; she has also taught at many colleges, summer programs, and institutions, including at Hollins University as the 2020 Louis D. Rubin Jr. Writer-in-Residence. She has received grants and awards from the National Endowment for the Arts, the New York Foundation for the Arts, the Foundation of Contemporary Art, and others, and she is Emeritus Fellow for Black Earth Institute and organizer of the American Poets Congress. More at www.psjones.com.

Having grown up near New York City, **Lisa Kellman** was exposed to artistic and creative ideas from a young age. She studied textile production and calligraphy in her teens and early twenties. She moved to Los Angeles in 1976 to study ethnomusicology at UCLA but switched to Women's History, as she was inspired by the emerging women's movement of the time. She became involved with hand-bookbinding and letterpress printing prior to moving to San Francisco. As she developed her skills in book arts, her activism grew, landing her at The Women's Building in San Francisco. This led her to the cocreation with Deborah Costello of Black Oyster Press and the publication of their women's poetry anthology. In the late 1980s she became involved with groups that were fighting against US intervention in Latin America and performed at San Francisco clubs and at venues supporting progressive movements. In 1995 she and her partner opened an herb and holistic healing store, the Scarlet Sage Herb Co., which they ran for twenty years. They built a strong community centered around healing and empowering people to take charge of their own health. She continues to pursue her lifelong interests of music, holistic healing, gardening, women's rights, and social and environmental justice.

Martha King, born in Virginia in 1937, attended Black Mountain College in the summer of 1955, and soon after left the South for San Francisco, where she met and married the artist Basil King. They moved to New York City in 1958 and have lived in Brooklyn since 1967. They have two children and four grandchildren. Retired from her day jobs—in mainstream book publishing and later as editor-science writer at the National Multiple Sclerosis Society—Martha's recent books are her memoir *Outside / Inside, Just Outside the Art World's Inside* (2018) and crime thrillers featuring the painter and amateur sleuth Max Birtwhistle: *Max Sees Red* (2019) and *Max Turns Yellow* (2021). Currently she is devoting her time to cataloging Basil King's art works. See www.marthawking.com.

One of the major poets of the San Francisco Renaissance, **Joanne Kyger** was born in 1934 in Vallejo, California. After studying at UC Santa Barbara, she moved to San Francisco in 1957, where she became a member of the circle of poets centered around Jack Spicer and Robert Duncan. In 1960 she joined

398 List of Contributors

Gary Snyder in Japan and soon traveled to India where, along with Allen Ginsberg and Peter Orlovsky, they met the Dalai Lama—all experiences she has written extensively about. She returned to California in 1964 and published her first book, *The Tapestry and the Web*, in 1965. In 1969 she settled on the coast north of San Francisco. She published more than thirty books of poetry and prose, including *The Japan and India Journals: 1960–1964* (2015), *On Time: Poems 2005–2014* (2015), *As Ever: Selected Poems* (2002), and *About Now: Collected Poems* (2007), which won the 2008 Josephine Miles Award from PEN Oakland. She taught at Naropa University, the New College of California, and Mills College. In 2006 she was awarded a grant from the Foundation for Contemporary Arts. She passed away in March 2017.

Rose Lesniak's latest book, *What the Dogs Tell Me*, is a direct reflection of her love for the canine world and the poetry universe. She was born and raised in Chicago and graduated from Northeastern Illinois University with degrees in education and psychology. In 1977 Rose moved to New York City, where she founded Out There Productions. This all-purpose poetic collaboration included magazines, poetry and video performances, poetry writing classes, and the Manhattan Poetry Video Project, the very first poetry-music videos. *Billboard Magazine* called this spoken-word creation "a new short-form entertainment genre: poetry video." They were a direct precursor to the fledging music videos of MTV and premiered at the Public Theater hosted by Lou Reed. These performances introduced the wider world to established poetry legends like Allen Ginsberg, Anne Waldman, and Bob Holman. They also served as a teaching template for high schools and won a Blue Ribbon Award from the American Film Festival. Rose's books of poetry include *Young Anger* and *Throwing Spitballs at the Nuns*. Her work can be found in *The Partisan Review*, *Poets' Encyclopedia*, *Poetry Project Newsletter*, and numerous small press magazines. She was featured on *Life is a Killer* by Giorno Poetry Systems. Her many on-stage performances at the St. Mark's Poetry Project and numerous other venues were legendary. Rose moved to Miami Beach, Florida, where she worked as a child abuse investigator until becoming a Certified Dog Trainer and Canine Consultant.

Bernadette Mayer authored more than twenty-seven collections, including, most recently, *Milkweed Smithereens* (2022), *Works and Days* (2016), *Eating the Colors of a Lineup of Words: The Early Books of Bernadette Mayer* (2015) and *The Helens of Troy* (2013), as well as countless chapbooks and artist books. She received grants from the Guggenheim Foundation, Creative Capital, National Endowment for the Arts, and the Foundation for Contemporary Arts, and was the recipient of the 2014 Shelley Memorial Award from the Poetry Society of America. From 1980 to 1984 she served as the director of the St. Mark's Poetry Project; she also edited and founded 0 TO 9 journal and United Artists books and magazines. She taught at the New School for Social Research, Naropa University, Long Island University, the College of Saint Rose, Miami University, and at University of Pennsylvania as a Kelly Writers House Fellow. Her influence in the contemporary avant-garde is felt widely.

Eileen Myles (they/them, b. 1949) is a poet, novelist, and art journalist whose vernacular practice of mostly first-person writing has made them one of the most recognized writers of their generation. *a "Working Life" (poems)* came out in 2023 and *Pathetic Literature*, an anthology, was out in 2022. Their fiction includes *Chelsea Girls* (1994), *Cool for You* (2000), *Inferno (a poet's novel)* (2010), and *Afterglow* (2017). Writing on art was gathered in the volume *The Importance of Being Iceland: Travel Essays in Art* (2009). Earlier books of poetry include *evolution* (2018) and *I Must Be Living Twice: New and Selected Poems 1975–2014* (2015). *The Trip*, a super-8 puppets road film they wrote and directed, can be seen on YouTube. They've received many grants and awards including a Guggenheim & Warhol/Creative Capital Arts Writers Grant. They live in New York and Marfa, Texas.

Alice Notley was born in Bisbee, Arizona, in 1945 and grew up in Needles, California, in the Mojave Desert. She was educated in the Needles public schools, Barnard College, and The Writers Workshop, University of Iowa. She has lived most extensively in Needles, in New York, and since 1992, in Paris, France. She is the author of numerous books of poetry and of essays and talks on poetry and has edited and coedited books by Ted Berrigan and Douglas Oliver. She edited the magazine *CHICAGO* in the 1970s and coedited with Oliver the magazines *SCARLET* and *Gare du Nord* in the 1990s. She is the recipient of the *Los Angeles Times* Book Award, the Griffin Prize, the Academy

400   List of Contributors

of American Poets' Lenore Marshall Prize, and the Poetry Foundation's Ruth Lilly Prize, a lifetime achievement award. Notley may be most widely known for her epic poem *The Descent of Alette*. She is also a collagist and visual artist. Recent poetry collections include *The Speak Angel Series*, *Early Works*, and *Being Reflected Upon*; other recent books include *Telling the Truth as It Comes Up* (essays), and *Runes and Chords* (poem/drawings).

Maureen Owen is the former editor-in-chief of *Telephone Magazine* and *Telephone Books*, currently celebrated in a two-volume Among the Neighbors recap by The Poetry Collection at the University of Buffalo. Her latest title is *let the heart hold down the breakage Or the caregiver's log* from Hanging Loose Press. Another recent publication is *Poets on the Road* with Barbara Henning, a collaborative reading tour blog in print from City Point Press. Other books include *Edges of Water* from Chax Press and *Erosion's Pull*, a Coffee House Press title that was a finalist for the Colorado Book Award and the Balcones Poetry Prize. Her collection *American Rush: Selected Poems* was a finalist for the *LA Times* Book Prize and her work *AE (Amelia Earhart)* was a recipient of the prestigious Before Columbus American Book Award. She has taught at Naropa University, both on campus and in the low-residency MFA Creative Writing Program, and served as editor-in-chief of Naropa's online zine *not enough night*. She has most recently published work in *Three Fold*, *Dispatches*, *Positive Magnets*, *Hurricane Review*, the *Denver Quarterly*, *Blazing Stadium*, the *Brooklyn Rail*, the *Cafe Review*, and *Posit*. A recipient of grants from the National Endowment for the Arts and the Foundation for Contemporary Arts, she can be found reading her work on the PennSound website.

Margaret Randall (b. New York, 1936) is a poet, essayist, oral historian, translator, photographer, and social activist. She lived in Latin America for twenty-three years (in Mexico, Cuba, and Nicaragua). From 1962 to 1969 she and Mexican poet Sergio Mondragón coedited *El Corno Emplumado / The Plumed Horn*, a bilingual literary quarterly that published some of the best new work of the sixties. When she came home in 1984, the government ordered her deported because it found some of her writing to be "against the good order and happiness of the United States." With the support of many writers and others, she won her case, and her citizenship was restored in

1989. Throughout the late 1980s and early 1990s, she taught at several universities, most often Trinity College in Hartford, Connecticut. Randall's most recent poetry titles include *Vertigo of Risk, Time's Language II: Selected Poems 1958–2018* and *Home*; her recent essay collections are *Artists in My Life* and *Luck*. In 2020 her memoir, *I Never Left Home: Poet, Feminist, Revolutionary*, was published by Duke University Press. Two of Randall's photographs are in the Capitol Art Collection in Santa Fe. Her translations include *When Rains Became Floods* by Lurgio Galván Sánchez and *Only the Road / Solo el Camino*, an anthology of eight decades of Cuban poetry (both published by Duke), among many other titles. Randall received the 2017 Medalla al Mérito Literario from *Literatura en el Bravo*, Ciudad Juárez, Mexico, and in 2018 she was awarded the Poet of Two Hemispheres prize by Poesía en Paralelo Cero in Quito, Ecuador. In 2022 she earned the City of Albuquerque's Creative Bravo Award. She lives in Albuquerque with her partner (now wife) of more than thirty-eight years, the painter Barbara Byers, and travels extensively to read, lecture, and teach.

Jaime Robles is a writer and visual artist. She has two collections published by Shearsman Books (UK), *Anime Animus Anima* and *Hoard*, and has produced many artist books, including *Loup d'Oulipo, Letters from Overseas*, and *Aube/Afternoon*. Her bookworks are at the University of California, Berkeley; Yale University; and the Oulipo Archive in Paris, among others. While pursuing her doctorate in the UK, she created several environmental poetry installations, including *Autumn Leaving* and *Wall of Miracles*, which can be seen on her website, jaimerobles.com. She has collaborated with composer Ann Callaway to write the chamber opera *Vladimir in Butterfly Country*, based on Vladimir Nabokov's love of Lepidoptera. Her sound poems using field recordings from the Devon area can be found on SoundCloud at https://soundcloud.com/user-431180174/sets/passing-moments-2017.

Rena Rosenwasser grew up in New York City, where her passion for literature and the visual arts flourished. After graduating from Sarah Lawrence College, she settled in Berkeley, California, and continued her studies at Mills College (MFA). In 1974 she cofounded Kelsey Street Press and subsequently served as its director. When the press reestablished its collective nature, Rosenwasser remained a press member. She also initiated and produced a series of collaborations between poets and visual artists for the press. In 2000 she and the other cofounder, Patricia Dienstfrey, turned the press over to younger press members, while they remained available as mentors. Her poetry publications include *The Body and Film: Queer Registry* (2023), *Elevators* (Kelsey Street Press, 2011), *Dittany (Taking Flight)* (Mayacamas Press, 1993), *Unplace.Place* (Leave Books, 1992), and three collaborations with artist Kate Delos: *Isle* (Kelsey Street Press, 1992), *Aviary* (Limestone Press, 1988), and *Simulacra* (Kelsey Street Press, 1986). Her first volume of poetry was *Desert Flats* (Kelsey Street Press, 1979). Rosenwasser served as a board member of Small Press Distribution for more than twenty years; she has also served on the Literary Panel for the California Arts Council. She lives with her longtime partner and now spouse, Penny Cooper. Together they have a collection of contemporary art by women, which they began purchasing in the late seventies.

Poet, playwright, essayist, and founding editor of *IKON* magazine, **Susan Sherman**, has had twelve plays produced off-off Broadway, has published seven collections of poetry as well as an adaptation from Spanish of Pepe Carril's *Shango de Ima* (Doubleday, 1971), which she brought from Cuba in 1968. Her memoir, *America's Child: A Woman's Journey Through the Radical Sixties* (Curbstone Press), was published to critical acclaim in 2007. Her most recent books are *Nirvana on Ninth Street: Short Fiction*, with photos by Colleen McKay and an afterword by Rona L. Holub (Wings Press, 2014), and *The Light that Puts an End to Dreams: New and Selected Poems* (Wings Press, 2012), which was a finalist for the Audre Lorde Award for Lesbian Poetry.

Barbara Smith has played a groundbreaking role in opening up a national, cultural, and political dialogue about the intersections of race, class, sexuality, and gender. She has been politically active in many movements for social justice since the 1960s. Her extensive writings and activism as an independent book publisher made her among the first to define an African American women's literary tradition and to build Black women's studies and Black feminism in the United States. In recognition of her four decades of efforts as an author, activist, and independent scholar, she was nominated for the

Nobel Peace Prize in 2005, one of one thousand women from all over the globe who were nominated to call attention to women's extreme underrepresentation as recipients of this honor. In 2012 she was chosen for the AOL and PBS multiplatform Makers: Women Who Make America initiative that profiles distinguished women in all walks of life who have transformed the nation. She was cofounder and publisher until 1995 of Kitchen Table: Women of Color Press, one of the first US publishers for women of color. She resides in Albany, New York, where she served two terms as a member of the City of Albany's Common Council. She has edited several major collections about Black women; recent books include *Ain't Gonna Let Nobody Turn Me Around: Forty Years of Movement Building with Barbara Smith* (eds. Alethia Jones and Virginia Eubanks, SUNY Press, 2014) and the fortieth anniversary edition of *Home Girls: A Black Feminist Anthology* (Rutgers University Press, 2023).

Renee Tajima-Peña is an Oscar-nominated filmmaker who has become a chronicler of the Asian American experience through her films, including the civil rights documentary *Who Killed Vincent Chin?* and the road film in search of Asian American identity *My America . . . or Honk if You Love Buddha*; as series producer–showrunner of the docuseries *Asian Americans*; and, most recently, the May 19 Project, a social media campaign amplifying the legacy of AAPI solidarity with other communities, which she cofounded with Jeff Chang. Her other films and media projects include the *Best Hotel on Skid Row, The Last Beat Movie, Calavera Highway, New Americans (Mexico Story), Labor Women,* and *No Más Bebés.* Tajima-Peña's films have screened at the Cannes Film Festival, New York Film Festival, Sundance Film Festival, and the Whitney Biennial. She was awarded two Peabodys, the Guggenheim Fellowship, the USA Broad Fellowship, and Alpert Award in the Arts for Film/Video. She was formerly the managing editor of *Bridge: Asian American Perspectives*, a cultural critic for NPR, and was the only Asian American woman film contributor to a national publication while writing for the *Village Voice.* Tajima-Peña has been deeply involved in Asian American politics and arts movements and was part of the founding of the Center for Asian American Media and A-Doc/Asian American Documentary Network. In 2005 she launched the Graduate Program in Social Documentation at UC Santa Cruz. At UCLA she is currently a professor of Asian American studies, the director

404   List of Contributors

of the Center for EthnoCommunications, and holds an endowed chair in Japanese American studies.

Lisbet Tellefsen is an Oakland, California–based archivist, collector, and curator. In 1989 she cofounded *Aché: A Journal for Black Lesbians*, which she published until 1995. Her archives and collections focus on late twentieth-century political African Americana with specializations including Angela Davis, the Black Panther Party, and BIPOC LGBTQ+ history and culture. Her archives are a frequently used resource for academic research, film-media projects, and exhibits including *Angela Davis—Seize the Time*, which spawned a book by the same title. In addition to contributing a dozen pieces to the 2016 inaugural exhibit of the Smithsonian National Museum of African American History and Culture, more than one hundred objects from the Tellefsen Collection now reside in the permanent collections of the Smithsonian, SFMOMA, and the Oakland Museum of California. As an archival consultant and a dealer in things archival, she has worked with numerous clients to develop and place their personal papers and collections. In 2012 the Lisbet Tellefsen Papers were acquired by Yale University and were featured most recently in their 2022 exhibit *We Are Everywhere: Lesbians in the Archive*.

Rosmarie Waldrop is a poet, translator, and small press publisher born in Germany in 1935. At age ten she spent half a year acting with a traveling theater, but was happy when schools reopened and she could settle for the quieter pleasures of reading and writing. These she has pursued in universities (PhD at the University of Michigan) and in Providence, Rhode Island, with Keith Waldrop, who coedited with her Burning Deck Press. Her most recent poetry books are *The Nick of Time, Gap Gardening: Selected Poems, Driven to Abstraction*, and *Curves to the Apple* (all New Directions). Her novel, *The Hanky of Pippin's Daughter*, has been reissued by Dorothy, a Publishing Project. Her collected essays *Dissonance (if you are interested)* and a K. & R. Waldrop reader *Keeping the Window Open* are available from University of Alabama Press and Wave Books respectively. She has translated, from the French, fourteen volumes of Edmond Jabès's work as well as poetry books by Emmanuel Hocquard, Jacques Roubaud, and, from the German, Friederike

Mayröcker, Elke Erb, Elfriede Czurda, Ulf Stolterfoht, and Peter Waterhouse.

C. D. Wright was one of the most influential and vital North American poets of her generation. After her sudden, unexpected death in 2016, the *New York Times* obituary noted that she was so uniquely original that she "constituted a school of exactly one." Although she was known as a lyric and elliptical poet, she drew from narrative and documentary poetics to write books defined by their wry humor, their ethical orientation, and their inventive formal strategies. She grew up in the Ozarks of Arkansas as the daughter of a country judge and a court reporter. There she picked up a keen vernacular voice that came to characterize much of her writing. Wright was married to the poet Forrest Gander from 1983 until her death; they had one child, the artist Brecht Wright Gander. Among many prestigious honors, Wright received a MacArthur "Genius" Fellowship, a Guggenheim Fellowship, the National Book Critics Circle Award, the Lenore Marshall Prize, and the Griffin Poetry Prize. Since her death, the Foundation of Contemporary Arts has funded an annual C. D. Wright Prize, an annual C. D. Wright Women's Writers' Conference was launched, Brown University funded into perpetuity a C. D. Wright Memorial Lecture, and books of critical essays on her work and a "Collected and New Poems" are in the works.

Index

Abi-Karam, Andrea, 240–41
Aché, 6, 20; considering legacy of, 330–31; creating/documenting community, 327–30; genesis of, 321–23; genesis of editorial team, 325–26; themed issues, 323–25
ACJ. *See* American Citizens for Justice
"Acting Up!" (Heresies Collective), 267–69
address mailing lists, reliance on, 19–21
Adichie, Chimamanda, 42
Adisa, Opal Palmer, 240
Ain't Gonna Let Nobody Turn Me Around, 318
Aion (magazine), 7, 357
Alarcón, Norma, 360–61
Alcalá, Rosa, 241
Alcheringa (magazine), 102
Aldan, Daisy, 1–4; blurry oscillation between editor and writer, 27–28; moving from magazine to bound book, 8–14; reliance on address mailing lists, 19–20; and "scarcity aesthetic," 19
Allen, Donald, 1, 3, 10–12, 46, 72
ally, term, 268
AM Multilith, 273
America Is in the Heart (Bulosan), 145
America's Child: A Woman's Journey Through the Radical Sixties (Sherman), 112

American Booksellers Association, 317
American Citizens for Justice (ACJ), 148
American Poetry Review (*APR*) (magazine), 263–64
Angel Hair (magazine), 178, 355
Angel Hair Books, 91
Angelo, Valenti, 191
anthologies: anthology wars, 3, 46; considering scholar's introduction to, 23; and double issues, 124; evolution of, 1–4; moving from magazine to bound book, 8–15; shared affinity between, 12; uniqueness of, 22–23
Apocalypse Poetry Project, 210–12
APR. See American Poetry Review
Aquino, Corazon, 310
Areas of Silence (Sherman), 121–22
Arif Press, 188
Arnold, June, 358
Ashberry, John, 22
Asian American International Film Festival, 139–40
Asian Americans: addressing oppressed reality of, 357; joys and difficulties of collaboration, 146–47; and "looking back," 147–49; political and cultural movement in 1980s, 139–41
Asian Cine-Vision, 139
Asian Women United Collective, 113

407

408 Index

Auerhahn Press, 188
Autumn Leaving (Robles), 195
Avalanche (magazine), 88–89, 102
Avant Squares, band, 202–4
Ayumi: A Japanese American Anthology
 (Mirikitani, ed.), 7
Azalea (magazine), 360

Bake-Face and Other Guava Stories (Adisa),
 240
Bandanza, Richard, 286
Bang, Mary Jo, 164
Banks, Russell, 93–94
Bañuelos, Juan, 58
Baraka, Amiri, 34–35, 38–40, 64, 205,
 243, 253, 354
Barg, Barbara, 17; and changing tech-
 nology, 199–201; community
 and, 208–10; involvement with
 Out There, 198–99; and Language
 poets, 206–8; New York press
 of, 197; performances of, 202–4;
 pressure in publication, 204;
 publishing with smaller presses,
 205–6; typesetting technology of,
 197–98. *See also Out There* (maga-
 zine); Out There Productions;
 Power Mad Press
Barnett, Anthony, 51
Barone, Dennis, 15
Bartra, Agustí, 62
Basement Workshop, 140, 264, 357–58
Battlefield Where the Moon Says I Love You,
 The (Stanford), 272–74
Bay Area, new movements in, 186–87
BCUD. *See* Bolinas Community Public
 Utility District
Beam, Joseph, 327–28
Beatnik Hoax, 26, 48–49
Beaulines (newspaper), 245
Beluga & Bluebirds (Dechar), 292
Benitez, Zuleyka, 272
Bergen, Brooke, 154, 160

Berman, Richie, 189
Berrigan, Ted, 92, 151, 153, 169, 198, 285
Berssenbrugge, Mei-mei, 53, 237–39
Bettmann Archive, 280
Bissert, Ellen Marie, 359
Black Oyster Press, 291–95
Black Poets Speak Out, 267
Black Press Association, 317–18
Black Sun Press, 227
Blackburn, Paul, 61, 76, 177
Blue Smoke (magazine), 98–99
Blue Stairs, The (Guest), 239
Blurbs, 23, 103–4
Body Politic, 153–55
Bök, Christian, 167
Bolinas Community Center, 245
Bolinas Community Public Utility Dis-
 trict (BCUD), 245, 250
Bolinas Hearsay News (newspaper):
 approaching creative work, 248;
 being Wednesday editor for,
 249; community of, 246, 249–51;
 considering reprints, 247; first
 issues of, 246–47; foundation
 of, 245–46; genre of, 246; and
 immediacy of Internet, 249;
 localism of, 247–48; return reading, 249; technological changes
 at, 248
Bolinas Hit (newspaper), 245
Bolinas Journal (Brainard), 250
Booth, Miven, 335
Boston Eagle (magazine), 98
Brainard, Joe, 100, 155, 156, 250
Brathwaite, Kamau, 276
Breuer, Lee, 263
Bridge (magazine), 7; becoming involved
 with, 139–41; editorial staff of,
 142; fundraising and logistics
 at, 142–43; joys and difficulties
 of collaboration, 146–47; legacy
 of, 142; pieces in conversation,
 143–44; plurality of cultural

influences, 144–45; varied responsibilities at, 142

Brigham, Besmilr, 275, 276

Brilliant Corners (magazine), 181

Brodine, Karen, 225

Bronk, William, 51

Brooks, Gwendolyn, 212

Brown v. Board of Education, 35

Brown, Lee Ann: exploring connections, 335–41; poetry scene, 334–35; thinking about early days of Tender Buttons Press, 333–34. *See also* Tender Buttons Press

Bundy, Alison, 276

Bunker, Cameron, 185–86

Burke, Clifford, 186, 231

Burning Deck (magazine): distribution, 46–47; physical process of printing, 47; shift to books, 48; soliciting submissions, 46–47; starting, 45–46

Burning Deck Press, 26–27, 233; editorial role with, 49–50; full books, 51; future of, 53; manuscript acquisition process, 52; printing chapbooks under, 50–51; publishing works in translation, 52–53

Butler, Frances, 188

CAAM. *See* Center for Asian American Media

Caddel, Richard (Ric), 163

California Arts Council, 76

Callahan, Bob, 190

Callahan, Eileen, 185, 190

Callahan, Jennifer, 335

Callaway, Ann, 195

Camp Notes (Yamada), 310

Camp, James, 48, 50

Cannon, Steve, 264

Cardenal, Ernesto, 58, 62

Carrington, Lenora, 74

Carrington, Leonora, 62

Carroll, Paul, 151, 154–59

"Casabianca" (Hemans), 45

Castro, Fidel, 63–64

Cavanah, Claire, 335

CCLM. *See* Coordinating Council of Literary Magazines

Cecilia Vicuña: New and Selected, 241

Celebrated Running Horse Messenger, The (Phillips), 234

"Celebrating the Legacy of *Aché* Magazine" (Tellefsen), 328

Cellar Stories (bookstore), 275

Center for Asian American Media (CAAM), 143

Centering (Richards), 74

CHAIN (magazine), 4, 52–53, 225

Changing Woman (Hough), 77

chapbooks, 185, 197–98, 253, 322–23; and desktop publishing, 321–22; getting submissions for, 166–67; and Internet, 205–6; layout for, 179; from post-1974, 52; printing, 50–51; rebellious nature of publishing, 347–48; refusal of professionalism, 349; and taking over as editor of, 111–12; visual art in, 254; visuals in, 254; working on, 121–22, 126

Chapman, StuArt, 248

Char, René, 276

Cheang, Shu Lea, 141

Chen, Ching-In, 240

Chernoff, Maxine, 24; doing things more sporadically, 161–63; on explosion of new poets, 165–67; editing influencing writing of, 164–65; looking at gender balance, 161; printing escapades of, 152; soliciting through readings, 154–57; technical duties for production, 157–59; transition to *New American Writing*, 159–60. *See also New American Writing*; *Oink!* (magazine)

410   Index

Chiang, Fay, 6, 264, 265, 357–58
CHICAGO (magazine), 2–3, 153; curation of, 180–81; editing pieces for, 171; and editorial intentions, 182; entertainment factor in, 175; European editions of, 180–81; laying out pieces in, 179–80; memories of issues, 170; mimeographing and stencil-cutting, 170–71; open-field technique in, 176–77; ordering pieces in, 173–74; potential commentary of, 175–76; and sexism during time of, 171–73; soliciting poems, 169–70; starting, 169; staying connected to/joining poetry community, 173; talk of travel, 178–79; typing stencils, 174–75; utopian idea of poetry 24/7, 177–78
Chicago, Judy, 232
Childs, Lucinda, 73
Chin, Lily, 147
Chin, Rockwell, 140
Choy, Christine, 146
Clark, Jeff, 232, 240
Clark, Susan, 361
Clark, Tom, 169
Clennon, David, 286–87
Cohen, Robert, 66–67
Colin, Nancy, 114–15
Committee for International Poetry, 205
community: of Bolinas Hearsay News, 246, 249–51; creating/documenting, 327–30; group and community of small press publishing, 21–26; necessary interplay of community and audience, 24–25; orienting conceptions of, 21–26; publishing community, 274; sense of, 22–23, 35, 236; staying connected to/joining, 173
Comrade Is as Precious as a Rice Seedling, A (Aguilar), 310–11

Concordance (Berssenbrugge and Smith), 239
Conditions: Five (magazine), 303–5, 306, 315, 323
Coordinating Council of Literary Magazines (CCLM), 76, 93, 136, 214, 287
Copper Beech Press, 275
Corbett, Bill, 98, 101
Corinth Books, 41
Corno Emplumado, El (magazine): ambitions, 67; copyright page of, 67; Cuban issue, 62–69; finding printer for, 60; first issue of, 59; magazine production of, 59–60; memorable or remarkable issues of, 62; name origins, 55–56; photographs in, 61–62; removing cultural expression from politics, 56–57; representatives of, 60–61; translations, 62; traveling while editing, 65–67
Corporation for Public Broadcasting, 147
Costello, Deborah, 5, 291–95. See also Black Oyster Press
Coyote Books, 249
Cran, Rona, 24
Cranium Press, 186, 188
Creeley, Robert, 74, 162
Crocus/Sprouting (Robles), 189
Crumpacker, Caroline, 335
Cuba, interest in, 62–69
Cuentos: Stories by Latinas, 300
curator, term, 181–82
curse words, theory of, 208

Dambroff, Susan, 295
"Danger of a Single Story" (Adichie), 42
Dark Lyrics: Studying the Subterranean Impulses of Contemporary Poetry (Robles), 194
Daughters Inc., 358
Davids, Betsy, 188

Index 411

Dawson, Fielding, 41, 74, 253
Deanovich, Connie, 156
DeBoer, Bernhard, 38–39
Dechar, Lorie, 292
de Kooning, Elaine, 62, 64
Delbos, Stephan, 10–11
Delos, Kate, 233, 237
demands, balancing projects and, 235–37
Demetrakas, Johanna, 145
Demick, Jared, 46
Dennis, Donna, 156
DeNoyelles, Bill, 103
Devora, Natalie, 330
Dewey, Alice, 4, 8
Dewhurst, Robbie, 289
Dienstfrey, Patricia, 15, 242, 277; address coincidence, 227–29; advice for small presses, 243; asking for editorial input, 236–37; balancing projects and demands, 235–37; and Bay Area poetry scene in 1974, 225–26; and bridge between literature and visual art, 232–33; challenges of producing and distributing offset, 240; challenging parts of publication process, 241; choosing name for publishers, 226–27; collaborations, 237–40; early years of printing press, 229; emphasizing release parties, 33; favorite books printed at, 229–31; longevity of, 242; major changes at, 242–43; and mimeograph revolution, 17–19; moving away of letterpress, 234–35; recent favorite books of, 240–41; and release parties, 231–32; selecting manuscripts by consensus, 235; technological shift challenges-opportunities, 241. *See also* Kelsey Street Press
Diggs, Lucretia, 318–19

di Prima, Diane, 64, 354
Distressed Look (Kyger), 249
distribution, in midcentury, 19–21
Doctor Williams' Heiresses (Notley), 2
dodgems (magazine), 14, 26, 199; choosing name for, 279; choosing work for, 280–81; covers of, 280; dating issues, 286; differentiating from magazines, 279–80; and gender ratio, 283; and Internet causing loss of intimacy, 284–85; production of, 280; publishing magazine in relation to bands and music world, 281–84; as subsidiary of fido productions, 286–87; third issue of, 287–89
Doolittle, Hilda, 190
Doris, Stacy, 335
Dorn, Ed, 41, 74, 182, 188
Doubiago, Sharon, 276
Dover Publications, 307–8
Dragonwings (Yep), 148–49
Dreaming as One (Opstedal), 250
Drucker, Johanna, 188
Durand, Marcella, 129
Duane, Kit, 225
Dufresne, Mg, 242
Duncan, Robert, 153, 188
Duncan, Robert, 74
Dunn, Anne, 233
Duras, Marguerite, 37–38, 80

e-books, 249
Ebens, Ronald, 146
editing, 324, 357, 362; aggressive style of, 171; associate editor, 120; changing works, 92–93, 132; choreographing film, 147–48; design and, 237; difference between writing and, 79; discovering form in, 258; dividing responsibilities of, 86; editing as catch-all word, 27; and evolution of press

412 Index

editing (*continued*)
mission, 274; exercising editing muscle, 171; flexibility of role of editor, 26–29, 254; and funding, 99; gender and, 186, 283; "ideal" of "no unused spaces" in, 255; link between power and, 174; managing editor, 140, 146, 403; optimism in editing, 29; principle for, 182; process of, 293; providing feedback, 28; separating from writing brain, 117; showcasing, 28; similarity to grading papers, 307; specific genres, 305; while running press, 297–300; word choice for, 181–82
Ehrenberg, Felipe, 69
Elephants & Angels (Rosenwasser), 237
Elmslie, Kenward, 155, 156, 161–62
encuentro con Rubén Darío, El, 63
End of the Far West, The (O'Hara), 181
end papers, 311–12
Endocrinology (Berssenbrugge), 238–39
epicenters, poetry, 182–83
Epler, Barbara, 27
Equi, Elaine, 156, 164
Erzen, Tanya, 241
Esteves, Sandra Maria, 6, 265
Eva Awakening (Robles), 188–89, 192
Evans, George, 155
Evergreen Road Press, 248
EXTRATRANSMISSION (Abi-Karam), 240–41

Fair Play for Cuba Committee, 64
FAP. *See* Feminist Art Program at Cal Arts
Faulwell, Dean, 151, 159
Felipe, León, 62
Felter, June, 233, 237
Feminist Art Program at Cal Arts (FAP), 232
Feminist Studio Workshop, 291

Ferlinghetti, Lawrence, 39, 61, 64
fido productions, 280, 286–87
Findlay, Heather, 335
fine-press publishing, women interested in, 187–88, 344
Fisher, Holly, 145, 147
Five Trees Press: acquiring manuscripts, 191; addressing both visual and verbal arts, 189; books done by, 189–91; career highlights, 194–95; first books of, 188–89; most memorable project of, 192; overview of, 185; political climate influencing, 192; and predominantly male printing establishment of Bay Area, 187–88; release parties, 191–92; skills and interests for, 185–87
Fleming, Pippa, 321–25, 329
Floating Bear, The, 3, 354
Flynt, Henry, 126
Folder Editions, 13, 27
Folder (magazine), 3, 5; moving from magazine to bound book, 8–15
For Fidel (Dawson), 41
fore-intuition. *See* editor, flexibility of role of
Foss, Philip, 276
Found Life, A (Schneeman), 136
Founders' Syndrome, term, 242
Four Trains (Mac Low), 51
Frances Jaffer First Book Awards, 235
Francia, Luis, 140
Francis, Sam, 195
Frankl, Howard, 58
Fraser, Kathleen, 53, 361–62
Free Speech Movement, 186
Friedman, Ed, 215
Friedman, Richard, 153
friendship, 5, 8, 29, 64, 111, 156, 274, 300, 318, 343, 345; orientation of, 21–26
From Shadows Emerging: An Anthology of Bay Area Women Writers, 292–95

Gates, Rick, 140
Gay Activists Alliance, 360
Gay, Roxanne, 330
gender, 349; affecting work, 80–81; as bias, 52–53; exclusion, 25–26; foregrounding, 6–8; gender ratio, 283; as influencing publishing decisions, 52–53; issues, 259–60; legacy of gendered institutional disenfranchisement, 5; looking at gender balance, 161; parity, 283; treating as inconsequential, 4–5; tacitly gender-blind allegiances, 4–5. *See also* production technologies, gendering of
gendered institutional disenfranchisement, legacy of, 5–6
Genet, Jean, 37–38
genres, overlay of, 178. See also *CHICAGO*
Gerrey, Alta, 356–57
Giants Play Well in the Drizzle (magazine), 20, 28; assembling, 255–56; and changes in technology, 260–61; connections resulting from circulation of, 258–59; and gender issues, 259–60; naming, 257–58; publishing schedule of, 256–57; space as guiding editorial principal, 255
Gibbs, Joan, 360
Giménez, Carmen, 277
Ginsberg, Allen, 28, 40, 61, 76, 176, 181–82, 202, 205, 214–15, 217, 258, 285
Giorno, John, 212, 215, 217
Godzilla Asian American Artists Network, 140
Grabhorn Press, 187
Grahn, Judy, 356
Grand Permission: New Writings on Poetics and Motherhood, The, 236
Granta (magazine), 77
Grapevine (newspaper), 272–74

Grecourt Review (magazine), 72
Green, Paul, 52
Griffin, Joanna, 226
Griffith, Lois Elaine, 265
Grinnell, E. Tracy, 277
Grossinger, Richard, 71–72, 74, 76–77, 79, 82
group, orienting conceptions of, 21–26
Grove Press, 1, 36–38, 40
Guest, Barbara, 237, 239
Guidacci, Margherita, 229

Hackman, Neil, 210–11
Hagedorn, Jessica, 141
Hahn, Kimiko, 140
Hair-Raising, 231–32, 234
Hall, Carla, 242
Hall, Carol, 23
Hall, Donald, 23, 48, 171
Hardware Poets Occasional (magazine), 122
Hardware Poets Playhouse, 121
Hardware Poets Theater, 111–12
Harlem Renaissance, 328
Harryman, Carla, 155
Hart, Kitty Carlisle, 141
Havana Cultural Congress, 63
Hay, Deborah, 119
Hearsay. See Bolinas Hearsay News
Heath-Stubbs, John, 48
Heilig, Steve, 24
Heineman, Sue, 267
Hejinian, Lyn, 53, 109, 359–60
Helms, Jesse, 164, 202
Hemans, Felicia, 45
Hemingway, Ernest, 227
Hemphill, Essex, 329
Henderson, David, 264
Hennessey, Michael S., 10
HerBooks Feminist Press, 362–63
Heresies Collective, working with, 267–69
Hermes Free Press, 188

414 Index

Hesperidian Press, 121
Hewlett, Greg, 245
Hill Street Blues (television), 145
Hipparchia Press, 186
Hollo, Anselm, 61, 169
Holman, Bob, 197, 202, 218, 286
Holmes, Janet, 277
Home Girls, 303–5, 307, 308, 314–16, 323
Hoover, Paul, 151, 155, 163–64, 166
Hope, D. C., 48
Hornick, Lita, 3, 353–54
Hough, Lindy: choosing poems for anthology, 77–80; gender affecting work, 80–81; magazine distribution, 76–77; memorable issues of *Io*, 76; memories of first issue of *Io*, 71–73; printing technology, 82; self-publishing advice, 81–82; soliciting submissions for magazine, 73–76; written poetry versus oral poetry, 82–83. *See also Io* (magazine); North Atlantic Books
Hough, Polly, 72
Hours Press, 227
HOW(ever) (journal), 361–62
HOW2 (journal), 361–62
Howe, Fanny, 236
Hoyem, Andrew, 187, 191
Hunt, Erica, 236
Hwang, Roland, 148
Hyland, MC, 343–49
Hyner, Stefan, 28

identity politics, 5–6, 64, 266, 358
I Have Something to Say About This Big Trouble, 7
I Like You (Bandanza), 286
IKON (magazine), 5, 18, 20; *Art Against Apartheid* (issue), 113–14, 124–26; *Coast to Coast: National Women Artists of Color* (issue), 126; content generating activity, 116–19;

criticism of, 123–24; distribution of, 124–25; funding for, 113–14; general protest poetry in, 123; integration of graphics in, 114–15; magazine design, 115–16; offset printing, 122–23; selling on newsstands, 114; starting, 111–14; title, 115, 118–19; value of reading, 126; *Without Ceremony* (issue), 113, 126; and women's movement, 125–26
inheritance. *See* lineage, concept
Internet, and immediacy of, 249
interpersonal connections, conceptions of, 21–26
intersectionality, term, 268
interviews, 1–8. *See also* Barg, Barbra; Brown, Lee Ann; Chernoff, Maxine; Costello, Deborah; Dienstfrey, Patricia; Hough, Lindy; Jones, Hettie; Jones, Patricia Spears; Kellman, Lisa; King, Martha; Kyger, Joanne; Lesniak, Rose; Mayer, Bernadette; Myles, Eileen; Notley, Alice; Owen, Maureen; Randall, Margaret; Robles, Jaime; Rosenwasser, Rena; Sherman, Susan; Smith, Barbara; Tajima-Peña, Renee; Tellefsen, Lisbet; Waldrop, Rosmarie; Wright, C. D.
Io (magazine): as built home, 78–79; *Changing Woman* issue, 77–78; choosing poems for anthology, 77–80; memories of first issue of, 71–73; gender affecting work, 80–81; magazine distribution, 76–77; *Mind, Memory, and Psyche* (issue), 76; self-publishing advice, 81–82; soliciting submissions for magazine, 73–76; written poetry *versus* oral poetry, 82–83
Io Anthology, 72, 79
Irby, Ken, 188

Index   415

IS (magazine), 79

Jabès, Edmond, 52
Jackson, Gale, 126
Jackson, Lorri, 156
Jodorowsky, Raquel, 58, 60, 61
Johnson, Honor, 274
Jones, Hettie, 14, 126, 236; collating parties, 34–35; as editor of first three issues *Yugen*, 38–39; favorite part of magazine production process, 33–34; recalling release parties, 39–40; time at Totem Press, 41–43; working at *Partisan Review* and Grove Press, 36–38; on *Yugen* as "new consciousness," 35–36; *Yugen* issue 8, 40–41. See also *Yugen* (magazine)
Jones, LeRoi. *See* Baraka, Amiri
Jones, Patricia Spears, 6, 16–17; on necessary interplay of community and audience, 24–25; starting *W. B.*, 263–64; working with Heresies Collective, 267–69; working on *Ordinary Women*, 264–67. See also Heresies Collective, working with; *Ordinary Women* (anthology); *W. B.* (magazine)
Jordan, June, 263–64
Joyce, James, 117, 227
Judson Review, 121
Julian, Isaac, 327

Katzman, Allen, 121
Keller, Lynn, 6
Kellman, Lisa, 5, 291–95. *See also* Black Oyster Press
Kelly, Robert, 62, 76
Kelsey Street Press, 167; address coincidence, 227–29; advice for small presses, 243; asking for editorial input, 236–37; balancing projects and demands, 235–37; and Bay Area poetry scene in 1974, 225–26; and bridge between literature and visual art, 232–33; challenges of producing and distributing offset, 240; challenging parts of publication process, 241; choosing name for publishers, 226–27; collaborations, 237–40; early years of printing press, 229; favorite books printed at, 229–31; longevity of, 242; major changes at, 242–43; moving away of letterpress, 234–35; recent favorite books of, 240–41; and release parties, 231–32; selecting manuscripts by consensus, 235; technological shift challenges-opportunities, 241
Kennedy, X. K., 48
King, Martha, 17, 20; editing Two and Two Press chapbooks, 253–55; making *Giants Play Well in the Drizzle*, 255–61. See also *Giants Play Well in the Drizzle* (magazine); Two and Two Press
Kirsch, Andrea, 213, 216, 217
Kitchen Table: Women of Color Press, 6–7; and cover design, 309–11; curation of visuals, 306–9; editing while running press at beginning, 297–300; and end papers, 311–12; handling distribution, 306; intense proofreading jobs of, 299–301; looking specific genres, 305–6; political perspectives of Kitchen Table, 301–4; and press friendships, 318–19; project distribution, 303–5; and stationery design, 312–13; work of keeping Kitchen Table alive, 315–16
Kleinzahler, August, 155
Knott, Bill, 153
Koch, Kennth, 9, 22, 37
Koch, Peter Rutledge, 237, 239

416 Index

Kocot, Noelle, 164
Kostakis, Peter, 153, 163
Kramen, Cynthia, 265
Kraus, Chris, 202, 204
Kulchur (magazine), 3, 353–54
Kulchur Press, 353–54
Kyger, Joanne, 74; and 1971 oil spill,
    250–51; approaching creative
    work, 248; being Wednesday edi-
    tor, 249; community of *Bolinas
    Hearsay News*, 246, 249–51; con-
    sidering reprints, 247; first issues
    of *Bolinas Hearsay News*, 246–47;
    genre of *Bolinas Hearsay News*,
    246; and immediacy of Internet,
    249; involvement in founding of
    Bolinas Hearsay News, 245–46;
    localism of *Bolinas Hearsay News*,
    247–48; other publishing ven-
    tures, 250; return reading, 249;
    technological changes at *Bolinas
    Hearsay News*, 248. See also *Boli-
    nas Hearsay News*

Lamantia, Philip, 58
Land of Roseberries (Lowenfels), 62
Lansing, Gerrit, 76
Larson, Robert, 147
Las mujeres (*The Women*, Randall), 67–68
Lauterbach, Ann, 53, 156
Lee, Corky, 140, 142
Lee, Grace, 139
LaPalma, Marina, 225
Le Mieux, Dotty, 25
Lesniak, Rose, 26; and Apocalypse
    Poetry Project, 210–12; asking
    for donations, 217; Barg talking
    about, 217–18; facing challenges,
    218–21; involvement with *Out
    There*, 213–15; meeting Barbara
    Barg, 210–13. See also *Out There*
    (magazine); Out There Produc-
    tions; Power Mad Press

letterpress, 9, 189; advocates of, 17–18;
    chapbooks, 27, 50–51; editions,
    187, 226; printing, 51, 121, 189, 231,
    292; roots, 237. *See also* mimeo
Levenson, Roger, 186, 188
Levertov, Denise, 74, 80, 121, 185, 192,
    259
Lew, Walter, 140
Lewis, Harry, 126, 253
LGBTQIA+ movement, 316, 330–31
lineage, concept, 1–8
Lippard, Lucy, 267
Lisanevich, Xenia, 231
Lisbon & the Orcas Islands (magazine), 79
Lithocrafters, 82
Little Books / Indians (Weiner), 198
Little Magazine in America, The, 56–57,
    370n15
Little Red Book (Mao), 141
Llama's Almanac (magazine), 79
localism, *Bolinas Hearsay News* (newspa-
    per), 247–48
Longyear, Jeanne, 47
"looking back," forms of, 147–48
Lorde, Audre, 7, 126, 302, 312, 313, 315,
    329
Lost Ceilings (Hamill), 136
Lost Roads Press: aspirations for, 271;
    being woman editor at, 277;
    books published by, 276; continu-
    ing, 271–72; favorite part of pub-
    lishing process, 275–76; funding
    for, 276–77; marketing books of,
    273; mission of, 274–75; name for,
    271; printing process at, 272–73;
    production of books, 274–75; and
    publishing and writing culture,
    275; publishing community and,
    274; truffles, 273
Lotus Press, 7, 358–59
Lowenfels, Walter, 61, 62
Lucent Fire: New and Selected Poems, A
    (Jones), 269

Luschei, Glenna, 354–55
Lyons, Kimberly, 156
Lytle, Ellen Aug, 126

Mabou Mines, 263
MacAdams, Lewis, 250–51
Macdonald, Jennifer, 233
Mac Low, Jackson, 51
Mademoiselle (magazine), 10
Madgett, Naomi Long, 7, 358–59
Mailer, Norman, 64
Making the Park (Rosenwasser), 229, 234
Malanga, Gerard, 8, 89
Mallarmé, Stéphane 177, 230, 239
Mankovich, Ted, 136
Marcus, Sharon, 335
Martí, José, 62
Martin, Dawn Lundy, 326, 330
Martínez, Juan, 58
Martz, Sandra Kay, 362
masthead, 152, 246
Matson, Clive, 231
May, James Boyer, 12
Mayer, Bernadette, 14, 16, 17, 18, 19, 27, 74, 169, 215, 220, 336, 337; advice for young women wanting to do magazines, 101–2; coloring letters, 99–101; current project of, 108–9; discussing handling old writing, 103–4; editing *O TO 9*, 87; favorite time of year to write, 107; giving readings, 106; having devices, 94–95; on helpers, 87–88; ideal house of, 107–8; keeping in touch with New York scene, 89–91; on "last mimeograph magazine," 98–99; learning more about synesthesia, 105–6; reflecting on "happenings," 86; starting *O TO 9*, 85–86; talking about two-issue hurdle, 102–3; and United Artists Books, 89–94; working with writers, 94–96. See also

United Artists (magazine); United Artists Books; *O TO 9* (magazine)
Mayes, Frances, 274, 276
McAlmon, Robert, 227
McCauley, Robbie, 141
Memorial Sloan-Kettering Cancer Center (MSK), 256
Mesmer, Sharon, 156
midcentury, term, 4–5
Miles, Josephine, 187
Miles, Sara, 6, 265
Milk Quarterly, The (magazine), 153, 154
Mill Mountain Press, 273
Miller, Amy, 47
Miller, Cheryl, 185–87, 191
Miller, Christanne, 6
Miller, Richard, 9
mimeo, 46; aesthetic goals in relation to, 131–32; collation parties, 87–88; machines, 16–17, 87, 98–99, 152, 322; mags, 85, 98–99, 133, 263–64; mimeograph revolution, 4, 17–19; publication, 136, 249; technology, 17–19, 131
mimeograph. *See* mimeo
Mirikitani, Janice, 7, 357
Modulations for Solo Voice (Levertov), 192
Mondragón, Sergio, 58–59, 63, 65, 66, 69
Monk, Meredith, 73
Moore, Sabra, 267
Moreno, José, 62
Moriarty, Laura, 225
Morrison, Anna, 241
Morrison, Rusty, 277
"Moving the Image" (Tajima-Peña), 144, 147–48
Moyer Bell, 154, 275, 363
Moyer, Jennifer, 154, 363
MSK. *See* Memorial Sloan-Kettering Cancer Center
Muth, Thomas, 111
My America . . . or Honk if You Love Buddha, 145

418 Index

Myles, Eileen, 199, 204, 208, 215, 216, 266, 279. See also *dodgems* (magazine); mimeograph revolution

NAATA. See National Asian American Telecommunications Association
NAB. *See* North Atlantic Books
Nagel, James, 121–22
Nash, John Henry, 187
National Asian American Telecommunications Association (NAATA), 143
National Book Critics Circle, 8
National Endowment for the Arts (NEA), 25, 73, 76, 113–114, 125, 141, 241, 271, 276–77
NEA. *See* National Endowment for the Arts
Need: A Chorale for Black Women Voices (Lorde), 302
Nemeth, Terry, 73
Neurosuite (Rosenwasser), 234, 229–30
New American Poetry (anthology), 1, 3–4, 10–12, 72
New American Poetry and Cold War Nationalism (Delbos), 10–11
New American Poetry, term, 72
New American Writing (magazine), 20, 151, 155, 156; on explosion of new poets, 165–67; influencing writing, 164–65; special issues of, 163–64; sporadically doing things at, 161–63; transition to, 159–60
New Directions, 49
New Folder, A (Aldan, ed.), 1, 3–4; initial printing of, 13; moving from magazine to bound book, 8–15; as spectral version, 12–13
New Poets of England and America, 10
New York State Council on the Arts (NYSCA), 113, 136
New York Times, 299
New York Times Magazine (magazine), 134
New Yorker (magazine), 103, 182, 204

News from Niman Farm (MacAdam), 250–51
Nguyen, Huong Giang, 114
Nichols, Bob, 121
Nichols, Mary, 121
Nitz, Michael, 146
North Atlantic Books (NAB), 72–73
Notley, Alice, 2, 151, 153; on "curating" *CHICAGO*, 181–82; editing pieces for *CHICAGO*, 171; editorial intentions of, 182; laying out poems, 179–80; memories of *CHICAGO* issues, 170; mimeographing and stencil-cutting, 170–71; open-field technique in, 176–77; potential commentary of *CHICAGO*, 175–76; principle of being artist/poet, 175; and sexism, 171–73; soliciting poems, 169–70; starting *CHICAGO*, 169; talk of travel, 178–79; typing stencils, 174–75; utopian idea of poetry 24/7, 177–78. See also *CHICAGO* (magazine)
Nuclear Strategy and the Code of the Warrior, 79
Nuyorican Poets Café, 6, 205, 206–207, 264
NYSCA. *See* New York State Council on the Arts

O'Hara, Frank, 22, 33–34, 37, 174, 176–77
O'Brien, Marian, 238
Obama, Barack, 69
Obeying the Chemicals (Barg), 198
offset printing, 122–23
Oink! (magazine): activities of, 151–52; Chicago as word in, 156–57; doing things more sporadically at, 161–63; and explosion of new poets, 165–67; gender balance in, 161; influencing writing, 164–65; printing escapades, 152–53;

regarding title, 160–61; soliciting through readings, 154–57; special issues of, 163–64; technical duties for production, 157–59; transition to *New American Writing*, 159–60
Oliver, Douglas, 174
Olson, Charles, 74, 76, 80, 154, 177, 158, 260
One Million Poets, 267
Only Humans with Songs to Sing (Sherman, ed.), 124
open-field technique, 176–77. *See also* Olson, Charles
Opstedal, Kevin, 250
Ordinary Women (anthology), 6; favorite part of making, 265–66; idea for collection, 265; issues of representation and privilege, 268–69; putting together, 265; reception of, 266–67
Orlovsky, Peter, 40, 285, 336
Osman, Jena, 4
Our Bodies, Ourselves, 186–87
Out There (magazine): and changing technology, 199–201; geographic range of, 214; involvement with, 198–99; Rose Lesniak involvement in, 210, 213–15; women poets of, 215
Out There Productions, 213, 216; projects of, 221–22
Overstreet Printing, 272
Owen, Maureen, 16, 87, 172, 236; branching out into publishing books, 134–35; describing "scene," 129–30; discontinuing publishing, 133; editing magazine, 132; and Ma Bell in terms of inclusivity, 130–31; publishing at slower and steadier pace, 133; publishing poems under pseudonym, 132–33.
Owen, Patrick, 136. *See also* Owen,

Maureen; *Telephone* (magazine); Telephone Books
Oxford English Dictionary, 14, 314

Padgett, Ron, 169, 177
Page Mothers Conference, 4
Paley, Grace, 316–17
Paper (newspaper), 245
Paper Nautilus, 275
Papier-Mache Press, 362
Parenthood (film), 146
Paris Review (magazine), 49, 77
Parker, Pat, 329
Parkinson, Tom, 186
Parmar, Pratibha, 327
Partisan Review (magazine), 36–38, 40, 42, 398
Passionate Perils of Publishing, The (West and Wheat), 226
Patterson, Ian, 10
Pearlstein, Darlene, 153
Pearson, Norman Holmes, 190
Peculiar Motions (Waldrop), 233
Penguin Random House, 77
people, professionalization, 140. *See also* Asian Americans
Perelman, Bob, 155
Permission by the Horns (Kyger), 249
"Personal Poem" (O'Hara), 33–34
Petit, Simon, 205
Petrillo, Jim, 188
Phillips, Frances, 234, 242
Phillips, William, 37
Phony Express (magazine), 322
Pines, Paul, 126
Ploughshares (magazine), 77
Poet & The Dancer, The (Doolittle), 190
Poetry Project, 6, 18, 21, 26, 52, 86, 129–30, 206, 210, 215, 263–64, 285, 333
Poetry Project Newsletter (newsletter), 18, 199, 266
Poets & Writers (magazine), 81
Poets Press, 354

420   Index

Poulson, Lory, 232
Power Mad Press, 197, 212; and changing
    technology, 199–201; typesetting
    technology of, 197–98
Prisoners Legal Services, 280
production technologies, gendering of:
    changing technology, 199–201;
    distribution, 19–21; labor restric-
    tions, 15–16; mimeograph revo-
    lution, 17–19; and "scarcity aes-
    thetic," 17–19; setting type, 15–16;
    technological shift challenges-
    opportunities, 241; typing of
    stencils, 16–17; using letterpress,
    15; of o TO 9, 89
projective verse, 74
projects, balancing demands and,
    235–37
Prontuario (Moreno), 62
proofreading, 40, 47, 300
*Provisional Avant-Gardes: Little Magazine
    Communities from Dada to Digital*
    (Seita), 10
publisher, flexibility of role of, 26–29
Publisher's Weekly (magazine), 312–13
publishing, term, 335

Quivering Aardvark and the Jelly of Love, The
    (play), 48

race, 6–7, 25, 28, 35, 141, 146, 148, 263,
    268, 293, 302
race-blind, stance, 6
Rahv, Philip, 37
Rainer, Yvonne, 119
Rakosi, Carl, 155, 166
Ramholz, Jim, 154
Randall, Elinor, 62
Randall, Margaret, 20–21, 113, 119, 236;
    on alienation between two con-
    tinents, 56–57; interest in Cuba,
    62–69; knowing Spanish, 58–59;
    living as young woman, 57–58;

living in New York City, 55–56; on
    Philip Lamantia's apartment, 58;
    traveling while editing *El Corno
    Emplumado*, 65–67; working on *El
    Corno Emplumado*, 59–61. See also
    Corno Emplumado, El (magazine)
Rashomon (film), 145
Ratner, Rochelle, 126
recombinant (Chen), 240
Reed, Cannon & Johnson, imprint, 264
Regan, Julie, 335
Reid, Laurie, 233, 239
release parties, 14, 22, 39, 88, 97, 161, 191,
    231–32, 287
Reti, Irene, 362–63
return reading, 249
Rexograph, 279
Rexroth, Kenneth, 153, 186–87
Rezek, John, 154
Rice, Stan, 274
Rich, Adrienne, 265, 266–67
Richards, MC, 74
Rifkin, Libbie, 4, 8
Riggs, Marlon, 327
Rivers, Larry, 22, 156
Roberts, Renee M., 8
Robles, Jaime, 22; acquiring manu-
    scripts, 191; addressing both
    visual and verbal arts, 189; books
    done by Five Trees Press, 189–91;
    career highlights, 194–95; dif-
    ficulty finding publisher, 193–94;
    doctoral research of, 194; meet-
    ing Kathleen Walkup and Cheryl
    Miller, 185–87; most memorable
    project of, 192; political climate
    influencing, 192; predominantly
    male printing establishment of
    Bay Area, 187–88; release par-
    ties, 191–92; skills and interests
    of, 185–87. See also Five Trees
    Press
Rodgers, Carolyn, 355–56

roles, flexibility of, 26–29
Room of One's Own, A (Woolf), 1–2, 13, 103
Rose-Steel, Mike, 195
Rosenthal, Bob, 205
Rosenwasser, Rena, 5, 15, 17, 277, 294; address coincidence, 227–29; advice for small presses, 243; asking for editorial input, 236–37; balancing projects and demands, 235–37; and Bay Area poetry scene in 1974, 225–26; and bridge between literature and visual art, 232–33; challenges of producing and distributing offset, 240; challenging parts of publication process, 241; choosing name for publishers, 226–27; collaborations, 237–40; early years of printing press, 229; favorite books printed at, 229–31; longevity of, 242; major changes at, 242–43; moving away of letterpress, 234–35; recent favorite books of, 240–41; and release parties, 231–32; selecting manuscripts by consensus, 235; technological shift challenges-opportunities, 241. *See also* Kelsey Street Press
Rosenwasser, Robert, 238
Rothenberg, Jerome, 62, 74, 76
Roxburghe Club, 187

s/kins, 233
Saalfield, Catherine, 335
Saar, Alison, 233
Sable, Sheilah, 318–19
Sainer, Arthur, 111
San Francisco Chronicle (newspaper), 247
San Francisco Renaissance, 118
Sanders, Ed, 212
Saturday Night Live, 139
Scalapino, Leslie, 155

"scarcity aesthetic," 17–19
Schapiro, Miriam, 232
Schleifer, Marc, 64
schlock magazines, 102
Schneeman, George, 170, 179, 338
Schoolman, Jill, 277
Second Generation New York School, 4, 6, 24
Seiner, Arthur, 117
Sejourne, Laurette, 62
Selected Poems of Friedrich Hölderlin, 164
self-publishing, 5, 13–14, 18, 23, 27, 29, 81–82, 96, 349
Série d'Ecriture, 52
Serpas, Carlos Coffeen, 58
Setterfield, David, 73
Seventeen Syllables (Yamamoto), 311–13
SEW. *See* Society for Educating Women's
Shameless Hussy Press, 356–57
Shang-Chi and the Legend of the Ten Rings (film), 148
Shange, Ntozake, 226, 227
She Writes Press, 81
Shearsman Books, 194
Sherman, Susan, 5, 17–18, 64; chapbooks of, 121–22; life between genesis and funding, 119–21; offset printing, 122–23; starting *IKON*, 111–14; on value of reading *IKON*, 126; and women's movement, 125–26; working at *The Nation* and *Village Voice*, 61–63, 121, 253. *See also IKON* (magazine)
Shimoura, Jim, 148
Siete.de.Catorce (Seven of Fourteen), 69
Simic, Charles, 162
Simulacra (Rosenwasser and Delos), 237
Sixpack (magazine), 79
Skeezo Typography, 197
Slaves of New York (film), 201
Small Press Distribution, 273

422 Index

small press publishing, women in: flexibility of roles, 26–29; group and community, 21–26; moving from magazine to bound book, 8–15; origins, 1–8; predecessors, 1–8; siblings, 1–8; successors, 1–8
Small Salvations (Dienstfrey), 237
Small, Judith, 295
Smith, Barbara, 5, 7; and cover design, 309–11; curation of visuals, 306–9; editing while running press at beginning, 297–300; and end papers, 311–12; handling distribution, 306; intense proofreading jobs of, 299–301; looking specific genres, 305–6; political perspectives of Kitchen Table, 301–4; and press friendships, 318–19; project distribution, 303–5; and stationery design, 312–13; work of keeping Kitchen Table alive, 315–16. *See also* Kitchen Table: Women of Color Press
Smith, Kiki, 233, 238–39
Smith, Michael, 117
Smith, Patti, 282, 285
Snodgrass, W. D., 48
Snyder, Gary, 74
Society for Educating Women's (SEW), 111, 115
Songs for the Unborn Second Baby (Notley), 178
Sorrentino, Gil, 41
"Space Occupied: Women Poet-Editors the Mimeograph Revolution in Mid-century New York City," 24
Spahr, Juliana, 4
Spectacular Diseases Press, 52
Sphericity (Berssenbrugge), 238
Spicehandler, Steve, 136
Spicer, Jack, 188
spy in the audience, phrase, 26
Steele, Suzanne, 195

Stein, Charles, 76
Stein, Gertrude, 2, 74
Steiner, Rudolf, 13
stencils, typing, 16–17, 87, 158, 200
Stern, Steve, 276
Stone Wind (magazine), 154
Strand, Mark, 215
Strange Rain (Owen), 136
Studying Hunger Journals (Mayer), 105
Sulphur (magazine), 79
Surasky, Cecilie, 335
Symbiosis (Guest), 239
synesthesia, 105–6; coloring letters, 99–101
Sze, Arthur, 276

table of contents, 9, 21–22, 25, 108, 132, 152, 157, 325
table-top poetics, 236
Taggart, John, 276
Tajima-Peña, Renee, 7, 24; advice on "looking back," 147–49; becoming involved with *Bridge*, 139–41; joys and difficulties of collaboration, 146–47; on legacy of *Bridge*, 142; on relationship between poetry and film, 145; special report by, 143; working at *Village Voice*, 145–46. *See also Bridge* (magazine)
Tajiri, Shinkichi, 61–62
Tamalpais Press, 186, 188
Tasawassan (magazine), 99, 103
Telephone (magazine), 199; branching out into publishing books, 134–35; collation process at, 131; constant change and flux of, 133; discontinuation of, 133; editing magazine, 132; inviting contributions of innovative process, 131–32; Ma Bell in terms of inclusivity, 130–31; memorable issues of, 133; and 1999 "scene," 129–30; publishing

at slower and steadier pace, 133; publishing poems under pseudonym, 132–33

Telephone Books, 134; acquiring manuscripts, 135–36; lapse in book publication, 136

Tellefsen, Lisbet, 20, 24; considering legacy of *Aché*, 330–31; creating/documenting community, 327–30; genesis of *Aché*, 321–23; genesis of editorial team, 325–26; on themed issues, 323–25. *See also Aché*

temporal distance, 25

Tender Buttons Press. *See* Brown, Lee Ann

Third Woman Press, 360–61

Third World Press, 355–56

Third World Women, 265

13th Moon (magazine), 359

This Bridge Called My Back, 305

Thomas, Lorenzo, 169

Those Fluttering Objects of Desire, 141

Timmons, Matthew, 46

Tomkiw, Lydia, 156

Tong, Nancy, 147

Tongues Untied (film), 327

Tooth of Time Review (magazine), 79

Toothpaste (magazine), 79

Totem Press, 41–43

Trace (magazine), 11–12

translation, publishing works in, 52–53

Trouble in Paradise (Benitez), 272

Truck (magazine), 79

Trump, Donald, 69

Tsien, Jean, 145

Turkey Buzzard Review (magazine), 250

Turtle Island Press, 185, 190

Tuttle, Richard, 233, 237

Tuumba Press, 359–60

Two and Two Press, 17–18; editing chapbooks for, 253–54; incorporation of visual art in, 254; name of

publishers, 254; role in editing and making chapbooks, 254–55; space as guiding editorial principal, 255

two-issue hurdle, 102–3

type, setting, 15–16

typesetting, 15–21

typing, 15–21; reader/writer influence, 34; retyping, 16, 33–34; stencils, 16–17, 87, 158, 200

UCLA EthnoCommunications Program and Visual Communications, 143

ULAE. *See* United Limited Artists' Editions

Un coup de dés (Mallarmé), 8

United Artists (magazine), 17; envisioning, 89–90; funding for, 93; name for, 93

United Artists Books, 17, 104; distribution, 97; editing books, 92; memorable books, 92; publishing under, 96–97; release parties, 97–98; reprinting out-of-print titles, 93–94; typesetting books, 92

United Limited Artists' Editions (ULAE), 238

Utterances (Bronk), 51

Valda, Douglas Dunn, 73

vanity publisher, term, 14

Verityper, 272–73

Vermont Council on the Arts, 76

Vicuña, Cecilia, 233

Viewers Like Us (podcast), 139

Village Voice (newspaper), 117, 121, 145–46, 396, 403

Vincent Chin 40th Remembrance and Rededication, 148

visual art, incorporation of, 254

W. B. (magazine), 16, 263–64

424 Index

Wachtel, Chuck, 126

Wagan, Betsy, 47

Wakoski, Diane, 61, 74

Waldman, Anne, 74, 89, 169, 172, 202, 212, 355

Waldrop, Rosmarie, 26, 233, 277; admiring contemporary women writers and editors, 53; at Burning Deck Press, 49–53; distribution, 46–47; role in Beatnix Hoax, 48–49; shift to books, 48–49; soliciting submissions, 46–47; starting Burning Deck, 45–46. See also *Burning Deck* (magazine); Burning Deck Press

Walkup, Kathleen, 185–87, 191

Ward, Skye, 325

Warner, Brooke, 81

Watten, Barrett, 155

We Are Everywhere: Lesbians in the Archive, 328

Weber, Bruce, 126

Weiner, Hannah, 198

Weiners, John, 89

Whalen, Phil, 182

Whalen, Philip, 177

Wheeler, Susan, 164

Whigham, Peter, 186, 191

Whitaker, Keith, 238

White Rabbit Press, 188

White, Hazel, 242

Whitefield, Nancy, 245

Whitehead, James, 271–72

Whitney Museum of American Art Biennial, 140

Who Killed Vincent Chin? (film), 145, 146

Wiebe, Dallas, 48

Williams, William Carlos, 103, 177

Wilson, Erin, 242

Wolff, Rebecca, 277

Wolgamot Interstice, The, 48–50

Wolin, Harvey, 56, 58

Women & Children First (King), 54

women of color, showcasing, 6–7

women's movement, 5, 125, 228, 293, 316, 397

Women's Press Collective, 356

Wong, Nellie, 294

Woolf, Virginia, 1

World, The, 141, 355

Wright, C. D., 20, 236; aspirations for Lost Roads Press, 271–72; and Verityper, 272–73. *See also* Lost Roads Press

Wright, Franz, 276

writer, flexibility of role of, 26–29

Wu, Shanlon, 140

Yamada, Mitsuye, 300, 310

Yamamoto, Hisaye, 300, 311–13

Yellow Press, 153

Young Feminists, 215

Young, Virginia Brady, 13–14

Yugen (magazine), 3, 14; collating parties, 34–35; first three issues of, 38–39; issue 8, 40–41; magazine production process at, 33–34; as "new consciousness," 35–36; *Partisan Review* and Grove Press in relation to, 36–38; recalling release parties, 39–40; secondary title of, 35–36

Z Press, 162

Zahn, Curtis, 11–12

Zedong Mao, 141

Zephyrus Image, 188

0 TO 9 (magazine): distribution of, 88; editing, 87; helpers, 87–88; production technology, 87; short run of, 88; starting, 85–86; Street Works as culmination of, 86–87

Zia, Helen, 148

Zimmerly, Vanessa Kauffman, 242

zines, 5, 130, 132, 330, 349

Zombie Notes (Owen), 135